The Politics of Downtown Development

✦

The Politics of Downtown Development

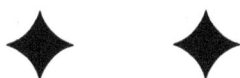

Dynamic Political Cultures in San Francisco and Washington, D.C.

Stephen J. McGovern

THE UNIVERSITY PRESS OF KENTUCKY

Publication of this volume was made possible in part
by a grant from the National Endowment for the Humanities.

Scholarly publisher for the Commonwealth,
serving Bellarmine College, Berea College, Centre
College of Kentucky, Eastern Kentucky University,
The Filson Club Historical Society, Georgetown College,
Kentucky Historical Society, Kentucky State University,
Morehead State University, Murray State University,
Northern Kentucky University, Transylvania University,
University of Kentucky, University of Louisville,
and Western Kentucky University.

Editorial and Sales Offices: The University Press of Kentucky
663 South Limestone Street, Lexington, Kentucky 40508-4008

02 01 00 99 98 5 4 3 2 1

Library of Congress Cataloging-in-Publication Data

McGovern, Stephen J., 1959–
The politics of downtown development : dynamic political cultures in San Francisco and Washington, D.C. / Stephen J. McGovern.
p. cm.
Includes bibiliographical references and index.
ISBN 0–8131–2052–7 (alk. paper)
1. Urban renewal—California—San Francisco. 2. Urban renewal—Washington (D.C.) 3. Central business districts—California—San Francisco. 4. Central business districts—Washington (D.C.) 5. Political culture—California—San Francisco. 6. Political culture—Washington (D.C.) 7. Political participation—California—San Francisco. 8. Political participation—Washington (D.C.) I. Title.
HT177.S38M34 1998
307.3′42176′09753—dc21 97–53074

To My Parents
Sheila and John McGovern

Contents

Figures, Tables, and Maps

Figures

Tables

Maps

Preface

This is a book about how the political culture of cities shapes local politics. It is also about how the people who live and work in cities shape the local political culture. In brief, the argument is that people who engage in various forms of political activity inevitably have an impact on the ideas, values, beliefs, and practices that constitute the local political culture and that those cultural impacts then have important ramifications for the content of public policy.

The specific context for this examination of the relationship between political participation, the local political culture, and urban policy making involves the issue of downtown development. Many political scientists have noted the centrality of land use issues to urban politics. According to Paul Peterson, for example, "Urban politics is above all the politics of land use, and it is easy to see why. Land is the factor of production over which cities exercise the greatest control."[1] Stephen Elkin writes, "Land use is at the core of the vital concerns of citizens. It affects neighborhood quality, crime, and schools." Consequently, "any discussion of the public interest in the contemporary city must . . . concern itself with land-use patterns."[2] And of all land use issues, downtown development has dominated the urban policy agenda. Downtown development has been the preferred urban revitalization strategy among civic and business leaders ever since the end of World War II. As such, it has been a lightning rod for money and power in American cities, and thus a vibrant breeding ground for political conflict. Downtown-oriented interests have repeatedly clashed with neighborhood groups troubled by the costs and unfulfilled promises of rapid growth.

My interest in the politics of downtown development long precedes my days as a scholar. Like many ideas for books, the genesis for this one was wrapped up in the personal life of the author. I grew up in New York City—just below the Upper East Side of Manhattan not far from the East River. It comes as a surprise to many when I tell them that the area was not always the affluent enclave that it is today. As recently as the late 1960s, it was an economically and ethnically diverse place. My day-to-day existence revolved around the elementary school across the street, the creaky old gymnasium around the corner, and the dirt field underneath the Fifty-Ninth Street Bridge. I had more than a dozen friends living in the turn-of-the-century, four-story walk-ups that lined many of the streets for blocks. Their names were a testament to what a melting pot the neighborhood was: Jose Perez, William Maggio, Kurt Schumann, Pat Boyle, Jose Andujar, Alan Schultz, and Laura Kowalski. It was a good time and place to be a kid. The neighborhood was colorful, cohesive, and lively.

And then, quite suddenly, conditions changed. The school was torn down and replaced by a towering office building, and many of my friends' homes were likewise cleared to make way for highrise, luxury apartment buildings. The candy store where I faithfully bought my baseball cards became a boutique. The five-and-dime on Second Avenue lost its lease. My friends moved away, and before long so did our family.

My parents tried to explain to me that the world was changing and that this was progress. A good thing. I was not convinced. For years I wondered whether the neighborhood transformation that I had experienced in New York City had to have happened. Was it really an inevitable outcome of sweeping forces in our society? Was it something that could have been modified or reversed? What kinds of people wielded the power necessary to preserve or reconstruct a neighborhood? Such questions stayed with me through the years and influenced how I thought about local politics and particularly land use politics. To what extent does the public sector have the capacity to guide the development of cities, and who exactly controls the public sector anyway?

With issues like these percolating in my subconscious, I suppose it was only natural that I would be attracted to the world of political science. And when it came time to choose a dissertation topic as a graduate student at Cornell University, I knew that my firsthand experience with urban development in New York City would be a major influence. I ended up deciding to undertake a comparative case study of the relatively recent politics of downtown development in San Francisco and Washington, D.C., partly because those cities satisfied the social scientist's need for cases that would allow me to evaluate my hypothesis while controlling for competing variables, but also because those two cases offered fascinating stories of ordinary people struggling to manage the growth of their cities. Immersing myself in the politics of downtown development in San Francisco and Washington, D.C., promised to throw light on the linkages between grassroots activism, political culture, and public policy. I hope that this book accomplishes that.

I deeply appreciate the many people who helped me to complete this study. To start, I thank my dissertation committee for according me the freedom to venture away from Cornell's traditional focus on the institutions of government and into the often murky domain of political culture. Although this was unfamiliar turf for them, my committee always encouraged me to "be bold" and trust my instincts. More specifically, it was Martin Shefter's provocative seminar "Political Change" that first prompted me to question institutionalist explanations and challenged me to document whether and how ideas matter in politics. From the beginning, Pierre Clavel's enthusiasm for my project kept me going. Theodore Lowi's wisdom, energy, and integrity were a source of inspiration; after working so closely with him over the years, I can easily see why he has been at the pinnacle of this profession for so long.

Other scholars deserve my gratitude too. Sheldon Wolin's stay at Cornell was all too fleeting, but during his time in Ithaca, he forever altered how I think about politics. I add my name to the lengthy list of students who have been profoundly touched by his extraordinary vision. Others in the Cornell community who assisted me along the way and otherwise contributed to my intellectual development include Rich Strean, Scott Wilson, David Patton, Michael Marks, Linda York, Patty Hipsher, Suzanne Mettler, Francis Adams, Paul D'Anieri, Dennis Merryfield, Colin MacLeod, Avigail Eisenberg, Geoff Waite, Jeremy Rabkin, Elizabeth Sanders, and all of the folks at the Cornell-in-Washington Center, especially Jack Moran and Steve Jackson. Finally, a Mellon grant from Cornell University allowed me to devote a full year to research in Washington, D.C.

A number of individuals at Temple University were invaluable to my growth as an urbanist: Mark Pfeifer, Stephanie Wood, Leslie Martin, Dana Hanchin, Jenna Allen, Solomon Jones, Sharon Leacock, Todd Margasak, Lane Johnson, Barbara Ferman, Joe Schwartz, and the hundreds of other undergraduate and graduate students who made teaching urban politics such a joy. In particular, I want to thank Susie Clampett-Lundquist, Neil Donahue, Marshall King, and Cameron Voss for their support; their willingness to risk speaking out about the importance of teaching is Temple University's best hope of someday remembering that its primary mission is to educate its students.

I am indebted to Jeffrey Henig, Richard DeLeon, Todd Swanstrom, Dan Schulgasser, and the anonymous reviewers at the University Press of Kentucky for their comments on the manuscript; their astute observations and constructive criticism made it a much better product. And Lois Crum did a splendid job copyediting the manuscript.

As for the research phase of the product, I am extremely grateful to the dozens of people who agreed to be interviewed. Those interviews are the heart and soul of this book. Chuck Thomas, Richard Pachter, and Terry Chin were kind enough to give me delightful places to stay during my many months in San Francisco; moreover, their genuine interest in my work and our numerous conversations about city politics made my research all the more exciting.

My sister, Susan McGovern, also put me up for extended periods while I was in San Francisco. More importantly, she has taught me through her teaching and political work volumes about the theory and practice of democracy. She's also a really good sister. My parents, Sheila and John McGovern, have always been there for me. This book is dedicated to them.

Finally, I can not even begin to describe how essential my wife, Lisa Baglione, has been to completing this book. As a fellow political scientist, she has the training and knowledge to help me work through perplexing conceptual and methodological problems and perceive new ways of understanding and explaining the data. No one's intellectual contribution to this project was more vital than Lisa's. Her generous willingness to take on the family financial burden at the beginning and end of my research was also crucial. But most importantly, it was Lisa's unwavering confidence in me and her whole-hearted emotional support and love that sustained me. This book would not have happened without her.

Part 1
Introduction

✦1

Interpreting Downtown Development

The Conventional Interpretation

From the vantage point of city leaders in the middle of the twentieth century, urban America was at risk. Broad societal forces were exerting a powerfully decentralizing influence over life in the metropolis. Changes in lifestyle preferences made millions yearn for single-family homes with spacious yards and two-car garages in tranquil suburbs far from the congested city. Changes in transportation technology enabled first the upper class and then the middle class to act on those yearnings. Perhaps most importantly, changes in the global economy led to a steady decline in manufacturing in U.S. cities as corporations shifted production first to the suburbs, later to the Sunbelt, and still later to Third World nations offering low labor costs and minimal government regulation. Deindustrialization devastated urban neighborhoods. When plants shut down, long-time residents were forced to relocate in search of job opportunities; local shop owners lost customers and community institutions—schools, clubs, and churches—faded from the scene. As the urban tax base eroded, city officials were left with dwindling resources to cope with ever mounting problems. Poverty, crime, and homelessness steadily increased, prompting even more residents and businesses to flee what had become a seemingly hopeless situation. Decay and despair set in.[1]

At the same time, however, some of these observers detected a silver lining in the dark cloud of global economic restructuring. Although the move from an industrial to a service- and information-based economy did not bode well for neighborhoods dependent on manufacturing, some civic and business leaders contended that the outlook for cities was far from gloomy. They reasoned that as a relatively affluent and highly educated nation, the United States was well positioned to flourish as a postindustrial power in the new world economy. Those observers further maintained that the downtown business districts of major U.S. cities would be the natural hub of postindustrial activity. Downtown was the ideal location for a conglomeration of corporate headquarters and the plethora of business entities that would be needed to serve them. Much of the infrastructure was already in place. A wave of skyscraper construction during the first three decades of the century had provided office space for companies seeking a home base. In addition downtown-centered mass transit systems existed to facilitate commuting between the increasingly popular suburbs and the urban core. And street-level retail and commercial establishments that had been operating for decades would continue to cater to the swelling population employed in the downtown highrises. In sum, changes in the private sector pointed to where cities needed to head in order to survive and prosper. The rise of a postindustrial economy meant that the downtown business district was where the action would be in the years to come. Downtown America would lead the global economy in the postwar era.[2]

Accordingly, the policy response to economic restructuring was clear to the civic and business leaders of U.S. cities by midcentury. Although societal transformations were exacting the most damaging costs in industrial neighborhoods, diverting substantial resources to revitalize those neighborhoods would only delay the inevitable and prolong the pain brought on by deindustrialization and suburbanization. Instead, city leaders concluded that urban policy ought to be consistent with the potent forces that were reshaping how Americans lived and worked. And that required concentrating most of the city's scarce resources in the one area that promised the greatest return on investment—the downtown business district.

Downtown development offered an enticing vision of what cities could become in a fast-changing world. But city planners also realized that a great deal of work had to be done. The Depression and World War II had brought a virtual halt to downtown construction, and so by the late 1940s business districts were looking dreary at best and dilapidated at worst. Moreover, adjacent neighborhoods had been neglected and were experiencing serious social strains. In the broader context of mass suburbanization and deindustrialization, cities simply did not appear to be likely places for business growth and prosperity. Persuading large corporations and the vast array of business-support firms that downtown business districts were, indeed, the most desirable sites for economic investment would be a challenge. Bold plans were needed.[3]

Those plans called for extensive physical redevelopment of the downtown core. Infrastructure improvements, new highway construction, mass transit upgrading, and the demolition of poor residential neighborhoods that abutted the downtown business district became central features of urban renewal. Downtown properties that were being used for low-intensity purposes would be purchased and cleared by city governments pursuant to their eminent domain power. The increasingly valuable real estate would then be used for civic purposes or sold at bargain basement prices to private developers, who would then build office towers, hotels, and upscale housing, all of which would boost the investment potential of the downtown district.[4]

Apart from physical redevelopment, planning for downtown growth was also attentive to the value of projecting the right kind of image. As the competition for economic investment heated up, cities would have to convince potential investors that they offered "a good business climate." And in the minds of city leaders this meant limiting governmental intrusions that might inhibit economic growth. Minimal regulations and low taxes indicated that a city had the proper attitude toward business. To the extent that government did have a role to play in development matters, business leaders felt it ought to be a constructive one; cities would be expected to promote business growth, not just through infrastructure improvements, but by offering private investors special inducements such as tax abatements and sweetheart land sales. If a city was reluctant to project a probusiness image through its public policies, potential investors were ready to look elsewhere for a more favorable business environment. The combination of physical redevelopment and fostering a probusiness image constituted the cornerstone of most cities' downtown development strategies.[5]

In the early years, downtown development was easy to sell to the general public. City planners painted an alluring picture of a reinvigorated downtown driven by Fortune 500 companies and dozens of law firms, accounting firms, banks, insurance companies, and advertising agencies. Hotels and restaurants would thrive. Retail businesses ranging from giant department stores to small corner shops would flourish. Downtown expansion would stimulate job growth and tax revenue, and all of this newly created wealth would spill over into the surrounding neighborhoods and improve the material well-being of all urban residents. Civic pride would be restored. Citizens would once again have confidence in the future of cities.

Meanwhile, the anticipated costs of downtown development seemed trivial. To make room for the new office buildings, hotels, and convention centers, a few downtown neighborhoods might experience some disruption. Some long-time residents and small-business owners would have to be relocated. But the removal of old and decaying neighborhoods in favor of an expanding downtown business district that promised to enrich the area's population seemed like a small price to pay.

Moreover, the city's interest in exploiting the ongoing transformation to a postindustrial economy by aggressively pursuing downtown development seemed even plainer when alternative paths to urban revitalization were contemplated. Should city officials attempt to address the ravages of deindustrialization and suburbanization more directly by appropriating substantial resources for neighborhood development, upper-income taxpayers and large businesses would surely resent having to foot the bill. To them, such governmental activism would mean a decline in public services and higher taxes. Their response would be to flee the city in search of a more hospitable climate elsewhere. The consequences of such additional capital flight would be devastating. Continuing depletion of the tax base would further constrain cities from responding to chronic social problems. The urban crisis would continue to intensify. The threat of capital mobility only reinforced the conviction of city leaders that a policy of aggressive downtown development was the sole viable strategy for rebuilding urban America.

This practitioners' view of the city's interest in downtown development is expressed most forcefully in the academic literature by Paul Peterson in his influential book *City Limits.*[6] Peterson's study of the deep constraints on city policymakers is grounded on the primacy of market forces. In his view cities are locked in a fierce competition with one another to attract and retain mobile wealth. Local governments therefore have a strong incentive to avoid redistributive policies aimed at ameliorating urban inequalities. A consistent commitment to development policies would be more likely to keep mobile capital within the city. Peterson argued that to protect the public fisc, cities were limited to policies that developed wealth rather than redistributing it. In an environment that was so closely attuned to the pressures of market forces—both the transformation to a postindustrial economy and the increasing mobility of postindustrial capital—only a strong program of downtown development seemed rational.

This perspective had important ramifications for the policy-making process. With the city's interest in pursuing downtown development so certain, the need for public debate seemed superfluous. Public participation in the development process was deemed inefficient, even counterproductive. Again, Peterson's view captures the thinking of downtown elites: "By keeping mass involvement at the local level to a minimum, serious pressures for policies contrary to the economic interests of the city are avoided." All that was necessary was for experts skilled in the professions of planning, finance, law, architecture, and engineering to *administer* a program of downtown development. In many large cities an intricate network of private development corporations and quasi-public agencies assumed responsibility for the complicated task of rebuilding the downtown business district; much of its activity took place behind closed doors, out of the public eye.[7]

Popular reaction to downtown development took several paths. Many citizens came to see downtown development as the exclusive domain of skilled professionals trained to resolve highly complex matters. Lacking experience in the practice of governing, those individuals were inclined to defer to the experts downtown. Other citizens were more skeptical of the wisdom of downtown elites, but they too opted not to participate in the political process, believing that their participation would not amount to very much; in their view downtown development policies really were a response to market forces over which individuals had little control. But some citizens did get involved. Those who were directly threatened by downtown development were the most likely to band together and troop down to city hall to voice their opposition. They immediately ran up against a brick wall, however, in the form of a tight-knit coalition of public and private elites determined to maintain the course of rapid growth. This coalition of city politicians, real estate developers, corporate lawyers, financiers, architects, engineers, labor union officers, newspaper editors, and others with a strong interest in downtown expansion was in no mood to entertain criticism of its policies from isolated segments of the community. Such groups, which scholars dubbed downtown growth machines or downtown growth coalitions, sternly lectured protesting citizens about the city's overall interest in pursuing downtown growth and rarely wavered from their plans. In most cases disgruntled neighborhood groups soon discovered that they were no match for the powerful downtown growth coalition.[8]

For many, the early results of downtown development efforts were encouraging. Pittsburgh, an aging center of steel manufacturing, was among the first cities to anticipate how changes in the global economy might adversely affect its prospects, and so city leaders moved aggressively to rebuild their downtown business district. The strategy seemed to pay off as large corporations relocated their headquarters downtown, thus stimulating considerably more business expansion in the area. When the steel mills began to close in the ensuing decades, Pittsburgh was able to absorb the costs of economic transformation and glide relatively smoothly into the emerging postindustrial economy. Other cities, including Philadelphia, New Haven, and Boston, also reported success with their redevelopment programs. Later, cities such as Baltimore and San Antonio provided more evidence of downtown-led urban rejuvenation. By the same token, Rustbelt cities that failed to revitalize their downtown districts risked disaster when the inevitable decline in manufacturing occurred. The misfortunes of Gary, Indiana, another steel center, served as a lesson to city planners of what might happen if little or no action were taken to rebuild downtown cores.[9]

As downtown development progressed through the 1960s and 1970s and then boomed in the 1980s, progrowth enthusiasts were pleased. Public policies were consistent with private sector forces, and popular support for downtown development as the chief vehicle for rebuilding cities seemed widespread. Most citizens appeared content to allow the experts at city hall to carry on with existing policies and practices. No other urban revitalization strategy seemed to offer the same promise of jobs, tax revenue, and general prosperity. Downtown development was the hope of the cities.

An Alternative Interpretation

The conventional interpretation of the origins and evolution of downtown development seems plausible, reasonable, and even desirable given the political culture of most American cities during the postwar period. If one were to reinterpret the story of downtown development by positing an alternative political culture, however, a very different story might unfold. In an alternative cultural milieu, popular perceptions of downtown development might deviate markedly. What is regarded as rational and wise according to the conventional view might be perceived as irrational and foolish, and vice versa. The shift in consciousness, in turn, might generate a new form of politics surrounding downtown development with sharply diverging policy outcomes.

Such a reinterpretation of downtown development might begin with the sweeping societal forces that were reconstructing the urban landscape of the twentieth century. As in the conventional interpretation, such societal transformations as suburbanization and deindustrialization would be seen as having a devastating impact on cities. But the reaction to those transformations would vary. In the conventional interpretation, suburbanization and deindustrialization are regarded as natural and inevitable forces beyond the power of individuals to influence. Public policy that seeks to resist such forces is considered a futile exercise, a squandering of scarce resources. Only public policy designed to go with the flow and capitalize on the positive aspects of such forces would be deemed a constructive use of resources. Under this perspective, private-sector trends determine public policy choices. Such an understanding of the relationship between the private and public sectors made the downtown development policies adopted in most American cities seem perfectly rational.[10]

But in an alternative political culture, citizens would be less likely to interpret societal changes in such a deterministic manner. While acknowledging the impact of suburbanization and deindustrialization on urban life, citizens would be inclined to reject the notion that they were at the mercy of transformations emanating from the private sector. They would question, for example, just how "natural" these transformations were. Was suburbanization simply a consequence of changes in popular tastes, technology, and the economy (that is, changes in the private sector)? Or did human beings acting through governmental processes and institutions play a significant role as well by heavily subsidizing middle-class housing and highway construction? In other words, to what extent did the public sector help shape popular tastes, technology, and the economy? To what extent are public- and private-sector activities inextricably intertwined? The same analysis could be applied to deindustrialization in urban neighborhoods and the growth of a postindustrial economy in downtown business districts. Were such trends a reflection of purely private-sector phenomena? Or were public policies such as extensive government efforts to promote high-tech business growth in the suburbs and the Sunbelt and corporate services in downtown business districts even more decisive in influencing events? The point is that in an alternative political culture citizens are less likely to view societal forces as natural and inevitable phenomena beyond human control; indeed, such forces are just as likely to be seen as the product of human control. Consequently, if the public sector is perceived to be at least partially responsible for the urban problems caused by deindustrialization and suburbanization, then it follows that the public sector ought to be able to contribute to the formulation of possible remedies.[11]

The shift from a fatalistic to a more activist consciousness has important implications. If citizens do not believe they have the power to shape events, they have little incentive to participate in public life. Fatalism breeds political passivity. But in a political culture in which citizens believe that what happens in the political realm matters, active engagement in public life would be more common. At a minimum, they would pay attention to what goes on. There would be a heightened sensitivity to the formation and consequences of public policy. Policies that generate negative impacts are particularly likely to capture the attention of an engaged citizenry.

Applying some of these alternative values and assumptions to the issue area of downtown development, citizens might be more acutely aware of the direct costs arising from the rapid expansion of the downtown business district. Some might perceive a noticeable deterioration in the quality of life. Many of those who live or work downtown might object to the crush of new high-rise towers that block sunshine and turn city streets into dark, windswept canyons. Others might resent the environmental harm caused by the increased traffic congestion in the downtown core. Still others might lament the loss of historic buildings to make room for soulless, box-like behemoths of glass and steel. In the eyes of such citizens, downtown development would mean that old city charms would vanish in favor of modern office buildings and concrete parking garages. The vitality of downtown life would be under assault.

The material impacts of aggressive downtown growth might also be perceived more readily in an alternative political culture composed of actively engaged citizens. Apart from the most obvious costs associated with the direct displacement of residents and small-business owners caused by demolition and new construction, citizens might be more attuned to the indirect costs that ripple out from downtown. For instance, some might detect a steady rise in property taxes and rents, and thus additional rounds of displacement beyond the downtown business district. Others might complain about mounting traffic congestion, not just downtown but also on the neighborhood avenues and boulevards leading to downtown. Others might criticize the extra burdens on the public transit system that result when thousands of new employees begin to commute to new downtown jobs.

By the same token, citizens might be suspicious of the promised benefits of a downtown-centered postindustrial economy. Downtown development might create jobs and generate tax revenue, but would those benefits find their way to the residents of struggling urban neighborhoods? Or would most of the good jobs leak to suburbanites? And how much tax revenue would be available for the neighborhoods after taking into account the city's practice of providing substantial tax abatements to downtown investors, not to mention the revenue that would be needed to supply services to an expanding downtown center? The image of downtown wealth flowing to surrounding neighborhoods would be regarded with considerable skepticism.

Indeed, citizens in an alternative political culture would be more likely to perceive downtown growth as leading to an uneven pattern of urban development in which the downtown core flourishes while surrounding neighborhoods continue to be neglected. The long-term prospects for a city undergoing such a pattern of development would not be considered bright. People would foresee the neighborhoods' declining standard of living, which would continue to hasten middle-class flight, thus further eroding the city's tax base. The resulting additional cuts in public services would lead to a deepening slide in the quality of urban life and yet another round of middle-class flight. Decay and dilapidation would blight broad sections of the city. Under such circumstances even the prosperous downtown business district would be seen to be at risk. In short, a consistent pattern of uneven development would be viewed as inimical to the city's long-term interests.[12]

In an atmosphere of popular skepticism over the wisdom of a policy agenda that would lead to such an undesirable outcome, it is predictable that doubts would arise regarding the architects of the city's downtown development strategy. The tendency to defer to the skilled expertise of elite policymakers in ascertaining what policies would advance the city's interest would fade. Citizens would begin to take more initiative in charting the future development of their city. After all, it is they who directly experience the costs and benefits of downtown development as they go about living their lives in the neighborhoods, so they are better positioned to evaluate the city's interest. And since downtown development affects urban groups in a variety of ways, broad public debate would be encouraged to ensure that all interests would be heard and responded to.

In summary, the central features of this alternative political culture would be a vigorous and expansive public sphere characterized by widespread popular engagement in the political process. City government would assume an activist stance in minimizing the costs and maximizing the benefits of downtown development. The principal goal would be to promote a more equitable development of the city.

In this political culture, certain kinds of public policies that seem reasonable when viewed through another cultural lens are perceived as rather dubious. For example, the policy of offering a vast array of inducements to businesses contemplating investment in the downtown core no longer is interpreted as a wise strategy of capitalizing on a natural and inevitable process of economic restructuring. Instead, the policy is viewed as exacerbating the problem of uneven development. Perpetuating such a self-defeating policy is seen as illogical. A more equitable development of the city, in this view, calls for a scaling back, or even an abandonment, of business inducements to promote downtown development.

In a political culture that respects the capacity of the public sector to influence urban conditions, citizens would feel comfortable backing policies aimed at regulating the pace and character of downtown growth. Strict governmental restrictions on the height, bulk, and perhaps overall number of new development projects would be viewed favorably as a means to moderate the negative impacts of rapid downtown growth.

Moreover, government might be employed proactively to ensure that whatever negative impacts remained would not fall disproportionately on the backs of neighborhood residents; instead, those agents who caused the negative impacts might be required to assume responsibility for them by taking appropriate mitigation measures. For example, if a commercial office developer constructed a fifty-story office building that employed three thousand people, half of whom would take public transit to and from work each day, one negative impact might be an overcrowding of city buses and subways. The developer could be required to offset that impact of the development project by contributing funds to provide new buses or subway cars. Likewise, if the same project cut into the affordable housing supply by introducing an additional three thousand prospective residents into the city, it would be reasonable to require the developer to contribute funds for the production of affordable housing to offset the increased demand. If the developer stands to benefit from a commercial office project because the downtown-centered postindustrial economy is thriving, the same developer could be held accountable when a project generates costs for the surrounding community. Public policies might take such thinking one step further and hold downtown developers accountable for the promises they make when seeking official permission to proceed with their projects. One often-heard promise, for example, is that new commercial office buildings will create jobs for city residents. But rather than relying on the market to ensure that this happens, city government might enact a law that simply requires developers to honor such a promise. All of these public policies adopted through an activist government open and accessible to ordinary citizens in the neighborhoods would help to ensure a more equitable development of the city.

The previous account of the policies associated with such an alternative political culture is by no means a hypothetical scenario. In fact, it is a reasonably accurate description of the politics of downtown development in at least three major U.S. cities during the 1980s—San Francisco, Boston, and Seattle.[13] In each of these cities, neighborhood residents disgruntled with downtown development challenged the downtown growth coalition and were eventually able to reverse the long-entrenched pattern of downtown business prerogative in policy making in favor of development policies that more directly responded to neighborhood concerns. For instance, all three cities came to view business inducements such as tax abatements and density bonuses as "business giveaways" and thus moved to scale back the use of inducements or in some cases eliminate them altogether. Careful government regulation of downtown development also characterized policy making in all three cities. Height and bulk restrictions are commonplace in most cities, but in these three cities such restrictions were rigorously enforced. San Francisco, in its desire to curb the adverse impacts of rapid growth, went so far as to set a limit of five hundred thousand square feet of new commercial office development per year, the strictest downtown building regulation in the nation. And finally, all three cities enacted various so-called linkage policies to hold developers accountable for the negative impacts of their projects and to ensure that downtown development really would be linked to development in the neighborhoods. In all three cities, citizen participation in the development policy-making process was widespread.

In the conventional interpretation of downtown development, a prevailing assumption was that an activist government intruding upon the "natural" market forces determining land use patterns would yield a hostile business climate inhibiting economic investment. But even though downtown business leaders in San Francisco, Boston, and Seattle certainly grumbled about the enactment of regulatory and redistributive policies, the downtown real estate market in each of those cities remained red hot throughout the 1980s. In fact, a startling situation developed in San Francisco by the end of the decade. After city voters passed a citizens initiative imposing an annual cap on downtown commercial office development, developers began to compete among themselves for the privilege of obtaining a limited number of office development permits each year. That competition impelled developers not only to comply with the various linkage measures mandated by law, but to offer funds for affordable housing, mass transit, and job training above and beyond what the linkage laws required. In other words, investor prerogative was turned on its head; instead of cities competing with each other for investment dollars by providing myriad inducements, potential investors competed with each other for the privilege of building their projects in San Francisco. The political culture that fostered such alternative downtown development policies was itself reaffirmed and strengthened as the policies were implemented and became institutionalized. Even those groups that had originally been skeptical of or hostile to the neighborhood-based policy initiatives came to see them in a new light. Some even came to share the prevailing neighborhood perspective that such policies advanced the long-term interests of the city by promoting balanced and equitable growth. Consequently, the alternative political culture in these cities became even more deeply entrenched, a condition that continued to shape the politics of downtown development in remarkable ways.

The Constitutive Impact of the Local Political Culture

The two contrasting interpretations of the politics of downtown development illuminate how the surrounding cultural context shapes political consciousness. Individuals in different political cultures may look at the same set of facts underlying the contemporary urban crisis and the most common policy response to that crisis and yet reach very different conclusions about their interests and options. That is because when individuals affected by downtown development think about their interests, evaluate the wisdom of public policies, and calculate the costs and benefits of various courses of action, they do their thinking, evaluating, and calculating through a cultural prism. The resulting interpretation of what has happened and what ought to be done is guided by whatever ideas, values, beliefs, and practices happen to predominate in that city at that time. Decisions about interests and options "make sense" to individuals depending on the nature of the local political culture. In short, the preceding two interpretations of downtown development establish at least a prima facie case that the local political culture matters a great deal in shaping the politics of downtown development.

Most scholars have analyzed development politics in objective terms, however, as if the political culture did not color perceptions of interests and options. Especially prominent in this regard is Paul Peterson, who contends in his book *City Limits* that the development policies advocated by downtown growth coalitions advance the objective interests of the general public. Those policies often do seem compelling to a wide range of urban groups, but that is largely because the prevailing political culture in most U.S. cities favors the policy preferences of downtown-oriented elites. Where an alternative political culture thrives, those very same policies no longer appear as rational and desirable as Peterson would have us believe. Where an alternative political culture thrives, an entirely different set of development policies is perceived to further the city's interests. Peterson's failure to recognize the constitutive impact of the local political culture seriously weakens his analysis of city politics.

Peterson is hardly the only culprit. Surprisingly few political scientists have considered how the cultural realm affects urban politics. One exception is Jeffrey R. Henig, who reflects on the link between political culture and popular mobilization in asking why citizens victimized by the current urban crisis do not rebel more often and more forcefully. He compares the quiescent 1980s with the activist 1960s and notes how the public philosophies that prevailed during the two eras differed. Activists in the 1960s were influenced by a political culture that respected the public realm. Government intervention to promote equality of opportunity had been legitimized by the success of New Deal programs, and popular participation in politics was tolerated, even celebrated at times. Given this atmosphere, urban residents were more likely to perceive their interests and political options in ways that favored support for grassroots mobilization. By the 1980s, however, the public-oriented ideology of the 1960s had given way to a cultural environment that accentuated the private sphere and individualist paths to self-fulfillment. Henig argues that it is too simplistic to say that the subsequent decline in collective political action is attributable, as rational-choice theorists would have it, to aggrieved citizens coolly assessing their situations and deciding that the benefits of participating in a movement are not worth the costs. Rather, one must also consider how the overarching political culture can "skew the conceptions upon which individuals' calculations are based." Henig asserts that "the distinction between practical obstacles that hamper mobilization among individuals who are alert to their common interests and other obstacles that make it difficult for people to interpret accurately what their interests really are is significant. Although the latter are conceptually and empirically more elusive, they may provide the more valuable insights into the background of political quiescence."[14]

Along similar lines, Michael P. Smith notes that most political scientists overlook "the subtle ways that dominant beliefs and the ritual acts that reinforce such beliefs limit the range of political actions and public policies that various cultures come to define as legitimate." Furthermore, according to Smith, "future research in urban studies would benefit from a close examination of the cultural and ideological process that determine how people in particular national and local cultural settings come to define their values and interests, prior to the point where 'interests' are either mobilized into politics or deflected from consideration. In particular, urban researchers must adequately account for the current decline in social protest activities and class-based political mobilization at the very time that objective economic conditions and government fiscal austerity are worsening the plight of many working people."[15]

In general, the "local cultural settings" that characterize most American cities mold popular perceptions of self-interest and the public interest regarding downtown development such that only a narrow range of public policies are seen as legitimate, and this has important ramifications for political activity. Even neighborhood leaders advocating political change may not conceive of certain ideas, goals, and policies because they are too far removed from the bounds of what is considered proper and realistic. Moreover, even if activists do have alternative policies and strategies to suggest, rallying a citizenry that has been culturally conditioned to look upon existing arrangements as natural and inevitable becomes an onerous task.

But although the cultural context often constrains neighborhood-based protest directed against downtown growth coalitions, it is also possible that the cultural context may have the opposite effect. It is conceivable that an alternative political culture could actually assist neighborhood activists in mobilizing citizens to challenge downtown-led regimes and fundamentally reorder the policies that guide downtown development. If the local political culture does occupy a crucial role in clashes between neighborhood residents and downtown growth coalitions over development policy, the precise nature of that role still needs to be spelled out. The principal goal of this book is to elucidate how the local political culture matters in shaping the politics of downtown development.

✦2

Political Culture and Political Change

The Silent Revolution

Some of the most provocative research on the relationship between political culture and political behavior during the past two decades has come from Ronald Inglehart and his followers.[1] Inglehart has argued that during the post–World War II era, the citizens of advanced industrial nations have experienced a cultural transformation marked by a move away from materialistic values such as economic and physical security and toward postmaterialistic values such as individual autonomy, self-expression, and quality of life. At a more specific, issue-oriented level, this has meant a departure from the more traditional preoccupation with economic growth, employment, wage levels, and law and order in favor of a deeper concern for environmental protection, nuclear disarmament, women's rights, and tolerance for alternative lifestyles.

The primary impetus for what is nothing less than a "silent revolution" has been the widespread peace and prosperity that most advanced industrial nations have enjoyed over the past five decades: Because "an unprecedentedly large portion of Western populations have been raised under conditions of exceptional economic security," more and more people have been able to "take this kind of security for granted." As a result, "economic and physical security continue to be valued positively, but their relative priority is lower than in the past."[2] The resulting shift toward a postmaterial culture, which first became widely evident during the 1960s, has progressed steadily through the decades as younger generations with "new orientations" replaced older generations with "traditional values and norms."[3] Inglehart's claims about the nature and the extent of the cultural transformation are buttressed by an enormous body of comparative survey data measuring popular and elite opinion in twenty nations over a period of two decades.

Inglehart then explores the political implications of the spreading postmaterial culture. He believes that the greater sense of economic and physical security associated with a postmaterial society leads to "a growing potential for citizen participation in politics" and that the quality of that participation is inevitably better because of the expansion of formal educational opportunities. As citizens acquire more sophisticated political knowledge and skills, Inglehart asserts that they are no longer content to limit their involvement in politics to simply casting a ballot in periodic elections. In a postmaterial society, citizens insist on assuming a more active role in shaping the actual governing process between elections. "Elite-directed" politics gradually gives way to "elite-directing" politics.[4]

At this level of political activity, the possession of political skills becomes essential, according to Inglehart: "Special skills are prerequisite to playing an effective role in the politics of an extensive political community." Citizens who hope to direct elites in the making of public policy must develop a capacity "to manipulate political abstractions and thereby to coordinate activities that are remote in space and time. Without such skills, one is more or less doomed to remain outside the political life of a modern nation-state."[5] The need for political sophistication expands as the world becomes ever more complex.

In Inglehart's scheme, much of elite-directing politics might be considered unconventional or outside the bounds of "normal" political institutions. Perhaps the most visible manifestation of this form of political behavior in the postmaterial era is the social movement. The inclination of aggrieved individuals alienated from mainstream politics to join grassroots protest movements is hardly a new phenomenon. But whereas old social movements often involved conflicts over material resources that pitted one social class against another, new social movements are organized around alternative sources of collective identity such as ethnicity, age, gender, and sexual orientation. Moreover, the values and goals that are thought to enhance the quality of life in a postmaterial society transcend class boundaries since members of all social groups are potentially affected. Prominent examples of new social movements include the peace, antinuclear, environmental, women's rights, and gay and lesbian rights movements. In the context of institutional politics, new social movement activity has provided essential support for the emergence of alternative political parties such as the Greens in various European countries.[6]

Inglehart's theory that the transformation from a materialist to a postmaterialist culture accounts for changes in political behavior has generated substantial interest in the academic community and a long list of scholars who have utilized important aspects of his approach in their own work.[7] It is easy to see why. His cultural analysis helps to explain why there has been a decline in traditional forms of political participation such as political parties and electoral voting but a rise in other forms of political expression such as new social movements. Moreover, the proliferation of postmaterial attitudes, beliefs, and values would also seem to explain why the most forceful proponents of social change have not been members of the working class as Marxist theory had predicted, but members of the middle class who are dissatisfied with the quality of their lives.

Application of Inglehart's postmaterialist theory to the realm of urban politics has also yielded promising research. Donald L. Rosdil, who has perhaps been most directly influenced by Inglehart, has sought to demonstrate the connection between American cities that have adopted progressive policies and the postmaterial culture that pervades those cities. Where postmaterial values are missing, Rosdil contends that the likelihood of progressive policies will be significantly diminished. Mark E. Kann's *Middle Class Radicalism in Santa Monica* and the case studies of Burlington, Vermont, and Berkeley, California, in Pierre Clavel's *Progressive City* provide additional confirming evidence for Inglehart's theory of the relationship between political culture and local politics.[8]

The notion that a postmaterial culture leads to a fundamental change in political behavior is not entirely convincing, however. When Inglehart's theory is applied to the realm of urban politics (and given the emphasis on participatory politics, one would assume that the local level of politics would be most favorable to his theory), one difficulty is its limited generalizability. Inglehart's brand of postmaterialism seems to be confined to a handful of small, middle-class, college towns. In larger cities the spread of postmaterial values has had a much smaller impact on politics. In part this is because Inglehart seriously overestimates the extent to which material values have been in decline. A growing percentage of people may indeed value environmental protection, nuclear disarmament, and freedom of expression, but that does not mean that most of these same people do not attach a high level of significance to their material well-being. Job security, a decent income, and upward mobility all still matter a great deal to people who hold postmaterial values, not to mention the majority of individuals who, even according to Inglehart's own research, retain a materialist mindset.[9] The continuing importance of material values and aspirations may impede the radical potential of postmaterialism in the political sphere.

In addition, Inglehart may have underestimated the downside of the transition from an industrial to a service- and information-based economy. Although millions of individuals have benefited from the increase in high-paying jobs as professionals and business executives, the new economy has also entailed an expansion in low-paying, low-status employment. As union-based, well-paying manufacturing jobs have diminished, millions of working-class citizens have been forced to accept significant cuts in wages and benefits in an increasingly polarized workforce. This segment of the population has had little choice but to dwell on issues of economic security.[10] Nor have more privileged groups been as immune from materialistic worries as Inglehart would suggest. The wave of mergers and acquisitions that swept the country during the 1980s and the corporate downsizing that has continued into the 1990s have compelled even the beneficiaries of global economic change to think long and hard about their material status.

Hence, there is ample reason to believe that at least in the United States millions of people have embraced materialism with renewed vigor. And the ramifications for the political sphere are clear. New social movements guided by a postmaterial perspective may persist, but they do so in a political environment that has seen Ronald Reagan triumph as the dominant political figure of late-twentieth-century America and the Republican Party emerge as the nation's majority political party. Finally, the broad popularity of conservative leaders such as Margaret Thatcher, Helmut Kohl, and Jacques Chirac in recent years indicates that a politics sparked by a thriving materialist culture is not confined to the United States.

Inglehart might respond to such criticism by emphasizing that the pace of cultural change is gradual. He acknowledges that even by the year 2000, materialists will still outnumber postmaterialists and that far-reaching changes in political behavior in large cities and entire nations will therefore be slow in coming. He writes, "Cultural theory implies that a culture cannot be changed overnight. One may change the rulers and the laws, but changing basic aspects of the underlying culture will take many years."[11] But this points to a second problem with Inglehart's theory—its strikingly deterministic character. According to Inglehart, cultural change in advanced industrial society is a response to broad societal changes and intergenerational population replacement; any role for human agency in promoting cultural change is minimal. Even theorists of new social movements write as though activists were simply exploiting *preexisting* changes in popular consciousness in their efforts to bring about political changes. This perspective undervalues the role of individuals in engendering cultural or political change through their own efforts, especially in contexts where an alternative worldview does not already predominate.

These two weaknesses in Inglehart's theory—the lingering pervasiveness of materialist values, beliefs, and aspirations and the minimal role accorded to individuals as agents of cultural change—cast doubt on the notion that a rising postmaterial culture is the inevitable catalyst for fundamental political change. In fact, when activists with a postmaterial worldview participate in the political realm in hopes of effecting significant policy reform, their impact is likely to be limited. Advocating postmaterial issues when a substantial majority still views politics through a materialist cultural lens turns out to be a hard sell. Green issues simply do not resonate when so many people are worried about job security, health insurance, and paying the rent. Indeed, social movements propagating postmaterial goals run a risk of provoking genuine resentment among the majority, who may see the activists as elitist snobs, utterly out of touch with the mainstream.

Notwithstanding these problems, Inglehart's theory is valuable because it underscores the fact that culture matters in shaping politics. The basic insight that the overarching culture molds perceptions of interests and options, thus influencing political behavior, remains sound. Furthermore, Inglehart's specific focus on postmaterialism as an agent of political change is instructive. He makes a convincing case that postmaterial values have spread widely in advanced industrial societies in the decades since World War II and that those values constitute a clear alternative to a dominant culture that reaffirms the legitimacy of existing power structures. It is therefore possible to conceive of postmaterialism as a kind of breeding ground for protest movements directed against ruling elites and the structures that sustain their power. But apart from a few small middle-class communities where postmaterialism really does flourish, the Inglehart scheme does not persuasively explain how or why cultural change may generate fundamental political change.

A better cultural theory of political change would recognize a greater role for human agency as well as the radical potential embedded in persisting material concerns. After all, why assume, as Inglehart does, that a materialistic culture is necessarily a conservative one? It may be possible for activists to appeal to the material concerns of the majority, but do so in ways that avoid reaffirming the political culture that inhibits fundamental political change. The proper kind of grassroots activism might transform the prevailing political culture so that individuals come to perceive their interests and options through a different cultural prism, producing a shift in consciousness that would then facilitate real political change. In sum, an alternative model of cultural/political change suggests that a less deterministic approach that is more grounded in the everyday, material concerns of the majority may be more fruitful. That model is provided by the theorist who has been most influential in searching for a bridge between the economism of orthodox Marxist theory and cultural theory—Antonio Gramsci.

Gramsci's Theory of Cultural Hegemony/Counterhegemony

Antonio Gramsci's theory of cultural hegemony/counterhegemony has been extensively analyzed elsewhere, so a relatively brief overview of his insights into radical change will suffice here. The quandary that Marxist scholars such as

Gramsci faced in the 1920s and 1930s was: Given striking inequalities in wealth and power in Western industrial nations, why had working-class people not rebelled against their capitalist rulers? Marx had predicted that as capitalism experienced increasing internal contradictions, and as objective conditions worsened for the proletariat, oppressed workers would throw off their chains and demand fundamental change. But although revolution had come to Russia, the working class in most industrial nations remained quiescent. Gramsci sought to develop a theory that would account for this unexpected popular passivity by considering how individual perceptions of societal and political conditions were shaped by the prevailing culture. "The major premise of Gramsci's theory of revolution," according to Gramscian scholar Joseph V. Femia, "is that objective material interests are not automatically or inevitably translated into class consciousness. In contrast to the mainstream of Marxist analysis, Gramsci understood that responses are invariably culturally conditioned, that political action—even in the long run—cannot be conceived as an 'objective' calculating of costs and benefits, for the very definition of what constitutes costs and benefits necessarily presupposes some framework of values and categories which does not itself merely reflect 'external reality.'"[12] That preexisting "framework of values and categories," Gramsci came to believe, reflects the needs and interests of the dominant groups in society. It is through that cultural framework that powerful groups are able to secure the consent of the masses to existing arrangements. More specifically, subordination had been achieved not through coercion, but because the dominant groups had succeeded in persuading the masses of the legitimacy of both the prevailing distribution of wealth and power and the values, beliefs, and norms that determine how that distribution occurs.

Gramsci's most intriguing contribution to radical political theory was his notion of cultural hegemony, which he conceived of as "the 'spontaneous' consent given by the great masses of the population to the general direction imposed on social life by the dominant fundamental group; this consent is 'historically' caused by the prestige (and consequent confidence) which the dominant group enjoys because of its position and function in the world of production." Another student of Gramscian theory, Carl Boggs, expands on the all-important concept of hegemony:

> It encompassed the whole range of values, attitudes, beliefs, cultural norms, legal precepts, etc. that to one degree or another permeated civil society, that solidified the class structure and the multiple forms of domination that pass through it. The arenas of ideological-cultural transmission are infinite: the state, legal system, workplace, schools, church, bureaucracies, cultural activities, the media, the family. Hegemony quite clearly embraces far more than single, well-defined ideologies (e.g. liberalism) that can be said to reflect (and mystify) the interests

> of dominant classes. In capitalist societies it might include not only the competitive individualism diffused by liberalism but also the social atomization and depoliticization produced by bureaucracy, the fatalism instilled by religion, the state-worship fanned by nationalism, and the sexism which grows out of the family. . . . Whatever the patterns, Gramsci observed that ruling elites always sought to justify their power, wealth, and status *ideologically,* with the aim of securing general popular acceptance of their dominant position as something "natural," a part of an eternal social order, and thus unchallengeable.[13]

In short, the dominant classes exercise hegemonic power when their ideas, values, beliefs, and practices saturate a society's culture.

At the same time, Gramsci was very much aware that subordinate groups were not exactly enchanted with their difficult and sometimes oppressive circumstances; hence, the internalization of the dominant class's view of the world was far from absolute. Accordingly, Gramsci asserted that popular consciousness was "fragmentary, incoherent and inconsequential." He elaborated on this condition of contradictory consciousness:

> The social group in question may indeed have its own conception of the world, even if only embryonic; a conception which manifests itself in action, but occasionally and in flashes—when, that is, the group is acting as an organic totality. But this same group has, for reasons of submission and intellectual subordination, adapted a conception which is not its own but is borrowed from another group; and it affirms this conception verbally and believes itself to be following it, because this is the conception which it follows in "normal times"—that is when its conduct is not independent and autonomous, but submissive and subordinate.

So, for example, factory workers perceiving their immediate circumstances during "normal times" may despise their boss for ordering them to work under miserable conditions, and yet because they have internalized the capitalist principle of managerial prerogative, they simultaneously respect the right of the boss to issue such an order. Gramsci summarized his conception of popular consciousness this way: "The active man-in-the-mass has a practical activity, but has no clear theoretical consciousness of his practical activity. . . . One might almost say that he has two theoretical consciousnesses (or one contradictory consciousness): one which is implicit in his activity and which in reality unites him with all his fellow-workers in the practical transformation of the real world; and one, superficially explicit or verbal, which he has inherited from the past and uncritically absorbed."[14]

Unfortunately for proponents of radical change, the consciousness inherited from the dominant classes tends to prevail over the incipient ideology that is implicit in the workers' daily experiences. As Femia explains,

> consent . . . emerges not so much because the masses profoundly regard the social order as an expression of their aspirations as because they lack the conceptual tools, the "clear theoretical consciousness," which would enable them effectively to comprehend and act on their discontent—discontent manifest in the activity which unites them "in the practical transformation of reality." . . . Because it is devoid of overall direction or purpose, this action is sporadic and ineffective. The average person lacks the means with which to formulate the radical alternative "implicit in his activity." On the one hand, his education has never provided him with the ability to manipulate abstract symbols, to think clearly and systematically; on the other hand, all the institutional mechanisms through which perception is shaped—the schools, the Church, the conventional political parties, the mass media, even the trade unions—in one way or another play into the hands of the ruling groups.

Gramsci believed that the political consequences of such a "disjointed and episodic" conception of the world were grave. Although the subordinate classes may occasionally react to their oppression by rebelling (e.g. insubordination, strikes, riots, etc.), most will find it difficult to sustain such a rebellion. They simply lack the means to transform perceptions of what they experience in daily life into a coherent worldview that would unify the subordinate classes in a potent oppositional movement. The result is a kind of paralysis: "the contradictory state of consciousness does not permit of any action, any decision or any choice, and produces a condition of moral and political passivity."[15]

Gramsci argued that revolutionary struggle, at least in the industrial West, could succeed only if an attempt to gain state power were preceded by an extended campaign to transform the contradictory consciousness of subordinate groups into a coherent conception of the world based on their practical activity. Without this initial effort to transform consciousness, which he called a "war of position," any seizure of state power, which he labeled a "war of maneuver," would be doomed to fail because "the momentarily triumphant revolutionary forces would find themselves facing a largely hostile population, still confined within the mental universe of the bourgeoisie." Therefore, Gramsci insisted that revolution was possible only after a cultural transformation had enabled the working class to develop its own hegemony of ideas, values, beliefs, and practices: "A social group can, and indeed must, already exercise leadership [that is, be hegemonic] before winning governmental power (this is one of the principal conditions for the very conquest of such power)."[16]

But how would such a cultural revolution occur? How would contradictory consciousness ever evolve into the kind of critical consciousness necessary for enduring political change? To start, Gramsci rejected all deterministic variants of cultural/political transformation. He dismissed the Marxian notion that economic change manifested by declining conditions under advanced capitalism would impel oppressed workers to rise up in rebellion. Nor did he believe that other forms of broad social change would inevitably reorder popular values and beliefs such that individuals would perceive of their interests and options in radically new ways. Rather, Gramsci insisted that revolutionary consciousness would have to be the product of human action. More specifically, revolutionary leadership would have to come from "intellectuals"[17] who have the capacity to see the world clearly, distinguish among competing worldviews, and assist subordinate classes in developing a coherent understanding of existing conditions.

Gramsci's intellectuals would be "organically" tied to the subordinate classes through familial relations and institutional associations such as the workplace. This bond would encourage a more genuine understanding of the conditions and aspirations of oppressed groups. Gramsci believed that the intellectuals, to further cement that bond, always needed to be actively engaged in the practical life of subordinate groups so that they would be well positioned to validate the masses' embryonic understanding of power relations inherent in their daily activity and expose the legitimizing ideologies of the dominant classes. This close proximity between the leaders and the masses was essential for transforming popular consciousness from its conflicted and passive state into a coherent and revolutionary state.[18]

Gramsci anticipated that this process of transforming mass consciousness would take place within the myriad associational contexts of civil society, wherever subordinate groups were bombarded by conflicting visions of the world. The workplace was one obvious site where incipient understandings of power relations would collide with the learned ideologies of the hegemonic culture. But the schools, the media, the church, and any other societal institution of ideological diffusion also represented potential sites for cultural contestation in a massive "war of position." As mass consciousness gradually becomes less contradictory and more coherent within each associational context, a counterhegemonic worldview emerges, paving the way toward a sweeping cultural transformation.

Cognizant of the immensity of the task of waging such a vast counterhegemonic war within civil society, Gramsci saw the need for some kind of overarching structure to motivate and guide the effort. In another important departure from orthodox Marxism, Gramsci sought to restore politics as a central category of revolutionary change. Here inspired more by Machiavelli than Marx, he saw the political sphere as the arena in which human beings could best control their own destinies. And within the political sphere, Gramsci identified the modern political party as the ideal catalyst for exciting the passions of "a dispersed and shattered people" behind a "national popular collective will."[19]

Gramsci's political party would fulfill two functions. First, it would play an educative role as the primary agent for transforming mass consciousness. Second, it would play an organizational role as the main institution overseeing and coordinating the multitude of counterhegemonic struggles going on throughout civil society.[20] As the various subordinate groups developed a clearer conception of the world, the political party would work to nurture class alliances under a unifying counterhegemonic vision. The resulting "historical bloc" would then be poised to create history by turning its hard-earned cultural power into far-reaching political power.

For Gramsci, then, the key to revolutionary change was collective struggle aimed at transforming a culture that produced a contradictory consciousness in the minds of subordinate groups, a condition that inhibited sustained popular protest while bolstering the power of dominant groups. Such a struggle would be fought on two fronts: (1) at the grass roots within the numerous institutions of civil society and (2) within the political realm by a radical political party providing intellectual and organizational leadership. Persistent collective action would subvert the hegemonic culture that legitimized existing power structures while advancing a counterhegemonic vision of the world that would fundamentally alter how individuals decided what was natural, reasonable, and desirable. As popular conceptions evolved, the barriers to lasting political change would fall away.

The Mechanics of Cultural/Political Change

Gramsci's theory of hegemony/counterhegemony was bold and original. It has influenced generations of scholars, activists, and politicians not only in Italy but all over the world. But when one attempts to apply Gramscian theory to a particular context such as the politics of downtown development, two problems stand out. First, it is breathtakingly ambitious. The proposition that fundamental political change could occur only after an extended campaign of counterhegemonic struggle within all institutions of civil society would give even the most ardent revolutionary reason to pause. In fact, the kind of sweeping change that Gramsci envisioned has never taken place in a Western democracy, and one must wonder whether it ever could.

The remedy for this first problem may simply be a lowering of horizons. Most obviously, the concept of "fundamental change" need not be confined to a colossal shift from capitalism to socialism. Also, it may not be necessary to fight and win a "war of position" in all institutions of civil society before a change in political power can even be contemplated. Even Gramsci seemed to acknowledge this by according the political party the principal role in promoting revolutionary change, and thus treating the political sphere as the central arena of counterhegemonic struggle. Furthermore, within the political realm, it may not be essential to rely so heavily on a political party; other institutions might also fulfill the functions of political education, organization, and coalition building. This kind of flexibility in thinking about Gramscian theory enhances the potential for expanding the range of workable applications in politics today.[21]

The second limitation of Gramscian theory is a lack of precision in specifying the mechanisms of cultural/political change. The general components are readily apparent—an ongoing collective struggle at the source of popular discontent, guided by indigenous leaders and coordinated by an overarching political party—but exactly how this vast grassroots movement is supposed to transform the contradictory consciousness of the masses remains sketchy.

The Prison Notebooks highlights the role of ideas. What is needed is a vision to excite the passions of the masses. That vision must resonate with the incipient knowledge that subordinate groups acquire simply by living their day-to-day lives and at the same time squarely contest and undermine the hegemonic vision that so favors the dominant groups. Such a vision is essential to transforming contradictory consciousness into a single and coherent conception of how the world operates.

The problem is that Gramsci's discussion of counterhegemonic activism is heavily tilted toward the idealist realm. More is needed than just a counterhegemonic vision, or a set of revolutionary ideas. Gramsci would no doubt concur. Despite his emphasis on the importance of ideas, he could never be pigeonholed as an idealist, for he always appreciated the dialectical relationship between ideas and structures. Nevertheless, what is missing from his theory of revolutionary change is sustained attention to how concrete practices interact with an all-encompassing vision of radical politics. At times Gramsci does make cryptic references to how this dialectic works in an actual context. For example, when he points to the Jacobins of eighteenth-century France as a model of counterhegemonic activism, he notes how well their "language, their ideology, their methods of action" meshed in responding to the immediate needs and aspirations of subordinate groups.[22] What made the Jacobins such a powerful counterhegemonic force was that their discourse and conduct conformed to an appealing vision of change. Anything short of this congruence between a clear vision of radical change and conforming practice and their influence would have been much weaker. In other words, had the Jacobins offered a vision that blended aspects of the old aristocratic order with the new bourgeois order, or engaged in practices that sent out mixed signals, their ability to undermine the hegemonic culture would have been diminished. Popular consciousness would have remained conflicted. People would have continued to interpret their interests and options through a cultural prism that inhibited alternative ways of seeing and organizing the world. And yet Gramsci neglected to elaborate on the concrete practices of counterhegemonic activism, or how those practices would interact with oppositional ideas to transform popular consciousness.

In sum, Gramsci's theory of hegemony/counterhegemony is a powerful one in terms of potential applications; his analysis of revolutionary change would appear to be relevant in countless contexts. But the very breadth of his theorizing points to another limitation for particular studies. In any given case, it will be necessary to elucidate the substantive content of competing worldviews or conflicting hegemonies. What exactly is the hegemonic political culture? And what exactly should be the content of an opposing counterhegemonic vision? The core notion of human struggle to engender cultural/political change remains a constant; but any Gramscian analysis of an oppositional movement challenging elite power structures would always have to specify the composition of clashing visions of the world. Put simply, how can Gramsci's theory of radical political change be applied to contemporary politics?

The Content of Political Cultures

Before tackling the complicated task of describing the variety of relevant political cultures, it is necessary to examine the meaning of political culture. Early definitions were widely influenced by the pioneering research of Gabriel A. Almond and Sidney Verba, who set out in the years following World War II to ascertain why some political systems were vulnerable to fascist and communist revolutions while others developed into or remained liberal democracies. Focusing on the political cultures of different nation-states, they found that societies in which individuals exhibited a balance of deferential and activist attitudes toward their political system were most likely to nurture stable democracies. Almond and Verba's conceptualization of political culture accented the psychological or subjective orientations of individuals toward politics. They wrote in *The Civic Culture:* "The term political culture refers to the specifically political orientations—attitudes toward the role of the self in the system." An entire generation of political scientists embraced this definition as well as the use of mass survey instruments to measure popular attitudes and beliefs in a wide variety of cases.[23]

In time, a new wave of scholars surfaced to criticize the Almond and Verba conception of political culture as simply an aggregation of popular attitudes and sentiments toward the political system. They maintained that although attitudes and sentiments were significant, it was also important to pay attention to "recurring patterns of manifest behavior." As he endorsed the position that political culture should be viewed as a psychological *and* behavioral concept, political scientist Robert C. Tucker, a student of Soviet politics, indicated that anthropologists had influenced his thinking: "Their culture concept covers what people culturally do as well as what they culturally feel and think." Indeed, Tucker's understanding of political culture as a concept that embodies mindsets and conduct is consistent with how the broader notion of culture is viewed by most contemporary anthropologists. For instance, David M. Fetterman asserts that "definitions of culture typically espouse either a materialist or an ideational perspective. The classic materialist interpretation of culture focuses on behavior. In this view, culture is the sum of a social group's observable patterns of behavior, customs, and ways of life. The most popular ideational definition of culture . . . [emphasizes] the ideas, beliefs, and knowledge that characterize a particular group of people. . . . Obviously, ethnographers need to know about both cultural behavior and knowledge to describe a culture or subculture adequately."[24]

The current study of political culture and political change in American cities conceives of political culture in the more comprehensive manner as the constellation of ideas, values, beliefs, *and* practices that constitute the polity of a given society. Note, however, that this formulation of political culture does not yet address the question of what ideas, values, beliefs, and practices are relevant. Surely not just any aspect of knowledge or behavior associated with the political system ought to matter,[25] but only those that are in some sense fundamental. This, of course, leaves much unresolved.

Assistance in identifying what is truly fundamental may be found by considering previous attempts to elaborate the substantive content of political culture. Daniel J. Elazar's study of American political culture is a good place to start because it has attracted considerable scholarly attention, much of it focused on his classificatory criteria. In contrast to Louis Hartz's well-known thesis that Lockean liberalism has always dominated American politics,[26] Elazar contends that American political culture is actually an amalgam of three distinct subcultures, each associated with a particular region of the country. First, a moralistic political culture developed in Puritan New England in which government was seen as a positive force in promoting a moral society; all citizens were encouraged to participate in the public realm in a cooperative endeavor to further the common good. Second, an individualistic political culture emerged in the mid-Atlantic region. Here, the individual pursuit of private gain regulated only by the marketplace was considered the surest route to a well-functioning and prosperous society. The government's role was limited to ensuring that the marketplace remained in sound working order; political participation was not valued, since politics was perceived to be the province of permanent politicians whose behavior was often corrupt. Finally, a traditionalistic political culture, characterized by a strictly hierarchical view of the political world, took root in the South. Power rested in the hands of established elites who had secured their preeminence in the community through generations of family connections. They exercised political power in a paternalistic manner and discouraged citizen engagement in politics. The purpose of government was to preserve the traditional way of life. Elazar argues that as settlers from each region migrated to other parts of the United States, they carried with them their own distinctive conception of political life. Over time, the three political subcultures blended together to form a uniquely American political culture.

Elazar's attempt to classify political subcultures has been criticized by Richard Ellis on the ground that his cultural categories were derived inductively from regional variations in the United States, which caused Elazar to confuse a cultural category with a particular historical example of the cultural category. For instance, a traditional political culture is equated with the political culture of the South; but this ignores the reality of cultural deviations from traditionalism within the South, while overlooking the extent to which aspects of a traditionalism existed in New England and the mid-Atlantic region. Ellis asserts that "the fundamental weakness" of Elazar's cultural categories is that they are "neither mutually exclusive nor exhaustive."[27]

One classificatory scheme that was derived deductively, and thus presumably avoids the problems of Elazar's approach, is the cultural typology constructed by anthropologist Mary Douglas and applied to the field of political science by Aaron Wildavsky and his associates.[28] That typology is based on "the axiom that what matters most to people is their relationships with other people and other people's relationships with them." How individuals interact in society varies according to two dimensions, which Douglas labeled "grid" and "group." The grid dimension refers to the degree to which individuals perceive themselves to be restricted in their actions, and the group dimension refers to the degree to which individuals see themselves as belonging to a group. These two dimensions, constraint on action and group identification, constitute the core elements of a culture, and taken together, they delineate four distinct "ways of life." The typology of cultures associated with Douglas's grid-group dimensions appears in figure 2.1.

Each cultural variant reflects a distinct pattern of ideas, values, beliefs, and social relations. In an individualistic culture, individuals experience a high level

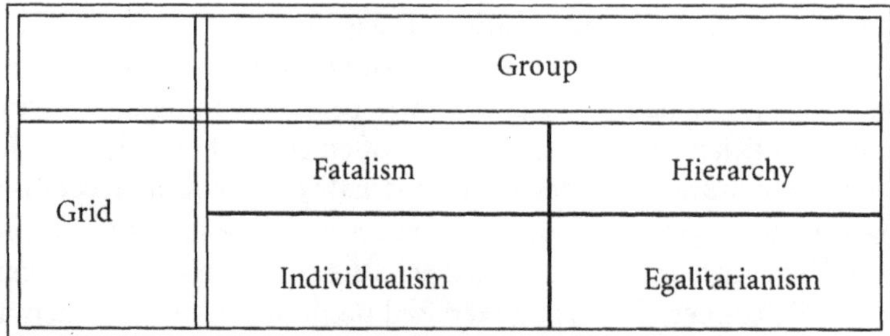

Fig. 2.1. Douglas-Wildavsky typology of cultures

of autonomy; bound neither by group responsibilities nor societal prescription, they feel free to pursue their own goals unconstrained by others in society. A prosperous business owner operating in a free market exemplifies the individualist culture. At the other extreme is a hierarchical culture. This social context is marked by well-defined group boundaries and extensive prescriptions regarding individual conduct. Individuals are constrained by clearly defined group controls and must conform to the rules appropriate to their assigned role. Order and efficiency are valued. An example is a well-run bureaucracy. An egalitarian culture is characterized by strong group identification and minimal prescriptions. Egalitarians reject the societal constraints imposed in a hierarchical context. With no one in charge and decision making by consensus, internal conflicts may be difficult to resolve. This, in turn, inclines egalitarians to build a "wall of virtue" separating the group from "the nasty, predatory and inegalitarian outside world," thus reinforcing a strong sense of group boundedness. Examples of an egalitarian culture can be found in the Green Party and the Clamshell Alliance. Finally, individuals who experience binding prescriptions but are excluded from group membership make up a fatalistic culture. Their social situation is disheartening. Their autonomy is sharply limited and they endure a high level of isolation. Slaves and prisoners live in a fatalistic culture.[29]

Wildavsky believed that each of the four cultural variants represents a way of life that, in turn, influences how individuals come to formulate their interests and how societies end up choosing which public policies to pursue. In other words, basic divisions over individual preferences and collective policies are grounded in variations in the structuring of social life. Patterns of social relationships are associated with distinct visions of politics.

Although the grid-group typology helps to classify a wide range of social relationships, the scheme does not translate easily into an adequate classification of political cultures. Social breadth comes at the expense of political relevance, especially if the focus is on urban politics in the United States. Although individualism and hierarchy are readily apparent in any quick survey of urban politics in America, the significance of the other two cultural variants—egalitarianism and fatalism—is less certain. First, as conceptualized by Douglas and Wildavsky, the egalitarian way of life is reminiscent of the social environment of a California commune in the 1960s. Individuals are free to pursue whatever lifestyle they wish, but that freedom leads them to divorce themselves from the rest of the world that does not share their values. Over time, there is a tendency to hunker down with like-minded souls, which only intensifies the egalitarians' growing sense of isolation. Such a cultural existence can certainly be linked to a vision of politics. Wildavsky and his colleagues cite the Green Party to exemplify the egalitarian culture; at the opposite end of the political spectrum, a right-wing militia might fall within the same cultural category. But how common is such a political culture in American politics, and especially urban politics? Even more marginal to contemporary urban politics is the fourth cultural variant of the Douglas-Wildavsky typology, fatalism. Subject to a high level of prescription and disconnected from society, individuals in a fatalist culture are barely visible in the political arena. Wildavsky and his colleagues go so far as to equate their condition with that of prisoners and slaves.

The deductively derived grid-group typology succeeds in establishing mutually exclusive cultural categories, in contrast with Elazar's classificatory model. It falls short as a mechanism for classifying political cultures, however. The problem is that the Douglas typology was developed by an anthropologist who was mainly concerned with illuminating cultural patterns based on varying *social* contexts. But if the goal is to better understand *political* life, then it might be more fruitful to construct a typology of political culture derived from dimensions that go to the heart and soul of politics. The appropriate place to search for such dimensions would be in the realm of political philosophy, where for centuries philosophers have contemplated issues that reflect fundamental tensions in political life. As perhaps the first renowned classifier in political thought, Aristotle may be helpful in identifying suitable criteria for a typology of political cultures.

Aristotle devised a classification scheme of political systems or "constitutions" around the categories of who rules and for what purpose. As for the former, the choices were limited to the one, the few, or the many. As for the latter, authority could be employed to promote either private or public ends. The six constitutions produced by such dimensions can be seen in figure 2.2.

Aristotle's typology contained a strongly normative thrust. Although not as elitist as his mentor, Plato, he nonetheless believed that ideally the few people possessing the most merit should rule. Likewise, Aristotle followed the ancient

	Sovereignty			
		One	Few	Many
Role of State	Public-Oriented	Monarchy	Aristocracy	Polity
	Private-Oriented	Tyranny	Oligarchy	Democracy

Fig. 2.2. Aristotle's classification of political systems. From Barker, *The Politics of Aristotle*, book 4, ch. i-xiii.

Greek respect for the public sphere. He was so committed to pursuit of the common good that he viewed any deviation by rulers toward a preoccupation with private interests as a "perversion" of the "right" constitution. Therefore, for Aristotle any of the constitutions listed in the top row of figure 2.2 would be preferable to those in the bottom row, and of the public-oriented constitutions, an aristocracy would be the most desirable.

Of course, Aristotle's own inclination toward rule by the few and for public ends did not always persuade subsequent philosophers. Proponents of democracy, for example, departed from the elitist preferences of Aristotle and Plato by advocating rule by the many. However, this certainly did not settle the issue of who should govern. Even self-proclaimed democrats continued to split over just how much power should be invested in the many as opposed to the few. Liberal democrats subscribed to majority rule, but only on the condition that the decisions of the majority did not infringe on individual rights. Representative democrats believed that the people should rule by casting votes for candidates for public office in periodic elections, but once the elections were over, the people should defer to the wisdom and experience of public officials who have mastered the art and science of governance.[30]

And with respect to the role of the state, political philosophers became increasingly conflicted with the rise of Christianity and capitalism. Many came to appreciate the virtues of the private sphere. Classical liberals lacked the confidence in the public sphere that so pervaded the Greek polis. Instead, they looked to the private market as providing the most efficient and ultimately the fairest mechanism of developing and distributing the goods and services of a society. Classical liberals believed that a limited state would maximize the freedom of individuals to pursue their own conceptions of the good life. This pursuit of self-interest by free and autonomous individuals would yield a contented and prosperous society. Meanwhile, Rousseauian republicans, communitarians, and radical democrats responded to the liberal critique by continuing in the Aristotelian tradition that sees an expansive public realm as essential to the development of virtuous character and society's well-being.[31]

The point is that political philosophers have been debating the questions of who should rule and what is the proper scope of government for centuries. These questions raise tensions that go to the very core of politics, tensions that are as alive in American politics today as ever. It is therefore no coincidence that contemporary political scientists who have tried to classify visions of politics have addressed, intentionally or unintentionally, these same core issues. Both Elazar's categories of political culture—individualism, traditionalism, and moralism—and Wildavsky's cultural variants—individualism, hierarchy, egalitarianism, and fatalism—concern themselves, directly or indirectly, with the questions of who should govern and what is the role of the state. If the recent efforts of political scientists to describe and classify political culture are considered in light of the preceding overview of the history of political thought, it is now possible to arrive at some conclusions about what kinds of ideas, values, beliefs, and practices are fundamental to politics.

The new typology of political cultures being proposed here remedies the problems that flawed previous classificatory schemes by using dimensions that produce categories of political culture that are both mutually exclusive and relevant to contemporary urban politics (see fig. 2.3).

All four political cultures promise their own visions of the good life, but their pathways differ substantially. The animating value of a privatist political culture is the generation of wealth through the pursuit of individual self-interest. If all individuals are allowed to pursue their interests freely, the assumption is that society as a whole will be better off. Accordingly, the role of government is limited to ensuring the continuous operation of a thriving market, thus maximizing the opportunity of autonomous individuals to seek their fortune. In a privatist political culture, however, individual autonomy is not synonymous with individual equality. Privatists assume inherent inequalities among people; those inequalities mean that some individuals will prosper more than others. Likewise, it is natural that some will come to wield more power than others. The power wielded by deserving elites is then utilized to ensure that the public sphere never threatens to overwhelm the private sphere. In a privatist milieu, the state is meant to serve the market.

Empirical examples of a privatist political culture abound. In American political history, Alexander Hamilton's vision of the nation's development was grounded on privatist principles. First, Hamilton expressed strong faith in the marketplace as the driving engine of economic growth, but jump-started by a government capable of building the necessary infrastructure and providing

	Source of Power	
		Elite	Mass
Scope of Government	Broad	Managerialism	Progressivism
	Limited	Privatism	Populism

Fig. 2.3. Typology of political cultures

the necessary protection for infant industries. Second, he believed that America's economic development policies would be devised and implemented by individuals of grand vision, energy, and intelligence, like Hamilton himself. The privatist spirit suffuses the politics of U.S. cities. Sam Bass Warner's study of the evolution of the city of Philadelphia in *The Private City* is an excellent illustration of elite power combined with a weak public sector. More recently, a plethora of studies of urban power relations have described a policy-making process guided by market forces and firmly under the control of a coalition of public and private elites. Some explicitly use the terminology of privatism.[32]

The polar opposite of privatism is progressivism. In a progressive political culture, popular control over vital decisions is extensive, both through direct participation in policy making and through mechanisms that enable the general public to exert significant influence over their representatives in government. The public sphere in a progressive political culture is vibrant and expansive. Progressives seek to use the powers of government to remedy the inequalities produced by private market forces that divide people and foster social alienation. Minimizing inequality has the desirable effect of nurturing a sense of community, an appreciation for what brings people together rather than what splits them apart. As individuals with diverging backgrounds and perspectives participate in public life, citizens develop a richer understanding of the interconnectedness of the larger community. A single-minded preoccupation with self-interest is replaced by a concern for the common good. In this way a progressive political culture leads to a stronger commitment to community, equity, and empowerment.

Urban scholars who have tried to distinguish the typical privatist city from a progressive city have employed similar criteria. For example, after presenting a collection of case studies of local public-private partnerships slanted in favor of downtown business elites, Derek Shearer outlines a progressive alternative. He identifies three elements that define a progressive approach to urban development:

1. balanced economic growth: urban development should proceed so that there is an equitable distribution of the costs and benefits of growth;
2. citizen participation: the political process should be structured to promote extensive popular engagement in all decisions materially affecting the development of the city; and
3. human scale: the physical environment of the city should facilitate social interaction of people in pleasant public places.

The implicit assumption of the first and third criteria is that an activist government is relied upon to ensure equitable growth and a human-scale, built environment; that view of the state is consistent with a progressive vision of politics, as is the second criterion's exalting of popular empowerment. Pierre Clavel has utilized similar standards in his writings about progressive cities in the United States, and those standards have been applied in more recent case studies. Finally, Edward G. Goetz has noted how the federal government's retrenchment in the area of housing and urban development policy has unleashed a torrent of grassroots organizing in cities, resulting in an unexpected revival of progressive politics at the local level. Increasing citizen engagement in the public sphere has led, Goetz contends, to a proliferation of innovative public policies enacted by local governments trying to fill the vacuum left by Washington's retreat from urban affairs.[33]

A managerial political culture is characterized by an activist public sphere dominated by highly skilled and experienced elites. Order, efficiency, and a wise use of resources are the highest virtues in promoting the general welfare. Historically, the reform era of the early twentieth century was probably the pinnacle of managerialism in city politics. The reformers believed that only public authority was sufficient to counteract powerful and corrupt private interests such as the robber barons. And to the extent that government needed to play an aggressive role in rooting out corruption in the private sector, public authority had to be extended to the right kind of individual. Reformers, who tended to come from relatively privileged backgrounds, stressed the need for professional expertise in solving complex problems brought on by the strains of rapid urbanization during the nineteenth and early twentieth centuries. Only those individuals with the requisite training in engineering, planning, law, and other professions had the competence and character necessary to respond to the urban crisis and manage city affairs properly.

Managerialism flourished again during the 1950s and 1960s when city planners, who typically value an activist government led by professional experts, became a decisive influence in the implementation of urban renewal policies. The arrogance of such planners/power brokers as Robert Moses and M. Justin

Herman contributed to the sudden collapse of managerialism in city politics when citizens mobilized against the massive displacement of long-time residents caused by urban renewal.[34] So intense was the backlash against elite rule that federal policies of the Great Society era required the maximum feasible participation of local residents in the development and implementation of neighborhood revitalization programs. In time, however, the rush toward citizen empowerment provoked its own reaction and a gradual move back toward the managerial respect for training and expertise in the administration of public policy. More recently, although it is still considered bad form to openly criticize the value of popular empowerment,[35] actual practice suggests that the "managerial mood" is alive and well. For example, there has been a rash of state takeovers of city school districts on the ground that local officials are not up to the task of running inner-city schools efficiently and competently.[36]

Finally, a populist political culture is associated with popular rule and a distrust of large institutions that infringe upon individual autonomy. In principle, populists wholeheartedly subscribe to the notion of government by the people as a force for good. But in the real world, they know that as government expands, the people inevitably lose control over decision making. Elites step into the resulting vacuum and begin to exercise power. Notwithstanding their promise to govern in ways that promote the general good, elites always have their own self-serving agenda that often runs counter to the interests of ordinary citizens. Big government comes to be perceived as a corrupt institution. The solution is not to reform the government to guarantee accountability (a futile endeavor), but to limit the scope of government. In a populist political culture, scaling back big government (and big business) is the best hope of ensuring that the people will be able to exercise control over their own lives.

Given their mutual desire to promote individual liberty by limiting the public sphere, populism and privatism would appear to have much in common. But the two visions differ over the question of who should govern. Populists favor small government in order to maximize the opportunity of ordinary people to hold power. By contrast, privatists regard the idea of popular empowerment as naive. They believe that since human beings have varying levels of intelligence, integrity, and ability, it is natural and desirable that some individuals will rise to the top and wield a disproportionate amount of power. With their egalitarian sensibilities, the populists reject the privatists' hierarchical view of government.

Much has been written about the populist rebellion in American cities in recent years, but usages of the term vary, thus causing some confusion. For instance, Todd Swanstrom examined the populist rebellion in Cleveland during the 1970s. But the rebellion led by the youthful, neighborhood-oriented politician Dennis Kucinich was not a "populist" one as the term is being defined here. This is because although Kucinich denounced the elite rule of downtown business leaders and veteran politicians beholden to them and demanded greater control by neighborhood residents, he also favored extensive use of public authority to promote equity throughout the city. For example, he supported the city's takeover of private utilities to lower utility bills. Such a commitment to the public sector, along with his support for popular rule, would make Kucinich a progressive, not a populist, under the proposed typology.[37]

A better representation of urban populism would be Philadelphia's mayor in the 1970s, Frank Rizzo. The son of Italian immigrants and raised in a working-class neighborhood, Rizzo never graduated from high school but made a name for himself by ascending to the top of the city police department before being elected mayor in 1971. His scorn of downtown elites and devotion to neighborhood residents (at least in predominantly white ethnic neighborhoods) was unquestioned. At the same time, Rizzo was never a strong proponent of government activism. Although he was a registered Democrat, Rizzo's suspicion of big government endeared him to national Republicans such as Richard Nixon.[38]

More recently, the influence of a populist political culture in U.S. cities is evident in the rush of local governments to privatize public services in order to cut costs and raise productivity. The proliferation of business improvement districts is another example of the populist vision. Rather than depend on the city to keep commercial corridors clean and safe, business owners band together in a business improvement district, impose essentially a new tax on themselves, and then use the funds to hire private entities to do what the city has neglected to do.[39] Both privatization and business improvement districts reflect a populist lack of confidence in the public sector and a desire on the part of individuals in the private sphere to assume more power in directing their own affairs.

The typology proposed here is based on dimensions that are internally coherent and fundamental to politics. The questions of who governs and what is the role of government have been at the center of debates in political philosophy for centuries, and those debates remain as robust today as ever. The four political cultures that emerge from these two pivotal dimensions are thus immediately relevant to understanding contemporary American politics, and especially contemporary urban politics.

A Model of Transformative Politics

Now that a clearer conception of the meaning and varieties of political culture has been established, our focus turns to specifying how political culture actually matters in the case of downtown development. In the vast majority of U.S.

cities since the end of World War II, the political culture that has been hegemonic has been privatism. Land use politics in particular has operated in a cultural environment characterized by a strong faith in the marketplace as the key to urban development and confidence in elites, from both the private and the public sectors, to oversee growth strategies. The ideas, values, beliefs, and practices associated with a privatist political culture have been conducive to a particular package of public policies regarding urban development. For the most part, city leaders have eschewed government action that might unduly interfere with entrepreneurs wishing to do business in urban centers; this has meant an avoidance of regulatory and redistributive policies. On the other hand, government intervention that seeks to promote business activity is deemed desirable; development policies such as infrastructure improvements and business inducements have, therefore, become common features of an approach to urban development pervaded by privatist principles. In sum, a privatist political culture has facilitated a market-led, elite-controlled approach to urban revitalization that generally reflects the policy preferences of downtown-oriented interests.

But in some large American cities, neighborhood groups became increasingly disenchanted with the unfulfilled promises and unexpected costs of downtown development policies. They engaged in extensive grassroots protest to effect a very different package of policies. First, neighborhood activists sought to roll back the broad array of business inducements, which many saw as nothing but business giveaways at taxpayers' expense. Second, they backed regulatory policies that would impose restrictions on downtown development in order to better control the societal costs of rapid growth; such polices ranged from stricter enforcement of traditional zoning laws to annual caps on downtown construction. And third, activists pushed for policies that would ensure a more equitable distribution of the costs and benefits of downtown development; for example, so-called linkage policies sought to ensure that downtown growth really would improve living conditions for neighborhood residents in the form of more affordable housing, better public transit, more day care centers, and more jobs for city residents. Thus, in addressing the issue of downtown development, grassroots activists argued in favor of a mix of developmental, regulatory, and redistributive policies that would more favorably reflect the needs of urban neighborhoods. This study assumes that success in getting such a package of policies enacted and implemented over an extended period of time would constitute a significant change in the politics of downtown development.

The argument presented here is that the path to fundamental political change is via fundamental cultural change. But the theory of cultural/political change on which the present work is based deviates from or advances previous theories in important ways. First, it differs from the deterministic analysis of

Ronald Inglehart, which views cultural change as the product of underlying social and economic forces, by according a much more substantial role to purposive human action in transforming popular consciousness. Moreover, that process is furthered by appealing not just to the postmaterial concerns of individuals, as Inglehart would suggest, but to the material concerns as well. Consequently, the theory being advanced here more closely resembles Gramsci's approach to radical change. But I attempt to extend the Gramscian framework by giving substantive content to the notion of conflicting worldviews and by dealing more concretely with the interaction of ideas and structures in promoting cultural/political change.

With respect to the politics of downtown development, if we assume that the cultural context does affect how the myriad groups and individuals in a city assess their situations and evaluate their alternatives, then it becomes crucial for neighborhood activists challenging the downtown growth coalition to confront the privatist political culture. That hegemonic culture systematically slants perceptions of interests and options in favor of the preferences of the downtown growth coalition and against those of neighborhood residents.

To overcome the cultural hegemony of downtown elites, a grassroots movement must satisfy two conditions. First, there must be a coherent oppositional vision of politics—one that both resonates with the actual experiences of disgruntled groups and subverts the hegemonic worldview that legitimizes the status quo. Second, there must be a congruence between that vision and the discourse and conduct of the challenging movement. Such a congruence sharpens the coherence of the counterhegemonic vision and facilitates the transformation of popular consciousness from a contradictory and passive state to a clear and activist state. As the typology presented in this study indicates, the political culture that most directly opposes the hegemonic privatist vision is the progressive vision. Therefore, a grassroots movement seeking fundamental cultural/political change regarding downtown development is most likely to succeed by projecting progressive ideas, values, and beliefs, *and* by engaging in practices consistent with such a vision.

Most grassroots activists earnestly claim that they do precisely this when battling the downtown growth coalition. I suggest the contrary, however, and contend that although most activists purport to seek a progressive vision characterized by popular empowerment and a vigorous public sphere, close scrutiny of their discourse and conduct reveals, as Gramsci might have predicted, a more conflicted state of mind. Grassroots activism often more closely reflects a managerial vision (an expansive public sphere but one dominated by elites) or a populist vision (mass power but also a deep suspicion of government). Theoretically, even managerial and populist activism could work to undermine the hegemonic culture since aspects of each are diametrically opposed to the core features of privatism, but such activism is of questionable counterhegemonic value. The mixed signals of the protest movement actually reaffirm key elements of the privatist vision, and given the power of that hegemonic vision, even the oppositional aspects of populist and managerial activism run a serious risk of failing to convert the contradictory consciousness of neighborhood residents into a coherent conception of how downtown development might operate differently. As a result, grassroots activism grounded in managerial or populist (or even occasionally privatist) ideas, values, beliefs, and practices experiences much frustration in its attempts to bring about reform; indeed, such forms of collective action tend to strengthen the grip that downtown growth coalitions maintain over downtown development policy making.

Counterhegemonic activism, that is, activism aimed at promoting fundamental cultural/political change, is most effective when characterized by a coherent progressive vision and practices that are clearly consistent with that vision. As the ideas, values, beliefs, and practices of progressive neighborhood activists proliferate in a society, the old hegemonic culture (privatism) dissipates and is gradually replaced by the emergent counterhegemonic culture (progressivism). That transformation in culture, in turn, opens up possibilities for a long-term transformation in city politics.

✦3

The Empirical Framework

Case Selection

To evaluate the relationship among grassroots activism, the local political culture, and downtown development policy, I employ a comparative case study method. The politics of downtown development in two major cities during the 1970s and 1980s—San Francisco and Washington, D.C.—are examined. At first glance it might seem that San Francisco and Washington are an odd pairing for a comparative case study. The former is an ethnically diverse city of colorful neighborhoods, quirky charms, and breathtaking natural beauty. San Franciscans are portrayed in the national media as socially offbeat, economically comfortable, and culturally cosmopolitan. They are a contented people and with reason. The crime rate is low, recreational space is ample, public transportation is excellent, and the city government has a reputation for getting things done. The quality of life is good. San Francisco is proud of its positive image.

The popular image of Washington, D.C., in contrast, is hardly positive. A steady stream of newspaper and magazine stories have recounted the mounting woes of the nation's capital: impoverished neighborhoods struggling with drug infestation, teenage pregnancies, violent crime, and diminishing economic opportunity; an escalating suburbanization rate that has drained the city's middle class (white and black), depleting the District of desperately needed tax revenue; a deepening fiscal crisis that has resulted in round after round of budget cuts and reductions in public services; and a deteriorating standard of living.[1]

At the center of this grim portrait is a city government accused of mismanagement and corruption. And at the center of that government is Marion Barry, the mayor of Washington for all but four years since 1978. The son of a sharecropper, the first member of his family to attend college and graduate school, and a prominent activist during the civil rights movement, Barry moved to the District in 1965 and quickly rose to the pinnacle of local government. As mayor, he enjoyed growing popularity until his administration was rocked by a series of scandals that forced the resignation and imprisonment of a number of high-ranking city officials. Barry himself became the target of several investigations by the federal government, acting on tips that the mayor was using cocaine. These investigations, along with the subsequent prosecution of the mayor, triggered a backlash among the city's largely black population. Although most Washingtonians had their own doubts about the mayor's integrity and competence by the late 1980s, many African Americans came to view the federal government's repeated investigations of Barry as at best a form of racial harassment and at worst a conspiracy by a powerful white minority to undermine black self-determination in the city. Whatever the case, the mayor became a symbol of racial pride and most black residents rallied behind him. Although Barry was eventually convicted and incarcerated for six months, he returned to local politics, getting himself elected as an at-large member of the District Council and then as mayor in 1994, thus completing a stunning political comeback. Nevertheless, Washington's problems continued to accumulate so that even Barry felt compelled to request the extraordinary intervention of the federal government. In 1995 Congress appointed an emergency control board to supervise local government operations in hopes of turning around the city's desperate situation. If San Francisco appeared to be a model of urban success, Washington had come to be seen by the nation as a city of monumental misfortune.[2]

Although recent events have understandably provoked contrasting popular images of San Francisco and Washington, this has not always been the case. Indeed, for most of the 1970s and 1980s, the time period with which this study is primarily concerned, the two cities were strikingly similar with respect to key social, economic, and political characteristics, and both have had parallel experiences regarding downtown development. San Francisco and Washington each pursued aggressive downtown growth policies during the 1970s and 1980s under the direction of powerful growth coalitions. In each case rapid downtown expansion sparked extensive neighborhood-based opposition. Yet, whereas the San Francisco grassroots movement succeeded in bringing about far-reaching changes in development policy, the Washington grassroots movement had only a marginal impact. The puzzle addressed in this study is why the two protest movements produced such different outcomes.

Urbanists and social movement theorists have pointed to a wide assortment of factors in trying to explain clashes between neighborhood groups and downtown elites over public policy. Some scholars build on Paul Peterson's analysis of the structural constraints facing local governments to identify variations in the potential for progressive policy making. Peterson would argue that all American cities are deeply limited when it comes to pursuing a progressive agenda through regulatory and redistributive policies because of the threat of capital mobility. That threat alone exerts a disciplining effect on city officials who might otherwise feel compelled to respond to neighborhood demands.

City officials recognize the risk that capital flight poses to the public fisc and thus conclude that their city has an objective interest in avoiding progressive policies that might prompt businesses and upper-income taxpayers to relocate.

But even if one accepts Peterson's conception of objective interests, most scholars detect some variation in the exposure cities have to the threat of capital disinvestment.[3] Cities that offer minimal amenities are presumably more vulnerable than those with abundant amenities. San Francisco and Washington both fall into the latter category, which helps to explain why both cities have experienced very high levels of demand for downtown investment throughout the postwar years (see table 3.1). Investors know that San Francisco is a beautiful and charming locale with a vibrant business community. Washington's principal competitive advantage is that it is the site of the federal government; numerous businesses, particularly law firms, trade associations, and other lobbyists, find it essential to be based close to the nation's center of political power. Keenly aware of such attractions, businesses are more willing to pay a premium in order to locate in downtown San Francisco and Washington. The threat of capital mobility is thus lower than in many other U.S. cities, which means that at least the *potential* for progressive policy making is higher. In this respect, therefore, the growth-control movements in San Francisco and Washington had similar opportunities to affect downtown development policies.

Whether neighborhood-based activists have the capacity to exploit such opportunities is another question. In San Francisco and Washington there was ample reason to believe that grassroots protest aimed at the downtown growth coalition would be effective. In predicting the outcome of popular protest, social movement theorists have emphasized the role of grievances, resources, and opportunities in the political structure. Significant differences with respect to any of these variables might account for the contrasting experiences of grassroots movements in the two cities. But the similarities far outweigh the differences: San Francisco and Washington were both hotbeds of neighborhood activism.

First, citizens in San Francisco and Washington had cause to feel aggrieved because of downtown growth. After many years of central city stagnation and decline, both cities embarked on determined campaigns to rebuild their downtown business districts. As the pace of development accelerated in the 1970s, however, urban residents began to encounter pressures from rapid growth: rising housing costs, retail displacement, traffic congestion, pollution, and mounting burdens on public services such as mass transit. Others sensed that downtown prosperity was not leading to any noticeable improvement in the material condition of their neighborhoods. In short, citizens in both cities were sufficiently disgruntled over downtown development policies to back neighborhood-based protest movements seeking major policy changes.[4]

Table 3.1. Downtown Office Construction in Major U.S. Cities, 1955-1982 (in thousands of square feet)

City	Downtown Office Space
New York	140,950
Chicago	43,248
San Francisco	26,102
Washington	25,874
Houston	24,492
Dallas	18,655
Los Angeles	16,749
Boston	16,725
Denver	16,440
Philadelphia	13,943

SOURCE: *Development Review and Outlook, 1983-1984* (Washington, D.C.: Urban Land Institute, 1984), 74.

Second, resource mobilization theorists point to the capacity of social movements to mobilize resources such as leadership, money, and skills in predicting the likelihood of success. Each city offered a substantial reservoir of resources with which to challenge the downtown growth coalition. To start, a host of socioeconomic indicators demonstrate the middle-class composition of both cities' population, a condition that many political scientists contend favors mobilization prospects. That Washington qualifies as a middle-class city is surprising to some, because of its notoriety in the 1990s. But for decades the city has been home to a large population of white and black residents who have benefited by holding government jobs that provide good wages and benefits. That steady base of employment has given District residents a comparatively comfortable standard of living vis-à-vis residents of other U.S. cities.[5] Among the twenty-five largest American cities, San Francisco and Washington rank one and two in per capita income (see table 3.2). As table 3.3 shows, the distribution of household income in the two cities is quite close as well. The two cities have similar and comparatively low poverty rates (see table 3.4), and their residents also have comparable educational levels, as indicated by table 3.5.[6] Thus, citizens in both San Francisco and Washington, D.C., enjoy a relatively high level of economic security that, in turn, gives them a similar opportunity to participate in grassroots politics.

That middle-class citizens have taken advantage of that opportunity in San Francisco over the years is hardly a surprise. But it is reasonable to wonder whether Washington's middle-class citizens would be as inclined to participate in local politics given that they lacked the power to elect their own government

Table 3.2. Per Capita Money Income in Twenty-Five Most Populated Cities in the United States (based on 1989 incomes)

San Francisco	$19,695
Washington	$18,881
Dallas	$18,737
Seattle	$18,308
San Jose	$16,905
San Diego	$16,404
New York City	$16,281
Los Angeles	$16,187
Denver	$15,590
Boston	$15,581
Indianapolis	$14,478
Houston	$14,306
Phoenix	$14,078
Jacksonville	$13,661
Columbus	$13,151
Chicago	$12,899
Philadelphia	$12,091
Baltimore	$11,994
Memphis	$11,682
New Orleans	$11,372
Milwaukee	$11,106
San Antonio	$10,885
El Paso	$9,603
Detroit	$9,443
Cleveland	$9,258

SOURCE: U.S. Census Bureau, *1990 Census, Population, Social and Economic Characteristics, Urbanized Areas* (Washington, D.C.: Government Printing Office, 1992), 47-69.

representatives between 1874 and 1974. Notwithstanding the absence of home rule for such a lengthy period, Howard Gillette's recent book *Between Justice and Beauty* on the political history of Washington, D.C., makes it clear that the District has had a long tradition of citizen activism on the part of white and black residents. For example, during the 1930s when FDR's New Deal greatly expanded the size of the federal government, causing the capital's population to swell, the city experienced a severe housing crunch. Gillette describes how white and black civic associations played a vigorous role in the formulation and amendment of local housing policies to alleviate the crisis. And following World War II, grassroots activism in the African American community soared

Table 3.3. Distribution of Income by Household in San Francisco and Washington, D.C.(based on 1989 income)

Household Income	% of Households SF	DC
Less than $14,999	21.8	23.7
$15,000 to $24,999	15.1	17.3
$25,000 to $34,999	15.0	14.7
$35,000 to $49,999	17.2	15.6
$50,000 to $74,999	16.5	14.4
$75,000 to $99,999	6.9	6.4
$100,000 or more	7.4	7.8

SOURCE: U.S. Census Bureau, *1990 Census, Population, Social and Economic Characteristics*, table 148, Income in 1989 of Households, Families, and Persons (Washington, D.C.: Government Printing Office, 1992).

in response to the city's urban renewal program, which destroyed black neighborhoods and displaced thousands of residents and businesses.[7]

The tradition of citizens in San Francisco and Washington taking a direct role in the actual governing of their cities—what Ronald Inglehart would call "elite-directing politics" as opposed to "elite-directed politics"—has continued into the present period. The clearest examples of a flourishing grassroots activism in both cities are seen in the willingness of citizens to employ various tools of direct democracy to go over the heads of elected officials in the executive and legislative branches of city government and appeal directly to the general public. In recent years San Franciscans have used the citizens initiative and referendum to shape public policy with respect to education, social welfare, and urban development. Washingtonians have relied on the same mechanisms to affect policy on capital punishment, homelessness, and bottle deposits and to impose term limits on locally elected officials.

Moreover, citizens in San Francisco and Washington who do choose to participate in local politics tend to hold left-of-center views on issues and back left-of-center candidates for public office. For example, voters in both cities have shown a consistently strong preference for Democratic Party candidates in recent presidential elections (see table 3.6). Broad popular support for left-of-center perspectives provides further evidence that San Francisco and Washington are well endowed with the kinds of resources that would fortify a grassroots challenge to the downtown growth coalition.

A third school of thought in social movement theory focuses on the political opportunity structure. Political scientist Sidney Tarrow, who has been at the forefront in applying this approach to explain the formation and evolution

Table 3.4. Percentage of Population with Income below Poverty Level in Twenty-Five Largest Cities in the United States (based on 1989 income levels)

San Jose	9.3
Seattle	12.4
Indianapolis	12.5
San Francisco	12.7
Jacksonville	13.0
San Diego	13.4
Phoenix	14.2
Dallas	16.0
Washington	16.9
Denver	17.1
Columbus	17.2
Los Angeles	18.4
Boston	18.7
New York City	19.3
Philadelphia	20.3
Houston	21.0
Chicago	21.6
Baltimore	21.9
Milwaukee	22.2
San Antonio	22.6
Memphis	23.0
El Paso	25.3
Cleveland	28.7
New Orleans	31.6
Detroit	32.4

Source: U.S. Census Bureau, *1990 Census, Population, Social and Economic Characteristics, Urbanized Areas* (Washington, D.C.: Government Printing Office, 1992), 47-69.

of social movements, defines political opportunity structure as those "consistent . . . dimensions of the political environment which encourage or discourage people from using collective action." He proceeds to identify four changes in the opportunity structure that are most likely to enhance the prospects of popular protest movements: (1) an expansion of access to political institutions, (2) shake-ups in governing alignments among elites, (3) divisions among elites, and (4) the availability of influential allies. The mobilization potential of a social movement is a reflection of subordinate groups seizing and exploiting such political opportunities. The theory has been used to analyze numerous social movements in American politics such as the civil rights movement, the women's movement, and the peace movement.[8]

Table 3.5. Educational Attainment of Individuals Twenty-Five Years and Older in Twenty-Five Largest Cities in the United States

City	% with Bachelor's Degree or Higher	% High School Grad or Higher
Seattle	37.9	86.4
San Francisco	35.0	78.0
Washington	33.3	73.1
Dallas	31.6	77.5
Boston	30.0	75.7
San Diego	29.8	82.3
Denver	29.0	79.2
San Jose	25.3	77.2
Houston	25.1	70.3
Columbus	24.6	78.7
New York City	23.0	68.3
Los Angeles	23.0	67.0
New Orleans	22.4	68.1
Indianapolis	21.7	76.4
Phoenix	19.9	78.7
Chicago	19.5	66.0
Jacksonville	17.9	76.4
San Antonio	17.8	69.1
Memphis	17.5	70.4
El Paso	16.2	65.3
Baltimore	15.5	60.7
Philadelphia	15.2	64.3
Milwaukee	14.8	71.5
Detroit	9.6	62.1
Cleveland	8.1	58.8

SOURCE: U.S. Census Bureau, *1990 Census, Population, Social and Economic Characteristics*, table 3 (Washington, D.C.: Government Printing Office, 1992).

In this comparative case study, there are two ways in which the political structure in San Francisco and Washington may yield diverging opportunities for grassroots protest aimed at downtown elites: Washington's unique political system, in which the federal government is accorded formal powers over city affairs, and possible differences in the level of cohesion among downtown elites and neighborhood residents in the two cities. First, it is conceivable that Washington's institutional arrangement may produce rhythms in local politics that are utterly foreign to any other U.S. city. Although Washington was granted

Table 3.6. Voting Results in Recent Presidential Elections

	Washington %	San Francisco %	U.S. %
1996			
Clinton (D)	85	72	49
Dole (R)	9	15	41
Perot (I)	2	3	8
1992			
Clinton (D)	86	73	43
Bush (R)	9	18	38
Perot (I)	4	9	19
1988			
Dukakis (D)	83	73	46
Bush (R)	14	26	53
1984			
Mondale (D)	85	67	41
Reagan (R)	14	31	59
1980			
Carter (D)	75	52	41
Reagan (R)	13	32	51
Anderson (I)	9	16	6
1976			
Carter (D)	82	52	50
Ford (R)	17	40	48

home rule in 1974, as the nation's capital it still cedes some official authority to the federal government. For example, the city is barred from taxing federal property within the District. The U.S. government also retains some control over the city's criminal justice system through its power to appoint prosecutors and judges. And most importantly, the Congress maintains a veto power over all city laws.[9]

In practice, however, Washington's political institutions are not so unusual. Congress compensates for the partial loss of taxing authority by paying the city an annual lump sum. Moreover, although the federal government has veto power over city laws, it actually used that power only three times during the first twenty years of home rule. At the same time, Congress has often exercised its prerogative to challenge local policy making by introducing resolutions expressing disapproval of a particular piece of legislation enacted by the District government. (Most of these disapproval resolutions have been sponsored by Republican lawmakers who wish to register their opposition to liberal policies adopted by the city on such issues as gun control, affirmative action, rent control, and disinvestment in South Africa.) But the disapproval resolutions are not in any way binding and thus have little or no influence on city policy making. It is conceivable that this might change if the Republican Party were to control both houses of Congress and the White House, but the norm of Democratic Party control or a divided national government has meant that federal intrusions into District affairs have been relatively infrequent and insignificant.

With respect to most issues, the city of Washington functions very much like any other American city. This is particularly true of downtown development. The city editor of the *Washington Post* said as much in a commentary on the first decade of home rule: "Take a look around downtown Washington. For better or worse, over the past decade—the home rule decade—it's been almost totally redone. Look at all the new office buildings, the new plazas. Regardless of what anyone thinks about them (some find them ugly, monotonous, undistinguished), they were built with the guidance of the District's local elected officials. . . . The pace, location and density of development have all been decided largely by the city's local elected officials. . . . The city government sets the tone for development."[10] Washington, like San Francisco, was run during the 1970s and 1980s by a downtown-led regime committed to the aggressive development of its downtown business district. Rapid development, in turn, provoked a growth-control movement that was typical of the kind of growth-control activism found in many other cities. Thus, with respect to land use politics, Washington's political institutions had little or no unusual influence.

A second way in which the political opportunity structure may have rendered the growth coalition more vulnerable to grassroots protest in one city than the other concerns the degree of cohesion among downtown elites and neighborhood residents. For example, divisions within the downtown growth coalition may have given neighborhood activists a chance to mobilize enough popular support to push through major policy changes. The potential for this kind of division appeared to be greater in Washington, where Mayor Marion Barry led an uneasy alliance between public and private sector elites. Before becoming mayor, Barry had been a militant leader in the civil rights movement, and his uncompromising stance on racial matters often alienated the predominantly white downtown business establishment. Even after Barry was elected into office, the obvious differences in backgrounds and leadership styles created some tension between the mayor and downtown business leaders. But by and large, the mayor was soon able to find ways to cooperate with downtown interests, and the latter's support for Barry grew throughout the building boom of the 1980s.

In San Francisco, Mayor Dianne Feinstein enjoyed a cozy relationship with the downtown business community from the start, and with good reason. The mayor and downtown business leaders had much in common—privileged backgrounds, similar social connections, and like goals and visions. Feinstein was enthusiastically supported by the downtown business community in her first run for mayor, and for the most part she could count on strong business support throughout her tenure in city hall. Thus, cohesion among ruling elites in Washington and San Francisco was quite strong throughout the 1980s, although Barry at first had to work harder than Feinstein at establishing a cooperative alliance.

Cohesion among neighborhood activists is almost always problematic in large American cities, and Washington and San Francisco followed this pattern. The same racial polarization that initially created tension between the Barry administration and downtown business leaders caused problems for grassroots activists trying to build a unified neighborhood movement. Washington had always exhibited a high level of racial segregation in terms of residential patterns. The problem was compounded by the fact that the wealthiest neighborhoods in the city, concentrated in the northwest quadrant, tend to be overwhelmingly white. Physical separation often breeds suspicion, fear, and ignorance. And this predictably makes the task of organizing a broad-based neighborhood movement all the more difficult. Absent unity, it becomes easier for the downtown growth coalition to pursue a divide-and-conquer strategy, thereby emasculating fledgling grassroots challenges to its power.

To a considerable degree, racial divisions in San Francisco are no less striking. Although San Francisco is not a southern city with a history of legally mandated segregation, it has always been characterized, like virtually all American cities, by pervasive de facto segregation and discrimination.[11] One historian found that despite its reputation for civility and tolerance, for much of the early twentieth century "most whites [in San Francisco] perceived blacks as an inferior racial caste and restricted their progress socially, politically, and economically." And as the city's black population rapidly increased during World War II and in the decade after, "white prejudices became even more virulent." In their research on race relations in the United States, Douglas S. Massey and Nancy A. Denton found that black-white segregation in the San Francisco metropolitan area is comparable to that in other metropolitan areas and is particularly similar to segregation in the Washington area.[12] The social and political consequences are the same. Misunderstanding and prejudice among racial and ethnic groups is also intense in San Francisco, thus presenting grassroots activists with the same formidable challenges to find ways to overcome such barriers and forge a unified oppositional movement against downtown power. Certainly, elites in San Francisco tried everything possible to foment discord among the city's diverse groups, from co-opting prominent neighborhood leaders to inciting fierce neighborhood competition for scarce resources. The threat to neighborhood cohesion in both cities was always substantial.

Given all of the similarities regarding the potential for a reordering of downtown development policy, it is not surprising that strong grassroots protest movements did emerge in San Francisco and Washington, nor that the two protest movements shared a number of characteristics. Each growth-control movement seemed to contest the basic tenets of the privatist political culture that pervaded both cities during most of the post–World War II era. Activists in San Francisco and Washington, D.C., rejected the hegemonic preference for a minimalist government whose main purpose in land use matters was to facilitate the impulses of private market forces favoring downtown growth. Instead, activists called for a proactive government that would control the negative impacts of urban growth by adopting a variety of regulatory policies. In addition, activists subscribed to the view that the immense wealth being generated by downtown development should not simply enrich downtown interests but should be spread more evenly throughout the city. Since public officials could not be trusted to carry out such regulatory and redistributive measures, given their comfortable relationship with progrowth interests, activists insisted on structural reforms to guarantee broader citizen influence. Through their own participation in government, activists wanted to make sure that downtown development proceeded in a way that protected what they viewed as the public interest.

Thus, conditions related to urban politics, and particularly development politics, in San Francisco and Washington were quite similar. Both cities experienced massive campaigns to rebuild their downtown centers. Such campaigns, in turn, inspired grassroots movements to challenge the downtown growth coalition. Each movement proclaimed its support for such progressive goals as the empowerment of ordinary citizens, the strengthened regulation of urban development, and the promotion of equitable growth.

But that is where the similarities end; the outcomes of community-based struggles against downtown power diverged sharply. After years of grassroots activism, the San Francisco movement largely realized its progressive vision. By the late 1980s it had succeeded in imposing strict limits on commercial office development in the downtown district. It had pushed the city to enact a series of linkage policies designed to hold developers accountable for the costs their projects imposed on the rest of the city and for the promises they had made in securing official approval for their projects. And the San Francisco movement had raised popular awareness of land use issues and stimulated broad-based engagement in the policy-making process. In his book on San Francisco politics, political scientist Richard E. DeLeon gives this assessment:

"Under progressive leadership, San Francisco has asserted its local autonomy, expanded the public sphere, politicized and democratized the planning process, spurned the dictates of investor prerogative, severely restricted business use of its open space, and inured itself to threats of private-sector disinvestment. The progrowth coalition of downtown business elites, labor unions, and city hall officials that controlled the city's economic and physical development for a quarter of a century is now in pieces, its vision for San Francisco discarded, its relentless building of highrises checked, its hegemony in land use and development erased."[13] By the end of the 1980s the downtown growth coalition had crumbled and the politics of downtown development had been transformed.

By contrast, the Washington growth-control movement's impact on local development politics was marginal at best. The only significant growth limits it secured were a series of downzonings to protect residential neighborhoods from commercial encroachment. Otherwise, Washington witnessed little change in the regulation of downtown building or in the city's practice of granting generous inducements to business to encourage development. Efforts to promote equitable growth produced some results, but the city's housing linkage policy was paltry compared to the impressive linkage programs adopted in San Francisco. Finally, although citizen influence over urban development increased in some middle-class neighborhoods, most Washington neighborhoods continued to play only a minimal role in the policy-making process. In the early 1990s the downtown growth coalition's lock on power remained as secure as ever.

In selecting the cases for this comparative case study, the most prominent explanations for social movement success have been held constant. There was little or no difference between San Francisco and Washington with respect to the influence of grievances, resources, or opportunities in the political structure. Moreover, the risk of capital mobility as a deterrent to alternative approaches to downtown development was roughly the same in each city. The reason for the divergent outcomes of the neighborhood-based movements in San Francisco and Washington involves the capacity of neighborhood-based groups to engage in a form of grassroots activism that could transform the previously hegemonic privatist political culture into a newly hegemonic progressive political culture.

An Ethnography of Cultural/Political Change

Evaluating whether neighborhood groups will be effective in challenging downtown-led regimes by transforming the local political culture requires a three-step process. First, it is necessary to scrutinize the kind of activism employed by neighborhood groups in order to illuminate its *cultural content.* The purpose is to determine the degree to which the ideas, values, beliefs, and practices of the activists were consistent with a particular vision of politics—privatism, managerialism, populism, or progressivism. The second step is to assess the *cultural impact* of grassroots activism. How did grassroots activism affect perceptions of self-interest and the public interest by various urban groups such as city planners, business leaders, and neighborhood residents? Did grassroots activism transform perceptions of the political options available to citizens in contesting downtown development policy? Changes in consciousness may reflect a broader transformation in the local political culture. Third, it is necessary to ascertain whether changes in the local political culture led to enduring *changes in downtown development policy.*

The third phase is the most straightforward. If downtown development policy continues to emphasize strong developmental policies with minimal regulatory and redistributive policies, then the impact of neighborhood-based activism will have been ineffectual. On the other hand, if downtown development policy evolves into a mixture of restrained developmental policies and aggressive regulatory and redistributive policies, then grassroots activism will have accomplished its goals.

But the question of how to measure the cultural content and cultural impact of grassroots activism is more complicated. Given that political culture represents the central concept in this study, it makes sense to study it the way an anthropologist would—ethnographically. The virtue of ethnography is that it enables a researcher to obtain a rich contextual understanding of a given cultural environment and provide descriptions and explanations from the perspective of individuals and groups within that environment. An ethnographic approach assumes that the members of a culture may hold multiple perspectives of social reality and that it is the purpose of the researcher to uncover those perspectives through becoming immersed in the culture. The attention to multiplicity of meanings is especially relevant in this study, which hypothesizes that an oppositional movement contesting a hegemonic political culture may inspire a proliferation of political cultures. As a result, various urban groups may interpret the politics of downtown development in very different ways. An ethnographic approach, with its sensitivity to context, nuance, and complexity, offers the best means of revealing multiple perspectives and how those perspectives may or may not evolve in light of a grassroots challenge to downtown power.[14]

But multiple perspectives of what exactly? As discussed in chapter 2, this study adopts a definition of political culture that analyzes how individuals think *and* behave with respect to the political system. That means that the focus will be on the ideas, values, beliefs, and practices as they relate to two fundamental dimensions of politics: Who governs? and What is the role of the state?

Illuminating the cultural content of grassroots activism, therefore, requires examination of the discourse and conduct of the activists themselves regarding the questions: Who should wield power over development decision making? and To what extent should the public sphere exert control over downtown development? Obviously, the degree of scrutiny is important here: a superficial review of the rhetoric and behavior of activists may suggest a progressive disposition toward popular empowerment and an activist government, whereas a more intensive study may disclose that grassroots activism should be more closely associated with a managerial or populist political culture. Exposing the gap between a rhetorical commitment to a progressive vision and the actual commitment to another vision of politics in practice will be an important goal of this ethnographic undertaking.

Once the cultural content of the grassroots activism has been established, it is then necessary to determine the cultural impact of that activism. This calls for attention to the discourse and conduct of urban groups significantly affected by downtown development. To what extent has grassroots activism altered these groups' orientations toward the two key dimensions of political culture? To what extent has the hegemonic privatist culture been transformed? If there has been change, how has the discourse and conduct of urban groups concerned with downtown development come to reflect the ideas, values, beliefs, and practices of a progressive, managerial, or populist political culture?

To assess the cultural content and impact of grassroots activism in San Francisco and Washington, two main measurement strategies were utilized: depth analysis of historical records, government documents, and local periodicals and newspapers; and intensive interviews with nearly one hundred neighborhood activists, city planners, politicians, attorneys, journalists, and business leaders. The former was especially helpful in providing insights into the nature of each city's political culture in the past and how activists thought and behaved in the early years of taking on the downtown growth coalition. But the interviews were essential to supplying a deeper understanding of what really impelled growth-control activism and what effect it had on the perceptions of other groups in each city. The interviews enabled individuals affected by downtown development to express their own interpretations of land use politics in their own terms. Consequently, they provided a valuable mechanism for understanding the multiple perspectives that compose a political culture and how that culture may have changed over time.

Interviewees were selected on the basis of their connection to downtown development and their capacity to offer a broad range of views on land use politics. First, every effort was made to interview all individuals deemed to have been major "players" in clashes between growth-control movements and downtown growth coalitions. Thus, for example, anyone whose name frequently appeared in local newspapers in connection with downtown development was contacted. In addition, the first and second sets of interviewees were asked to recommend individuals who played a significant role; those people were also contacted. The only category of individuals who proved difficult to track down were current high-ranking public officials, who were simply too busy and perhaps too wary of the political ramifications of giving long interviews to scholars asking probing questions about controversial issues. On the other hand, interviews with top public officials who had recently left their government positions and suddenly had the time and even the desire to reflect on their tenure in office proved to be particularly rewarding.

The other criterion for selecting interviewees, besides relevance to development politics, was a diversity of perspectives. Of course, the starting point in this study of the effects of grassroots activism on development policy making was to scrutinize the ideas, values, beliefs, and practices of the activists. Hence, a substantial number of interviews were conducted with activists, but activists from a wide variety of neighborhoods, backgrounds, and perspectives. Also, to document the impact of grassroots activism throughout the city, it was necessary to interact with a range of groups having some connection to downtown development, groups that may have held very different views from those of the activists. Business leaders, corporate attorneys, city planners, and neighborhood leaders who had traditionally supported the progrowth agenda were interviewed in order to give a more thorough portrait of the city's political culture. Interviews continued to be conducted from each discrete group until the saturation point had been reached, until nothing significantly new was being revealed about how a particular group perceived the politics of downtown development.

As for the actual interviews, interviewees were informed that the study was for a doctoral dissertation that would hopefully be published as a book. Permission was always requested to tape record the interviews to assure accuracy, and all except one interviewee agreed. The interviews tended to run long; every interview but one lasted at least one hour, and one lasted nearly ten hours over the course of three days. Many interviews were purposefully scheduled at the end of the work day so that interruptions would be minimized and interviewees would feel more relaxed and willing to speak at length.

In general, a semistructured interview was used. There was always a basic checklist of questions or issues to raise, but the order changed depending on the context of each interview. A priority was given to establishing a natural conversation. So even though there were predetermined themes, they were discussed at various points depending on when it was appropriate. Developing a comfortable rapport was crucial to open and honest exchanges. Often at the beginning of an interview, interviewees would reiterate standard lines typically associated with their group's view of downtown development (for example, a developer might initially complain about linkage fees deterring new investment in the city), but as the interviewees continued to talk, they often acknowledged changes in their perspectives (maybe the linkage fees have not really slowed the building boom after all). The frequency with which this occurred testifies to the value of an ethnographic approach in capturing the workings of contradictory consciousness. Relying on a simple questionnaire to obtain data, by contrast, would have missed the complexity of popular and elite interpretations of downtown development and the subtle ways in which those interpretations were evolving.

The semistructured format had two additional advantages. First, it facilitated natural conversation flow that enabled interviewees to speak in their own words, use their own terminology and categories of meaning, and offer their own reflections, judgments, and experiences with minimal cues from the interviewer. Second, a preset checklist provided structure to the interviews while limiting the scope of the subject matter. Although questions tended to be open-ended, standard themes such as individual orientations to control over decision making and the role of the state vis-à-vis the market were considered as interviewees recounted their experiences with the politics of downtown development. This helped to systematize the collection and analysis of what turned out to be a large body of data.

Once the interviews had been transcribed, the transcripts were coded and indexed based on categories derived from key concepts and themes. In this way it was possible to identify consistent patterns regarding, for example, orientations to power and the scope of government. These patterns shed considerable light on the cultural content and impact of grassroots activism on downtown development policy making in San Francisco and Washington. In short, the ethnographic approach was crucial to documenting the dynamics of cultural and political change in each city.

Conclusion

The puzzle that these introductory chapters address is why so few grassroots movements seeking to challenge the power of downtown growth coalitions have experienced lasting success. Many prominent scholars of urban politics have completely overlooked the role of the local political culture in shaping perceptions of interests and options in ways that strongly favor the perspective of downtown elites. Other political scientists have recognized the constitutive impact of the political culture but have employed an excessively deterministic and overly narrow conception of cultural change. This study of the politics of downtown development, however, builds on Gramsci's theory of cultural hegemony and counterhegemony in positing a more dynamic explanation of political change, one that takes account of both material and postmaterial concerns.

The capacity of neighborhood activists to effect enduring reforms in local politics turns on their ability to project a vision that contests and undermines a privatist political culture that privileges elite control and market-dominated approaches to dealing with chronic urban problems and at the same time advances a progressive political culture that privileges broad-based engagement in public life and an activist government promoting equity throughout the city. An effective counterhegemonic movement also requires that activists engage in practices that are consistent with their oppositional vision, a point that may seem obvious, but in an environment characterized by the cultural hegemony of privatism and a deeply conflicted mass consciousness, maintaining a congruence between vision and practice often proves difficult. To the extent that neighborhood activists are able to fulfill each of these conditions of counterhegemonic protest, the discourse and conduct that they inspire proliferate throughout the local political culture, transforming it in the process. Cultural change then paves the way to lasting political change. Just how compelling a theory of political change this proves to be depends, of course, on evidence gleaned from the real world of city politics.

Part 2
San Francisco

✦

✦4

The Hegemony of Privatism (1)

Like most large American cities after World War II, San Francisco embarked on a determined campaign to rebuild its downtown business district in anticipation of the rise of a postindustrial economy. The early redevelopment of downtown San Francisco has been well documented by other scholars, notably Frederick Wirt, Chester Hartman, and John Mollenkopf;[1] this chapter begins by briefly recounting that story in a way that highlights the ideas, values, beliefs, and practices that propelled the building boom. It then examines the first outbreak of grassroots opposition to the city's progrowth policies. The initial battles between the downtown growth coalition and neighborhood residents took place in the context of a privatist political culture that privileged market forces and elite control. So powerful was the hegemony of privatism in San Francisco development politics that even much of the early grassroots protest was characterized by a privatist outlook. The results were disappointing. Unable to transform the local political culture, the first growth-control activists were consistently and decisively defeated. No real hope for political change materialized until a new wing of the growth-control movement emerged a few years later with a very different vision of politics.

Downtown Development

America's mass migration from the cities during the years following World War II sparked a boom in construction of suburban subdivisions, shopping malls, and freeways. Because the public and private sectors were preoccupied with the task of suburban development, the nation's central cities experienced a period of neglect and decline. The urban infrastructure began to decay and property values dropped. For many political leaders, the trend toward promoting suburban growth instead of the rebuilding of downtown centers was a tolerable, even desirable, phenomenon. Many came to view Los Angeles as a model for a new kind of lifestyle. By dispersing and decentralizing its downtown business district, Los Angeles planners moved the workplace closer to suburban residents instead of requiring suburban residents to commute long distances to their jobs every day. The formula proved to be immensely popular, as middle-class families relished the opportunity to own their own homes and still live only a short distance from work. Many western cities embraced the Los Angeles model of development during the postwar years.[2]

Other cities were less certain of the attractions that suburban-style growth seemed to offer. San Francisco was one city that decided not to follow in the footsteps of its southern neighbor. Instead, San Francisco's civic and business leaders chose Manhattan as their model of development. In their eyes Manhattan, with its sleek steel and glass skyscrapers and dynamic downtown life, conjured up appealing images of wealth and power.

Apart from aesthetic considerations, rebuilding San Francisco's downtown core made good economic sense given the nation's transition from an industrial economy to a postindustrial economy dominated by corporate headquarters, business service firms, advanced technology, and communications. The locus of economic activity in American cities was shifting from older, industrial neighborhoods to downtown business districts. If San Francisco was going to take advantage of this seemingly irreversible trend, it would have to make its downtown core attractive for business investment. The fact that the city stood to benefit enormously from anticipated leaps in the volume of Pacific Rim trade during the coming decades was not lost on local business leaders. Perched in the middle of America's West Coast, San Francisco was well positioned to link the rest of the nation with what many believed would soon be the booming economy of the Far East.[3]

But if city leaders were going to realize their dream of making San Francisco America's gateway to Asia, much needed to be done to revitalize a downtown business district that had stagnated amid suburban prosperity during the postwar years. To attract multinational corporations and their support network of attorneys, accountants, bankers, and communications specialists, a sustained commitment to the expansion and modernization of downtown would be essential. And yet, despite a general consensus on what needed to be done, simply getting started proved to be an obstacle. Construction was delayed by political corruption and mismanagement. As the years passed, the city's leaders grew increasingly frustrated by their own paralysis. City Planning Director Paul Opperman pointed out that San Francisco was losing jobs and residents to the suburbs and warned that downtown would soon become "a ghost town" unless decisive action were taken. He urged downtown business leaders to "get together and figure out a priority list with the city."[4] Opperman's appeal to the business community to take the initiative became a familiar refrain in the 1950s. One business leader commented, "In Pittsburgh, where they got it all done, they had the Mellons on their side. In Chicago where they are starting to work, they have the head of Marshall Field. Where are the bankers, the heads of oil companies?" The *San Francisco Chronicle* editorialized that the only way the city would reenergize itself was to entrust the execution of development policies to "a handful of absolutely top-flight men, broadly representative of the downtown community, chosen for their imagination, their drive, their proven capacity to get things done. . . . The key people in this picture are the people who make up the business community of San Francisco."[5]

In 1955 business leaders heeded the call to action. Investor Charles Blyth and industrialist James Zellerbach recruited some of the city's most prominent corporate executives and formed the Blyth-Zellerbach Committee to oversee the rebuilding of downtown. That committee assumed responsibility for generating the necessary financial, technical, and administrative resources. Real estate magnate Ben Swig reflected the committee's confidence: "The whole San Francisco skyline is going to change—though not all at once of course. We're going to have a great building wave. Money is going to ease up. We're going to become a second New York."[6]

For technical guidance the Blyth-Zellerbach Committee retained a respected planning consultant named Aaron Levine, based in Philadelphia, to spell out the steps San Francisco would need to take to redevelop downtown. After conducting his own study, Levine presented his report to the committee. He first commended the Blyth-Zellerbach Committee for taking the bull by the horns and thus filling a serious leadership vacuum. In fact Levine urged the committee to expand its role by adding to its ranks "several men who will be representing the top executive level of the City's business community during the next 10 to 15 years." But aggressive business leadership, Levine cautioned, would not be enough. Key government bodies such as the City Planning Department and the Redevelopment Agency were understaffed, underfunded, and hampered by outdated, inefficient practices. Since these departments would inevitably serve important administrative and planning functions, they needed to be modernized and replenished with resources adequate for the massive tasks ahead. Finally, Levine recommended the establishment of "an independent citizen organization to assist the planning program" and to overcome the public "apathy and usually opposition and resentment to most planning proposals."[7]

The Blyth-Zellerbach Committee followed Levine's advice. It expanded its own size and role in directing the "Manhattanization" of San Francisco. The committee also lobbied public officials to upgrade the city's planning institutions. The most important move in this regard came in 1959 when Mayor George Christopher appointed the nationally renowned M. Justin Herman to head the

San Francisco Redevelopment Agency (SFRA).[8] Herman quickly expanded the SFRA staff and obtained considerable increases in federal funds to carry out ambitious urban renewal programs. The Blyth-Zellerbach Committee also created the San Francisco Planning and Urban Renewal Association (SPUR) to promote comprehensive planning and generate popular support for downtown growth. Though nominally a citizens organization, SPUR was initially funded by the Blyth-Zellerbach Committee as well as other downtown interests, and several of its directors were powerful business leaders.[9] By the late 1950s a powerful growth coalition capable of rebuilding downtown San Francisco had emerged.

In searching for appropriate development sites, progrowth enthusiasts soon zeroed in on what they felt had become a conspicuous eyesore—the city's large produce market, which occupied land adjacent to where Market Street, downtown's main thoroughfare, runs into the San Francisco Bay. Though the market was popular with local residents, the Blyth-Zellerbach Committee asserted that it was dirty and raised a mere $250,000 in property taxes for city coffers.[10] The first redevelopment project in 1959 was to clear out the produce market and commence construction on a fifty-one acre site of immensely valuable real estate. The planned complex of office buildings, hotels, and luxury housing, which would eventually include the Embarcadero Center and the Alcoa Building, was named the Golden Gateway.

Pleased with its initial effort, the city's downtown growth coalition set out to follow the same formula in subsequent years. The objective was to convert low-intensity and inefficient uses of land to high-intensity and more productive uses. Large parcels of property just south of Market Street fit those criteria perfectly. Although the South of Market area was home to thousands of lower-income residents and dozens of small businesses, the Blyth-Zellerbach Committee believed the city would be better served by replacing existing tenants with new commercial office buildings, hotels, and a convention center. The San Francisco Redevelopment Agency under M. Justin Herman was charged with using urban renewal mechanisms to carry out the South of Market redevelopment, along with many other downtown projects.[11]

Over the next fifteen years, a period that spanned three mayoral administrations, San Francisco witnessed the construction of over 19.4 million square feet of new commercial office space in the downtown area (see table 4.1). By the mid-1970s the downtown growth coalition felt that it had made giant strides in accomplishing its mission. The skyline, now dominated by the Bank of America building, the Transamerica Pyramid, and numerous other highrises, had changed dramatically, and most San Franciscans were pleased with the transformation. Writing in 1974, political scientist Frederick Wirt found "general popular support of highrise development." Even many activists who would later attack downtown development were relatively satisfied. Sue Bierman, who would go on to become one of the city's most visible critics of downtown growth from her position on the City Planning Commission, acknowledged that she liked the "bright lights" of the new highrises and "found downtown pretty exciting." Another growth-control activist recalled his favorable impression of downtown when he first moved to San Francisco in the 1970s: "Everyone loves the skyline. You cross the bridge and the buildings are gorgeous, man it's so pretty. People work there and it's jobs and everything like that."[12]

Broad popular support for downtown development made public officials even more disposed to cooperate with progrowth advocates in the private sector. Wirt reported that public officials fully shared the Blyth-Zellerbach Committee's "urban vision of San Francisco as a new regional and national administrative center, in which highrises were essential and beneficial components."[13] In short, the city's downtown growth coalition was well on its way to realizing its development goals by the early 1970s. The public-private partnership was functioning smoothly, and San Francisco residents seemed content to maintain the course.

The Privatist Political Culture

This brief review of the origins of downtown development in San Francisco provides some insights into the underlying values and beliefs driving land use politics during this period. First, city leaders expressed great faith in the workings of market forces. They interpreted changes in the global economy as giving San Francisco an opportunity to prosper as a center of international commerce by linking the United States with the expanding economies of the Pacific Rim. They also viewed the natural currents pushing America from a manufacturing-based economy to one based on business services, information, and technology as a positive trend. With its advantages in human and physical capital, San Francisco was strategically positioned to flourish in the evolving economy. A revitalized and robust downtown business district was all that was needed. The city's elite were convinced that transforming San Francisco into a West Coast version of Manhattan would bring unprecedented wealth and prosperity to its citizens. Frederick Wirt observed that growth advocates "have totally accepted the national wisdom that equates change with improvement, more with better and higher with best. For them to believe otherwise is unthinkable."[14]

Meanwhile, there seemed to be minimal concern about the negative consequences of vigorous downtown development. For example, John Mollenkopf discovered that most city planners were oblivious to the fate of residents living

Table 4.1. Development of Downtown Office Space, San Francisco, 1959-1974 (in gross square feet for structures ten stories and higher)

Year	Square feet
1959	1,427,000
1960	836,000
1961	270,000
1962	N/A
1963	1,219,000
1964	N/A
1965	1,529,000
1966	1,027,000
1967	2,046,000
1968	186,000
1969	3,173,000
1970	1,853,000
1971	N/A
1972	1,858,000
1973	2,633,000
1974	2,548,000
Total	19,405,000

SOURCE: Department of City Planning, reprinted in Gerald Adams, "A Hard Look/The Battle of the Skyscrapers," *San Francisco Examiner and Chronicle*, January 26, 1979, A6. (Note that the 19.4 million square foot total does not include figures for three years between 1959 and 1974.)

in the Western Addition, a lower- and working-class neighborhood within close commuting range of downtown, and thus an appealing site for urban renewal. He points to an early study urging redevelopment of the Western Addition because "it is close to the financial district . . . and contains slopes on which apartments with fine views can be erected." The same study later declares: "In view of the characteristically low incomes of colored and foreign-born families [in the Western Addition], only a relatively small proportion of them may be expected to be in a position to occupy quarters in the new development."[15] It is safe to say that progrowth advocates in the 1950s and 1960s were not particularly sensitive to how downtown development might adversely affect at least some San Francisco residents.

When city planners occasionally recommended stronger controls on downtown growth to mitigate negative impacts, business leaders insisted that government intervention had no place in what they felt was a market-driven phenomenon. Many examples could be cited. In 1957, when city planners suggested that limits on the floor area ratio of new commercial office buildings might be necessary to avoid excessive congestion in the financial district, real estate interests unanimously rejected the plan and insisted that no new government limit be placed on downtown construction. They claimed that existing building code restrictions and market forces would be sufficient to prevent excessive construction.[16] From an early date, proposals to regulate the pace and character of downtown development were condemned as needless governmental intrusions that would only harm San Francisco's reputation as a budding commercial and financial capital. A Chamber of Commerce official declared in 1963 that "tinkering with the floor area ratio downtown is hazarding the welfare of the city and adversely affecting the business climate." Planning Director Allan Jacobs commented that the San Francisco chapter of the American Institute of Architects "seemed philosophically in tune with Ayn Rand's Howard Roark" and was "at heart opposed to any zoning."[17]

By and large, the city's leading politicians followed the laissez-faire approach to downtown development. In the 1950s Mayor George Christopher generally sided with the business perspective, asserting that he did not want the city's zoning code to "restrict private capital." Several years later, Planning Director Jacobs recalled that Mayor Joseph Alioto was anything but an advocate of deliberate, controlled growth: "I [did] not [kid] myself about Alioto's being a planner's mayor. He was not. My initial sense was that he was highly development-oriented, even when development might be ill-placed, and that he would not be terribly concerned with long-range views. His early addresses, in which he talked about his 'Darwinian theory of urban development,' confirmed my fears."[18] The privatist political culture was thus characterized by a strong hostility toward almost any aspect of governmental regulation of downtown development. Moreover, any notion that government might intervene to promote a more equitable distribution of the costs and benefits of downtown growth through redistributive policies was essentially unimaginable at this point.

Despite the virtual absence of regulatory and redistributive policies, government was not entirely invisible in the city's privatist political culture. Local government was expected to facilitate market trends by actively contributing to redevelopment efforts. This entailed prodevelopment policies such as infrastructure improvements in the downtown core and inducements to businesses considering investment in San Francisco.

But even a limited, facilitative role for government posed a problem for progrowth proponents. In keeping with the privatist spirit of the era, most business leaders lacked confidence in the capacity of public officials to do their part in devising and carrying out progrowth policies. To some extent their position was justified; the government's ineptitude and corruption had frustrated development plans for a decade following World War II. On the other hand, as the Levine report had confirmed, key city agencies suffered from inadequate funding and antiquated technologies. In any event, the perception of governmental incompetence was accompanied by a deep-seated faith in the ability of business leaders to execute complex tasks. Consequently, pivotal actors interested in the city's development looked mainly to the business community to provide leadership and the necessary resources to rebuild downtown San Francisco.

The confidence in business leadership was so strong and pervasive that no one objected to the secretive mode of operating employed by the downtown growth coalition. In discussing the Blyth-Zellerbach Committee, Chester Hartman cites a *Business Week* article that reported: "Zellerbach and his collaborators have no by-laws, no written policy, no executive director and keep no minutes. They regard the absence of such organizational trappings as prerequisites to their operations."[19]

The growth coalition's shunning of publicity had an important consequence; it inhibited popular awareness of downtown land use issues and kept public participation in the development decision-making process to a minimum. When he took over as director of the City Planning Department in 1967, Allan Jacobs discovered that the notion of city officials trying to encourage citizen participation in the planning process had not occurred to many people. At his first "staff-initiated general community meeting," Jacobs found that "many people in attendance had never heard of the Department of City Planning." He recalled that "the nature of the questions and the demands led me to conclude that few high ranking city officials had ever been to a neighborhood meeting. Indeed, one speaker said that I was just there for the publicity and that people had better make their demands known then because they weren't likely ever to see me again."[20] The lack of popular awareness of downtown development issues helped business leaders to wield broad influence over policy making.

The City Planning Department under Jacobs actually tried to depart from standard privatist practices by encouraging citizen participation in the policy-making process and slowing the pace of the building boom to ensure prudent planning. But such deviations from the hegemonic norm encountered powerful resistance. The seven-member City Planning Commission would often reject staff recommendations provided by the Planning Department regarding particular projects. Moreover, it was not long before developers realized that they could simply bypass Jacobs's Planning Department and make their appeals directly to the Planning Commission, the Board of Supervisors, and the mayor, where they would almost always find a receptive audience.[21]

It is clear, then, that the early phases of the redevelopment of downtown San Francisco occurred within a distinct cultural context. The political culture assumed that downtown growth was consistent with broad changes in the global economy and was thus an inherently positive goal that should be pursued aggressively. The Manhattanization of San Francisco would generate unprecedented benefits that would flow sooner or later to all urban groups. Whatever negative consequences might arise from rapid growth were dismissed as marginal irritations or ignored altogether. There was no suggestion that the growth coalition was obligated in any way to take responsibility for the costs of downtown development on adversely affected citizens beyond the payment of just compensation for takings of property and perhaps some assistance in relocating. Local government's role in executing the downtown revitalization would be a limited one. Regulatory policies were seen as unwarranted interference with the market, and redistributive policies linked to downtown development were never even considered. Progrowth advocates had minimal confidence in the capacity of political leaders to set and implement land use policies; consistent with their distrust of the public sphere, they also saw little value in promoting citizen participation in the planning process. Instead, they felt that the job of guiding downtown development should be entrusted mainly to business leaders, who would rely from time to time on the counsel of specialists in planning, engineering, architecture, and a few other professions. These ideas, values, beliefs, and practices shaped the perspective of nearly all groups connected with downtown development in the 1950s and 1960s. Privatism dominated the local political culture; the worldview of the downtown growth coalition was hegemonic.

The Emergence of Grassroots Opposition

Although a broad consensus throughout the city supported downtown growth, undercurrents of opposition became apparent in the late 1960s as the first decade of downtown development was drawing to a close. The most obvious outbursts of protest occurred in a couple of neighborhoods undergoing extensive urban renewal, the Western Addition and the South of Market. Plans to evict hundreds of residents and demolish entire blocks of homes and small businesses in order to make room for new office buildings, hotels, a convention center, and upscale housing prompted many citizens to organize and fight city hall.[22]

But the first citywide campaign to limit downtown development also began to take shape during this period, and that campaign represented the start of the San Francisco growth-control movement. The impetus for the movement came from several sources. As the environmental movement gathered steam throughout the United States, some citizens began to contemplate the environmental consequences of rapid downtown growth. They pointed out that highrise development was attracting thousands of new commuters to the financial district every day and that many of them drove automobiles. The escalating influx of commuters and cars increased traffic congestion on the area's highways and bridges and clogged downtown streets. This, in turn, exacerbated the city's problem with air and noise pollution. Moreover, erecting several skyscrapers each year was devouring open space, blocking sunlight, and turning downtown into a grid of shaded wind tunnels.

Another group, which never had been captivated by the Blyth-Zellerbach Committee's aesthetic vision of San Francisco as a modern, postindustrial headquarters city of towering highrises, also began to express its reservations about redevelopment of the downtown business district. It preferred the old San Francisco, a place of immense natural beauty, colorful neighborhoods, and singular charms and thus questioned the logic of a massive rebuilding program to transform the city into another Manhattan.[23] The concern of these preservationists turned to alarm as construction through the 1960s caused the demolition of a growing number of historically significant structures and as the new highrises obscured the city's dramatic hills and magnificent vistas.

These two groups perceived their interests and the city's interests regarding downtown development as different from the interests of the downtown growth coalition. Unimpressed by promises of a prospering postindustrial economy, the opponents of aggressive growth saw mainly the threats posed to San Francisco's environment and cultural heritage. When the U.S. Steel Corporation announced plans to construct a forty-story office building and a highrise hotel directly on the waterfront, just south of the centrally located Ferry Building, environmentalists and preservationists were outraged. The structures would have been the first highrises on San Francisco Bay, a prospect that they condemned as an unconscionable blight on the city's beauty. They sprung into action and helped to block the project.[24]

Protest directed against individual projects soon expanded into a broader attack against the city's overall policy regarding downtown development, thanks to yet another source of popular discontent. Perhaps the most important stimulus for the emergence of a *citywide* movement to limit downtown growth was a fear that commercial office development would begin to spread beyond the downtown business district and into middle-class residential neighborhoods. The first major highrise proposal to galvanize sustained grassroots opposition was the plan to build the Transamerica Pyramid. Environmentalists and preservationists opposed the project for the reasons mentioned above, but this time they were joined by residents living in the adjacent neighborhood of North Beach. To be located at the outer edge of downtown, the giant Transamerica Pyramid loomed as an ominous threat to the community.

Activists from these three groups came together in 1970 to form the first organization concerned with downtown development's impact on urban life—

San Francisco Tomorrow (SFT). However, SFT's spirited campaign against the Transamerica Pyramid never attracted much public interest in neighborhoods beyond the immediate vicinity of downtown. Allan Jacobs, the city planning director at the time, recalled the lack of public concern over the issue: "If the public had cared enough, it could have influenced the outcome, perhaps to the extent of overcoming the influence of the mayor and chief administrative officer. But the public was not sufficiently aroused. Either people did not know about the proposal and its implications, or they did not feel the issue was of major concern, or, alternatively, they may have known about the proposal and favored it. It seems reasonable to conclude that . . . not enough people considered one oddly shaped building in a questionable location enough of an issue to merit greater involvement."[25] Although the Transamerica Pyramid was eventually built, the organizing of SFT encouraged a core of growth-control advocates to step up their efforts to combat the so-called Manhattanization of San Francisco.

Citywide opposition to the downtown growth coalition shifted into a higher gear in 1971 when a number of neighborhood leaders reacted to mounting fears that highrise development was about to spill over into their communities. Suddenly, highrise apartment buildings were being proposed in such residential areas as Russian Hill, Telegraph Hill, and Nob Hill, all of which were within a short commuting range of downtown offices. The most important leader of this expanded opposition was a garment manufacturer living in Russian Hill named Alvin Duskin. He described his reasons for getting involved: "I was born in San Francisco, my business is here, I'm raising my kids here. And I walk out of my door in the morning and I look around and say 'Is this what I had in mind? Do I want this? Who asked me about this? . . . This is my town. Why is all this happening?' And nobody asked me. And I go around and I talk to my friends, and we say we don't like what's happening and nobody asked us. So let's do something about it."[26] At bottom, Duskin was motivated by anger over his inability to shape land use decisions that had the potential to greatly alter the quality of his life.

Duskin was not a typical business person; he had once worked with the famed community organizer Saul Alinsky, an experience that deeply affected his view of politics. His response to the sense of powerlessness over urban growth that he felt was extremely important. Duskin reasoned that because the mayor and the city legislature seemed firmly committed to a program of aggressive highrise development, conventional political strategies centering around the lobbying of public officials were doomed to fail. He concluded that the downtown growth coalition was so well entrenched in city government that the regular institutions of representative democracy offered little hope for a change in policy. So Duskin and his allies turned to alternative institutions of direct democracy.

They decided to take their case directly to the people through a citizens initiative. If city officials were reluctant to enact a law controlling downtown development, the citizens of San Francisco would take matters into their own hands and adopt their own law.

In early 1971 Duskin recruited a number of young, energetic volunteers to help him draft a proposal, get it placed on the ballot, and then run the campaign to persuade 50 percent of the voting public to support it in the November election. Two of those volunteers, Sue Hestor and Charles Starbuck, would go on to play highly visible roles in the city's growth-control movement. Duskin drafted a simple initiative that would impose a severe height limitation of seventy-two feet on all new buildings throughout the city. He realized that such a strict height limit was probably unrealistic, but he believed that forceful advocacy of an extreme position would generate more publicity and serious discussion of the problems of downtown development. He explained: "One of the things I learned from my long apprenticeship with Saul [Alinsky] was that if you're going to do any type of community organizing . . . you really go for something that probably is beyond what you're going to get. . . . What you get is probably all you could have gotten in the first place."[27] In any event, backers of the measure managed to collect enough signatures to get the initiative placed on the November ballot.

During the campaign, supporters of the initiative contended that the Manhattanization of San Francisco was permanently altering the city's character and destroying its "Mediterranean feel."[28] They also appealed to environmentally concerned citizens by arguing that highrise development was worsening the city's air quality, eliminating open space, and blocking sunlight in downtown corridors. Finally, they insisted that highrise development posed a threat to the quality of life not only in the downtown area but in the surrounding neighborhoods as well. That threat was both direct in the sense that highrises were now being advocated by the downtown growth coalition in nearby neighborhoods and indirect in that downtown expansion was responsible for various spin-off costs such as traffic congestion and a scarcity of parking throughout much of the city. The initiative campaign marked the first time grievances against the city's progrowth agenda had been aired in public on a citywide basis.

The Duskin initiative campaign attracted enough media publicity and generated enough public discussion to make growth advocates nervous. For the first time the city felt compelled to reign in the building boom. In August 1971 the city adopted an Urban Design Plan prepared by the Planning Department. One aspect of the plan imposed a set of restrictions to improve the architecture and design of new highrises. Until then the downtown growth coalition had

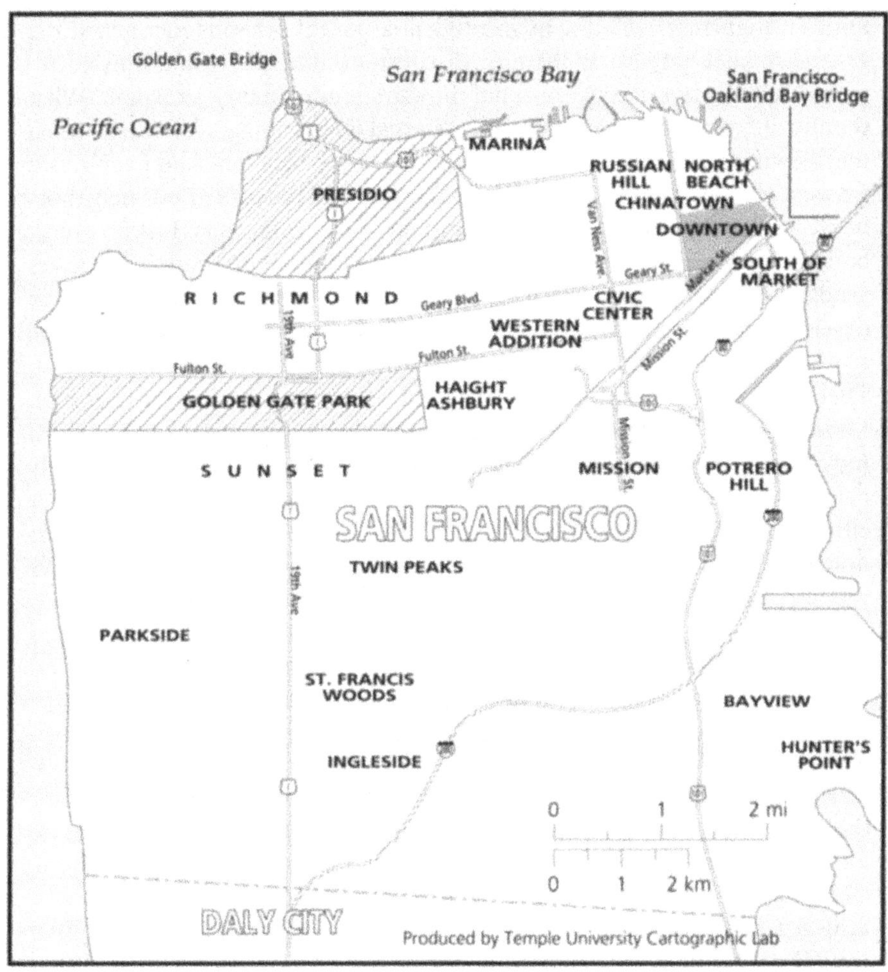

fought even this mild form of regulation as an unnecessary intrusion into private-sector decision making.[29] But realizing that such guidelines would appease the preservationists, progrowth advocates relented.

More importantly, another aspect of the Urban Design Plan called for a rezoning of much of the city. The plan established strict interim height controls on new development in all residential communities outside the downtown district, to be followed by a formal, permanent downzoning in 1972. Under the proposed guidelines, no new building could exceed forty feet in residential neighborhoods. These two measures had their desired effect. The design regulations mollified some segments of the preservationist community, and the limit on highrise development in residential neighborhoods dampened the general public's interest in the growth-control initiative. Duskin himself remembered the devastating impact of the city's action on the campaign: "What the city did, which was very smart, was started downzoning. . . . Because when they downzoned Russian Hill, I lost half of my organization. And people said we won, y'know. They said it's hopeless downtown. We won in our neighborhood. . . . And the campaign, we just lost all of our volunteers. I mean everybody just walked."[30] It was a brilliant strategy; although progrowth advocates grudgingly conceded to a partial expansion of government regulation of urban development, those regulations had only a slight impact upon the area of the city where development was most profitable—the downtown business district. There, commercial office growth promised to continue as vigorously as ever. Meanwhile, the Urban Design Plan utterly deflated the nascent growth-control movement's momentum. In November the initiative was overwhelmingingly defeated by a vote of 62 percent to 38 percent. The Duskin forces ran another citizens initiative campaign in June 1972, this time offering a somewhat less draconian height limit (160 feet) on highrise construction, but that initiative was also rejected by San Francisco voters 57 percent to 43 percent.

Notwithstanding the ultimate outcome of each initiative campaign, this initial wave of grassroots activism did have some impact on the local political culture. The Duskin forces contested the growth coalition's assumption that San Francisco had a unitary interest in promoting aggressive downtown development by pointing out negative impacts on the environment, the city's historical heritage, and the quality of life in the neighborhoods. Given those costs, the privatist practice of market-driven, elite-controlled policy making was no longer acceptable to the activists. Instead, they demanded progressive reform: a heightened level of government regulation of downtown development to be achieved through broad-based popular control in the form of a citizens initiative. The Duskinites thus seemed to pose a genuine counterhegemonic challenge to the downtown growth coalition.

As the previously obscured costs of rapid growth were highlighted, the notion that government ought to play a more assertive role in controlling those costs began to sound more reasonable. That position gained legitimacy when the city moved, under pressure from the citizens initiative campaign, to impose design restrictions on new construction and limited highrise building beyond the downtown core. Although these actions had little direct bearing on the downtown building boom, they did alter the prevailing belief that *any* form of government regulation would be anathema to the fortunes of the city.

The Duskin initiative campaigns also affected conceptions about who ought to exercise power over development decision making. By utilizing the citizens initiative as the chief mechanism for battling the downtown growth coalition, the activists advanced the progressive principle that ordinary people ought to have ultimate control. This constituted a decisive shift away from the privatist practice of relying on experienced experts to determine and implement whatever policies they judge to be in the public interest.

But a closer look at how the Duskinites actually behaved reveals deviations from their purported commitment to a progressive vision of political change and thus limitations on their counterhegemonic potential. The main problem concerned the question of who should wield power. Although Duskin obviously endorsed the idea of citizen empowerment as evidenced by his use of the citizens initiative, the centralized organization of the campaign undermined its progressive impact. In fact, long-time activist Calvin Welch recalled the "elitism" of the Duskin campaign: "It was a very top-down campaign. I mean Alvin ran it. There was no neighborhood organization, no field force, no campaign coordinator—Sue Hestor kind of functioned as that role, but basically she was the administrator of the system of Alvin Duskin. And Alvin would sit in his office and get his brainstorms and go off, do them, usually events, you know, that aimed at gathering a crowd." The top-down nature of the Duskin campaigns tended to inhibit broad-based grassroots organizing, thus constricting opportunities for ordinary citizens to get involved in land use politics on a more substantial level.[31]

The elitism of the early growth-control activists had important ramifications. The Duskin campaigns simply failed to connect with most San Francisco voters, who viewed the initiatives as something that mattered only to a few narrow groups with an odd set of priorities. To the average San Franciscan, the relatively affluent residents of near-downtown neighborhoods such as Telegraph Hill and Russian Hill sought to restrict highrises simply because they wanted to preserve their scenic vistas. And criticisms of the adverse impacts of downtown development on the environment and the aesthetic charm of the city did not concern working-class residents in outlying neighborhoods, who were more interested in how the building boom affected the city's economy.

Frederick Wirt's 1974 analysis of the Duskin campaigns is pertinent: "High-rise opponents might claim to speak for the city's people, but it was unclear how well they represented those who lacked a view of the bay or who cared little for arguments concerning aesthetics." In fact, many San Francisco workers were hostile to the Duskin forces. Alluding to the growth-control activists, one union member remarked: "Some of these guys wouldn't know a worker if he bit them.... Eight-hundred guys sitting in our hiring office waiting for work ... a lot of them black ... and the conservationists are screaming about the U.S. Steel project blocking the view. View? How many working people have a view?

That project means jobs—and that's what counts."[32] Duskin himself conceded that the campaigns failed to reach out to key segments of the city's population:

> We had good support among the people who were being evicted around Yerba Buena. So there were a lot of South of Market groups there. . . . I don't think I made any contact with [the] Asian community at all on these issues. They just never related to it, never got into it. . . . And what would now be called the YUPPIES . . . that was really a strong group of people, urban professionals wanting to live in San Francisco and didn't want to see the quality of life deteriorate. It was never, it was never a strong black issue. It was never really a strong issue in the Mission [with] the Hispanic community.

Duskin's recollection of where the campaign resonated with voters is confirmed by actual voting patterns. The two growth-control initiatives won in affluent areas such as Pacific Heights and Russian, Nob, and Telegraph Hills but were defeated by sizable majorities in virtually all working- and middle-class communities, including predominantly minority neighborhoods such as Hunters Point and Chinatown.[33]

In summary, the Duskin campaigns' centralized organization and their inability to connect with ordinary voters were interrelated. The top-down structure hampered efforts to develop grassroots organizing throughout the city. This meant that although growth-control leaders were in tune with the wishes of their friends and neighbors regarding land use matters, they had little idea how citizens from other neighborhoods thought about downtown growth. The one issue that did arouse broader concern was the possibility that highrise development would spread to residential communities throughout San Francisco. But once the city declared its intention to downzone those communities, most voters saw no good reason to back the initiatives. Environmental and aesthetic impacts on downtown hardly seemed compelling to the majority of San Franciscans. In their view only the downtown growth coalition was speaking to their more materialistic concerns about the need for economic growth and expanded employment opportunities. As a result they were particularly receptive to the growth coalition's dire warnings about what would happen to the city if growth-control activists succeeded in imposing strict regulations on downtown development. Most voters continued to subscribe to the privatist belief that government interference with market forces was a dangerous proposition. Moreover, the failure of the Duskinites to draw ordinary people into the political process, other than on election day, had the effect of reinforcing popular beliefs that downtown development was a complex issue best left to the skilled experts. In other words, the Duskinites' elitism unwittingly strengthened the downtown growth coalition's claim to authority on development matters and thus reaffirmed the privatist privileging of elite control. With the privatist political culture flourishing, the downtown growth coalition's policies continued to appear reasonable and desirable to most San Franciscans. Put simply, the Duskinites were out of touch with the mainstream.

The Building Boom Continues

With the Duskin initiatives soundly defeated, the growth coalition proceeded with its plans. Downtown development in San Francisco progressed in the 1970s as it had during the previous decade. Each year several highrise office buildings were added to the city's skyline. A metropolitan light-rail system, the Bay Area Rapid Transit (BART), was completed in the early 1970s to facilitate suburban commuting to the downtown core. Construction of a state-of-the-art downtown convention center also got under way during this period. Progrowth enthusiasts applauded the downtown building boom as a generator of jobs, tax revenue, and economic prosperity.

Yet the initial burst of growth-control activism sparked by Alvin Duskin and his supporters had raised public awareness of the issue of downtown development and thus altered popular perceptions. As the years passed, many San Franciscans began to perceive a striking imbalance in how City Hall dealt with downtown vis-à-vis the neighborhoods. Many felt that a succession of mayors culminating with Joseph Alioto, a former corporate attorney and head of the San Francisco Redevelopment Agency, had been overly solicitous of the wishes of powerful interests downtown while demonstrating only sporadic concern for the needs of neighborhood residents.

With Alioto prevented by law from seeking a third term as mayor, an opportunity arose in 1975 for a progressive state senator named George Moscone to take advantage of the deepening downtown-neighborhoods rift. Moscone set out to build an extensive grassroots network by promising to redirect political power in the city away from downtown and toward the neighborhoods. He proved adept at reaching out to urban groups long ignored by downtown-oriented politicians—Asians, Latinos, African Americans, and gays and lesbians. The timing for a neighborhood-based, grassroots mayoral campaign was just right. In November Moscone defeated conservative supervisor John Barbagelata and moderate supervisor Dianne Feinstein.

After Moscone's victory, hopes ran high among growth-control activists that the pace of downtown expansion would be slowed. Early actions by the new mayor raised expectations even higher. He fulfilled a campaign promise to regulate downtown development more carefully by appointing an entirely new Planning Commission including well-known growth-control advocates Sue

Bierman, Ina Dearman, and Charles Starbuck. Moscone asserted: "[The new appointees] recognize our critical need for jobs in San Francisco, while also understanding we cannot have rampant, unchecked development which we will be ashamed of 20 years from now. I think they represent a commitment to preservation of our neighborhoods in the planning process." Expecting a change in policy, activists set aside any thoughts of putting another growth-control initiative on the ballot and focused on other issues.[34]

But to the activists' dismay, the Moscone administration did little to alter the city's downtown development agenda. Planning Commissioners Bierman, Dearman, and Starbuck frequently questioned the value of new projects and often voted against them, but they constituted a minority on a seven-member commission that remained strongly in favor of rapid growth. Starbuck recalled that business interests consistently had "good access" to the Planning Commission, that they were "always present when big decisions were made." Even more disappointing than the Planning Commission's ineffectiveness at reigning in the building boom was the mayor's performance. Moscone proved to be reluctant to get involved in the development issue. When he did speak up, it was often in support of the growth coalition. For instance, in a 1978 letter to the publisher of the *San Francisco Chronicle,* he boasted: "Since January, 1976, when my Planning Commission took over, not a single *major* project has been turned down." The pace of development in 1977 and 1978 had, in fact, returned to the preelection levels, thus leaving many growth-control advocates confused and uncertain what to do. Activist Gerald Cauthen said, "[Moscone] promised more representative commissioners and he did it, so all of us went to sleep.... He put on strong people and took a hands-off attitude.... The pressures should have been kept up by neighborhood groups, but they thought all was well."[35]

In November 1978 the entire city was shocked when Mayor Moscone and Supervisor Harvey Milk were assassinated by a former supervisor, Dan White, while at work in City Hall. That tragedy thrust the president of the Board of Supervisors, Dianne Feinstein, into the mayor's office, a development that further solidified the bond between city government and the downtown establishment. Unlike Moscone, whose power base had been rooted in the neighborhoods, Feinstein had always benefited from a close relationship with downtown business elites.

Few were surprised when Mayor Feinstein began to take steps to *accelerate* the pace of downtown development. She pointed to the low vacancy rate in downtown offices as justification for forging ahead with new commercial office construction. In 1980 she replaced two members of the Planning Commission who had consistently raised concerns about downtown development with individuals who could be counted upon to provide consistent support for new development projects.[36] One of her new appointees, Jerome Klein, was quoted as saying, "She appointed me. She has my vote." Mayor Feinstein also pressured Moscone's planning director, Rai Okamoto, to step down in favor of her choice, Dean Macris. With new personnel in place and a renewed commitment to downtown development in the mayor's office, the city embarked on an unprecedented building spree (see table 4.2).[37]

Few public officials ever called for any pause in the building boom. One exception was Richard Sklar, the general manager of the Public Utilities Commission, who would periodically voice concern over the adverse consequences of rapid growth on the public transit system and the city's infrastructure; but those concerns swayed few votes on the Planning Commission. Sklar himself commented at one point: "[The Planning Commission] certainly hasn't turned down any projects during my lifetime in the city and I don't think it will. All it does is tinker with the facades on buildings, [make] occasional changes with the outline and shadow patterns and get a few amenities here and there, but development continues at the developer's pace, limited only by the economics of building highrises." And in 1981 Planning Commission President Toby Rosenblatt essentially agreed with Sklar: "If one looks back at the last five years, which is the time I've been on the Commission, ultimately we have not denied permits for any office building presented. . . . There were two buildings, maybe three, that were denied initially but those developers returned with alternative plans that we approved."[38]

Not only were office projects being approved at a record pace, but many of the new buildings were massive in height and bulk. Although the city regulated the density of office space by setting a maximum floor area ratio of fourteen to one, it also provided ample loopholes for developers to build bulkier, and thus more lucrative, buildings. The chief loophole was a density bonus system that enabled developers to increase density to as much as twenty-five to one in exchange for design amenities that would somehow benefit the public. Developers were all too happy to include in their projects, for example, a low-cost pedestrian mall or atrium, when it gained them the opportunity to tack on an additional fifty thousand square feet of office space that they could rent out to corporate clients at twenty-five to forty-five dollars per square foot. The economic windfall was substantial.

Abuse of the density point system was an especially sore point for growth-control activists. For instance, the Bank of America building, the city's tallest structure, was granted a density bonus in exchange for a public plaza; however, the plaza turned out to be heavily shaded and rarely used by the public. Another office building, at 525 Market Street, was granted an additional ninety thousand square feet of space in exchange for a pedestrian access tunnel to a

Table 4.2. Development of Downtown Office Space, San Francisco, 1976-1985 (in millions of square feet)

1976	0.2
1977	1.3
1978	1.9
1979	4.2
1980	1.9
1981	3.8
1982	4.6
1983	3.8
1984	3.4
1985	2.8

SOURCE: San Francisco Planning Commission and Redevelopment Agency

BART station. Not only was the deal a bad one for the city, according to activists, but after getting the density bonus, the developer reneged on the promise, citing an engineering problem as his excuse.[39]

Therefore, despite the brief challenge to the downtown growth coalition posed by George Moscone's mayoral campaign in 1975, the downtown building boom continued to roll along throughout the 1970s. As in the previous decade, a privatist political culture continued to thrive in San Francisco. Downtown elites retained tight control over development decision making, and they used their power to minimize governmental interference with market forces. Some regulation in the name of prudent planning had become accepted practice, but sizable loopholes in the law undermined efforts to manage the negative impacts of accelerated growth. Privatist ideas, values, beliefs, and practices enabled the downtown growth coalition to dominate the politics of downtown development.

But although a particular political culture may be hegemonic in any given society, alternative ways of imagining political life can usually be found as well. This was certainly the case in San Francisco in the 1970s. The first episode of growth-control activism hinted at such an alternative vision of land use politics; a few years later, a new wave of activists emerged with a much more coherent oppositional vision. The new activists revitalized the stagnant growth-control movement and made it a potent force in San Francisco politics by the 1980s. The roots of their rise to power and the genesis of their worldview deserve attention.

The Origins of Progressive Activism

Many San Franciscans had been drawn into political activism during the 1960s by the civil rights and antiwar movements, but few of these people had paid much attention to local politics. Bruce B. Brugmann, the publisher of the city's leading progressive newspaper, recalled: "There was a war going on. And all of us who were around at the time, every essence of our being was involved in fighting that war. The war lasted, U.S. involvement, until '72 or '73. . . . It was a hairy time."[40] Traditional local concerns such as education, police protection, and land use planning seemed inconsequential in comparison to the weighty issues in the national and international spheres.

Ironically, it was a national election campaign that prompted younger activists to think about municipal issues for the first time. In 1972 many of San Francisco's activists joined the presidential campaign of Senator George McGovern. The campaign was a genuine grassroots effort that called upon volunteers to walk precincts and knock on thousands of doors. That experience with community-based campaigning required young activists to leave the familiar environs of college campuses and such centers of hippie culture as the famed Haight-Ashbury district and venture into middle- and working-class neighborhoods to mobilize support for the McGovern candidacy. The resulting face-to-face interaction between activists and ordinary citizens enabled activists to learn about issues that were of pressing concern to San Francisco voters, issues that more often than not pertained to such mundane matters as the lack of street parking and inadequate service delivery.[41]

Although McGovern lost the 1972 election, the campaign had two important consequences for the San Francisco growth-control movement. First, it had the effect of introducing young activists back into their own neighborhoods and acquainting them with local issues that concerned most voters. And second, it alerted them to the political potential of grassroots organizing around neighborhood issues. Activist Calvin Welch reflected upon the significance of the 1972 presidential campaign: "[Many of us] became very much involved in the McGovern campaign in '72 . . . which was . . . probably the best grassroots national political campaign ever devised. And there were precinct organizations created in San Francisco around the McGovern presidential campaign. And that educated a large number of heretofore only campus-based student activists . . . especially white activists, [who] came to understand that there was a role, an organizing role, to be played in white neighborhoods and that if the proper kinds of issues were developed, there could be created common political causes with the black neighborhoods, Hispanic neighborhoods, and Asian-based neighborhoods."[42] Activists who had been eager to advance their conception of social justice through national or global politics suddenly, in the aftermath of Nixon's landslide victory, redirected their sights toward local politics.

In searching for "the proper kinds of issues" to organize around, Welch and other like-minded activists sought to distance themselves somewhat from the hippie movement, which was still flourishing in certain sectors of the city. Although sympathetic to many of that movement's values and goals, Welch felt that its political appeal was limited in that the social and cultural concerns of the hippies simply did not connect with most San Franciscans. Believing that "the great Achilles heel of the hippie movement" was its lack of an "economic base," Welch recalled coming to the realization during this period that the most promising way to promote political change was to apply broad principles of justice to "rather provincial neighborhood issues" that really mattered to ordinary people.[43]

The issue that these activists first seized upon in the early 1970s was the problem of real estate speculation in residential neighborhoods. Absentee owners would buy up three or four adjoining Victorian homes, demolish them, and erect large stucco apartment buildings, a process that somehow resulted in even higher housing costs. Activists capitalized on mounting resentment in the neighborhoods to push through more than a dozen neighborhood-initiated downzonings to deter speculative ownership practices.

That experience confirmed the activists' hunch that the key to effective grassroots activism was to identify issues of material concern to a wide variety of neighborhood residents. In this case organizing around the rising cost of housing and the changing character of the neighborhood proved successful. Welch recalled, "We had gotten over three hundred people from this neighborhood to City Hall. We had blue-haired old ladies, property owners, black folks who at the time lived in some numbers in this neighborhood, low-income folks, college professors, district merchants. . . . We thought we had come up with a nice synthesis. It was a way, a vocabulary, a set of issues that created common ground." Moreover, the downzoning campaigns gave "thousands of people . . . first-hand experience" interacting with local government and prepared them for future mobilization efforts.[44]

As these young activists sought to mobilize citizens around pressing local issues, they came to believe that the city's political system was fundamentally biased against neighborhood interests. In particular, they attacked the city's at-large system for electing representatives to the Board of Supervisors because they felt it diverted attention toward downtown. The activists believed that a district election system would favor candidates who would be more attuned to neighborhood matters. After a substantial commitment of time, energy, and resources over a four-year period, neighborhood activists succeeded in getting a citizens initiative approved by city voters in 1976 that required the city to replace the at-large system with district elections.[45]

As with the neighborhood downzonings, the struggle for district elections was as significant as the actual outcome in terms of defining the motivating vision of what would soon become a reconstituted growth-control movement. That struggle educated many San Francisco residents about the role of the Board of Supervisors and local government in general. According to Welch:

> I mean when we first hit the streets in '73 with a petition to change the way in which the Board of Supervisors were elected, we found we had to conduct a local civics lesson. . . . Nobody knew even that there was a Board of Supervisors. Now that's hard to understand now given the fact that the Board of Supervisors is everybody's kicking board. But in the '60s and '70s, the Board of Supervisors, city government was almost this invisible thing, y'know. No one paid any attention to it. It was third-rate political types. . . . The progressive democratic tradition in San Francisco was to ignore local government and look to state government or Congress. So third-raters basically inhabited City Hall. The press didn't cover it. It was amazing. We'd be standing out on a street corner asking people to sign a petition to require elections by district instead of at-large and people would say "the Board of what? Is that like the Board of Education?" So I mean we found ourselves conducting a civics class on street corners.[46]

In short, both the neighborhood downzonings and the campaign for district elections enabled a new breed of community activist to develop an increasingly coherent vision of politics, one that was strikingly at odds with the hegemonic worldview of downtown elites. The counterhegemonic perspective that was surfacing by the late 1970s celebrated a vigorous public sphere dominated by ordinary citizens.

But it was not until the end of the 1970s that these progressive neighborhood activists began to focus on downtown development as an important issue in local politics. Quite suddenly, many activists came to the realization that the building boom downtown was having a negative effect in neighborhoods with respect to rising housing costs and residential displacement. Calvin Welch recalls: "I'm telling you, the rapidness . . . What happened in, it seemed like overnight, was that relatively stable neighborhoods in which we had based relatively stable neighborhood organizations, overnight those people were gone." Although activists had long known about gentrification in downtown neighborhoods and in urban renewal areas, they had not considered the possibility that downtown development was exerting displacement pressures in the city's many outlying neighborhoods too. Activists believed that with the construction of several highrise office buildings every year, thousands of new employees—many of whom were high-salaried executives and professionals—were moving to San Francisco and bidding up the price of housing. Many long-time residents who found their rents and property taxes soaring were forced to relocate. Moreover, residential displacement was accompanied by commercial displacement as service and specialty retail businesses adjacent to downtown started to lose their leases and move to outlying neighborhoods, thus driving up commercial rents there and putting pressure on existing neighborhood merchants:

> So we started seeing a real displacement of neighborhood-serving retailers.... Shoe repair shops, mom and pop grocery stores, mom and pop cleaners suddenly were replaced by trendy ... bars, trendy boutique clothing stores, offices, architecture offices, accountants, tax consultants, environmental EIR preparers. ... And suddenly people started, I mean, it was like waking up and finding the city was losing its character.... This became very jarring to people. Nothing is more familiar, plays into one's concept of neighborhoodness, than, y'know, the local merchants that have been there forever that you've used, especially like grocery stores and shoe repair shops.[47]

Neighborhood activists concluded that such adverse impacts on neighborhood life were a good reason to seek more stringent controls on downtown expansion.

The cultural content of the new wave of growth-control activism could be anticipated based on the activists' first experiences in city politics. They clearly evinced a strong commitment to popular empowerment. Their willingness to conduct "a civics class on street corners" and their emphasis on issues that genuinely mattered to ordinary people demonstrate their determination to get citizens actively engaged in public life. The activists' attachment to the principle of inclusion is further evidence of their support for popular empowerment. The neighborhood downzoning campaign aspired to mobilize diverse groups including "blue-haired old ladies, property owners, black folks ... low-income folks, college professors, district merchants." This mirrored the diversity of the activists themselves, who came from Latino, Asian, and African American neighborhoods, as well as white middle- and working-class areas. Activists from predominantly minority neighborhoods had a special interest in land use issues based on their unhappy experiences with previous urban renewal programs. Welch explained:

> Well, in the Latin, Asian, and black community, there was a common enemy around the development issue and that was the San Francisco Redevelopment Agency, which ... had established a redevelopment area in the Western Addition and Bayview/Hunter's Point, the two principal black neighborhoods, and by the early 1970s was seeking to establish a redevelopment area in Chinatown and the Mission. So basically the entire eastern half of San Francisco, [which] had 90 percent of the people of color, would basically be one huge redevelopment area,

> and the goals of redevelopment were very obvious. It was displacement of existing populations and economic uses and the replacement of those by a totally new economic base, a kind of Pacific Rim–oriented, a much more nationally oriented economic system.[48]

The key point is that this emergent wing of the growth-control movement emanated from a multiracial and multiethnic core of activists devoted to the idea of getting citizens—all citizens—participating in the development decisions that were shaping their lives.

This attachment to popular empowerment was accompanied by a faith in government action to ameliorate inequities caused by the marketplace. Suspicious of private-sector forces, the activists felt that only an actively engaged citizenry working through the machinery of democratic governance could assure a satisfactory standard of living. Thus, even before the new activists exerted their influence within the growth-control movement, the key elements of their vision were apparent. Their discourse and conduct manifested a clear commitment to a progressive vision of politics, a vision that stood in striking contrast to the privatist political culture that had long dominated San Francisco politics.

Conclusion

Development politics in San Francisco during the first three decades after World War II resembled the development politics of most other large American cities. A coalition of downtown-oriented elites coalesced around the goal of rebuilding the downtown business district to attract new economic investment. In San Francisco the dream of progrowth advocates was to transform the city into a West Coast Manhattan and America's gateway to the Pacific Rim. Realizing the dream simply required respect for the powerful market forces that were pushing the city to its destiny as an international center of commerce along with guidance from the civic and business leaders who had the wisdom to see that the goals were attained. The privatist vision of downtown development commanded widespread support from the general public.

The building boom had already entered its second decade before San Francisco witnessed any serious opposition to the progrowth agenda. The initial wave of growth-control activists led by Alvin Duskin rejected the downtown growth coalition's faith in the private sector. The Duskinites maintained that an activist public sphere was necessary to ensure an orderly and tolerable development of the city. But the Duskinites sent out mixed signals regarding the question of who should control the public sector. On one hand, they seemed to deviate from the privatist vision's preference for rule by skilled experts by using the citizens initiative as a primary instrument of land use policy making. On the other hand, the Duskinites exhibited elitist tendencies by concentrating power in the hands of a few white, upper-middle-class citizens.

The ramifications of this managerial approach to politics were important. Opposition to the downtown growth coalition was based on the relatively narrow perceptions of the Duskinites, who objected to rapid downtown development mainly on postmaterial grounds. But an initiative campaign that stressed the aesthetic and environmental costs of downtown development did not affect how the materialistic majority conceived of downtown growth. Most San Franciscans remained preoccupied with material concerns such as job opportunities and economic growth. Only the downtown growth coalition was addressing those concerns by warning that government interference with market forces would kill the building boom and ruin the city's economy. Given the hegemony of privatist ideas, values, beliefs, and practices, that message rang true. Even worse for growth-control advocates, the elitism of the Duskinites reinforced the hegemonic tendency of ordinary citizens to respect the wisdom of skilled experts. In the early 1970s, that meant San Franciscans were content to defer to the trained professionals who had directed downtown development for the past two decades.

The second wave of growth-control activists, which emerged in the mid-1970s, offered a more thorough challenge to the privatist political culture. The new activists shared with the Duskinites a confidence in government action to remedy market flaws, but they differed with respect to the question of empowerment. They built their approach to politics around issues that directly affected a wide spectrum of people and an organizing strategy that sought broad-based popular involvement. The commitment to an expansive government controlled by ordinary people represented the opposite of the privatist vision of the downtown growth coalition. The progressive vision of these new growth-control activists was thus a clear challenge to the ideas, values, beliefs, and practices that had guided downtown development since the 1950s. The counterhegemonic potential of this revitalized oppositional movement was unmistakable.

✦5

Progressive Activism

Expanding the Public Sphere

The 1979 Citizens Initiative Campaign

Throughout the 1970s, the one organization devoted to limiting downtown growth was San Francisco Tomorrow (SFT). SFT was composed mainly of white, middle-class professionals concerned about the building boom's effect on San Francisco's aesthetic and environmental character. The organization advocated stricter zoning regulation to ensure a more orderly development of the city. It had supported the early Duskin initiatives and then backed George Moscone's mayoral candidacy in 1975 after Moscone had promised to impose restrictions on highrise construction. As it became clear that the city would maintain its progrowth course, however, especially after Dianne Feinstein became mayor, SFT decided to turn to a citizens initiative as the only hope for preventing the further Manhattanization of San Francisco.[1]

Gerald Cauthen, the president of San Francisco Tomorrow, explained in January 1979 why his organization was backing a new growth-control initiative: "It's more than just losing views. . . . People are reacting to congestion, to the loss of historic, beautiful old buildings, and to a downtown that is getting drearier, darker, and windier."[2] Although Cauthen asserted that more was at stake than lost vistas, his comment suggests that SFT's primary concerns in 1979 continued to be aesthetic and environmental.

Meanwhile, the progressive contingent of the growth-control movement had become disenchanted with the postmaterialist perspective of SFT. Welch described his view of the organization as it existed in 1979: "There's a lot of Republicans, OK, in the conservationist movement. And San Francisco Tomorrow included large numbers of Republicans who were basically what we've come to call tree ecologists as opposed to urban environmentalists who basically had the mythical world, mythical agrarian vision of what environmentalism was all about. It was parks and trees and vistas and green things, small furry mammals. Had nothing to do with people." Another veteran progressive activist referred to SFT in these terms: "They're like living in Hobbit Land. They feel threatened by urbanity, by modernity. They come from the suburbs. They come here to a city and say, 'Gee, this city would be really great if it were just the suburbs.' . . . I think a lot of it is very right-wing, status quo, pull up the drawbridge sort of mentality, and that's insanity."[3] The progressives argued that in its zeal to protect the environment and historical buildings from commercial office expansion, SFT had been utterly oblivious to how the building boom had affected the material well-being of most city residents with respect to housing, small businesses, and employment. They went on to contend that the material impacts of rapid growth were so serious that broader action was needed than the simple zoning controls sought by SFT. The progressives decided to break off from SFT and form their own organization, San Franciscans for Reasonable Growth (SFRG). That group also advocated placing a citizens initiative on the November 1979 ballot, but an initiative motivated by a different vision of politics.

The first general strategy meeting to draft a highrise-limit initiative took place on January 24, 1979, under the auspices of SFT. The SFT contingent argued for a narrow initiative that would impose only height and bulk limitations upon new office buildings. Such an initiative would be patterned after the Duskin initiatives earlier in the decade but would be more lenient in setting restrictions (for example, a height limit of twenty-five floors instead of only seven or sixteen).[4]

Activists from SFRG took a more ambitious position. In addition to the regulatory limits on height and bulk proposed by SFT, they introduced a novel redistributive element. SFRG contended that the initiative should obligate developers of commercial office buildings to ameliorate the burdens that their projects create for neighborhood residents. The idea was that although developers had the right to develop their properties, they also had the responsibility to exercise that right in ways that did not harm the community. Since the progressives believed that commercial office development was harming the community, the city needed to hold the developers accountable. A journalist covering the event described the thrust of the SFRG proposal: "At the January 24 meeting, one camp argued that the initiative ought to address the social problems that highrises create. For example, suggestions were offered to add language to the measure that would compel developers to add housing to their highrise plans, to implement minority recruitment programs and to pay the costs of increased public services their projects require such as MUNI." In advocating this more aggressive approach to regulating downtown development, activist John Elberling said: "I feel my plan is more creative. . . . These buildings make a lot of money for their owners, and I think they should return some of that money to the rest of us who have to put up with the problems they create."[5]

More specifically, if downtown growth was constricting the supply of affordable housing and overburdening the public transit system, then SFRG activists argued that the city should impose exactions on new commercial office development and then use the revenue raised from the exactions for affordable housing production and public transit improvements. Such a redistributive policy would mitigate the negative impacts of rapid growth and ensure a more equitable distribution of the costs of downtown development. The SFRG proposal was a true innovation in the politics of downtown development; no other major city in the United States had ever implemented a similar mandatory mitigation measure.

Moderate and progressive activists struggled over the ensuing four weeks to draft an initiative that reflected both perspectives on controlling downtown development. San Francisco Tomorrow president Gerald Cauthen expressed some support for the rationale underlying the latter group's strategy but then sided with the former group: "We want to be democratic, but we can't add everything that is on everybody's shopping list."[6] On February 25 the SFT board of directors voted unanimously in favor of a compromise initiative that would subsequently be certified as Proposition O to be included on the November ballot. On the regulatory front, the initiative would lower the height limit from 700 feet or fifty-five stories in the heart of the financial district to 260 feet or twenty stories. It would also reduce the density of new office buildings downtown by decreasing the floor area ratio from fourteen to one to eight to one and eliminate the density bonus point system that had enabled developers to increase density to as much as twenty-five to one in exchange for design amenities.[7]

The redistributive component turned out to be a somewhat watered-down version of the SFRG proposal, which had called for mandatory mitigation fees on any new commercial office project. The compromise version continued to require the provision of off-site mitigation measures, but it offered developers a variety of compensatory density bonuses so as not to discourage future development. Under the initiative's guidelines, developers would be permitted to exceed established floor area ratios if they agreed to (1) preserve historic buildings in perpetuity, (2) build additional housing on or within five hundred feet of the proposed development site, or (3) provide "significant public benefits" in the areas of public transit, energy conservation, pedestrian environment, or housing construction elsewhere in the city.[8]

Calvin Welch believed that the compromise reached in Proposition O represented an important transition in the city's growth-control movement because for the first time the debate was framed not only in terms of aesthetic impacts, but in terms of economic impacts. The compromise demonstrated not only a "change in thinking" about downtown development, but also a willingness by divergent groups within the movement to put aside differences and work together: "[Proposition O] was like the duck-bill platypus. It was neither fish nor fowl. It didn't clearly come down on one side of the issue but tried to be a bridge in order to try and keep what it perceived to be . . . the political constituency out there that was interested in economic development but not wanting to break with the Duskinite, more established environmental group. So they saw themselves engaged in this great coalition and compromise." SFT's Gerald Cauthen agreed: "This initiative is one I think both sides can live with."[9]

The shift in substantive policy goals in the 1979 citizens initiative campaign was not the only departure from the earlier Duskin initiatives. Progressive activists also wanted to alter the *process* of grassroots organizing. The 1979 campaign would not be patterned after the centralized, hierarchical system utilized by growth-control activists at the beginning of the decade, but after the decentralized grassroots efforts used during the 1972 McGovern presidential campaign and the campaign for district elections in 1976. Sue Hestor, who had participated in the previous growth-control initiative drives, remarked: "Duskin relied on a few stars. We've worked in the districts to build up a solid organization."[10] The progressives were determined to take advantage of that growing base of community organizers. They also promised to reach out to diverse urban groups affected by downtown development and include them in the running of the campaign. It was hoped that attention to matters of common concern such as housing and transportation would give groups long overlooked by business elites an incentive to focus on issues of downtown development. In summary, the shift in policy goals and organizing methods signaled the emergence of a form of grassroots activism that was consistent with a progressive vision of politics and strikingly different from the dominant privatist vision.

The campaign in support of Proposition O had a profound effect upon the public discourse surrounding urban development in San Francisco. The principal message of the growth-control movement during the spring, summer, and fall of 1979 was that the city's aggressive promotion of commercial office development in the downtown business district was hurting more than it was helping San Francisco, and this time the new emphasis on material issues caught the attention of ordinary citizens.

For instance, progressive activists argued that downtown development was contributing to the city's shortage of affordable housing in three ways. First, the actual construction of highrise office towers sometimes necessitated the destruction of existing housing, a circumstance that led directly to the displacement of numerous lower- and working-class residents in the downtown area. Second, downtown development contributed to sharply rising property values not only in the financial district but in surrounding residential neighborhoods. That trend, in turn, further fueled real estate speculation, thus exacerbating the affordable housing crisis throughout the city. Third, the building boom was attracting tens of thousands of new employees to occupy the new highrise offices. This put considerable upward pressure on housing prices as the new employees, many of whom tended to be relatively affluent professionals or business executives, were able to outbid many native residents when competing for a citywide supply of housing that was increasing but only at a very slow rate.[11]

In addition to the link between downtown development and the scarcity of affordable housing, progressive activists tried to illuminate other costs of rapid downtown growth such as the mounting burdens on the municipal transit system, MUNI; city buses, streetcars, and trolleys were overflowing during rush hour. Traffic congestion was spreading beyond the downtown business district. And simply finding a parking space anywhere near one's residence was becoming an ordeal. Activists blamed all of these transportation problems on downtown development.

Along with highlighting the material costs of downtown growth in San Francisco neighborhoods, progressive activists began to emphasize how the purported benefits of urban development had not panned out to the degree that many groups might have hoped or expected. In particular, they argued that downtown development was not doing much for the less privileged groups in the city. Developers and their allies in local government had always promised that the building boom would produce new jobs for lower- and working-class citizens, many of whom had lost good jobs with the decline of the city's manufacturing base during the postwar era. In the 1979 initiative campaign, progressives contended that most employment opportunities in the new highrises benefited suburban commuters and upper-income professionals. Most city residents, they claimed, were left with lower-paying service and maintenance jobs.

Another promised benefit of downtown growth was that it would generate tremendous revenues for the city through commercial property taxes. But progressives criticized this position on three grounds. First, they asserted that even if the city was obtaining higher tax revenues, those revenues were not finding their way to the people who most needed them. City services in the poorer neighborhoods remained inadequate. The prosperity being created downtown seemed to be having little impact on the less privileged sections of San Francisco.

Second, the progressives argued that a substantial portion of the new tax revenues would have to be allocated to pay for the heightened demand on services produced by the building boom. They pointed to a warning issued by

William Evers, the president of the mayor's Economic Development Advisory Council, in a January 1979 newsletter. Particularly in light of Proposition 13's[12] limits on property taxes, Evers wrote that downtown growth raises "the question of the city's ability to provide services for those working in this space. After [Proposition 13], can the public infrastructure (parking, MUNI) keep up with the demand? This is something to ponder—we have a problem."[13]

Finally, progressive activists were able to derive significant political gains by arguing that Proposition 13 had shifted the burden of property taxes from commercial property owners to residential property owners. This is because under Proposition 13 a building's property tax could only be raised 2 percent a year unless that building were resold, thereby establishing true market value. Since houses are sold much more often than highrise office buildings, assessment of residential property would take place more frequently, thus keeping up with sharply rising property values in California. Therefore, activists charged that downtown's share of the city's property tax burden would decline.[14] That meant that San Francisco's neighborhoods were subsidizing to an increasing degree the services required by the downtown business district.

All of these arguments about downtown development attracted more public attention than they normally might have because 1979 was also a mayoral election year and San Franciscans were especially attuned to local politics. Moreover, Mayor Feinstein's chief opponent, Quentin Kopp, a member of the Board of Supervisors known for his relatively conservative position on most local issues, perceived a chance to capitalize on rising antigrowth sentiment and endorsed Proposition O at a press conference on September 13 at the Golden Gate Bridge toll plaza. Kopp called the initiative a "modest" measure that would "help redirect city policy in favor of San Francisco residents first as opposed to out-of-towners." The president of the Board of Supervisors, John Molinari, also endorsed the growth-control initiative, which enjoyed strong support in early voter opinion polls.[15] Downtown development thus became a hot issue in the mayoral campaign as well.

Dianne Feinstein found herself in a difficult position. She had always been a strong believer in the virtues of downtown development and since becoming mayor in November of 1978 had advocated a policy of accelerated growth. But Feinstein was also a shrewd politician. As the fall campaign got under way, she sensed that the growth-control movement was becoming a significant force. The mayor therefore opted to stay neutral on Proposition O. At one point she seemed to endorse the adoption of "highrise controls in the office building area," but administration assistants later explained that she simply wanted to shift commercial office development from the area north of Market Street to the area south of Market Street.[16] Throughout the campaign Feinstein continued to juggle the issue by meeting with both neighborhood organizations that supported the citizens initiative and downtown business leaders who vehemently condemned the measure; she studiously avoided taking a stand one way or the other.[17]

With Proposition O gaining momentum, and with Mayor Feinstein reluctant to take a public stand on the issue, progrowth interests finally began to act. They established a coalition called San Francisco Forward (SFF), composed mainly of business and labor groups. In a September 6 press release, SFF warned that Proposition O would "bring increased unemployment, urban sprawl and economic stagnation" to the city.[18] The Chamber of Commerce called the initiative a "legal nightmare," predicting it would take years of litigation to clarify its meaning and constitutional status. Moreover, the Chamber argued that the initiative violated "good urban planning principles," would reduce tax revenues, hamper city services, reduce opportunities for blue-collar employment, engender unanticipated problems such as low-rise sprawl, and "add immeasurably to the negative business climate image of San Francisco." The business lobby was particularly effective at stoking fears that the growth-control initiative would cause a loss of construction jobs among minority groups: "Seventy per cent of city construction jobs are held by San Francisco residents. A downturn in the construction industry will see the rule of 'last hired, first fired' operate with a vengeance in such [predominantely black and Latino] neighborhoods as the Western Addition and Mission."[18] In late September the Chamber of Commerce offered its own plan to control downtown development. It proposed lowering the maximum height of 700 feet to 575 feet and requiring office buildings to be somewhat less bulky. At the same time, the Chamber condemned the notion of planning by citizens initiative and urged a return to "the normal city legislative process."[20]

The downtown growth coalition's extensive command over financial, technical, legal, political, and media resources enabled it to wage a devastating counterattack against Proposition O. Downtown elites contested every argument made by the neighborhood activists while pressing their own case for a continuation of existing development policies. And the growth coalition made sure that its position was made known to San Francisco voters. It outspent the growth-control activists ten to one to pay for prominent billboard advertising and a series of mass mailings. The city's major newspapers, the *Chronicle* and the *Examiner*, published editorials denouncing the initiative in terms that mirrored the perspective of progrowth advocates.

The prodevelopment message began to resonate with the public. In trying to assess their interests and the city's interests, citizens considered the competing arguments of the growth coalition and the growth-control movement by looking through a cultural prism that—despite the counterhegemonic efforts of the activists—still skewed interpretations in favor of a privatist worldview. Opinion polls showed a steady slippage in support for Proposition O during the fall. When voters entered the polling booths in November 1979, they were swayed by the vision of an elite-supervised, market-driven expansion of the downtown business district that would generate substantial benefits for all. The initiative was defeated by a 54 percent to 46 percent vote.

Despite the outcome, the 1979 campaign succeeded in altering the discourse concerning downtown development. The phrase "negative impacts" gained common usage, whereas a decade before most citizens never even conceived that downtown growth could have adverse consequences in residential neighborhoods. Activists also succeeded in getting people to consider the "responsibility" that developers owed to the larger community for "mitigating" the negative impacts of their downtown office projects. They managed to focus public attention on the underlying fairness or unfairness of an urban development policy that generated tremendous wealth in the downtown business district but minimal improvements in the neighborhoods. Their calls for a vigorous public sphere to regulate downtown development and promote a more equitable distribution of the costs and benefits of growth set the agenda for the 1979 campaign and dominated the terms of debate. The evolving nature of the discourse, as well as the closer electoral outcome as compared to the results of the 1971 and 1972 growth-control initiatives, suggests that counterhegemonic activism was starting to make a dent in privatism's hegemonic grip over the local political culture.

Furthermore, cultural change was beginning to inspire political change. Following the 1979 campaign, Planning Commission president Toby Rosenblatt conceded that some new restrictions on downtown highrises were a "foregone conclusion." In January 1980 the Planning Commission voted unanimously to impose a one-year moratorium on "developer bonuses" that allowed developers to build denser office buildings in exchange for aesthetic amenities. Also, Mayor Feinstein picked up on an argument made by growth-control advocates when she told business leaders in January 1980 that "the dominant majority of new jobs go to non–San Franciscans" and urged them to hire locally.[21] Finally, the city engaged a private consulting firm to conduct a study of six proposed plans for downtown development, three of which were offered by the Chamber of Commerce, the City Planning Department, and growth-control advocates.[22] Such post-election moves indicated at least the possibility that the city was for the first time contemplating alternative approaches to its long-standing commitment to aggressive downtown development.

But perhaps the most dramatic evidence that counterhegemonic activism in the 1979 initiative campaign had affected how city officials conceived of downtown development involved the issue of developer exactions. The activists had made an impression. City officials now began to acknowledge the existence of negative impacts associated with rapid growth and join with the activists in insisting that the developers be held accountable for those impacts through mitigation measures that came to be known as "linkage" policies.

Linkage as a Counterhegemonic Device

The fact that growth-control activists were able to convince city officials to seriously consider linkage as a public response to the inequities of market-driven development pressures is itself something of an accomplishment given the rather radical nature of the practice. To appreciate the counterhegemonic significance of linkage in contributing to cultural/political change in San Francisco, it is necessary to take a close look at the origins of linkage and its rising influence in the context of growth-control activism.

Developer exactions were not exactly unheard of in the 1970s. For instance, developers of suburban subdivisions often had to pay exaction fees to finance the construction of streets, sidewalks, sewers, and other infrastructures to service the new development. The rationale was that the taxpayers of a municipality should not get stuck paying the bill for costs arising from a project that stood to enrich a private developer. Later, the principle was expanded to require developers to offset the anticipated increased demand for recreation and education generated by a suburban development by helping to pay for new parks and schools. Although they grumbled about these exactions, developers also realized that the new amenities made their developments more attractive and thus more lucrative. So both on-site and near-site exactions associated with suburban subdivisions became relatively common.

Exactions related to urban development projects also existed, but they were less ambitious. First, they were limited to mitigating adverse effects felt at the project site, as opposed to the surrounding area. Second, they tended to be confined to infrastructure improvements (for example, expanding a subway station) or aesthetic additions (for example, a public plaza). Urban developers tended to go along with such exactions because they enhanced the value of the project in the eyes of potential investors and because they usually did not cost very much in the context of a multimillion dollar project.[23]

What San Francisco's growth-control activists were proposing beginning in the late 1970s was a very different animal. They were demanding that developers pay substantial exaction fees to ameliorate the adverse social impacts of downtown office development not just at the project site or in the immediate vicinity, but *throughout* the city. More specifically, developers would be required to pay fees based on the amount of commercial office space in their projects to help offset the negative impacts on the city's housing shortage and public transit system.

Developers reacted with considerable hostility. Not only would exactions to finance such off-site amenities put a significant dent in their profits, but developers believed that the new amenities would do little to increase the value of their projects to potential investors and tenants. Moreover, such exactions conflicted with cherished beliefs about the inherent wisdom of urban development and the folly of government sticking its neck in where it did not belong. To downtown business leaders, there was no doubt that the kinds of linkage policies being proposed by growth-control activists contradicted common sense. The fact that no American city had ever before required private developers to assume responsibility for the broad social costs of their projects only confirmed their instinct that linkage was a pernicious idea.

Nevertheless, growth-control activists felt they had solid grounds for linkage based on their interpretation of environmental law. The legal origins of San Francisco's linkage policies can be traced to the nation's first major environmental protection law, the National Environmental Policy Act (NEPA). That statute, adopted in 1969, directed federal agencies to conduct detailed studies of all federal actions that potentially affect the environment to assess the environmental impact of the proposed action and any less demanding alternatives. Congressional enactment of NEPA led many state legislatures to follow suit. In 1970 California adopted its own version, the California Environmental Quality Act (CEQA), which obligated state agencies to accord "major consideration" to "preventing environmental damage" in regulating activity that affects the environment. Like the federal law, the state statute mandated the preparation of environmental impact reports to identify the adverse environmental effects of projects and how those adverse effects might be minimized.[24] In 1976 the California state legislature strengthened CEQA by adding an explicit mitigation requirement. Section 21002 provides that if an environmental impact report reveals that a project would significantly affect the environment, then the responsible public agency "should not approve" the project "if there are feasible alternatives or feasible mitigation measures available which would substantially lessen the significant environmental effects of such projects." The statutory duty to mitigate negative impacts represented an important victory for environmentalists, but that duty was not absolute. The statute also gave state agencies discretionary power to approve projects that adversely affect the environment in cases where "specific economic, social, or other conditions make infeasible such project alternatives or such mitigation measures." The state regulatory guidelines spell out the escape route more clearly: "If the benefits of a proposal project outweigh the unavoidable adverse environmental effects, the adverse environmental effects may be considered 'acceptable'" and the project may be approved.[25] Under CEQA, therefore, state agencies charged with approving projects that significantly affect the environment were left with two choices: (1) make sure that the negative impacts were mitigated or (2) find that the overall benefits of a project outweigh the negative environmental effects. An elaborate public process was established so that environmental harms arising from development projects were, at a minimum, identified and analyzed, and perhaps mitigated.

By the late 1970s, growth-control activists in San Francisco had come to view the environmental review process required by CEQA as providing an excellent vehicle for exposing problems associated with downtown development.[26] They started by using data contained in the environmental impact reports to highlight the ways in which commercial office development directly harmed the environment by significantly increasing the number of people commuting to downtown by automobile. This, in turn, aggravated traffic congestion not just on city streets but on highways and bridges leading to downtown. The resulting air and noise pollution was growing year by year.

Given these findings, activists could argue that downtown growth should be curtailed and that whatever development was allowed to continue should be mitigated by bolstering the public transit system. Activists charged that since private developers were the ones who had largely created the environmental problem in the first place, they should be obligated to remedy the problem by paying to expand and improve mass transit. The environmental review process thus gave growth-control activists a legal mechanism to advocate transit linkage.

Advocating housing linkage based on environmental law called for a more clever line of argument. Activists contended that downtown development had contributed to rising housing costs throughout the city, thus squeezing much of the working and middle class out of the housing market. Tens of thousands of people who worked downtown were thus forced to seek housing in the suburbs and commute to work every day. This increase in suburban-urban commuting exacerbated the environmental problems discussed above. One mitigation strategy was to improve mass transit, but another, activists insisted, was to compel commercial office developers to build or rehabilitate affordable housing within the city and thereby lessen pollution-producing commuting.

Growth-control activists thus believed that they had a logical argument for linkage policies grounded in environmental law, and so they set out to use those legal arguments to pressure city planners to force commercial office developers to agree to mitigation measures with respect to public transit and housing. At first the chosen forum for applying pressure was the one provided by the law. The California Environmental Quality Act required public hearings to evaluate the environmental impact of proposed highrise projects. Activists seized this opportunity to influence development policy.

Participating in public hearings enabled the activists to reshape the public discourse by (1) emphasizing the mounting costs and limited benefits of downtown development; (2) broadening the debate over the impacts of growth beyond purely environmental and aesthetic concerns; and (3) suggesting that developers who caused such negative impacts bear the cost of mitigating them. One long-time city planner, Alec Bash, attributed considerable importance to the environmental review process, and particularly the public hearings to evaluate the environmental impact reports, in facilitating an atmosphere conducive to the formation of linkage policies: "I think [the environmental impact reports] did a tremendous amount to changing the way that development happens because they got official information out to people that people could use, whether they believed and trusted the reports or not. They could use the reports as a vehicle for articulating what the problems were, and the environmental review process created a public forum for debating those types of impacts. They legitimized a whole area of inquiry and provided the opportunity for the public voice to be heard in a formal way."

As San Francisco activists became increasingly adept at pointing out the costs of downtown expansion, city planners felt greater pressure to respond. They began to insist on more elaborate preparations of environmental impact reports for new commercial office buildings. Once the Planning Department was able to obtain hard data on adverse environmental impacts caused by highrise development, it would then have legal authority under CEQA to require developers to mitigate those negative impacts by, for example, providing funds for more buses and affordable housing. But having the legal authority to require mitigation is not the same as having the political power to take such a step, and in the late 1970s the Planning Department was reluctant to do so.[27]

But being stymied on the administrative front did not last long. The 1979 citizens' initiative campaign gave the push for linkage a major lift. Grassroots organizing heightened popular awareness of the negative impacts of downtown development on mass transit and housing, and demands that developers do something to mitigate those impacts sounded reasonable to most citizens. As linkage attracted more and more public attention, the idea sounded increasingly plausible to city planners as well.

With the growth-control initiative enjoying broad support in public opinion polls throughout most of 1979, the Planning Department began to implement on an ad hoc basis its first linkage policies. The transit linkage measure required developers as a condition for official approval of downtown office buildings to "participate in a downtown assessment district or similar fair and appropriate mechanism, to provide funds for maintaining and augmenting transportation service."[28] The policy was a weak one since it was premised on the establishment of some yet unspecified mitigation procedure. With no assurance that such a mechanism would actually be created, transit linkage was not perceived by developers as a matter of great concern at that time. The Planning Department's first housing linkage policy in 1979 also posed little apparent threat to developers. It merely required that developers use "good faith efforts" to build housing somewhere in the city to mitigate the increased housing demand created by their projects. Housing linkage was thus a purely voluntary arrangement between the city and commercial office developers.[29]

Despite the tepid nature of these first linkage policies, their adoption by the Planning Department was a milestone. San Francisco became the first major city in the United States to endorse the idea that developers of commercial office buildings generate adverse social costs and that the government should intervene to obligate developers to accept responsibility to the larger community for ameliorating those costs. This marked a decisive shift away from the privatist faith in market forces and toward a progressive use of the public sphere to promote greater social equity.

Again, growth-control activism clearly contributed to this early process of cultural/political change. Participation in the environmental review process and especially the citizens initiative campaign in 1979 had transformed the discourse of development policy making and changed perceptions about what was possible and desirable. This, in turn, created sufficient public pressure on city officials to prompt them to step away from their close alliance with the downtown business community. The city planning director at the time, Rai Okamoto, confirmed that the 1979 initiative campaign had been "very important" in fostering a climate that enabled city planners to move ahead, albeit tentatively, with linkage policies.[30]

After the 1979 initiative campaign, growth-control activists sought to maintain the pressure on the city to strengthen its linkage policies. But the focal point of grassroots organizing shifted from the citywide level to the neighborhood level. In the spring of 1980, three major hotel chains—Ramada, Holiday Inn, and Hilton—announced plans to build hotels in the Tenderloin, a neighborhood valued by the hospitality industry because of its proximity to downtown, North Beach, Chinatown, Union Square, and many other prominent tourist destinations. But the Tenderloin was also home to tens of thousands of residents, many of whom were lower-income and elderly and who were facing rising housing costs. Fears of gentrification were quickly confirmed when the city reappraised land values surrounding the sites for the planned hotels from thirty-two to fifty dollars per square foot. That move prompted dozens of residential hotels in the area to convert to more profitable tourist uses, which further intensified displacement pressures on local residents.[31]

Tenderloin residents joined together in the summer of 1980 and formed the Luxury Hotel Task Force (LHTF) to combat gentrification of their neighborhood spurred by the three hotel proposals. On one level the LHTF activists wanted to block construction altogether, but because city officials supported the hotels,[32] they mainly focused on compelling the hotels to assume responsibility for the harms their projects would cause for the community. The LHTF demanded (1) one-to-one residential housing replacement or renovation for each of the anticipated 2,215 rooms in the three hotels and (2) that half of the hotels' workforce consist of Tenderloin residents.[33]

The hotels responded with dismay. They contended that, given the number of new jobs and additional tax revenue that the projects would produce, the community should be trying to entice development instead of attempting to extract concessions to mitigate alleged costs to area residents.[34] Meanwhile, during public hearings to review the environmental impact reports for each project, LHTF activists filled the hearing room and presented documented testimony on the adverse impacts expected from development of the hotels. The Planning Department ultimately sided with the Tenderloin residents by confirming the existence of negative impacts and recommending that the hotel developers be obligated to mitigate those impacts.[35]

Eager to begin construction on what they believed would be lucrative investments, Holiday Inn and Ramada finally gave in to certain linkage measures. They accepted a plan for preferential hiring of local residents and each agreed to pay two hundred thousand dollars for community projects. Ramada also agreed to participate in an Urban Development Action Grant (UDAG) project assembled by Mayor Feinstein by providing a $1.1 million loan to help renovate residential hotels in the neighborhood. Finally, Holiday Inn promised to pay fifty cents per occupied room per day into an affordable housing subsidy fund.[36] The important point is that grassroots pressure in the Tenderloin dovetailed with the ongoing efforts of growth-control activists elsewhere in the city to make linkage an increasingly accepted practice in land use policy.

Institutionalizing Linkage

But for linkage to move from an ad hoc policy to a consistently applied law, it soon became apparent that activists and sympathetic city planners would have to win over the mayor and other influential public officials who still feared that mandatory linkage would alienate business and discourage investment in the city. What gave the growth-control movement's advocacy of linkage a decisive boost in securing Feinstein's support was an event that had nothing to do with growth-control activism in San Francisco—the passage of Proposition 13 in 1978. That proposition was expected to slash property tax revenues and produce a crisis in local government financing throughout California. In searching for new revenue sources, Mayor Feinstein informed the Public Utilities Commission (PUC), the government agency responsible for overseeing the city's public transit system, that she wanted a doubling of the transit fare from twenty-five cents to fifty cents. Although San Francisco had one of the lowest transit fares in the country, the PUC was still reluctant to proceed with such a stiff increase for fear of losing ridership and encouraging greater automobile use.

At this point, growth-control activism also influenced PUC deliberations regarding Feinstein's request for a large transit fare hike. One PUC member, John Sanger, was concerned about asking neighborhood residents to accept such a burden when it seemed that the growing demand for transit service was largely a consequence of the downtown building boom. He said, on the equity issue: "I came from the neighborhoods. I was a neighborhood leader. I had my own neighborhood association. I wasn't anti-downtown, but I did believe in downtown paying for things that served them. . . . There was a lot of controversy [over the issue]: Was downtown a drain on the rest of the city or a net contributor? And I was a believer at that time that we weren't deriving enough revenue from downtown." On his own initiative, Sanger, who was both a planner and a lawyer, began to investigate the legal possibilities of imposing a transit impact fee on commercial office developers to pay for anticipated increases in future operating requirements caused by the building boom. His research convinced him that California courts would uphold such a fee if the city could convincingly document that a "rational nexus" existed between new office development downtown and increased burdens on the public transit system. Sanger described how he calculated what an appropriate transit impact fee would be:

> One of the impacts of all downtown office buildings to continually show up in these EIRs was increase in ridership on the MUNI and the question of . . . what increases in capacity and cost would accrue to MUNI by reason of those demands. So we were involved in projecting, MUNI would have to increase its service by X to accommodate the demand from this building. That would translate into increased operating deficits of Y because there was pretty good data . . . on how much MUNI lost per passenger. . . . And then we would project out what the capital requirements would be. And this was actually in the end how I came up with the five dollars [fee]. It had to do with a present value of future operating deficits and capital requirements, which I then derived on a per square foot basis.[36]

Confident that he had established an adequate factual foundation to demonstrate the requisite connection between downtown office growth and the burden on MUNI, Sanger moved to couple Feinstein's desire for a doubling of the transit fare with his own proposal for a five-dollar-per-square-foot transit fee on new commercial office development downtown.

In 1979, in the midst of the citizens initiative campaign to control downtown development, the PUC adopted a resolution approving a fare increase from twenty-five to fifty cents and at the same time calling upon the Board of Supervisors to enact into law the five-dollar-per-square-foot transit impact fee to accommodate the anticipated increase in ridership arising from the building boom. Sanger was certain that growth-control activism connected with that 1979 campaign provided the political impetus to get the transit linkage fee off the ground: "There's no question that the neighborhood movement, the growth-control movement at least led to the strong sentiment that downtown 'had to pay its own way.' It was viewed that the city had to ensure that that growth did not become a burden to the city because of the threat to services. There was also the sense of fairness that riders were going to pay more than the office developers who were profiting over the growth of downtown."[38] Despite public pressure from the initiative campaign, the Board of Supervisors declined to act on the PUC's resolution urging adoption of a transit linkage ordinance. One of the main obstacles was Mayor Feinstein, who remained wary of the whole idea of linkage.

But the evolving political environment soon changed the mayor's mind. In early 1980, anticipating a widening budget deficit caused by Proposition 13's stiff restrictions on property taxes, Feinstein went ahead with her plan for a 100 percent boost in MUNI fares.[39] San Franciscans reacted angrily. Not only was the fare hike seen as draconian, but many citizens had been influenced by the previous fall's initiative campaign, which had contended that the building boom was responsible for increased demands on MUNI. They concluded that a 100 percent fare hike unfairly penalized neighborhood residents when downtown interests really should be footing the bill.

As public hostility toward the fare hike mounted, Feinstein decided to reconsider transit linkage. In April 1980 she threw her support behind the PUC resolution calling for a 100 percent fare hike *and* a mandatory fee of five dollars per square foot on developers of new commercial office buildings to raise $5 million annually for MUNI construction projects downtown.[40] With this move, the mayor, in effect, sided with the growth-control movement's position that downtown developers should be held accountable for the costs that their projects create on city services such as MUNI.

Downtown opposition to the linkage measure was intense.[41] Real estate interests launched a massive lobbying effort, and six weeks after proposing the mitigation measure, Feinstein quietly withdrew her support for it.[42] But the mayor had genuinely come to believe that the transit linkage policy was both fair and appropriate. Early the next year, Feinstein tried to revive the measure once again. On April 20 the Board of Supervisors, ignoring business opposition, adopted two pieces of legislation requiring downtown to pay a greater share for MUNI. First, it adopted Feinstein's proposal to levy on developers a one-time fee of five dollars per square foot of new office space. And second, in an even more ambitious move, the board established a special assessment district downtown that would allow the city to collect an annual transit fee from all existing downtown property owners. Together, the two measures were expected to raise as much as $30 million in annual revenue.[43]

The downtown growth coalition bitterly attacked both ordinances. Conservative supervisor Wendy Nelder called the linkage fee a "dangerous precedent" and predicted, "This is one more measure that is going to chase businesses out of San Francisco." An official with the Building and Construction Trades Council warned, "They're going to kill the goose that laid the golden egg." And a developer condemned the linkage ordinance as "one of the most outstanding examples of municipal avarice I've ever seen."[44] The business community was particularly "furious" with the mayor, whom they had always counted on as a reliable ally on land use issues. The chairman of the Chamber of Commerce remarked, "I've supported Dianne Feinstein and have always liked her personally, but I would have to say the business community is troubled." A developer promised that the linkage policy would be challenged in court: "[Business leaders are] not like the activists who march into her office. Businessmen don't act this way. But they're getting together a big legal fund to fight these things."[45]

Under pressure from downtown business interests, Mayor Feinstein decided to abandon the transit assessment district but stood firm in her commitment to the transit impact fee, signing the linkage measure into law. The institutionalization of mandatory linkage was an important turning point in the evolution of San Francisco's politics of downtown development because it further legitimated the progressive notion that government intervention was necessary to promote a more equitable distribution of the costs of vigorous growth. Significantly, too, the mayor's continuing support for linkage in the face of business opposition encouraged activists to press for the extension of linkage into other policy domains.[46]

The city had begun to experiment with housing linkage as early as 1979. Lu Blazej, a long-time official at the Planning Department, remembered that city planners under Director Rai Okamoto would point out in negotiations with developers the connection between downtown office development and the city's affordable housing shortage. At that early date, however, the city would merely require the developer to use "good faith efforts" to build housing somewhere in the city to mitigate the increased housing demand created by their projects. Housing linkage was thus a purely voluntary arrangement between the city and developers.[47]

As with transit linkage, the 1979 citizens initiative campaign played a significant role in transforming housing linkage from a weak, voluntary arrangement to a mandatory policy. Growth-control activists emphasized throughout the campaign how downtown development had exacerbated the affordable housing crisis by causing the demolition of existing housing, sparking rampant speculation in near-downtown neighborhoods, and attracting tens of thousands of new employees to the downtown skyscrapers who then bid up the cost of housing throughout the city. All of this put an enormous strain on the city's housing stock, which had increased only marginally over the past decade. As a result, activists claimed that the building boom was causing housing costs in residential neighborhoods to soar. Many San Franciscans found the argument convincing. After the initiative campaign, city planners felt compelled to pursue housing linkage more aggressively.

But not all city officials were eager to push for a mandatory policy. Planning Commission President Toby Rosenblatt said it would be inappropriate to impose a mandatory scheme at a time when the city was undertaking an extensive study of downtown development. He advised waiting until a downtown plan had been completed. Despite continuing advocacy from growth-control activists, Rosenblatt's position on linkage prevailed through 1980 and into early 1981. The city's housing linkage policy continued to be a soft one replete with loopholes allowing developers to minimize their involvement in the program. For example, the Planning Commission voted in December to require one developer to build eighty-nine residential units as a condition for allowing construction of an eighteen-story office building; but the city left a sizable escape route by releasing the developer from the housing obligation if future highrise developers refused to abide by similar linkage arrangements.[48]

In early 1981 activists got some help from the city's new planning director, Dean Macris. Housing linkage first caught Macris's attention when it emerged as a policy proposal during the 1979 initiative campaign; after the campaign, activists continued to push for linkage in public hearings examining the environmental impacts of proposed office projects. Macris remembered, "The Calvin Welches and Sue Hestors and all of them were talking about it." The planning director soon concluded that housing linkage was "a damn good idea," but he felt that he would have to lobby strategically to win converts within city government. "I first had to convince the president of the Planning Commission, Toby Rosenblatt, who is a highly respected guy. . . . And when he bought the idea, then I thought I had enough clout behind me, because he was always considered a voice of reason in the administration, to go convince the mayor." Still, convincing Mayor Feinstein to apply linkage principles to housing would be a tough sell. Macris recalled broaching the issue with the mayor for the first time: "I mean Mayor Feinstein had to be convinced to do this. I remember when I talked to her and said that what we wanted to do next year is mandate a housing revenue from developers, her response was, 'You're going to do what?!' Those were brand new ideas."[49] But Feinstein had already decided to support transit linkage, and holding developers accountable for their impacts on the city's housing stock seemed just as reasonable as holding them accountable for their impacts on public transportation.[50]

Moreover, it is important to keep in mind that Feinstein and other city officials were evaluating linkage in a context in which growth-control activists were continually pointing out the adverse impacts of rapid downtown development in the neighborhoods and demanding that the city force developers to mitigate those impacts. It seems likely that the mayor was influenced by the impacts/mitigation and rights/responsibilities discourse propagated by the growth-control movement during the 1979 initiative campaign and in subsequent years. For by April 1981 Mayor Feinstein had decided to back a stronger housing linkage policy too.

With Feinstein on board, Macris's Planning Department adopted a set of guidelines known collectively as the Office Housing Production Program (OHPP), which required commercial office developers to build or rehabilitate housing to accommodate at least some of the demand generated by their projects.[51] The mandatory housing linkage policy was the first of its kind anywhere in the United States. Adoption of the housing and transit linkage policies legitimated the arguments of the growth-control movement and constituted undeniable evidence that privatist ideas, values, beliefs, and practices were experiencing some erosion. Counterhegemonic activism was changing popular and elite perceptions of downtown development. A progressive vision was gaining ascendancy.

The Backlash

Not surprisingly, the downtown business community was not about to cave in. Many progrowth advocates recognized the radical nature of linkage, and they attacked the practice on several grounds. First, some questioned the causal connection between new highrises and the citywide shortage of housing. They asserted that immigration from Asia and Latin America had also contributed to the affordable housing squeeze,[52] not to mention the activists' own efforts to downzone residential neighborhoods throughout San Francisco. Second, developers argued that they did not create downtown growth; rather, they simply responded to a preexisting demand for office buildings, and therefore developers should not be held responsible for conditions that they did not create in the first place.[53] Third, developers objected to the politically expedient practice of "demonizing" highrise office developers. One land use attorney queried whether it was "fair to select out various classes of businesses or business activities and say you, you, and you have to pay an additional fee for child care . . . or housing, but you, you and you don't. . . . In San Francisco, retailers do not pay any linkage fees. Why not? They don't have employees who have children? They don't have employees who need housing? They don't create people who come to work on public transit? Why not is because retailing is a centerpiece of San Francisco." Another corporate lawyer, Zane Gresham, elaborates on this point by noting that it was "relatively easy" for the city to impose linkage exactions on developers who were "very often from out of town," lacked a strong political constituency backing their interests, and "looked like they were very prosperous because it was a time when developers seemed to be making a lot of money."[54] According to this reasoning, it was unfair to adopt a "last guy in town pays for everything attitude" while exempting retailers and veteran San Francisco developers who had already built commercial office buildings. Finally, the most common argument was that the city's linkage policies would foster an antibusiness climate and thus deter future development.[55]

When the city adopted a transit linkage ordinance mandating a five-dollar-per-square-foot exaction fee for new commercial office development, a consortium of developers retained one of the most prestigious law firms in the city, Pillsbury, Madison, and Sutro, and filed a lawsuit challenging the legality of the measure. The ensuing litigation prevented the city from appropriating the revenue collected from the exaction fees to go ahead with transit improvements; instead, the linkage revenue was placed in an escrow account pending the outcome of the lawsuit. Hence, actual mitigation of the negative impacts of downtown development on the mass transit system was delayed for years as the case meandered through the California courts.

Interestingly, the downtown business community's response to the *housing* linkage policy was much less confrontational. The Chamber of Commerce did not exert its potent lobbying influence upon the administration, and no lawsuits were filed at this early stage to challenge the OHPP policy. Toby Rosenblatt, president of the Planning Commission at the time, noted that the business community's reaction to housing linkage was surprisingly quiet: "The most . . . dramatic condition [for building permit approval] that's been applied required the developers to create housing. . . . I expected some resistance from them, but the developers acceded, at least at the commission meeting, to that condition without any argument." City planner Lu Blazej believed that "the demand for office space was so great in the early '80s that [developers] were willing to go along with [linkage]." And planner Alec Bash recalled the initial reaction to linkage among real estate interests as one of "kicking and screaming, but happy to get their projects approved at the same time." He continued: "These were first imposed during a boom time in development here. . . . My people were happy to be getting the approvals, and if it took that kind of mitigation or exaction, they were happier to have that than have the process tell them you can't build something."[56]

But it is not clear how compelling this explanation is for the differing reactions to the two linkage policies. The hot real estate market would presumably have the same effect on developers with respect to both linkage policies. Moreover, the ideological objections discussed above would seem to apply to both. A better explanation would address the varying form and content of each policy. One distinction was that the transit policy was enacted by the Board of Supervisors as a formal ordinance and therefore carried greater legal stature. By contrast, the Planning Department's policy was just that, a departmental policy, and thus was perhaps less threatening. Another distinction concerned the nature of the exaction. The transit linkage ordinance mandated a five-dollar-per-square-foot fee on all commercial office developments; there were no exceptions. The housing linkage policy required some form of housing mitigation but offered considerable discretion to developers on how to fulfill the requirement. It is possible that developers saw opportunities to comply with the policy in ways that would not be too onerous.

If ideological objections to the adoption of housing linkage were surprisingly muted, the same cannot be said for the actual implementation of linkage during the ensuing months. Most importantly, developers complained that the lack of standards led to egregious acts. Planner Lu Blazej gave some indication of how planners put together linkage deals by saying, "We were breaking new ground in a way with how far can you push; it was really kind of a touchy-feely [process]." Dale Carlson, a businessperson who supported neighborhood activists, observed some of these ad hoc negotiations. He remarked, "The Planning Commission would play let's make a deal and there were no standards. They just sort of went from project to project and got what they could." Carlson proceeded to describe a typical scenario: "You know the developer would go in and try to negotiate a deal with the city's planning director. If the planning director would ask for $200,000 for affordable housing mitigation, the guy would say 'Gee, I can't afford it. The project won't pencil out. I'll give you $75,000.' The planning director would come back and say that's not enough and they would go back and forth and settle at $100 grand or $125 grand. I don't think anyone at the Planning Department ever went out and verified any of the numbers."[57]

Business leaders attacked the standardless procedure because it sometimes left them vulnerable to what they felt was "legal extortion" in situations where the developer had already invested a considerable amount of money but still needed at least one additional permit from some city agency. Attorney Zane Gresham referred to one incident in particular as an example of "an abuse of the process": the city extracted an additional sizable sum from a developer of a highrise office building at 345 California Street when he applied for a permit to install an elevator. Gresham declared, "That's another example, if you look at it, of why business people generally feel uncomfortable about exposing themselves to the potential vicissitudes of the process in San Francisco.... A sense of decency. Just because you have potential leverage and potential opportunity, you don't always press it because it's not appropriate. It's not fair."[58] In sum, although the business community objected to the entire concept of linkage on ideological grounds, it was furious with the actual implementation of the housing component. Business leaders were particularly exasperated by the absence of any standards to ensure predictability[59] and to guard against the possibility of "extortion" when they were in vulnerable positions.

For their part, neighborhood activists were also less than thrilled with the Planning Department's ad hoc implementation of housing linkage. Except for a few isolated incidents, they were convinced that the deals being cut did little to mitigate the building boom's impact on the *affordable* housing crisis.[60] In particular, growth-control activists criticized the policy for allowing developers to satisfy the housing mitigation requirement by building *market-rate* housing.[61] For instance, city planners proudly announced in January 1982 that a developer had promised to set aside six floors of a twenty-four-story office building for housing. But the new housing consisted of forty condominiums priced between $350,000 and $600,000, far beyond the means of most San Franciscans. Reflecting on that policy, activist Sue Hestor estimated that "tens of millions" of dollars were squandered because the original linkage policy supported by Mayor Feinstein channeled most funds into market-rate housing instead of affordable housing.[62] By the end of 1982, activists were questioning whether their efforts had done very much to promote a more equitable development of the city.

Furthermore, activists were even more doubtful that their efforts had led to a more controlled development of downtown. Although key city officials like Dianne Feinstein, Dean Macris, and Toby Rosenblatt had decided to support linkage, they remained firmly committed to aggressive promotion of commercial office development. Despite the apparent weaknesses in the linkage policies, the city continued to approve practically every highrise project that was proposed. In June 1982 Richard Sklar, the head of the Public Utilities Commission, announced that the building boom was putting an intolerable strain on the city's public transit system. He urged the Planning Commission to oppose new downtown projects unless additional funds were provided to allow MUNI to keep up with increasing demand. When the city ignored his warning and proceeded to approve each new highrise proposal, Sklar lashed out at the rubber-stamp mentality of the Planning Commission: "People no longer believe this is a place where projects are argued. . . . This commission changes a color, shaves a few feet off and saves an old wall. . . . I know this commission has never turned down a highrise and won't for the next four or five years."[63]

Absent meaningful controls on the rapid pace of downtown growth, many activists had serious reservations about the wisdom of linkage. Some feared that Mayor Feinstein was exploiting linkage as a way to co-opt the growth-control movement. In other words, linkage could be used to obtain considerable resources for public transit and housing, but only on the condition that downtown development be allowed to proceed according to market demand. The activists believed, however, that downtown development was already out of control. Calvin Welch explained: "The only way [linkage] would generate that much money is if we said, 'OK, fellas come on in!' But we couldn't; that wasn't our agenda."[64]

Indeed, frustration turned to bitterness for many activists who more than two years earlier had agreed to forgo another citizens' initiative campaign to impose limits on commercial office highrises while the city conducted a comprehensive environmental analysis of the cumulative impacts of downtown expansion. Periodically in 1981 and then again in 1982, the city assured community groups that the study was nearing completion and would soon be available to the public. But as 1983 approached, the long-awaited Downtown EIR remained shrouded in secrecy as downtown development continued at an unprecedented pace.

Thus, neighborhood activists believed that city officials were responding to the downtown business community's backlash against the growth-control movement in worrisome ways. Downtown's gravitational force was once again pulling City Hall into its orbit. The downtown-led regime, which had seemed to be becoming unglued during the 1979 citizens initiative campaign, was regrouping. Land use policies were once again reflecting the priorities of the growth coalition. With the renewed attack against progressive proposals for controlled and equitable growth came a revival of privatist discourse and a strengthening of privatist values and assumptions within the city's political culture. Sensing power slipping away from them, growth-control activists decided to return to the 1979 strategy of appealing directly to San Francisco's voters because, as Tony Kilroy of San Francisco Tomorrow asserted, "it is the only way to make city officials pay attention to us."[65]

The 1983 Citizens Initiative Campaign

Several community meetings were held during the first few months of 1983 to plan a strategy for the new initiative. There was general agreement at the outset that unlike previous campaigns this would not simply be an anti-highrise initiative. Activists wanted to avoid being portrayed as knee-jerk naysayers opposed to any and all forms of development. Rather, they sought to present a positive alternative, a plan that would both control downtown development by minimizing negative impacts and promote equitable growth.[66]

From there, however, the consensus began to break down as the old split within the growth-control movement resurfaced. The moderates associated with SFT focused on the need for more intelligent planning by arguing for an initiative to amend the San Francisco Charter to compel the city to comply with its own master plan, a broad set of guidelines that was supposed to serve as the basis for city planning for housing, transportation, park maintenance, and other services. At the time, San Francisco was the only city in California that was not obligated by law to follow its master plan. One activist declared, "The Master Plan is beautifully worded, and it's being totally ignored by the mayor and the planning commission."[67]

One of the more vociferous representatives of the progressive wing during the 1983 campaign was David Looman, a political consultant with considerable experience running local election campaigns. Until that year, however, Looman had not played a particularly active role in the growth-control movement. He described how he came to formulate his position on a proper campaign strategy:

> It was when I began studying the issue that it got clear to me—O.K. here are the social impacts, here's the real problem; I can now understand the issue well enough to frame up, and that it has all these destructive impacts. It was then my theory [that] what kind of issue ought to be on the ballot was that we oughta make these kinds of special impacts concrete by writing an [initiative] which included mitigation for these kinds of social impacts. . . . The '83 measure is kind of a portmanteau issue—it's got all the planning stuff and then it's got all the mitigation goodies. And the mitigation goodies are in there because I said they had to be.[68]

The 1983 initiative was thus another compromise between the two wings of the growth-control movement. The initiative contained provisions requiring the Planning Department to revise the state-mandated Master Plan to make it internally consistent and to rewrite the downtown zoning code to conform to the Master Plan.[69] But the initiative also called upon the Board of Supervisors to enact three linkage ordinances to mitigate the adverse effects of the city's progrowth policies. The first would reaffirm and strengthen the transit impact mitigation fee by requiring a developer of commercial office space to "pay for the costs of additional MUNI capacity to accommodate the demand generated by the project." Activists believed that phrasing the ordinance in this way would require the Board of Supervisors to raise the fee from its existing level of five dollars per square foot.[70] The second ordinance would close the most serious loophole in the Planning Department's housing linkage policy by requiring commercial office developers to provide not just market-rate housing, but *affordable* housing within San Francisco to offset the increased demand created by their projects. The third ordinance extended the practice of linkage into a new policy domain; it would establish a comprehensive job training and placement program aimed at ensuring that San Francisco residents, "especially the long-term unemployed and underemployed," obtain "the greatest feasible number of new jobs"[71] generated by downtown office development. The 1983 initiative's stress on promoting an equitable distribution of the costs and benefits of downtown development represented the most forceful expression of progressive policy goals by the growth-control movement to date. Signatures were collected and the initiative was certified for the November ballot as Proposition M.

Linkage became the central organizing principle of the Proposition M campaign in 1983. David Looman was convinced that the earlier initiatives had lost because most ordinary people did not care about the "fluffy-duffy, urban amenities, good views kind of shit" that was so important to the moderate growth-control advocates. Instead, this campaign would emphasize that "the reason why [the city] ought to limit downtown growth was because it had deleterious social impacts." And "the scaffolding for getting the message across . . . was the addressing of the social impacts through the mitigation measures. That kind of concretized it."[72]

The progressives also recognized the need to expand their appeal to previously neglected groups in the city. Calvin Welch described the 1983 campaign strategy:

> So we began working, trying to reform, recreate, reestablish the same kind of neighborhood and community coalition that we had done around district elec-

> tions around growth-control. We did not start out with assembling environmentalists. We basically assembled the district election coalition. Some of that coalition, of course, included environmentally active organizations. But we did not set out to first win over the environmentalists and then ink blot out from there. We started out to create a new constituency for commercial office development controls that dealt with people who were . . . concerned with economic development policy. . . . So we set out to identify and involve a whole different set of players. . . . We got many people of color involved who were interested in affirmative action, and employment and economic development. We got neighborhood groups which had never been involved, especially those neighborhood groups that had most actively fought the loss of neighborhood-serving retailers.[73]

This commitment to building a broad-based, inclusive movement represented a striking departure from the early days when growth-control activism essentially consisted of Alvin Duskin and a relatively small group of white, middle-class professionals motivated by postmaterial goals.

Linkage proved to be an ideal mechanism for attracting new groups into the growth-control movement. At the crudest level, campaign chair David Looman foresaw that activists could simply sell the linkage components of Proposition M as: "There's some goodies in here for you!" For the seasoned precinct walker, it became possible to target discrete groups and address their concerns about negative impacts and how linkage could ameliorate those particular concerns. For example, one canvasser in 1983 described how he would initiate a conversation by asking a citizen about his or her opinions on downtown growth. That person might talk about how overcrowded MUNI buses create serious commuting hassles everyday. The canvasser could then point out how Proposition M sought to remedy the transit problem by requiring developers, who created the problem in the first place, to contribute money to a city fund to pay for more MUNI buses. Similarly, in working-class communities, the same canvasser could stress how the job training and placement ordinance would ensure that newly established jobs would go to city residents, and not to suburban commuters.[74]

There were many indications that the 1983 initiative would be warmly received by San Francisco voters. First, the previous years of grassroots activism had undermined the hegemonic assumption that market-driven downtown growth was necessarily a good thing for the city. Growth-control advocates had alerted citizens to the societal costs of rapid growth and had made a cogent argument for government regulation to control those costs. Second, activists had introduced the concept of linkage to San Francisco voters in the 1979 campaign and many had clearly approved of the idea of holding developers accountable for the adverse impacts of their projects. The city's actual implementation of housing and transit linkage policies further legitimated linkage and increased the likelihood that voters would support strengthening the practice and expanding it into other policy areas.[75]

The 1983 citizens initiative campaign jumped off to a promising start. Early public opinion polls showed that San Franciscans supported Proposition M by an overwhelming margin of 2.5 to 1. But the auspicious beginning soon gave way to growing doubts. One problem involved divisions within the growth-control campaign itself. Whereas the two contingents of the movement had coexisted satisfactorily during the 1979 campaign, mounting tensions could not be contained in 1983. The level of animosity is reflected in David Looman's comments years later regarding the moderates in the campaign whom he accused of being "reactionary" and "mindless technocrats" concerned only with "good views" and certain types of "urban amenities" to be secured by tinkering with the planning code. Looman deeply resented the fact that the linkage components of Proposition M had been "violently contested by all the planner types" within the movement because they "clutter up the measure" and deflect attention from the more serious problems of downtown growth. Looman recalled that Calvin Welch tried desperately to keep the two groups together, but the coalition collapsed under the strains of the campaign and many of the moderates bolted.[76] The campaign proceeded that fall, though weakened by the depletion of some veteran growth-control advocates.

An even more crippling blow to the Proposition M campaign came in August when the city finally released its long-awaited plan for downtown development. The so-called Downtown Plan immediately garnered a great deal of media hype. The *San Francisco Examiner and Chronicle* praised it as "the most famous urban design document in this nation right now." Most prominently, the Downtown Plan would encourage a shift in highrise construction from the north of Market area to the less developed South of Market area through changes in the zoning code; it would also halt highrise construction in Chinatown and parts of the Tenderloin. In addition, it would lower building densities by reducing permissible floor area ratios, though it would grant exemptions if developers were willing to build "parks and plazas" anywhere else in the district. As for mitigation measures, the plan simply reaffirmed the existing housing and transit linkage programs, though it did impose additional exactions to encourage open space and "urban art" such as murals and sculptures downtown. The plan devoted substantial attention—approximately 41 percent of the report—to the promotion of aesthetic amenities ranging from historic building preservation to tapered buildings to allow more sunlight to filter down to street level.[77] The Downtown Plan was exalted as the finest urban planning document in the United States mainly because of its attempt to steer commercial office development to a different part of the downtown district and because of its extensive attention to enhancing the architectural designs of new highrises.

Strategically, the Downtown Plan was a co-optive measure intended to undermine the growth-control movement, much as the Urban Design Plan had done twelve years earlier. The Downtown Plan enabled the Feinstein administration to contend that the city was moving affirmatively to remedy the problems addressed by the citizens initiative. In fact, Feinstein called the Downtown Plan "planning at its best" because it represented the culmination of three years of detailed study by objective, professional consultants.[78] The implication was that the citizens initiative was, by contrast, the hastily compiled product of biased amateurs.

Not surprisingly, growth-control activists were dissatisfied with the city's plan to regulate downtown development. In their view, the most significant fact about the Downtown Plan was that contrary to claims in the *San Francisco Examiner,* it would not cut commercial office development in half. Rather, the rate of growth would be reduced only 6 percent if the city's 1980 zoning code were to remain in effect.[79] Progressive activists were also unimpressed with the emphasis on aesthetic concerns as opposed to the socioeconomic issues that they felt really mattered to the majority of city residents.

The unveiling of the Downtown Plan in late August nevertheless gave progrowth advocates a much needed shot in the arm. In early September, downtown interests formed San Franciscans for Reasonable Planning and commenced an aggressive funding drive to pay for a mammoth media blitz in the final month before election day. The group sent letters to every highrise office developer and project sponsor who was seeking approval for a proposed building, requesting a ten-thousand-dollar contribution to help defeat Proposition M. In the end, the "No on M" campaign was able to outspend the growth-control campaign seven hundred thousand dollars to sixty thousand dollars.[80]

The downtown business community attacked the 1983 initiative as "one of the most seductively attractive, deceptively complex and potentially destructive propositions to reach our city ballot in decades." The executive director of the Chamber of Commerce, John Jacobs, asserted, "This pernicious proposal is an economic Molotov cocktail wrapped in an American flag."[81]

Underlying the hostile rhetoric was a privatist conception of how downtown development ought to proceed. The arguments were familiar. The downtown growth coalition reminded San Franciscans of the advantages of rapid development—job creation, revenue generation, and economic prosperity for the entire city. Government interference in what downtown leaders saw as a natural growth process threatened to wipe out all of those benefits by making the city an unattractive place to do business. The growth-control movement's agenda of regulatory and redistributive policies would send San Francisco down the path of urban decline that so many other American cities were now experiencing.

The downtown growth coalition also denounced the process through which grassroots activists were pursuing their agenda. Business elites attacked the very notion of setting land use policy by a citizens initiative, while defending existing institutions of representative government. They insisted that "San Francisco's mayor, Board of Supervisors, Planning Commission and City agencies are responsive to the changing nature of our city." Furthermore, they contended that the prevailing system was sufficiently open to democratic participation: "Use of established governmental processes to develop and implement planning policies and regulations offers all San Franciscans an opportunity to participate in the process." The Downtown Plan confirmed that the system was functioning properly. At the same time, the growth-control movement was depicted as "an unelected, unaccountable, special-interest group"[82] seeking to "wrest from elected and appointed officials alike the ability to protect and nurture this city's economy." The growth coalition's assault on Proposition M influenced public opinion as popular support for the initiative steadily declined in October. Activist Dick Grosboll observed: "People get scared about the business community and the opposition to limits on development. The campaigns really scare people off."[83]

The mainstream media also assisted the growth coalition. The *San Francisco Chronicle* and the *San Francisco Examiner* offered only minimal coverage of the campaign in support of the initiative, while continuing to follow the lead of San Franciscans for Reasonable Planning in singing the praises of the Downtown Plan. The tight connection between the city's largest newspaper and downtown interests was apparent in the *Chronicle*'s October 29 editorial attacking Proposition M. Much of the editorial was taken directly from the "No on M" campaign literature and from an editorial in *San Francisco Business*, the monthly magazine of the Chamber of Commerce. Activist Rene Cazenave described the growth-control movement's frustration with local newspaper coverage by the *Chronicle* and the *Examiner:*

> These guys tore us to pieces in the editorials and didn't give us a drop of ink [elsewhere in the newspaper]. The other side could fart somewhere and there'd be a front-page article. No matter what we did we didn't get coverage. So in this town, again, getting some money to mail and print literature is critical because the entire media becomes a propaganda tool of the other side. And I'm not exaggerating. Ask journalism schools throughout the country what they think of the major media in San Francisco.... It's considered the worst of any city.... It's not like the *Chicago Tribune*, which will give you the story but kill you on the editorial page.... It's as if we never existed.[84]

On election day, Proposition M was defeated by only two thousand votes, 50.6 percent to 49.4 percent. In assessing the outcome, analysts noted that public opinion in support of Proposition M reversed toward the end of the campaign as progrowth interests mounted a well-financed media blitz attacking the initiative. Calvin Welch commented: "We came so close. It was a David and Goliath contest. . . . We lost because the other side did 14 pieces of mail" financed by a campaign war chest in excess of six hundred thousand dollars.[85]

Yet the sharp imbalance in resources only partly accounts for Proposition M's narrow loss. The impact of the local political culture should also be considered. Despite the years of counterhegemonic activism waged by an increasingly progressive growth-control movement, a privatist worldview remained hegemonic in San Francisco. The political culture had been evolving toward a more progressive vision, to be sure, but activists had not yet succeeded in turning the cultural corner.

Consequently, although a vast majority of citizens were intuitively drawn to the growth-control movement, as indicated by early public opinion polls, once the downtown business community mobilized its potent machinery and saturated the city with its privatist message, the hegemonic political culture was greatly bolstered. San Francisco voters were bombarded with conflicting messages in the final weeks of the citizens initiative campaign. In trying to sort out those messages and determine where their interests lay, the voters looked at the campaign through a cultural lens that continued to privilege the perspective of the downtown growth coalition. The cultural bias was, of course, reinforced by a material bias that gave progrowth forces a vast advantage in terms of financial, technical, and communications resources. But the lingering influence of the hegemonic privatist culture proved decisive in the final days of the campaign, especially among certain urban groups that might have been expected to support a change in land use policy.

The city's African American community had ample reason to be distrustful of the downtown growth coalition. Ever since the days of urban renewal in the 1960s, progrowth leaders had promised black citizens that downtown development would bring jobs and economic prosperity to their neighborhoods, and yet those promises were not kept. Nevertheless, the growth coalition worked diligently in 1983 to secure the endorsements of prominent black leaders such as Supervisor Willie Kennedy and Speaker of the California State Assembly Willie Brown. These leaders were usually revered in the African American community for breaking into the white-dominated world of city and state politics, and so when they decided to oppose the growth-control initiatives, black citizens tended to follow suit. In keeping with the privatist preference for elite power, they deferred to established leaders even though they had done little to reform development policy. On election day, all three of San Francisco's black neighborhoods voted heavily in favor of the downtown growth coalition and against Proposition M.[86]

But the electoral outcome in 1983 was not entirely bad news for the growth-control movement. Although their efforts had fallen short, most observers agreed that all of the counterhegemonic activism was beginning to have an effect. Popular values, attitudes, and beliefs regarding downtown development were undergoing a transformation. The margin of defeat in the 1979 initiative had been 8 percent, but in 1983 the margin had shrunk to only 1 percent. Most were convinced that a more clearly drafted initiative, along with closer attention to grassroots activism in the African American community, would bring certain victory in the next campaign. David Looman was particularly confident of future success: "The ballgame's over at that point! When you lose by a vote and a half per precinct and are outspent fifteen to one . . . With another ten grand we would have won. . . . Everyone in town knew that the ballgame was over after M1. I mean they knew we had won, and it was just a matter of time before we put the nails in the coffin."[87]

Conclusion

The two principal elements of a progressive vision of politics are an expansive public sphere and popular empowerment. This chapter examined how the San Francisco growth-control movement engaged in a brand of activism that consistently advanced the notion that an activist government was needed to correct inequities created by downtown development policies guided by private market forces.

Activists did this by first calling attention to the existence of inequities generated by accelerated growth, and then insisting that the developers who were primarily responsible for the inequities had an obligation to the larger community to take mitigation measures. Redistributive policies, which came to be known as linkage policies, could be enacted by the city government to ensure that the costs and benefits of downtown development would be spread more fairly. When the downtown growth coalition resisted the growth-control movement's demand for linkage, activists stepped up their lobbying efforts in public hearings to assess the environmental impacts of proposed development projects. This practice, by itself, had an impact on the discourse and conduct of policymakers. But the broader impact on the local political culture came in 1979 and 1983 when growth-control activists waged intensive citizens initiative campaigns in which linkage played a prominent role. Although progrowth enthusiasts prevailed in each campaign, though by narrowing margins, the growth-control movement used the initiatives to undermine the privatist assumption that government efforts to make downtown development more equitable were naive, impractical, and doomed to fail. When the city actually adopted transit and housing linkage policies, and the downtown business community's dire warnings proved unfounded, the privatist vision suffered yet another setback. The progressive impulse to utilize the public arena to promote equitable growth was gaining legitimacy within the local political culture.

At the same time, however, activists realized that their efforts had done little to slow the furious pace of downtown expansion. The Feinstein administration seemed as committed as ever to aggressive growth. In fact, the mayor interpreted the 1983 election outcome as a mandate to expedite efforts to enact the Downtown Plan. Likewise, Planning Commission President Toby Rosenblatt remarked that the election was "an affirmation of the Downtown Plan and other plans as appropriate planning processes and that people don't want to plan by initiative."[88] In the eyes of growth-control advocates, development decision making remained in the hands of downtown-oriented elites who seemed oblivious to increasing protests in the neighborhoods. The activists concluded that it was time to intensify their pressure to advance the other key tenet of a progressive vision—popular empowerment.

✦6

Progressive Activism

Promoting Popular Empowerment

During the years following the 1983 citizens initiative campaign, a critical question underlying the ongoing battle waged by growth-control activists was, Who should control downtown development decision making? Most business leaders and city officials believed that land use policy making was properly the domain of the City Planning Department. After all, planners were specifically trained to assume responsibility for a task as complicated as charting the development of the city. It therefore made sense that citizens, interest groups, and other public officials should defer to their experience and skill. But the years of progressive activism were beginning to weaken the hegemonic tendency to follow the lead of trained professionals in the making of public policy.

The following exchange involving a journalist who has covered land use politics in San Francisco since 1977 illuminates the tensions at work within the local political culture at the time. Speaking of the city's lawmakers on the Board of Supervisors, the journalist remarked:

> A: They don't do anything original, really. These planning issues are so complex that all they can do is depend on expert advice. And their experts tell them thus and so and I think people like Calvin [Welch] think the Board is manipulated, y'know, they depend too much on the bureaucracy. They trust the bureaucracy too much because they don't have the time and expertise to go out and develop their own real knowledge of what the effects of these changes are going to be. So they depend on the bureaucracy and listen to it. And that's probably where Calvin's disdain comes from is they don't do any original work on their own. They just listen to the bureaucracy and the bureaucracy says this is a great plan, so OK, well, we'll pass it.
>
> Q: . . . Does the Planning Department have a monopoly on expertise over downtown planning?
>
> A: Yea, they're the experts. What can I say? I think zoning law is complex.[1]

On one hand, the above exchange highlights the privatist habit of deferring to "experts," by city politicians and even by the journalist himself. On the other hand, the journalist refers to the "disdain" of a growth-control activist for legislators who decline to seek their own conclusions; the expectation that lawmakers and citizens alike should search for answers through "original work on their own" is consistent with the progressive view that citizens should assume responsibility for political decision making. By the mid-1980s, after years of counterhegemonic activism, these two perspectives on who should decide planning issues were at war with each other.

Progrowth advocates pointed to the Downtown Plan as evidence that city planners had heard the voters' concerns about rapid growth and responded in a way that had won widespread praise. For their part, growth-control activists rejected the assumption that only city planners were qualified to make the hard policy choices regarding downtown growth. Basic land use issues, they insisted, were understandable to all citizens, not just the trained experts in the Planning Department. Moreover, activists questioned the presumed impartiality of planners. Despite four initiative campaigns calling for a slowdown in downtown expansion, the building boom in the mid-1980s stormed along as vigorously as ever, much to the satisfaction of the growth coalition. When planners cited new restrictions on density within the Downtown Plan as evidence of their responsiveness to neighborhood concerns about development, activists retorted that the Downtown Plan did not curtail growth rates at all; it merely shifted growth a few blocks away, thus doing nothing to alleviate the most serious problems caused by commercial office expansion. Furthermore, activists argued that the Downtown Plan's all-consuming attention to architectural and design amenities indicated that city planners were continuing to neglect the material concerns of less privileged groups in San Francisco. Lower-income and working-class citizens were concerned about securing good jobs; they did not care much about whether new highrises had gently tapering roof tops. Activists concluded that the city's conception of urban planning, as manifested in the Downtown Plan, all but ignored the pressing needs and interests of most of its citizens.

The growth-control movement's litigation campaign, participation in public hearings, and preparation of citywide and neighborhood planning studies all contributed to a widening sentiment that broad-based influence over decision making should be the norm. The fact that all of these practices were undertaken in the context of massive citizens initiative campaigns further reinforced the participatory thrust of the activists' vision.

The Litigation Campaign

The attack on the growth coalition's control over downtown development was waged on several fronts during the 1980s, but perhaps the most obvious damage to the authoritative status of "expert" planners was inflicted through the growth-control movement's litigation campaign. The organization San Franciscans for Reasonable Growth (SFRG) and its attorney Sue Hestor utilized lawsuits and the threat of lawsuits in ways that prompted citizens to reevaluate the policy-making process.

One tactic, a response to the Planning Commission's apparent rubber-stamp mode of reviewing highrise proposals, was to file lawsuits alleging that developers had failed to submit an adequate environmental impact report (EIR) under the California Environmental Quality Act. That statute mandated detailed descriptions of adverse environmental impacts caused by a project and required developers to offer mitigation measures or, alternatively, reasons that positive features of the project would outweigh the negative features. SFRG generally alleged in its complaints that the Planning Commission had given short shrift to the EIRs.

In January 1984 SFRG won a stunning victory when a unanimous appellate court chastised city planners in unusually blunt language for underestimating the environmental impact of four commercial office towers proposed for downtown.[2] In its opinion the court declared: "We remind those agencies directly responsible for compliance with the law . . . that they do a great injustice to both the developers and members of the general public by an insufficient evaluation of the potentially severe impacts upon the environment of San Francisco which result from construction of these types of projects." In particular, the court faulted city officials for not including in the city's cumulative impact analysis other development projects in the vicinity that were also being considered for approval. The court held: "An omission of such magnitude inevitably renders an analysis of the cumulative impacts inaccurate and inadequate because the severity and significance of the impacts will, perforce, be gravely understated."[3] As a result of SFRG's lawsuits, developers were forced to invest significant time and resources in the preparation of their EIRs. Before long, EIRs in San Francisco had acquired a reputation for being among the most thorough in the United States.[4]

This was important to growth-control activists because where the EIRs disclosed serious environmental impacts, SFRG would try to pressure developers into revising their project designs to remedy the negative effects. For example, it persuaded one developer to lower the height of its building to reduce the shadow it would cast over Portsmouth Square in Chinatown. Alternatively, SFRG would insist that developers with EIRs showing adverse impacts increase their mitigation efforts. Throughout the mid-1980s, a familiar scenario would be repeated. A developer seeking to build a commercial office tower would prepare an EIR and then enter into negotiations with the city over mitigation.

After a deal had been announced, SFRG would sue the developer claiming the EIR was still inadequate under the California Environmental Quality Act. Thereafter, the developer would enter into a second set of negotiations with SFRG attorney Sue Hestor in which the developer would inevitably agree to increase its contribution to the city's housing or transit linkage fund.[5] Hestor explained her purpose: "The city planning department hasn't followed the law, and I am making them."[6]

SFRG's negotiation of stronger linkage arrangements proved to be very successful. In March 1985 the *San Francisco Chronicle* reported that Hestor had filed lawsuits contesting the adequacy of EIRs for fourteen different highrise proposals. At the time, six of those suits were still pending. Of the eight remaining, SFRG won an appellate court ruling ordering developers of four projects to rewrite their EIRs to be in compliance with state law and settled the rest. Most of the $414,000 collected by SFRG from developers as part of those settlements was turned over to the city's housing linkage fund or was used to pay for new planning studies on downtown development.[7]

A particularly dramatic settlement was reached in the summer of 1986 in conjunction with what turned out to be the third tallest building in San Francisco. In 1982 the Planning Commission had approved the highrise project on the condition that it include eleven floors of market-rate housing. After construction had commenced, the developer, Norland Properties, announced that the market for high-priced condominiums had dried up and requested permission to build a luxury hotel instead to satisfy its housing mitigation obligation. The Planning Commission agreed, but SFRG appealed that decision to the Board of Permit Appeals. That body suspected that Norland had promised to build the housing initially only as a way to secure quick approval for its project, but all along had planned to build a much more lucrative hotel instead.[8]

With the Board of Permit Appeals suggesting bad faith by the developer, and growth-control activists angry about the loss of housing downtown, Norland Properties was faced with the unpleasant prospect of a tendentious lawsuit while in the midst of construction. Wishing to avoid costly litigation and accompanying delays, the developer agreed to: (1) pay $500,000 to an open-space fund to mitigate the harm caused by the forty-seven-story highrise shading Portsmouth Square in Chinatown; (2) pay $300,000 to the city's housing linkage fund for "permanently affordable" housing to be built by community-based nonprofit groups; and (3) pay $50,000 to the Friends of the Public Library for a downtown branch and another $50,000 to the main branch of the San Francisco Public Library.[9]

The recurrent pattern of SFRG negotiating better deals for the city than the Planning Department was a source of acute embarrassment for the Feinstein administration. On February 7, 1985, Planning Director Dean Macris tried to put an end to it. He held a closed-door meeting attended by various city officials and attorneys for the largest developers in which he expressed concern that the private-party settlements were tarnishing the image of the Planning Department by suggesting that the commission was doing a poor job of negotiating with the developers. Mayor Feinstein backed up Macris by formally asking the city's district attorney Arlo Smith to investigate SFRG and Hestor to determine whether there was any misconduct that might warrant a criminal prosecution. Smith conducted the investigation but was unable to uncover any evidence of wrongdoing.[10]

SFRG's ability to extract significantly higher mitigation payments from downtown developers called into question both the ability and the objectivity of city planners. Perceptions of city planners as skilled experts capable of carrying out the public interest were altered. Those in the downtown business community and in city government who had insisted during the 1983 citizens initiative campaign that development policy making was best left in the hands of professionals at the Planning Department were viewed with increasing skepticism by 1985. For many San Franciscans, opening up the planning process to community-based groups like SFRG seemed like a good idea. Influential columnist Herb Caen, a veritable San Francisco institution, wrote in October 1985: "We need a dozen Sue Hestors. There's not enough opposition to overbuilding in this city."[11] The privatist faith in elite control over planning was being undermined by progressive activism.

Another important aspect of the SFRG litigation campaign also affected popular consciousness. The litigation campaign revealed that commercial office developers, when pressed, were willing and able to pay much larger sums to the city's linkage funds than they or city officials had ever acknowledged. Contrary to claims by the Chamber of Commerce, extracting significantly higher linkage fees did not deter new economic investment. Developers remained as eager as ever to develop their still-lucrative downtown properties. That revelation constituted yet another blow to the privatist assumption that governmental intrusions into the downtown development market would kill the building boom.

Meanwhile, downtown interests felt unusually impotent in conducting their own litigation campaign against the growth-control movement. They had filed a lawsuit to contest the constitutionality of the transit linkage ordinance soon after it was enacted in 1981, but interestingly, developers never tried to challenge any of the other linkage policies that were later adopted. Some observers speculated that the expense of litigation was just too high. But Sue Hestor believed that the years of community-based organizing around the costs of downtown growth had created an environment that rendered such lawsuits politically undesirable:

> [Real estate interests] were in a situation where the people understood the issue, and if the developers had said, "We're not going to pay for housing, and we're going to sue if you impose it," they could have created a backlash where the people would have said, "No more buildings!" . . . It was not a no-cost challenge. The cost to them would have been that they would have had a very heavy political burden when they knew that the citizens were contentious and could always put an initiative on the ballot. So we were always ready to do another initiative and they knew it. And so because they knew that, I think they pulled their punches. Housing is a much more emotional issue than even transit is.[12]

Hestor's comment highlights the importance of the cultural context in which litigation strategy is formulated. To the extent that neighborhood activists were able to transform the city's political culture by awakening a more critical consciousness about the negative impacts of downtown growth and the responsibilities of developers to mitigate those impacts, it became easier to wage battles within the legal system. Hestor summed up how the efforts of activists had created a favorable political climate: "It was all in a context. It was not done, y'know, just a little lawsuit here and a little bit of asking for legislation here. We were asking for legislation, we were drafting initiatives, we were doing political organizing, we were suing [laughs]. And we had gotten to the minds of enough voters that the politicians were nervous . . . and that's a pretty big advantage. I mean, we worked like hell."[13]

The countervailing pressure created by the litigation campaign and other practices once again prompted a change in how the governing regime conducted its business. As in the period surrounding the 1979 citizens initiative campaign, city officials after the 1983 campaign felt compelled to adopt policy changes supported by the neighborhood activists. In August 1985 the Board of Supervisors elevated the status of the housing linkage program from a policy implemented on an ad hoc basis by the Planning Department to a full-fledged ordinance requiring developers of commercial offices in excess of 50,000 square feet to satisfy their housing mitigation duty by (1) building or rehabilitating housing themselves or (2) contributing an "in lieu" fee based on a set formula to a fund administered by the Mayor's Office of Housing. Under the new law, 62 percent of the new units were required to be affordable to lower- and moderate-income residents.[14] With this move the city plugged a giant loophole in the housing linkage policy that had allowed commercial office developers to satisfy their housing mitigation obligation by building any kind of housing; since luxury condominiums yielded much higher profits, developers had rarely opted to build affordable housing needed by lower- and middle-income residents. The new housing linkage law thus constituted a significant step in ensuring that downtown development would be more equitable.

At first glance it seems ironic that one of the more inherently elitist practices of the San Francisco growth-control movement—the litigation campaign[15]—would have a strong counterhegemonic impact in contesting privatist values and assumptions. Using lawyers with their exclusive, legalistic language and procedures hardly seems likely to contribute to advancing the progressive goal of popular empowerment. But despite the unavoidably elitist aspects associated with any litigation campaign, San Francisco activists managed to subvert the downtown growth coalition's claim to authoritative expertise over land use matters while promoting the progressive inclination to expand popular control. As Sue Hestor stressed, all of SFRG's litigation efforts took place within a larger political environment that increasingly privileged participatory values and practices. The citizens initiative campaigns of 1979 and 1983 provided a perfect complement to the litigation campaign. Legal arguments made in a courtroom or an administrative hearing room took on added force in light of the massive grassroots organizing going on in most neighborhoods throughout the city. As more and more citizens grew skeptical of the official line on downtown development and as the activists' credibility simultaneously increased, people began to reassess their interests. In this climate of shifting consciousness, it became easier for activists like Hestor to pressure city planners and developers into accepting progressive positions on growth limits, linkage, and citizen participation. The inside-outside strategy of combining elite-oriented litigation with mass-based organizing in the initiative campaigns proved to be a powerful tool of counterhegemonic activism.

Citizen Planning

The growth-control movement weakened the city's claim to expertise over downtown development by engaging in other practices apart from its litigation campaign. Most directly, it challenged official findings concerning the costs and benefits of downtown growth by conducting its own planning studies. That tradition had started in 1971 when the city's most prominent alternative newspaper, the *San Francisco Bay Guardian*, published "The Ultimate Highrise: San Francisco's Mad Rush toward the Sky." Timed to coincide with the first Duskin initiative campaign, the document presented numerous charts and tables warning of the dire consequences of overly zealous downtown development for neighborhood residents.

In 1975 the research and planning wing of the downtown growth coalition, San Francisco Planning and Urban Renewal (SPUR), responded with its own study. Activist John Elberling credited the SPUR study with "instituting the key concept of cumulative, long-term impact analyses of commercial development, and . . . raising the key issue of the adequacy of the City's housing supply for a growing white-collar workforce." Elberling also contended, however, that the SPUR study underestimated the extent of future downtown development, as the next decade of building confirmed, and thus erred in concluding that the city would be able to accommodate continuing office growth without resorting to increased government regulation.[16]

The 1979 citizens initiative campaign prompted the city to commission a new planning study to evaluate the costs and benefits of downtown development. A prominent consulting firm, Sedway-Cooke, was retained and requested to issue its report before the November election. City officials were confident that the Sedway-Cooke study would put to rest claims made by growth-control activists about problems produced by rapid downtown expansion. To nearly everyone's surprise, however, the Sedway-Cooke report called into question the growth coalition's claim that the fiscal benefits of downtown development outweighed the costs. It found that "before passage of [Proposition 13], it appeared that revenues generated in the Downtown exceeded costs incurred in the region by a narrow margin of not more than 5 percent. . . . The effect of [Proposition 13] is to reverse the relationship to the point where present costs may exceed revenues in the Downtown by as much as 25 percent." The study concluded that "new downtown development will not solve the city's growing fiscal problem; without new revenue sources, development will make it worse in the long run."[17]

Predictably, the Sedway-Cooke study caused the downtown growth coalition to scramble to save face. In 1980 the Chamber of Commerce retained the accounting firm Arthur Andersen and Company to reconsider the impacts question. This time the findings were much more to the liking of downtown leaders. The Arthur Andersen study found that the downtown business district produced 50 percent to 60 percent more in revenue than it cost the city to serve it. In reaching its conclusion, Arthur Andersen attributed the following major revenue sources to the downtown district: property taxes paid on district property; payroll and gross receipt taxes paid for enterprises located in the district; and sales and hotel taxes paid by district hotels and stores. To calculate costs, Arthur Andersen estimated the percentage of each city department's activities that could be attributed to serving the downtown highrise district and then determined the equivalent percentage of each department's budget. For example, the cost of providing fire service was derived by calculating the percentage of alarms and the number of department personnel in the highrise district compared to the rest of the city. The costs for each department were then added together to provide a total cost to the city for serving the highrise district.[18]

It was at this point that growth-control activists intervened. David Jones, a member of SFRG, issued his own analysis of downtown development's impact on the city. He began by highlighting what he felt was a crucial flaw in the Arthur Andersen methodology: the fallacy that "the highrise district, or for that matter *any* San Francisco district, should pay only for those specific activities occurring within its boundaries." Jones asserted that the Arthur Andersen study overlooked the fact that the city must provide a host of services such as health care, legal assistance, public safety, and recreation to citizens who cannot afford to pay for them. Since these costs are not reimbursed by the beneficiaries of such services, the entire city must share the tax burden. Jones noted that "the Arthur Andersen study assumes that none of the taxes for the downtown district are used to support these services." He then recalculated the revenues and costs connected with the downtown highrise district, mostly applying the same data used by Arthur Andersen, but this time taking into consideration the cost of services ignored by the accounting firm. For the fiscal year 1978-79, instead of a $17 million profit generated by downtown, Jones discovered a $52 million deficit.[19]

Arthur Andersen then responded to the SFRG report with yet another study reaffirming its earlier findings. Normally, an exchange of cost-revenue studies of downtown development would not attract a great deal of media attention, but David Jones's response to the follow-up study was so creative and amusing that the public did take notice. One commentator described the report this way: "Entitled '239-45 Bartlett Cost/Revenue Study,' it took Jones' own 4-unit house in the Mission District, applied the same 'accepted cost accounting methods' used in the Chamber/Andersen study and demonstrated that in 1980 the revenues generated from his house exceeded costs by 10,119 percent. The only logical policy, he concluded, would involve stopping all highrise construction and replacing it with 3-story, wood-frame residential construction to maximize city revenue." Jones readily admitted that the cost-revenue analysis of his own home was vulnerable to attack because he had assumed that his home incurred no costs for police, fire, public health, recreation, and many other city services. But he added: "Our response to this criticism is that we used the same cost accounting methodology as the Chamber of Commerce's Downtown Highrise Study. The extent to which our conclusion is ludicrous, exaggerated, distorted, or unwarranted because of the methodology chosen, the conclusions of the Chamber/Arthur Andersen study must be held equally so."[20] Jones and SFRG continued in subsequent months and years to issue additional studies of the impacts of downtown development on the city's fiscal status, employment trends, housing conditions, and other public services. These studies consistently challenged studies by the Planning Department and private consulting firms that had earlier been considered authoritative. In this way the growth-control movement steadily chipped away at the downtown growth coalition's traditional claim to expertise on development matters and therefore also at the privatist privileging of elite control over policy making.

Citizen Planning and the Case of Chinatown

The land use studies conducted by the citywide growth-control organization SFRG, in turn, inspired various neighborhood groups to undertake their own analyses of how downtown development was affecting their communities. The experience of growth-control activists in Chinatown, which borders the financial district, provides a case in point. Skeptical of the planning studies prepared by the City Planning Department and other consulting firms hired by the city or the Chamber of Commerce, Chinatown activists decided to assess the impact of downtown development on their own and propose appropriate land use policies.

It should be noted, however, that it took many years before Chinatown activists had the means and will to take such an initiative. Gordon Chin, a long-time progressive organizer in Chinatown, recalled the sense of powerlessness that he and his allies once felt: "I remember some hearings that we went to as younger activists in the early '70s, '71-'72. People from Chinatown came and went down to City Hall to protest the Golden Gateway Center as why [it] didn't have any low-income housing there. And it was, no one was listening. I mean we just didn't have the political and the organizing strength then to, y'know, question and change the powers that be." The first redevelopment project for Chinatown also illustrated the political weakness of community activists, according to Chin. That project, completed in 1971, consisted of a highrise Holiday Inn with one floor set aside on a lease basis for a Chinese cultural center: "That's all we got out of that. I'm not criticizing, y'know. The activists who were around back then who fought, and they had to fight even to get that, right. But if there was a proposal today for a major block, city-owned, for a new project, it would invariably be something much more community-oriented. It may be a smaller hotel combined with a mix of income ranges for housing, maybe a community center."[21] Another blow to progressive activists in Chinatown was the city's decision to allow the demolition in 1979 of the International Hotel, home to several dozen lower-income Filipinos. The action was widely viewed as further evidence of the city's insensitivity to the needs of lower-income residents of Chinatown.[22]

The lack of influence over large-scale projects in Chinatown such as the Holiday Inn and the International Hotel was a source of growing consternation for neighborhood activists. But another impetus to step up organizing activity was the ever mounting threat of commercial office development from the adjacent downtown business district. The most direct adverse impact, according to Chin, was the taking of sites that had long been earmarked for residential construction in and around Chinatown, especially Jackson Square, and using them to build highrise office buildings. The indirect impacts on housing costs and store leases in Chinatown were substantial. Chin commented:

> Before the rezoning, Chinatown was . . . commercially zoned as high density; [it had] as permissive zoning as parts of downtown. . . . It would have been permissible, legal for developers to come into Chinatown, right across the street, Kearny, Grant Avenue, and promote demolition, promote new construction of . . . major retail, office, and not even have to replace existing housing. So if you have that perspective, the development community sort of tempting the property owners [by emphasizing] well the higher zoning, the highest and best use, the property's worth more [and saying] "I want to build a project, I want to pay you $20 million for your land," then the property owner starts to think . . .[23]

Rising rents and lost leases prompted by the downtown building boom added to displacement pressures in Chinatown. Before long, neighborhood activists began to "look at the bigger picture, not only on a case-by-case basis, but to look at more comprehensive measures." According to another Chinatown activist, "We decided that rather than wait for the Planning Department to come up with a zoning of Chinatown and respond to it, we would do our own zoning plan."[24]

The decision to take the initiative on how land was to be used in their community was a key step in contesting hegemonic values that exalted elite expertise. But just as important for purposes of advancing a counterhegemonic vision of land use politics in their neighborhood was the way Chinatown activists went about assuming greater control over development issues. They believed that ordinary citizens had to play a prominent role. Simply transferring responsibility for zoning from elites in the City Planning Department to a handful of elites in a community office would not result in genuinely empowering Chinatown residents. To build neighborhood power, it would be necessary to bring the community along by laying a foundation for popular understanding of land use politics. Gordon Chin explained what needed to be done:

> We knew that when we first started [to think about doing a rezoning plan] as an organization that politically there was just no way. . . . The recognition was there that it would be a long-term struggle, that we needed to do an analysis, a lot of research, a lot of documentation, but more importantly, though, the community understanding of what all this meant. Zoning? How does that affect me? . . . There was a recognition that we had to talk about land use, simply how the land

was used. You have to educate people about how government impacts what can be built.

The task of educating Chinatown residents about complex concepts such as zoning, density bonuses, and transferable development rights was made more difficult by the fact that many of those residents were senior citizens from China who had never received much education either in China or in the United States.[25]

Given such obstacles, Chin believed that the only way to enhance popular understanding of the zoning process was to "start with real basic kinds of concepts around their day-to-day needs: bus service, playgrounds, housing . . . and sort of back into an understanding of zoning." City policy on housing was a good place for activists to begin their educational mission. The demolition of the International Hotel in favor of a planned office tower offered a graphic example of how government planning could adversely affect affordable housing opportunities in Chinatown. Activists also organized and strengthened tenant associations to push for rent control and protect against unjust evictions; fighting over such landlord-tenant issues enabled residents to learn broader lessons on how local government works. Since few residents owned cars, public transit was always a pressing issue. Activists organized residents to lobby for a new bus route through the neighborhood and bilingual bus schedules. Also, activists made inroads into gaining support from small-business owners by continuing to pressure the city to keep streets clean and well maintained and to prevent the closure of alleys needed for pickups and deliveries. Attention to such concrete issues enabled activists to "lay a basis in terms of community understanding of what this land use thing is all about."[26]

Having devoted several years to grassroots organizing around land use issues, activists set out to prepare their own neighborhood planning study, one that would demonstrate why downzoning would be necessary to preserve not only affordable housing and small businesses but also the cultural heritage of Chinatown. At the same time, other neighborhoods surrounding the downtown area such as North Beach, South of Market, and the Tenderloin were also reorganizing and preparing their own planning studies.[27]

Given the level of grassroots activism at the community level and at the city level around downtown development, it was impossible for the Planning Department not to take notice. Moreover, once the city was committed to rezoning the downtown district itself by lowering densities and imposing new design controls through the Downtown Plan, Chin believed that city planners felt compelled to agree to some kind of downzoning of adjacent neighborhoods such as Chinatown: "So people sort of saw the handwriting on the wall. The city sponsored processes, advisory groups, public hearings in each of the adjoining neighborhoods at different periods of time. In our case, we did our own study for them and the establishment did their own study and the city basically took parts of each [and adopted a new rezoning plan]." The rezoning of Chinatown effectively blocked the proliferation of highrises into the neighborhood, preserved affordable housing, and maintained the community as a thriving ethnic enclave and cultural center. In his two decades of grassroots activism, Gordon Chin regarded the rezoning of Chinatown as "probably the number one accomplishment"[28] of the Chinatown Resource Center.

What happened in Chinatown in the early and mid-1980s was not unrepresentative of grassroots activism in other in-close neighborhoods concerned with the adverse effects of downtown development. Activist Marcia Rosen commented:

> It was not only broadened participation, but we had a number of community groups really coming of age with a level of sophisticated participation. And we had a movement toward neighborhood zoning then. I recall the ring neighborhoods, the neighborhoods circling downtown that felt really vulnerable to development pressures. So Chinatown organized and got rezoning that protected affordable housing and that protected residential character from encroachments from downtown. The same thing happened with North of Market Planning Coalition in the Tenderloin and North of Market area. South of Market, which had started earlier with the fight against Yerba Buena . . . but then went on for a whole South of Market rezoning which . . . tried to preserve light industrial uses, allow some office building, preserve housing. . . . These neighborhoods organized . . . to protect themselves as well as participated in the greater discussion of the impacts of downtown development.[29]

The practice of citizen planning as a tool of growth-control activism undermined the privatist political culture while it promoted a progressive vision of land use politics in two ways. First, citywide planning studies such as SFRG's analyses of the costs and benefits of downtown development weakened the authoritative status of elite planning by the city by exposing its analytical problems and even ridiculing its results. Second, as the city's claim to exclusive planning expertise declined, neighborhood groups felt increasingly capable of conducting and advocating their own planning evaluations. The Chinatown example illustrates the progressive ideal; not only did community organizations act to take planning analysis into their own hands, but they did so in such a way as to include ordinary residents in the process. Educating the community about downtown development politicized it and, to some extent, radicalized it. Over a ten-year period, popular perspectives regarding the issue of who should properly control downtown planning experienced a thorough transformation.

The Downtown Plan

As the growth-control movement gained momentum in the 1980s, progrowth forces were increasingly put on the defensive. Their strongest attempt to take back the initiative was the Downtown Plan, first unveiled in August 1983 just as the 1983 citizens initiative campaign was picking up steam. As detailed in chapter 5, the Downtown Plan lowered building heights and densities and sought to shift commercial office development from the congested downtown business district north of Market Street to the adjacent area south of Market Street. The plan also sought to respond to complaints from the older, moderate wing of the growth-control movement that the building boom had turned downtown streets into dark and windy canyons and robbed the city of its unique character. Architecture critics praised the plan for promoting innovative designs to make downtown a more hospitable environment and for preserving historically significant buildings. Finally, the Downtown Plan added new linkage fees for child care, open space, and public art to go along with the transit and housing linkage policies already in place. City officials viewed the Downtown Plan with considerable pride, contending that it constituted clear evidence that "normal planning processes" were working well.

But growth-control activists answered that the city was still missing the point. Underlying the Downtown Plan was a conception of planning that remained largely consistent with a privatist vision of urban politics. The primary defect of the plan was that the overall amount of commercial office growth was not curtailed at all. Nor was there any indication that the city would scale back its practice of heating up an already hot market for downtown investment by offering inducements to potential investors. At the first public hearing for the Downtown Plan in 1984, growth-control activists denounced the plan for failing to consider the building boom's adverse impact on public services. One activist argued that "the city should reverse its thinking and tie future development to the availability of housing and transit rather than allowing construction and then trying to provide services." Others attacked the privatist assumption that downtown growth would inevitably increase prosperity in the neighborhoods. Yori Wade, chairman of the University of California Board of Regents, told the Planning Commission that he was

> deeply troubled [by the] assumption that by expanding the area devoted to highrise office building, we will be able to solve the economic, and by implication, the social problems that will face this city over the next two decades.
>
> There is no convincing evidence . . . that a southward march of downtown will meet the employment needs of our own young people coming out of our own high schools and community colleges or those persons who are unemployed.

> [Instead there is evidence] that the neighborhoods, small businesses and people most in need of economic assistance will be pushed out of our city.[30]

Growth-control activists concluded that any acceptable downtown plan would have to impose strict limits on new construction.

In addition to the need for tighter regulation, growth-control activists continued to harp on the equity issue. To the extent that downtown growth continued—and virtually no one supported a no-growth policy—they maintained that stronger policies were essential to ensure that downtown development really would benefit San Francisco residents. To this end activists demanded that downtown development and employment opportunities be explicitly linked. Vague promises from the growth coalition that city residents would find jobs in downtown office buildings were deemed unsatisfactory. At the same time progressive activists criticized the city's proposed extension of linkage to the policy areas of open space and public art. It was felt that these new developer exactions were aimed at satisfying upper-middle-class sensibilities and did little to benefit ordinary citizens who needed jobs and more affordable housing.[31] These criticisms of the Downtown Plan continued to be aired at future public hearings before the Planning Commission and the Board of Supervisors.

By May 1985 it became apparent that the Feinstein administration would be unable to secure the six votes on the Board of Supervisors necessary for passage of the plan unless it agreed to some form of annual limit on downtown office construction. Though previously resistant to any kind of fixed growth restriction, Mayor Feinstein now relented, proposing a cap of 950,000 square feet per year. That decision represented a major turning point in the evolution of land use politics in San Francisco. Even if Feinstein personally retained some doubt about the wisdom of imposing an annual limit on downtown growth, her endorsement of such a measure was an acknowledgment that a majority of the Board of Supervisors had come to share the growth-control movement's perspective on the need for a stronger public presence with respect to the future development of San Francisco. Counterhegemonic activism was having an impact on elite consciousness; the city's chief legislative body, and perhaps even the mayor herself, had apparently abandoned the privatist practice of allowing the market to determine the pace of downtown development in favor of expanded government regulation.

Predictably, Feinstein's move angered the downtown business community. Business leaders had always attacked the very idea of an annual limit on development. John Jacobs of the Chamber of Commerce argued: "If you put a cap on, the logical assumption is that it will never be removed. . . . It's like rent control. It gets tighter rather than weaker. Who's going to guarantee that it doesn't get worse?"[32] And in the final hearing before a Board of Supervisors' committee, Lee Dolson, a former supervisor testifying on behalf of the Downtown Association, contended that any annual restriction would be "an assault on the free market place" and drive business out of the city.[33]

But growth-control activists were not exactly thrilled with Feinstein's decision either. They attacked the mayor's proposed annual cap of 950,000 square feet as excessively generous and pushed instead for an annual limit of 500,000 square feet. Activists also objected to the late inclusion of a sunset clause that provided that the annual limit would expire after three years. Finally, they criticized the willingness of the board to exempt a large number of projects from the annual limit because developers of those projects had already invested significant time and money. The combination of an overly generous cap set to expire after three years with a large number of grandfathered projects rendered the Downtown Plan unacceptable in the eyes of most growth-control advocates.

Nevertheless, Feinstein's gesture was sufficient to woo undecided supervisors, and in September the board voted 6 to 5 to approve the Downtown Plan with the mayor's annual limit on downtown office building. Feinstein called the new law the most significant planning accomplishment during her tenure at City Hall. Despite some grumbling from the Chamber of Commerce, which was ideologically opposed to any annual restriction on overall development, business leaders generally supported the mayor's compromise. William Coblentz, one of the city's leading land use lawyers, said: "The Downtown Plan makes sense to me as a planning device and I am pleased that it passed. I think now we can have some perspective to see how San Francisco grows. Now I think we have a chance for controlled growth."[34] The *San Francisco Chronicle* also endorsed the Downtown Plan in an editorial, commenting favorably on the plan's responsiveness to "an apparent desire by many residents for new growth-controls." The editorial predicted that the Downtown Plan would "blunt, if not totally undercut, arguments for even more severe limits."[35]

The 1986 Citizens Initiative Campaign

If elements of the growth coalition felt comfortable with the amended Downtown Plan, the growth-control movement did not. Activists continued to regard the Feinstein plan, even with an annual restriction on downtown development, as inadequate. In January 1986 activists began to organize yet another citizens initiative campaign.

The growth-control movement had reason to be confident that this attempt to assume control over development policy making would finally prevail. Ever since the first initiative campaign in 1971, the margin of defeat had steadily narrowed (see table 6.1). Notwithstanding the mood of optimism, campaign preparations in 1986 were diligent and thorough. At initial meetings committees were formed to draft the initiative and oversee other crucial functions such as fund-raising, media relations, and citizen outreach. In assembling the committees, considerable attention was given to ensuring that all San Francisco groups were represented. Although inclusion had become a hallmark of the growth-control movement over the previous decade, the effort to include all urban groups was even more determined in 1986.[36]

Moreover, the initiative campaign's emphasis on a committee system minimized hierarchical tendencies and contributed to an egalitarian mode of operation. Andy Nash, a relative newcomer to the growth-control movement in 1986, could not help comparing the "autocratic" nature of mayoral and other local campaigns with the "very democratically run" growth-control campaign: "There was a group of people who put it together.... It was a real committee that did the work, and then there were subcommittees meeting at people's houses to do stuff."[37]

The new initiative, which, like the 1983 initiative, was labeled Proposition M, contained three sections. The first restricted downtown development by (1) abolishing the Downtown Plan's sunset clause and extending the 950,000 square foot cap on new office development indefinitely; (2) permitting only half of that annual limit each year until all of the projects currently in the planning "pipeline" were completed (activists estimated that, in effect, this provision would keep an annual limit of 450,000 square feet for ten to fifteen years); (3) exempting only buildings less than 25,000 square feet, as opposed to the 50,000 square feet allowed under the Downtown Plan; and (4) removing exemptions from the Plan that had not gained final approval from the city, but allowing San Francisco voters to grant such approval if so desired. (This fourth provision was aimed at removing the proposed Mission Bay project, a mammoth development just south of the downtown district, from the list of exempted projects under the plan).

The second section of Proposition M required the Board of Supervisors to consider adopting a new linkage program to employ local residents to be funded, if necessary, by a $1.50-per-square-foot fee on new office development. The justification for the additional linkage fee was based on a finding in the Downtown Plan EIR that city and regional transit problems would continue to worsen as downtown expansion proceeded. To mitigate that adverse environmental impact, the city would encourage downtown employers to hire local residents through the new resident placement and training program.

The third section required the city to revise its Master Plan to make it internally consistent and to add eight new priority policies. The latter consisted of a

Table 6.1. Electoral Results of Citizens Initiative Campaigns to Control Downtown Development, San Francisco, 1971-1983

Year	Outcome %	Gap %
1971	Defeated 62-38	24
1972	Defeated 57-43	14
1979	Defeated 54-46	8
1983	Defeated 50-49	1

statement of policy objectives phrased in short, simple sentences expressing the city's interest in providing affordable housing, promoting small-business and blue-collar jobs, preserving historical buildings, and protecting open space.[38] Considerable time and effort had been devoted to drafting the initiative, and when the task was completed, activists were eager to get on with the campaign.

Early in the Proposition M campaign, there were indications that this growth-control campaign would differ from previous ones. Soon after Mayor Feinstein announced that she would support an annual cap on commercial office growth, downtown business leaders expressed dismay over the changes in the city's development politics. The proliferation of linkage policies followed by the imposition of a mandatory limit on growth represented an increasingly intolerable state of affairs. Some lashed out at the Chamber of Commerce for failing to do enough to oppose government meddling. Land use lawyer Tim Tosta faulted the Chamber for neglecting to emphasize the positive attributes of the market-led downtown boom. He asserted: "There are things that are trade-offs to buses getting a little less comfortable and streets getting more crowded. Only the negatives have been debated." And in a more sweeping attack, real estate magnate Walter Shorenstein charged, "The Chamber is becoming a non-entity. . . . You don't have any kind of effective business leadership, contrary to when I was chamber president and we worked out a proper arrangement."[39]

Many in the downtown business community had tired of fighting growth-control initiatives every few years and then battling with determined activists during the interim periods. Sensing that public opinion was shifting away from their perspective, some felt resentful. Richard Morten of the Chamber of Commerce remarked, "There is substantial sentiment that maybe the city should suffer and feel economic pain." A development lawyer agreed that maybe a Proposition M victory would be a good learning experience for city residents: "Let them watch San Francisco wither, and then we can be sensible."[40]

Economic conditions also contributed to business complacency. The building boom had caused the office vacancy rate in the financial district to climb steadily from 1 percent in 1980 to 17 percent by 1986;[41] this, in turn, put downward pressure on office rents. Developers who had invested early on and already owned several commercial office buildings thus had some incentive to support growth restrictions as a way to lower the vacancy rate and raise the rents they could charge to their tenants.

Other developers and business groups, however, had an interest in continuing progrowth policies. Some were involved with projects that would be seeking city approval in 1986. But even some of these groups, as it turns out, became disillusioned with city politics and decided to sit out the "No on Proposition M" campaign. Jeff Heller, president of Heller and Leake Architects, recalled that his firm was seeking permission to build two highrise office towers in 1986 when Mayor Feinstein decided to impose a one-year moratorium on all commercial office development. The mayor believed that the moratorium would demonstrate the city's determination to get tough with developers and thereby undercut popular support for Proposition M. Heller described what happened: "So the deal is done. And no buildings are approved and, in fact, they say there's no need for these buildings. And, in fact, they whipped us a little bit as architects. They said, 'Well, they aren't compellingly wonderful architecture.' That was patently bullshit, the design part. That was just a good excuse." Feinstein's moratorium and her insensitive handling of real estate groups seeking to continue development projects "infuriated and demoralized" many business leaders. When Feinstein moved to rally the business community to oppose Proposition M in the fall of 1986, Heller and other traditional supporters of the mayor this time walked away.[42]

This marked the first time the downtown growth coalition had shown signs of internal dissension; until 1986 the various groups that had joined forces in support of aggressive downtown development had always operated as a cohesive unit. But the constant attacks by the growth-control movement were finally beginning to take a toll. Indeed, some commentators have argued that divisions within the downtown business community in the mid-1980s created a political opportunity that the growth-control movement was able to exploit.[43] But while the defection of some business interests in 1986 is relevant, the argument is overstated. First, although some veteran developers had a short-term interest in curtailing growth, most felt that commercial office expansion would decline anyway as a result of natural market forces; moreover, many developers remained resolute in their opposition to a government-imposed limit on downtown growth, especially one as severe as the one proposed in Proposition M. Second, if other members of the business community had gotten off to a slow start because of initial weariness in responding to yet another growth-control initiative, their spirits were revived as the campaign benefitted from the emergence of two unexpected forces opposing Proposition M. Both forces helped to make the 1986 initiative campaign a much closer contest than anyone had anticipated.

Filling part of the vacuum left by the initial defection of some downtown business interests was a group of housing developers based in the city's residential neighborhoods. Their principal spokesperson was Joe O'Donoghue, the president of the Residential Builders Association (RBA). O'Donoghue was not troubled by the initiative's limitations on downtown commercial office development or with the employment linkage program, neither of which affected his constituency. Rather, he was worried about the section of Proposition M that had the least impact on downtown development—the eight priority policies that were intended to guide future development throughout the entire city. The priority policy that O'Donoghue found the most objectionable was the one that sought to "preserve the character of the neighborhood." He feared that "the bureaucrats" in the Planning Department would use that particular policy to cave in to NIMBY (Not in My Backyard) sentiment "as a means for stopping our projects and practically shutting our industry out."[44]

Starting in August 1986, the RBA adopted the organizing strategy of the growth-control movement and mounted a grassroots campaign targeted at the city's more conservative western and southern neighborhoods. The choice of political strategy was consistent with the trend toward greater direct citizen participation in the city's land use politics, a trend set in motion by growth-control activists. Zeroing in on neighborhood churches for leafleting on Sundays proved to be a particularly effective tactic. O'Donoghue summarized the message that "his guys" were trying to get across: "This proposition, no matter how well-intentioned, is going to first of all affect the industry, primarily the small contractor, the regular carpenter, the regular tradesman. All we want to do is just build and, y'know, provide housing. . . . Now when we passed those leaflets out we generally had people who used to attend those parishes. . . . so the parishioners would recognize them. So it wasn't some outsider coming in to do the leafleting. . . . And I believe it worked very effectively." O'Donoghue also staged highly visible protest demonstrations to get media publicity. For instance, he organized a convoy of several hundred trucks and contractors' vans that ran from the western edge of the city through pivotal, swing neighborhoods all the way to City Hall, where RBA members held a large rally against Proposition M. Columnist Warren Hinckle described the protest this way:

> This was a grass-roots assembling of the family-oriented small construction workers who are the staple of San Francisco neighborhoods—the churches, the savings and loan depositors, the union members—who couldn't care a hoot about highrises (many of them have never even *been* in one, let alone built one) one

San Francisco

The Transamerica Pyramid (*above*) and the Embarcadero Center (*below*), a cluster of imposing office towers and retail facilities at the foot of Market Street, helped spur the downtown building boom of the 1970s and 1980s. (Courtesy of Chuck Thomas)

The Moscone Convention Center opened in 1981 as one part of the sprawling Yerba Buena project in the South of Market area. (Courtesy of Chuck Thomas)

The view of the expanding downtown skyline from the convention center. (Courtesy of Chuck Thomas)

(*Left*) Mayor Dianne Feinstein was an ardent defender of aggressive downtown growth. Her Downtown Plan sought to shift future highrise development to the South of Market area while encouraging more interesting architectural designs. (Courtesy of Office of Senator Dianne Feinstein)
(*Below*) An example of the new architecture inspired by the Feinstein administration's Downtown Plan is the Marriott Hotel at Yerba Buena. (Courtesy of Chuck Thomas)

(*Left*)Starting in the 1970s, some groups began to question the wisdom of rapid downtown development. Historic preservationists feared that the "Manhattanization" of San Francisco was robbing the city of its unique charm and turning downtown into a series of dark and forbidding canyons. (Courtesy of Chuck Thomas)

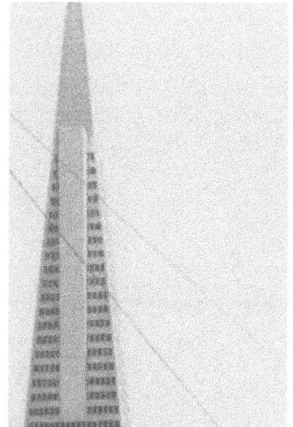

(*Right*) Residents of near-downtown neighborhoods such as Chinatown worried about the encroachment of commercial office buildings into their community. (Courtesy of Chuck Thomas)

Citizens from a wide variety of neighborhoods and civic organizations congregate at City Hall to express their support for the 1986 growth-control initiative, Proposition M. Veteran activist Sue Hestor appears in the foreground. (Courtesy of S.F. Information Clearinghouse)

(*Left*) Community activist Calvin Welch, one of the leaders of the San Francisco growth-control movement. (Courtesy of S.F. Information Clearinghouse)

Don't buy the developers' bull.
VOTE
YES on M

(*Right*) Growth-control advocates plastered this campaign poster all over the city as voters prepared to go to the polls in November 1986. (Courtesy of S.F. Information Clearinghouse)

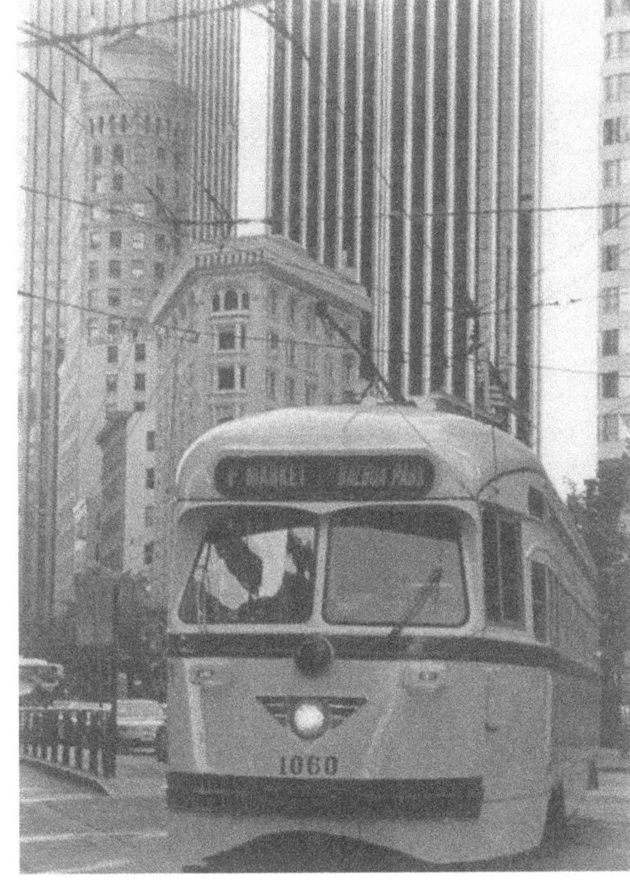

(*Above*) An affordable housing project in the Inner Sunset neighborhood funded in part with revenue raised from the city's housing linkage ordinance. (Courtesy of S.F. Information Clearinghouse)
(*Right*) The transit linkage ordinance enabled the city to expand and improve public transportation to accommodate the influx of commuters generated by downtown development. (Courtesy of Chuck Thomas)

(*Left*) Strict limits on commercial office growth have helped to preserve open space and sunshine in near-downtown neighborhoods. (Courtesy of Chuck Thomas)
(*Below*) Growth-control activists in San Francisco believe they have struck a balance between promoting equitable downtown development and safeguarding the quality of neighborhood life. (Courtesy of Chuck Thomas)

> way or the other but found their businesses threatened by Prop. M because the Yups who framed this once-thought-to-be-perfect proposition are so out to lunch in terms of the problems of middle class San Francisco that they are flushing the poor residential contractors down the toilet along with the rich highrise developers.[45]

Growth-control advocates were surprised to discover that Joe O'Donoghue's attack on the eight priority policies was resonating in the more moderate and conservative neighborhoods. Activist Ed Emerson recalled canvassing home owners in those neighborhoods and finding people expressing the O'Donoghue sentiment that Proposition M would create more "red tape" and "layers of bureaucracy," which would restrict their right to use their property as they wished.[46]

Growth-control activists scrambled to respond to this unanticipated and apparently growing source of opposition to Proposition M in the more conservative residential neighborhoods. Proposition M advocate Dick Grosboll credited the progrowth forces with clever campaigning: "They knew that if they campaign on the office development cap, they'll lose. . . . So they take unreasonably negative interpretations of other parts of the initiative" and invoke doomsday scenarios that are utterly unrealistic. For example, Grosboll said that Proposition M's priority policy of preserving parks and open space was distorted by opponents of the initiative to mean a complete ban on building on vacant lots; and the policy of maintaining the character of a neighborhood became a ban on eliminating porno shops. "As someone who participated in the drafting of the initiative, I know that those too-narrow interpretations were not the intent," Grosboll concluded.[47] Nevertheless, the RBA's grassroots tactics paid off as Proposition M's large lead in the polls began to shrink.

The other formidable force opposing the growth-control initiative was the mayor. Dianne Feinstein's role in the politics of downtown development had evolved over the years. In 1979 she had tried to steer a middle course between the downtown establishment and the growth-control advocates in the neighborhoods; she avoided taking a stand on that year's initiative until the final week of the campaign before giving Proposition O a weak endorsement. But over the next several years, Feinstein proceeded to make downtown development a cornerstone of her administration. She had worked hard to fashion land use policies that promoted downtown growth while at the same time imposing some controls. Her early support for linkage policies, aimed at forcing developers to mitigate the adverse consequences of commercial office development, helped to legitimate government intervention to advance equitable growth. The crowning jewel of her approach to downtown development was the Downtown Plan. In her mind the Downtown Plan represented a fair compromise between the progrowth and slow-growth contingents and, indeed, it had been praised by planners and architects throughout the United States.

In 1986 Mayor Feinstein remained deeply committed to the Downtown Plan and was dismayed that the growth-control movement had continued to push for even stricter limits on development, stronger linkage policies, and broader citizen control over policy making. She viewed the Proposition M campaign as an affront to her leadership and the expertise of her Planning Department. With the downtown business community taking a somewhat less aggressive stance, at least at first, Feinstein decided to take charge. Always a popular mayor, Feinstein proved to be highly effective at building an alliance between the traditional supporters of downtown development and homeowners in conservative neighborhoods anxious about excessively restrictive controls on their right to renovate their homes.[48]

The mayor moved quickly to capitalize on the success of the RBA's grassroots campaign by emphasizing the threats posed by Proposition M's goal of neighborhood preservation. She warned, "This measure will put a ball and chain around every neighborhood project." Feinstein then picked up a valuable ally. Quentin Kopp, San Francisco's long-time maverick politician and a hero to many of the conservative homeowners in the city's western and southern neighborhoods, announced his opposition to Propositon M on the ground that the initiative's "injurious and self-defeating language" would deter housing construction.[49]

Other traditional opponents of the growth-control movement seemed to be galvanized by the mayor's efforts and by the growing backlash against Proposition M in the city's more conservative neighborhoods. The Chamber of Commerce stepped up its usual critique of the growth-control agenda,[50] and the city's mainstream press published frequent editorials condemning the anti-business mood engendered by Proposition M: "Prop. M would send a chilling message to potential investors in job-providing establishments in this city. In the anti-business message it would transmit to the nation, it could expedite the flight already seen of many jobs to the far-out suburbs and cause a large revenue loss for the City. . . . What the City needs is not this knockout approach with a sledgehammer, but improved administration of the Downtown Plan."[51]

Along with trotting out the familiar privatist arguments about the dangers of regulatory and redistributive policies regarding downtown development, and warning against excessive citizen participation in the policy-making process, progrowth advocates resorted to other previously reliable strategies for undermining popular support for limiting growth. As in the past, the downtown growth coalition tried to fragment the growth-control movement through various co-optive strategies, most of which were directed at some of the city's poorest neighborhoods. Feinstein turned to her old friend Cecil Williams of the Glide

Memorial Church, a prominent figure in the African American community, for help. Williams responded by supervising the distribution of ten thousand pieces of literature intended to conjure up nightmarish images of a city so constrained by Proposition M that *all* kinds of development and rehabilitation would come to a halt. The literature showed a full-page picture of a cockroach and suggested that the growth-control initiative would keep people trapped in roach-infested ghettos by deterring new housing and employment.[52] At a press conference in the Tenderloin, Reverend Williams argued that the drafters of Proposition M "value buildings more than people. . . . They say 'stay in rat-and-roach-infested one-room homes and we will keep them as they are.'"[53]

The downtown growth coalition had reason to believe that the tactics employed by Cecil Williams would be particularly effective in the African American community. Progrowth forces had always counted on support from black voters to defeat prior citizens initiatives to limit downtown development. In 1983 the city's three largest black neighborhoods had voted 60 percent to 40 percent against the growth-control initiative. Black citizens had followed the lead of several well-known black leaders in rejecting the initiative for fear that it would eliminate jobs and any hope for economic revitalization in their neglected neighborhoods.

But in 1986 traditional progrowth arguments and efforts to co-opt the growth-control movement by mobilizing community leaders with strong ties to the downtown regime and by inciting racial and class-based divisions proved to be less effective. The first indication that the African American community was ready to take a new stance on downtown development came in September 1986 when a leading black politician, Supervisor Willie Kennedy, walked out of a meeting with Mayor Feinstein after announcing that she would depart from her 1983 position and now support the growth-control initiative.[54]

Kennedy's about-face coincided with an even more important development, the emergence of a strong grassroots challenge in the city's black neighborhoods to some of San Francisco's most powerful black leaders who had always opposed growth-control initiatives: State Assembly Speaker Willie Brown, Glide Memorial Church pastor Cecil Williams, Community College Board Member Amos Brown, and Redevelopment Agency Director Wilbur Hamilton. The formation of a new organization, Blacks for Proposition M, was announced at a September 25 press conference called by a group of black ministers that was led by Civil Service Commissioner Rev. Howard Gloyd. Other dissidents in attendance were Claude Everhart, chief aide to State Assemblyman Art Agnos, and Geraldine Johnson of the Coalition of Black Trade Unionists.[55] Highlighting the theme of how urban development had helped upper-middle-class whites while ignoring African Americans, Gloyd remarked: "There is no promised land on Fillmore. There is no opportunity on Fillmore. And the largest commercial development to take place in the area (the Safeway store) . . . is turned so that the wealthy from . . . Pacific Heights can shop without going through the Fillmore community."[56]

On the same day, the Black Leadership Forum, a group that had never supported a growth-control initiative before, voted forty-seven to thirteen to endorse Proposition M. The shift within the black community reflected increasing skepticism of Feinstein's record on urban development. A statement issued by Blacks for Prop. M declared, "The special interests have been claiming that blacks will lose construction jobs if Prop. M. passes. But we challenge the press to go to any construction site in San Francisco and count the number of blacks on the job, especially the number of blacks who are doing something more than being laborers." Geraldine Johnson said, "It looks like there are going to be two camps in the black community. And the traditional spokespeople for the black voters—the people the media looks to as representing the community—are rapidly losing their credibility."[57]

Activist Darryl Cox explained the change in black public opinion on development issues from one of hopeful acquiescence to one of critical skepticism.

> That was a long struggle to finally get black people to see that, y'know, where are the jobs? Look at the development that has gone on and where are the jobs? Y'know, the leadership couldn't show you the numbers. Unions were resistant [to black participation]. . . . Where are the jobs? They didn't exist. So, politically, in terms of electoral campaigns, and let me be clear, it wasn't that we were flat out opposed to development. We were saying if this is going to go on and these are the impacts, right, that it's going to have, we want some mitigation. Don't tell us that it's going to produce a certain number of jobs. Where are these jobs? Where are those blacks who are being trained?

New progressive activists in the African American community such as Geraldine Johnson, Darryl Cox, and Rev. Howard Gloyd joined forces with other progressive activists who were now solidly in control of the growth-control movement and built upon the theme of false promises made by developers in the past as a way of fostering a critical consciousness among San Francisco's African Americans. Calvin Welch described the basic campaign strategy: "In the end, it was going back and constantly reminding people, almost project by project, remember what you were promised on this? Did that happen? I think one of the most effective pieces of literature we did was a mailing to perennial black voters who were generally older people that just posed the question to them: How many of your grandchildren, how many of your friends do you know that work in an office building downtown?" Geraldine Johnson credited

"SFT, Sue Hestor, Calvin and all of them" for running an "inclusive" campaign with a simple, straightforward message that people understood. And indeed, the progressives' grassroots campaign brought results. Whereas in 1983 the growth-control initiative had been decisively rejected by the city's three African American neighborhoods, this time the same three neighborhoods approved Proposition M 55 percent to 45 percent, a turnaround of fifteen percentage points.[58]

The reversal in black attitudes toward controlling downtown development is not attributable to anything particularly new in growth-control activism. The 1986 citizens initiative campaign differed little from the two previous initiative campaigns in 1983 and 1979. Since the progressive wing of the growth-control movement had gained ascendancy, all of the campaigns had reflected the twin progressive values of empowerment and equitable growth through strong regulatory and redistributive policies. All of the campaigns had reached out to diverse urban groups, including the African American community, and tried to incorporate those groups into the grassroots movement.

Rather, what prompted the voting changes in 1986 was the ongoing transformation in the local political culture. Counterhegemonic activism had eroded the privatist tendency of black citizens to defer to established leaders, who happened to be closely connected to the mayor and the downtown business community. As time passed, citizens were more likely to evaluate their interests and options critically and take a more assertive role in making decisions about the future of their community. Although the basic arguments about downtown development's impact on the African American community had not changed much during the past seven years, by 1986 black voters were interpreting their situations within a very different cultural context. Given the increasingly progressive aura that pervaded San Francisco land use politics, growth-control arguments made more and more sense. By 1986 black voters were ready to abandon their traditional leaders and join other community groups in the mounting opposition to the downtown-led regime.

The evolution in popular consciousness that took place in the African American community was in many ways a microcosm of what was happening throughout San Francisco. When activists ran their first initiative campaign in 1971, voters analyzed that growth-control measure in a cultural context that had stressed privatist ideas, values, beliefs, and practices. Perceptions of self-interest and the public interest were heavily influenced by that culture. But fifteen years of progressive activism had dramatically recast the local political culture. Faith in the free market, elite planning, and the inevitable benefits of aggressive development had given way to support for broad citizen involvement in land use policy making and for an activist government to ensure that downtown development would be both limited and equitable. As a result, the way ordinary people interpreted the arguments of the growth coalition and the growth-control movement was bound to be different.

To fortify evolving perceptions of downtown development and guard against last-minute slippage caused by the inevitable media blitz that the downtown growth coalition unleashed toward the end of every initiative campaign, growth-control activists devised some clever strategies. The slogan that virtually everyone remembered from that campaign was "Don't Buy the Developers' Bull!" It was printed on signs and posters that were plastered all over the city. Under the slogan appeared a bull rampaging through the streets of downtown. The posters were so effective that activists soon began to distribute "Bull-Fact" sheets summarizing the growth coalition's position on a particular issue, followed by the growth-control movement's response.[59] Whereas in previous years voters might have been inclined to move toward the growth coalition's position on downtown development after a well-financed advertising campaign, this time they held firm. In the newly emerging political culture, San Franciscans increasingly regarded the traditional progrowth arguments as "just more of the developers' bull."[60]

As the campaign drew to a close, the growth-control movement accelerated its efforts, sending hundreds of volunteers to pivotal neighborhoods for canvassing and literature drops. Activists attended community meetings to make their case in informal settings. Leaflets targeted to specific groups such as small-business owners were distributed. None of these strategies were particularly new; the growth-control movement had run energetic grassroots campaigns since 1979. But this time the appeals for limited and equitable growth resonated with the voters. Despite the anticipated avalanche of "No on M" campaigning in the last two or three weeks, San Franciscans approved the citizens' initiative by a vote of 51.3 percent to 48.7 percent.

It is important to emphasize that the narrow margin of victory did not accurately reflect the extent to which San Franciscans had come to embrace the growth-control movement's perspective on downtown development. This is because a sizable percentage of citizens, especially in the southern and western neighborhoods, voted against Proposition M for reasons that had nothing to do with downtown expansion; instead, they had been persuaded by Joe O'Donoghue and the Residential Builders Association that the eight priority policies would inhibit neighborhood development. In 1990, when one final growth-control initiative to limit downtown development was on the ballot, many of these same voters revealed their true colors by siding with the growth-control movement. In fact, Calvin Welch noted that that particular constituency turned out to be one of the staunchest supporters of maintaining popular control over downtown expansion.[61]

Proposition M imposed the strictest limits on commercial office development ever witnessed in a major U.S. city. This alone was a remarkable achievement for the growth-control movement. But more significantly, the new law marked a stunning transition in power relations with respect to the all-important issue of urban development. The downtown growth coalition's once impenetrable lock on development policy had given way to a new coalition led by a diverse array of neighborhood groups with a very different agenda. Activist Tony Kilroy, who lived in the Richmond district, a key swing neighborhood that crossed over in 1986 and supported the growth-control initiative, summarized his impression of the change in development politics: "I think the peasants have just gotten better. The kings and queens don't have their way all the time. The peasants are better informed, better organized, better mobilized, have learned these tools better than they did before."[62]

Conclusion

Passage of the growth-control initiative, Proposition M, in 1986 is widely considered the symbolic triumph of the growth-control movement. Neighborhood activists had prevailed in two fundamental ways. First, elite influence over development decision making had seriously eroded. Most observers now felt that the city's many community-based organizations that made up the growth-control movement had gained substantial power. Second, growth-control activists were determined to use their power to remedy inequities resulting from an excessive reliance on market forces to distribute the costs and benefits of downtown expansion. In the years ahead, activists promised to continue advocating more regulatory and redistributive policies since in their view only an aggressive public sphere was capable of promoting limited and equitable growth.

By the end of 1986 the privatist political culture that had enabled the downtown growth coalition to thrive since the end of World War II had been discredited. In its place a progressive vision of politics was emerging as the new hegemonic political culture. In the years immediately following passage of Proposition M, as progressive practices such as growth limits, linkage, and citizen participation in land use decision making became increasingly routine aspects of the politics of downtown development, that political culture became even more entrenched. The political consciousness of all groups affected by downtown development was undergoing a remarkable transformation.

✦7

Cultural Change

The cultural impact of counterhegemonic activism in San Francisco becomes even more apparent by examining how perceptions of downtown development changed during the 1980s. The analysis presented here is structured, again, around the two key dimensions of politics: How did individual groups experience a change of consciousness regarding their involvement in local politics? How did they come to reconceive the role of government with respect to downtown development?

The General Public

By the late 1980s, after years of intensive counterhegemonic protest from progressive growth-control activists, the citizens of San Francisco had undergone a profound change in how they conceived of the city's land use politics. Most obviously, downtown development was no longer viewed as an inherently positive phenomenon. Activist Marcia Rosen reflected upon public perceptions of the building boom: "San Franciscans have felt generally that large-scale commercial development has never benefited . . . residents of San Francisco. . . . The benefits never trickled down. We didn't see increased health services, better libraries, better schools, better street cleaning, better pothole-fixing. . . . We continued to see development of this wealthy downtown neighborhood at the same time housing prices were escalating and were beyond the affordability of San Francisco residents. . . . So I think there was a fair amount of caution and pessimism about why do this. Who benefits? How does it affect me? How does it make my kids' schools better?" Accordingly, public confidence in developers as agents of economic revitalization plummeted. Another long-time activist remarked, "I think in this city you just go about anywhere and 'developer' is a nasty word. . . . Developers are not looked upon as anyone who is going to solve anyone's problems. . . . Minority groups, and particularly the black communities, still hope to get enterprise opportunities and jobs, but their cynicism is incredibly deep." These assessments were confirmed by a public opinion poll commissioned by the Catellus Development Corporation in 1990. It found that most citizens hold commercial office developers in low regard. Only 21.5 percent of the poll's respondents believed that a major developer would do what is best for the city; 66.5 percent disagreed.[1]

Distrustful of private market forces, San Franciscans abandoned their prior privatist belief in minimal government intervention in urban development by endorsing the strictest restrictions on office construction in the nation and a set of linkage policies aimed at promoting a more equitable economic development of the city. Four years after the city had approved Proposition M, public support for the measure had increased. In the 1990 poll by Catellus, respondents were asked whether the growth limits instituted by Proposition M were too strong, too weak, or about right. Only 15.5 percent answered "too strong"; 52.3 percent said "about right"; and 15.1 percent believed they were too weak.[2]

But if San Franciscans had grown suspicious of developers and other business elites, they were also skeptical of public officials. Hence, they embraced more vigorous government involvement in downtown development only on the condition that the nature of government itself change as well. Citizens rejected old practices that placed an overriding premium on skill and experience in dealing with development issues and demanded greater access to decision-making arenas. The most obvious manifestation of this cultural shift away from representative democracy and toward participatory democracy was the adoption of a new law governing downtown development by a citizens initiative; Proposition M's passage suggested that ordinary citizens were no longer willing to defer to city officials on major land use issues.

Underlying this citywide shift in the local political culture was a series of more subtle cultural transformations experienced by the many urban groups touched by downtown development. Four of the more important groups that underwent significant changes in how they conceived of downtown development are growth-control activists themselves, African American residents, city planners, and business leaders. Each of these transformations reveals a great deal about the overall political culture in San Francisco.

At one end of the spectrum, the growth-control movement developed, as the years passed, a more coherently progressive vision of political life. This is no small accomplishment since only a vision that offers a clear and consistent alternative to the privatist culture is most likely to engender widespread changes in consciousness and political activity. By contrast, a challenging vision that contains key elements of the dominant vision leads to confusion, or worse, a partial reaffirming of existing practices and power relations. The San Francisco growth-control movement's increasing cohesiveness and clarity of vision thus strengthened the counterhegemonic potential of its grassroots activism.

That counterhegemonic activism prompted groups from all over the city to reassess their interests and options according to a different set of ideas, values, and beliefs. The resulting change in thinking was particularly striking within the African American community. Once reliable supporters of the downtown growth coalition, African Americans in San Francisco responded to growth-control activism by thoroughly changing how they conceived of urban power relations and the role of government regarding downtown development. The transformation in consciousness and political behavior that this group experienced was among the most dramatic in the city.

The impact of counterhegemonic activism on city planners was interesting and important. City planners have traditionally seen themselves as occupying a position somewhere between the growth-control activists and the downtown business leaders. They felt it was their responsibility to weigh each side's position on downtown development and then recommend policies that advanced the public interest. In a privatist political culture, however, the evaluation process tended to be slanted in ways that favored elite power and market-driven approaches to redeveloping the downtown core. Counterhegemonic activism prompted city planners at all levels to reexamine old issues through a different cultural lens, and the consequences for day-to-day planning practice proved to be far-reaching for the politics of downtown development in general.

Finally, growth-control activism even brought about a noticeable transformation within the downtown business community. Although it would be inaccurate to claim that business elites fully embraced the progressive vision, the change in their discourse and conduct does indicate a significant departure from the unrelenting privatist outlook that characterized their participation in land use politics for most of the post–World War II period. The fact that business leaders have tolerated, and at times even welcomed, widespread citizen engagement in the political process and a more expansive role for government has helped to institutionalize progressive ideas and practices. What was once condemned as radical or foolish may now be considered practical and useful. Changes in the discourse and conduct of downtown business leaders, the group that was always the most hostile to the growth-control movement, thus represent some of the clearest evidence of a transformation in the city's political culture.

Although each group reacted to the counterhegemonic activism of progressive activists in different ways, taken together, each transformation contributed to the broader change in the city's political culture, a change that would enable a progressive politics of downtown development to take root and endure.

The Activists

The growth-control movement always advocated expanding popular control over development policy making. But in the initial years of the movement, practice did not always follow principle. For example, elite direction of the Duskin initiative campaigns undermined the counterhegemonic impact of their rhetorical commitment to citizen empowerment. Because leadership was so centralized, policy goals tended to reflect the perspectives and interests of a rather exclusive group of activists, most of whom were middle-class professionals. Consequently, the early growth-control movement emphasized aesthetic and environmental concerns while glossing over socioeconomic issues such as downtown development's impact on housing, small business, transit, and job opportunities. Such a restricted policy agenda gave little incentive for other groups to pay attention to the movement and get involved. Hence, the movement remained narrow and was easily marginalized by the downtown growth coalition.

But as the progressive wing of the growth-control movement gained power, the old rhetorical commitment to popular empowerment became much more meaningful. When progressives argued that "the people" should rule, they meant all people. They made a concerted effort to make growth-control activism a much more inclusive phenomenon. Veteran activist Sue Hestor believed that the strategy paid off: "[Grassroots activism] was much more focused in a couple of neighborhoods before. Now it's everywhere. The neighborhoods that really got up and in arms traditionally were the ones like Russian Hill, part of Nob Hill, places that had views, and that had basically upper-class people who were willing to wage fights. Now it's across all levels. People fight projects no matter where they are. I mean, I'm not saying all projects are fought, but I am saying it's not a factor of economics."[3] Urban groups that had once taken only a passive role in development politics became actively engaged in the planning process.

This is not to say that all groups in San Francisco felt empowered. Jim Wachob, an activist with a community organization in a white, working-class neighborhood in the southern part of the city asserts, "Historically, we've had problems with guys like Calvin [Welch] and those dudes, y'know. We've never been hooked into that whole planning kind of situation." Although Wachob believed that "things are comin' around on that," he maintained that his neighbors continue to feel alienated from the entire political process.[4] But by and large the insistence by progressive activists that urban groups long victimized by downtown-inspired land use policies be included in the growth-control movement yielded results. The city's black, Latino, and Asian communities became significant forces in land use politics.

The growth-control movement's efforts to recruit activists from diverse communities and then give them genuine influence over the direction of grassroots organizing inevitably widened the policy agenda to encompass the material concerns of a broad spectrum of citizens. Grassroots activism increasingly focused on the economic impacts of downtown development as well as the environmental and aesthetic impacts, a shift that attracted even broader support for the movement. And when activists called for a range of regulatory and redistributive policies so that the costs and benefits of urban development would be more fairly distributed, even more people joined the bandwagon.

The progressive commitment to inclusion and equity, in turn, influenced the outlook of previously moderate growth-control activists whose past policy interests revolved around the protection of their own neighborhoods' interests. For example, rarely did the upper-middle-class residents of the near-downtown neighborhood of Telegraph Hill consider how downtown development might be adversely affecting less privileged groups in other neighborhoods; they were too preoccupied seeking stronger zoning limits to block the encroachment of highrise office buildings on their neighborhood. But persistent progressive activism prompted Telegraph Hill residents to adopt a more civic-minded perspective on downtown development and support various redistributive policies. Telegraph Hill activist Denise McCarthy reported that her community endorsed applying an inclusionary zoning policy *in Telegraph Hill.* The local neighborhood association insisted that the developers of two large apartment complexes set aside at least 10 percent of the units for lower-income residents. Embracing the same perspective that inspired the rise of linkage policies, McCarthy asserted, "Affordable housing is so necessary that every neighborhood ought to swallow some increased density or . . . inclusionary zoning."[5]

Furthermore, members of the urban environmental organization San Francisco Tomorrow (SFT), which was founded in 1970 to promote sound planning principles as a way to minimize traffic congestion and air pollution, devoted considerable energy in the late 1980s to the rezoning of the South of Market district to protect existing blue-collar jobs. The president of SFT in the early 1990s, Andy Nash, agreed that the organization had undergone some changes in perspective. Traditionally, he said, much of SFT's support came from people motivated solely by a desire to protect their own neighborhoods. But Nash insisted that he and other SFT members came to reject the older NIMBY-like inclinations: "We can't just, y'know, roll up the door and say no more people can come in." The new SFT brought a "more balanced perspective" of regulating downtown growth and supporting policies that ensure that regulated growth will also be equitable. Progressive activist Marcia Rosen agreed that SFT had changed its orientation. Referring to negotiations between the developer and citizen groups over the Mission Bay project, she noted, "[SFT] initially came in with concerns about the traditional sort of traffic, waterfront, those kinds of concerns. But they really did buy into the affordable housing, jobs, housing-jobs imbalance kinds of issues."[6]

Finally, shifts in political consciousness were not limited to moderate activists. Even progressive activists changed how they thought about certain aspects of downtown development. For example, although they had always insisted that government ensure a more equitable distribution of the benefits and costs of urban growth, progressive activists did not always appreciate the full possibilities of linkage as a redistributive mechanism. At first some believed that the chief attribute of linkage was that it would serve as a deterrent to new commercial office development because the mitigation fees would make the cost of investment too prohibitive. Only after housing and transit linkage policies were actually being implemented and generating concrete results did progressives recognize their potential in promoting equitable growth. They soon called for a strengthening of existing policies and an expansion of linkage into other policy areas such as child care and employment.[7]

The African American Community

Although the African American community constitutes only about a tenth of San Francisco's overall population and is smaller in size than the Latino and Asian communities, it wields a disproportionate amount of influence in city politics. According to political scientist Richard DeLeon, "African Americans are now the smallest of the three major ethnic groups in terms of population size, but they have mustered the highest rates of voter mobilization, consensus on issues, and representation in government. Supported by political organization and leadership at the state and national levels, the city's African American leaders have converted limited numbers and economic resources into a power bloc to be reckoned with in local politics." Through the years, the African American community consistently used its influence to support the downtown growth coalition in opposing growth-control initiatives. At first glance, such support for the growth coalition was somewhat mystifying in light of urban renewal policies in the 1960s. Thousands of people had lost their homes and businesses and entire neighborhoods had been destroyed. The commercial and cultural center of black life in San Francisco, the Fillmore, had been wiped out. Nor did African Americans have reason to believe that economic development policies would improve as time passed. For example, in the late 1960s the Redevelopment Agency had promoted a giant industrial park, India Basin, to be located in Bayview/Hunters Point by promising local residents that the project would generate five thousand new jobs, of which twenty-four hundred would be earmarked for Hunters Point residents. India Basin was developed and it did provide thousands of new jobs, but Hunters Point residents saw few of the benefits. Of the twenty-four hundred jobs promised to them, only fifty-five had materialized by 1984. The companies that had received substantial incentives from the city to locate in India Basin failed to abide by their commitments to hire locally, and the city did little to enforce the contracts. Moreover, neighborhood businesses that had provided seven hundred local jobs moved out of the city, many displaced by the higher property values triggered by the India Basin development project. Not surprisingly, Hunters Point remained a blighted area, plagued by some of the city's highest unemployment and crime rates.[8]

Political support for the downtown growth coalition within the African American community is somewhat more comprehensible if one considers the co-optive tactics employed by progrowth advocates to smother the emergence of grassroots opposition. Beginning in the late 1960s, San Francisco mayors made a conscious effort to appoint blacks to high-ranking positions in city government. Within a few years, the heads of the Housing Authority, the Redevelopment Agency, and the Office of Community Development were all black. Ordinary citizens in the African American community were immensely proud of this first generation of black leaders to hold power beyond the confines of their own neighborhoods. Thus, although they were increasingly troubled by the development policies of the downtown growth coalition, most citizens found it difficult to openly question those leaders.[9]

By the early 1980s, however, growth-control activists were able to reach out and forge alliances with a new generation of black activists, who had become impatient with what they perceived as the empty promises of developers and the false assurances of older community leaders. In fact, the African American community offers an excellent illustration of how counterhegemonic activism inspired changes in consciousness that facilitated changes in politics. The first phase of the cultural transformation involved a loss of trust in government officials, including neighborhood leaders who had always vowed to look out for the interests of African Americans: "In the last five years, there's a general distrust of government, period. So whereas before they would tell you this was good for you, but you were too busy or didn't care. Now if government tells you it's good for you, you automatically think it's not.... Just because Ted Kennedy's liberal doesn't mean I'm going to sit there and close my eyes to everything he says, does, the way he votes on stuff. People, I think, generally do not respond to government in the way that they did." With regard to development proposals, African Americans are no longer satisfied with vague promises: "The political environment has changed. It is no longer possible to make those sorts of promises. People are not trusted. So if they want people to support their projects, things have to be explicitly stated. They have to talk about dollars and cents. They have to talk about jobs. They have to talk about what is this process going to be." Activist James Bell concluded, "So if I'm a developer and I'm coming to San Francisco, I can't just step in and pull wool over people's eyes. . . . I could do that in San Jose, but not here. I could do that in Oakland, but not in this city."[10]

As the 1980s progressed, feelings of distrust were accompanied by a mood of defiance. In 1986, only weeks before San Franciscans would vote on Proposition M, Geraldine Johnson was attending a meeting with Planning Director Dean Macris and other city officials to discuss how negotiations over the mammoth Mission Bay development project would be conducted. Johnson contended that the African American community should be represented at the bargaining table as a third or fourth party. Macris said that would not be necessary. Johnson asked, "Who's gonna fight for our interests?" Macris: "Oh, we will." Johnson: "Bullshit!" She described what then ensued: "I said to Dean Macris . . . 'Dean, where I come from, the people know that the only way to get a mule's attention is to pick up a two-by-four and hit 'em right between the eyes, and it seems that that's what we are going to have to do to you.' And leaving that meeting, my decision was that I was going to call, visit the thirty houses again to get support for Proposition M because it was gonna stop Mission Bay."[11]

A heightened realization of how developers and the city had misled the African American community in the past produced widespread distrust and defiance. That mood soon prompted people to take a more direct role in the development process. Johnson commented on rising levels of participation among African Americans in San Francisco land use politics: "Even though we came late to the development game, now that we are beginning to understand the interconnectedness of all of this, you see . . . a level of activism in this town that we have not seen at least—I came in '62, so I've been here 29 years—that has not happened up until this point."[12]

Rising levels of popular participation in land use politics are in no small measure attributable to the ongoing efforts of progressive activists. Geraldine Johnson described her approach to community organizing as follows: "There's about thirty households . . . that I tend to contact and ask them to bring in the neighbors and I try to explain the issue to them in that kind of cozy informal kind of setting where people can be relaxed and not feel stupid and not have to deal with how many square feet, how much of this . . . " In visiting people's homes, Johnson would talk with residents about planning issues and build on their growing skepticism about urban development by getting people to ask

"What's in it for my community?" The growth-control movement's practice of advocating linkage proved invaluable in mobilizing the African American community. Progrowth leaders had always assured neighborhood groups that downtown development would benefit them; linkage policies became a way of forcing those leaders to adhere to their promises. African Americans began to demand that promises regarding jobs and housing be explicitly stated in the form of legally enforceable linkage ordinances. As activist Darryl Cox put it, "you're not going to get the support of the black community by inviting various black leaders, y'know, to rubber chicken dinners and patting them on the back or paying a minister money. . . . If you want the support of the black community, then the black community has to be given something in return for its support. And the issue is . . . about contracts."[13]

Johnson and other activists believed that changes in the outlook and behavior of African American citizens in San Francisco had led directly to material improvements in what black citizens gain from development projects. But Johnson retained considerable skepticism about developers: "I would think that they know they have to do things differently, but if they could get away with doing the way they did in the past they would. . . . They will get away with as much as they can because that's the nature of the beast." What keeps the developers in line, Johnson believed, is the developers' knowledge that African Americans have developed a defiant consciousness that leads to active engagement in the political process. If San Francisco returns to the days of unfulfilled promises, the response this time, she predicted, will not be one of disappointed resignation and apathy, but of political retaliation. Johnson warns, for example, that if a major developer reneges on its employment commitments, community activists will sue the developer and "kick him in the ass at the ballot box."[14]

City Planners

In the privatist political culture, city planners conceived of themselves as objective professionals operating above the political fray, concerned only with overseeing the development of downtown according to sound planning principles. Dean Macris, who presided over the City Planning Department for twelve years during the height of San Francisco's building boom, saw himself as coming out of "a tradition of good planning," a tradition that assumed that if only "the politicians will keep their scummy hands off . . . we would get first-rate planning." Speaking of his approach to his job, Macris claimed, "I don't think in ideological terms. Anyone who is into causes loses me. This isn't a matter of causes; it's a matter of being smart. So ideology is not an issue with me. What is smart for the city? What makes sense for the city?"[15] But conceptions of "what is smart" or "what makes sense for the city" are shaped by the surrounding political culture. The city's growth-control movement played a decisive role in reshaping that political culture and in the process altering conceptions of "what makes sense," even in the minds of "objective" professionals such as Dean Macris.

Veteran city planner Alec Bash developed a view of the planning profession that is more sensitive to political realities than Macris's purely professional orientation. Bash began by observing how the political context changed and what that meant for city planning. He believed that San Franciscans went from being "very passive to being very active" during his twenty-year tenure at the Planning Department. He noted that "the planning constituency is much bigger, a lot more people care about it, they push very hard on things." As a result, Bash believed that planners in the early 1990s had a much different notion of what policy proposals would be practical. He explained that in the 1970s developers occupied a position on the far right of the ideological spectrum, with San Francisco citizens sitting only slightly to the left. Given that configuration, Bash said that a progressive planning agenda was impossible. By the 1990s he believed that the business community had shifted somewhat to the left, while San Francisco citizens had moved much further to the left. That, in turn, enabled the Planning Department to move considerably leftward as well, while continuing to occupy its traditional middle-ground position. Bash concluded: "We can accomplish a lot more when we have a very active citizenry that is trying to get as much out of the process, as much in mitigation and exactions. We can really use that."[16]

The influence of the growth-control activists on development policy making was confirmed by another long-time city planner: "We need the activists pushing, y'know, just to make it happen. . . . I mean we get away with what we do because we know that there's that counterbalancing force there. If you had a city that was really probusiness . . . they'd kind of laugh at you, go to the mayor, ignore you." Meanwhile, the activists were well aware of the kind of influence they exerted over city planners. Andy Nash observed:

> It's always a push. . . . The businesses want to maximize their profit, of course, and the government should want to maximize how much they get from them. So it's a tug-of-war, basically. And, unfortunately, the government people oftentimes become jaded. They just can't fight the developers because the developers . . . [have] got these high-powered attorneys who are going to convince you about everything . . . and they are relentless. And they're going to push, push, push. And so the reason Proposition M [prevailed] was that we pushed the city the other way. And I mean it's a beautiful thing when you think about it. . . . You could probably get [City Planning Director Dean Macris] to admit that it was much easier for him . . . with groups like us out there pushing the other way. So he came in as the reasonable guy. And I think he might admit that.[17]

Put another way, because of counterhegemonic activism, what city planners like Dean Macris considered reasonable by the late 1980s was strikingly different from what they had considered reasonable a decade earlier.

The cultural transformation brought on by the growth-control movement prompted important changes in how city planners think and behave with respect to downtown development. In the 1970s, then Planning Director Rai Okamoto's highest priority was "improving the quality of architecture" by attracting "world-class architects" to San Francisco. "I was concerned that San Francisco wasn't reaching as high or achieving as high quality architectural design as they might. And so whenever I had the opportunity I was advocating that we consider almost the world as our resource for getting architects." Other senior planners confirmed that architecture and design were the overriding concerns at the Planning Department. One recalled that Dean Macris used to say, "We're not social planners, we're physical planners."[18]

The consequence of this focus on architecture and design was that the social and economic impacts of downtown development tended to get short shrift. Activist Marcia Rosen remembered: "You used to talk to planners about child care and they would just look at you like 'What planet are you from?' y'know, they just didn't understand." Activist Sue Hestor recalled an incident in the early 1980s that illustrates how, given the hegemony of the privatist political culture, planning for social impacts simply did not make sense to city officials. Hestor and a number of social workers attended a Planning Commission hearing to lobby for a linkage fee for child care.

> Planning Commission [President] Toby Rosenblatt . . . went through the roof and he said, "Why are you here? This is the Planning Commission. Why are you not at the Social Services Department? This is a social services issue. It's not a planning issue." The Planning Commission only thought their responsibility was to do architecture. It was like planning doesn't exist. All we have to do is decide what color glass there should be in this building and what kind of notching we want, and cornices. Its concept of planning—'cause planning includes parks, child care facilities, police stations, the whole gamut of how a city is structured—was a foreign concept. And, y'know, it was rather astonishing. He really got irate that we had brought child care workers there.[19]

But growth-control activists forced city planners to conceive of planning as encompassing much more than bricks and mortar. Once linkage became institutionalized, planners came to see social and economic issues such as child care, housing, and employment as a necessary part of downtown development planning.

Also, progressive activists succeeded in changing how planners thought about linkage. In the late 1970s, when it was first being advocated, planners tended to dismiss the idea as utterly unrealistic; after all, no other U.S. city had mandated exactions from commercial office developers to counteract the social costs of their projects. But sustained pressure from growth-control activists persuaded the Planning Department to adopt a mild form of linkage with respect to mass transit and housing. When activists stepped up their pressure for stronger linkage policies, city planners at first balked, fearing that an expansion of linkage would kill off the building boom and steer new investment away from San Francisco. But continuing activism eventually convinced the city that it could push the envelope even further. By the mid-1980s the privatist assumption that redistributive policies and urban development did not mix had been turned on its head.

Finally, under the privatist vision of land use politics, planners were considered highly trained experts who were supposed to stay clear of the corrupting influences of politics. Their job was to identify the "best" policy and implement it. Citizen input would be tolerated, and at times even encouraged,[20] but citizen *control* over policy making was anathema. Even today, some senior officials in the Planning Department continue to view citizens initiatives to control downtown growth as inappropriate intrusions into their domain. But most city planners came to consider the use of initiatives as entirely reasonable. Such an increasingly prevalent perspective signals the fall of another tenet of the privatist vision amid an ascendant progressive political culture. Even Dean Macris agreed that although "neighborhood involvement is a growing movement around the country, . . . certainly San Francisco is in the lead." He observed that public officials in other cities are "in awe" of how citizens have pressed the city to control growth. Macris concluded that most American cities adhere to the concept of "building as a right. Here the concept doesn't exist."[21]

The Downtown Business Community

When analyzing the downtown business community's reaction to the changes brought by the growth-control movement, an appropriate place to begin is with Proposition M and its annual cap on highrise office building construction. Activists fought for fifteen years to obtain such a limit, and they were aggressively opposed by the city's real estate and business interests at every turn. Since Proposition M's passage in 1986, however, downtown's hostility to the growth-control initiative has diminished. Jeff Heller, president of one of the city's prominent architecture firms, criticized the competition that the Planning Department devised to determine which projects get selected each year, calling it "nasty, difficult and expensive" but then noted that Proposition M "created a certain level of crazed stability." He conceded, moreover, that the competition, which came to be known as "the beauty contest," encouraged a more orderly pattern of downtown growth and "better buildings" for the city.[22]

Some developers were not as immediately forthright in their assessment of Proposition M as Jeff Heller, though many, if pushed a little, arrived at a similar conclusion. The following exchange with developer Joe DeLuca is typical:

> Q: Is there anything the city can do over the next twenty years . . . to try and promote a [diverse urban environment]?
> JD: Yes, they can through managed growth. Managed growth, not reactionary growth, *not* acting by impulse to a condition, but by planning accordingly.
> Q: Isn't that what Prop. M tries to do, though?
> JD: *Tries* to do.
> Q: How does it fall short?
> JD: [Pause] At this point in time, I have to be brutally honest. I don't think it has fallen short.

DeLuca's reaction to Proposition M was common. Many business people who had predicted dire consequences for the city's economy if the initiative were approved, were hard pressed to identify how Proposition M had hurt San Francisco. One Chamber of Commerce official admitted, "We have a 4% unemployment rate and a 15% vacancy rate and you ask what's the problem—what are we supposed to complain about?"[23] Indeed, some business people gave Proposition M credit for keeping San Francisco's office vacancy rates relatively low compared to the disastrously high levels of most other large cities in the United States.[24] Another developer, Martin E. Brown of the Empire Group, pointed out that the highrise limit benefited banks and some developers who had an interest in maintaining a steady demand for office space. "Prop. M has increased the comfort level of lenders and investors who know that buildings are in short supply, and therefore, they feel safer."[25]

Another legacy of the growth-control movement is, of course, linkage. Roundly condemned by business as unfair and unconstitutional when it was first implemented, it later attained a wide measure of acceptance from the business community, if not enthusiastic support. The vice president of the Chamber of Commerce, Jim Lazarus, defended the legality of linkage by arguing that the city can demonstrate the requisite rational nexus underlying each of the linkage ordinances; moreover, he said the linkage policies constituted sound public policies, though he believed the fees had been elevated to a degree that they threatened to frighten away business.[26]

Others in the business community were not convinced that existing linkage fees discouraged economic investment at all. Bob Thompson, a corporate attorney who represented commercial office developers, was familiar with the argument that "you could lose development altogether if you make it too expensive. If you tap too much out of it, there is a point at which development will not continue." But Thompson went on to assert, "I think it's an untested theory because it's clear to me that exactions have never stopped a project. On balance, they're relatively a small proportion of the investment. They may eat into profits or they may enhance the loss, but they're not going to be a make-or-break issue for a project that's otherwise on the boards."[27]

Even a long-time critic of linkage, land use attorney Zane Gresham, acknowledged that overt business objections have subsided because many business people have simply "internalized" the policy. Furthermore, Gresham stated that some developers have actually used linkage to their advantage by bolstering their public image. He described how one developer told him that he thought child care linkage was the most "crazy ass thing I ever heard of," but he decided not to oppose it. "Instead what I'm going to do is figure out a way to cozy up to somebody who does child care and go parading around town that I'm a big child care advocate. It's politically attractive, it's a cheap buy, I'll do it!"[28]

Similarly, others saw linkage as a way to revive the dismal reputation that many developers had acquired. Vernon Schwartz, the chief executive officer of the Catellus Development Corporation, reportedly told his Mission Bay staff: "We're here for a long time; we need a good reputation. And the idea is that we've got property all over the country and we need to be thought of as a company that can work with government, that does the right thing. We need a good reputation." Some business leaders who observed how Catellus embraced the concept of negotiating with community-based groups over linkage arrangements were impressed with what the developer was able to accomplish. Attorney Bob Thompson commented: "I think Catellus is blessed with counsel—lawyers and political advisors—who have recognized that [linkage] is something they're not going to beat. That instead of . . . trying to make constitutional taking arguments that they ought to turn around and make it a plus. They know they're going to have to do this. Why not go into it? . . . They've done a splendid job of minimizing [problems] by going in and negotiating very astutely what those exactions ought to be . . . instead of challenging it. Had they challenged it, it would have been much worse."[29]

Other business leaders exhibited an even more striking change in outlook. Richard Watkins was the project manager for a commercial office tower that turned out to be the city's third tallest building. In 1982 he and his development company, Norland Properties, had agreed to a substantial housing linkage exaction in exchange for necessary construction permits. Four years later, Watkins reflected upon the practice of linkage in San Francisco's downtown development: "There is a social responsibility that goes back to the highest and best use of a valuable resource to the city—land. . . . The City is simply doing its job, recognizing that these projects have an impact on the environment, and saying, 'If you want to get that income stream, you've got to give something back.'" And attorney Marcia Rosen discerned a marked change in attitude on the part of developers and their counsel, based on her interaction with them: "We also, I think importantly, have built [linkage] into kind of the political-legal culture of acceptability within the development community in San Francisco. . . . I think if this were tried in some communities, there would be lawsuits immediately, but there is a certain acknowledgment here that there are some social . . . responsibilities that go along with development."[30]

The final legacy of the growth-control movement was the upswing in popular engagement in land use politics. Ordinary people became more aware of development debates and more likely to assume an active role in the political process. Some business people have accepted the ethos of participatory democracy regarding downtown development. Architect Jeff Heller said, "Big buildings are in the public realm, and therefore the public has a right to comment, control, and react to them and their desires. And that's one of the reasons we have always been comfortable with the public review process. . . . We were and still are advocating the business rights and interests, but at the same time we're trying to be sensitive to the people who react."[31] One builder even came to refer to community groups as "the conscience of the developer." He added, "But for the input of the community . . . [urban development] would be somewhat like a rampant car going downhill."[32] Such perceptions of growth-control activists are a far cry from those of a decade ago when the same people were "basically seen as outcasts, crazies."[33]

The business community's strategy for dealing with grassroots organizations concerned about the pace and character of downtown development evolved from one of hostile confrontation to one of constructive engagement. This transformation was best manifested by the Catellus Development Corporation, which commenced the largest development project in the city's history. It decided to pursue a "consensus-building process" that involved dozens of community meetings to work out conflicts and find common ground. Jim Jefferson, who worked as a consultant for Catellus, asserted that Catellus's strategy of embracing the community rather than fighting it attracted the attention of other developers who want to learn more about how to get development projects approved in San Francisco. He believed that other developers, even "mega-developers" such as Olympia and York, began to realize that the development process had changed in fundamental ways, that getting project approval required working with the community.[34]

In short, the business community retreated from its overwhelming opposition to linkage and growth limits and its deep suspicion of citizen participation in the development decision-making process. Some business leaders even came to view these progressive practices as positive attributes for their businesses and the city. In either case virtually all real estate interests adjusted to the change in the local political culture, as evidenced by their shifts in perspective and behavior.

Conclusion

Counterhegemonic activism produced a transformation in the political culture of San Francisco. Yet, that cultural transformation was not the kind of one-dimensional change that Marxian scholars might have anticipated. It was not simply a case of the workers of the world suddenly perceiving their oppressed state, casting off their chains, and demanding power. Individual groups in San Francisco experienced varying forms of transformations of consciousness. Taken together, those alterations created a very different cultural milieu, which, in turn, facilitated a transformation in political power.

There were commonalities in how diverse groups responded to the counterhegemonic efforts of growth-control activists. Most groups came to doubt the privatist assumption that a market-driven development of the downtown business district was an inherently positive phenomenon. Most came to perceive the social costs and limited benefits of the city's land use policies. Most came to adopt the progressive view that government action was needed to compel private developers to assume responsibility for how their projects adversely affect the larger community. Forceful government action to ensure equitable growth was widely accepted. And finally, there was broad support for the progressive value of popular control over downtown development.

Beyond these commonalities, however, different groups experienced different responses to growth-control activism. African Americans in some ways developed an individualistic orientation normally associated with a privatist culture. "What's in it for me?!" became a rallying cry in the city's black neighborhoods. But rather than continuing to look to the marketplace as the most dependable dispenser of goods and services, African Americans increasingly turned to the public realm. And, in another sharp break from prior practice, instead of relying on established political leaders to lobby for policy reforms, neighborhood residents became more self-assertive. Political passivity gave way to a sense of critical defiance of elite leadership and an unprecedented determination to participate directly in the shaping of one's own destiny.

Moderate growth-control activists were affected by the counterhegemonic practices of the progressive activists in another way. The premium placed on popular empowerment meant that in practice the growth-control movement became a broad-based, inclusionary movement representing diverse groups from all over the city. Exposure to a multitude of social groups and their varied needs and goals with respect to urban development had the effect of expanding the consciousness of activists who had once concentrated mainly on the postmaterial aspects of downtown growth. Adverse impacts on the environment and the city's cultural heritage remained important concerns for these activists, to be sure. But the shift to mass participation in land use politics alerted these activists to the material impacts of rapid downtown development too. Assuring downtown jobs for lower-income city residents became a priority. Protecting blue-collar employment in the light industrial South of Market neighborhood adjacent to the central business district also became a priority. Thus, moderate activists embraced the progressive principle of popular empowerment and in doing so they also came to embrace the progressive principle of using government to promote social and economic equity.

Counterhegemonic activism prompted city planners to alter their views on the nature of planning and, even more importantly, who should be making decisions on the future development of San Francisco. Whereas city planners once maintained a bricks-and-mortar perspective that limited government involvement in downtown development to physical development, contemporary planners came to adopt a more holistic approach that emphasizes the interconnectedness of social, economic, and physical planning. And planners largely relinquished their managerial beliefs about the necessity of trained experts making key decisions in favor of the progressive insistence that the citizenry should be the directing force. City planners came to see their primary role as one of simply providing guidance.

No matter how effective the counterhegemonic efforts of progressive activists were, no one would have expected downtown business leaders to adopt a progressive view of downtown development. Nor did this happen. But business leaders did show signs of moving away from the traditional privatist perspective. Publicly, they complained about government interference to regulate the pace and character of commercial office growth; privately, they conceded that the results of strict measures such as Proposition M were not so bad. Publicly, they complained about government interference to redistribute development-generated resources through linkage policies; privately, they admitted that linkage had not changed investment patterns much, and that there were even some positive aspects associated with linked development. Despite some noises of protest, business leaders went along with the changes pushed through by growth-control activists. And as those changes became institutionalized, they became part of the routine of land use practice and thus, ineluctably, a part of the consciousness of business leaders.

Different groups in San Francisco responded to the years of counterhegemonic activism by progressive activists in different ways. However, all underwent a decisive change in how they interpreted downtown development; those changes reflected the progressive vision of an expansive public sphere under popular control. Taken together, the individual shifts in consciousness amounted to a remarkable transformation in the local political culture. By the late 1980s San Franciscans had come to view land use matters through a progressive cultural prism.

✦8

Political Change

The years immediately following Proposition M's passage were crucial to determining the staying power of a progressive vision of land use politics. Leading scholars of urban politics, especially regime theorists, note that from time to time progressive candidates will get elected and progressive measures will get enacted into law. But whether progressives can hold onto power and govern effectively beyond the short term is another story. This is because downtown business interests use the many resources at their disposal to reward city officials who go along with their agenda and punish those who choose an alternative path. The gravitational forces that pull politicians into the downtown growth coalition's orbit are immensely powerful.

But traditional analyses of urban power relations that stress the role of material resources overlook how changes in the local political culture may alter how individuals, and even members of the downtown growth coalition, perceive their interests and options. The cultural transformation in San Francisco engendered by counterhegemonic activism established an atmosphere in which progressive political practices would continue to flourish. As such practices became institutionalized, they further solidified progressive ideas, values, and beliefs in the collective consciousness of the city, rendering the possibility of a resurgence of the old development policies less and less likely.

Development Politics after Proposition M

During the immediate post–Proposition M period, perhaps the first and most impressive indication that San Francisco was indeed undergoing lasting political change involved the metamorphosis of the growth-control movement's old adversary, Dianne Feinstein. Mayor Feinstein, who had just finished waging a skillful and energetic campaign against Prop. M, abruptly reversed course following the 1986 election. With only a year remaining in her term of office, and barred by law from seeking a third consecutive term, the mayor decided to cooperate with progressive activists. After a brief period in which she questioned the legality of Proposition M, Feinstein put aside her reservations about the initiative and ceased speaking out against the annual cap. With the issue of growth restrictions settled, the mayor turned her attention to other causes of concern to community groups. Calvin Welch, who had battled Feinstein for years, commented that Feinstein "became, y'know, the reformed alcoholic on affordable housing. She became a dynamo. She supported nonprofits, she agreed to reallocations of CDBG funds. . . . She supported individual projects. She mobilized the Planning Department and Redevelopment Agency towards affordable housing production. She recognized the primary role . . . of community-based nonprofit housing development corporations as the producers of affordable housing. She gave up this notion of trickle down."[1] Mayor Feinstein's shift on land use and housing issues in 1987 constituted firm evidence of the cultural/political transformation inspired by the growth-control movement.

Her successor did even more to sustain and cement that transformation. The progressive political culture proved to be ideally suited for the mayoral candidacy of state assemblyman Art Agnos. A former social worker with a long history of support for progressive issues, Agnos was able to build an impressive network of community-based organizations to work on his election bid. The grassroots strategy paid off as his standing in the polls steadily improved. On election day he won almost half the vote in a crowded primary and then defeated the moderate supervisor John Molinari with 70 percent of the vote in a runoff.

Throughout his mayoral campaign, Agnos reaffirmed his support for the growth-control movement's agenda, reminding voters that he had backed every growth-control initiative dating back to the early 1970s. He promised to use his power as mayor to further advance the principle of citizen participation in the policy-making process and to pursue regulatory and redistributive policies consistent with the spirit of Proposition M.

Once elected, Agnos in many ways kept his promises. With respect to popular empowerment, the mayor appointed a number of growth-control and affordable housing activists to key positions in city government. He virtually transformed the powerful Planning Commission overnight with three new appointments. Observers soon detected a change in how the Planning Commission conducted its business. The *Bay Guardian*, praising the commission's "record of openness" as "remarkable," reported that during the first six months of 1989 the Planning Commission "spent virtually no time in closed session," though they held twenty-four meetings totalling 131 hours. Planning Commission president Jim Morales said, "It is an obligation of government, and the planning process, to have as much public input as possible. . . . We are very proud of having a very open process and we try to accommodate all sides of an issue."[2]

With respect to regulating downtown development, Agnos moved to block the spread of highrise building beyond the traditional downtown district. This reversed one of the principal goals of the Feinstein administration's Downtown Plan—the shifting of commercial office development from the area north of Market Street to the area south of Market. Growth-control activists had always objected to the idea of creating, in effect, a second highrise district in a neighborhood that had long been home to much blue-collar industry and many lower-income residents. The battle lines were initially drawn in 1983 when Supervisor Bill Maher proposed a rezoning plan to protect the South of Market area from large-scale development. At the time, the Chamber of Commerce condemned the plan as an illegal infringement upon the rights of property owners to build revenue-producing offices. Opposed by the Feinstein administration, the plan went nowhere at first. But after 1987 the Agnos administration threw its weight behind the effort to limit highrise construction in South of Market. In March 1990, after intensive negotiations among the city, real estate groups, and community activists, the Board of Supervisors voted to approve a revised rezoning plan for the fifty-block South of Market district that would limit highrise office development to a few restricted areas and otherwise protect light industry, crafts, and small businesses ranging from print shops to film studios, as well as five thousand existing affordable housing units.[3]

Furthermore, the Agnos administration demonstrated support for the progressive goal of equitable growth by advocating a host of redistributive policies. It lobbied the Board of Supervisors to strengthen the housing linkage ordinance by raising the mitigation fee imposed on commercial office projects from $5 per square foot to $5.78 and by applying the measure to a wider range of office buildings. The previous ordinance applied to buildings fifty thousand square feet or larger, whereas the amended ordinance applied to buildings twenty-five thousand square feet or larger. By the end of 1990 the city had collected $29 million in housing linkage fees, which were used to build or renovate 5,690 housing units. The Agnos administration was particularly skillful in using locally generated revenue from housing linkage to leverage considerably greater sums from the federal and state governments and from private organizations. In 1990 San Francisco, which has one-third the population of Los Angeles, was able to raise three times as much revenue for housing from nonlocal sources as its southern California rival.[4] The Agnos administration's handling of the transit linkage program also helped to further entrench the practice of linkage in the local political culture. A 1991 report issued by the Planning Department stated that 144 office projects had contributed a total of $58.7 million. Much of that money had been tied up in escrow pending resolution of a lawsuit brought by a group of developers. But once a California appellate court upheld the constitutionality of the transit linkage ordinance in 1987, the Agnos administration was free to use that substantial sum to finance capital projects and pay for operating costs linked to the higher demand on MUNI generated by the downtown building boom.[5]

In addition, the Agnos administration advocated inclusionary housing policies, an alternative form of linked development. A typical inclusionary housing regulation requires developers of market-rate housing to set aside a fixed percentage of their apartment units for lower-income people in exchange for official permission to build. Along with creating more affordable housing, the policy advances the goal of fostering a stronger sense of community by integrating different socioeconomic classes within a neighborhood. When inclusionary zoning was first proposed elsewhere in the state in the late 1970s, the Building Industry Association and the state Association of Realtors pressured municipalities into abandoning dozens of proposals. *San Francisco Examiner* correspondent Bradley Inman wrote that inclusionary housing "symbolized the fears of government intervention and was treated as a threat to property rights." But by the late 1980s, the environment in San Francisco was conducive to such an initiative. The Planning Commission adopted an inclusionary housing policy that took effect in July 1990 requiring developers of projects of more than ten units to set aside 10 percent of their units as affordable.[6] That policy was expected to generate between 150 and 200 affordable housing units per year.

That same year, the Redevelopment Agency adopted an even more aggressive inclusionary housing policy for developments in urban renewal areas. Under the new rules, housing projects built on public land had to set aside at least four of every ten dwellings for low- and moderate-income buyers or renters and keep them at below-market rates for fifty years. Also, projects built on private land in renewal areas had to set aside one-fifth of the units for low- and moderate-income buyers or renters or pay a fee for a comparable number of units to be built elsewhere in the city. City officials anticipated that the new rules would generate five thousand affordable housing units during the next ten to fifteen years. Commenting on the new policy, Rick Devine, an analyst with a nonprofit organization that monitors housing development policy nationwide, said: "To my knowledge, this is the most stringent requirement in the country. San Francisco took the national lead with its office-housing mitigation fee [which extracts money for housing from office developers seeking to build in the city] and this takes the city a step further." Bill Rumpf, head of housing production and management at the Redevelopment Agency, emphasized the unusual character of the new rules by noting that inclusionary housing requirements are rarely imposed on developers who own their land in renewal districts.[7]

Of the variety of linkage policies advocated during the Agnos administration, perhaps the most innovative new linkage policy aimed at ensuring equitable growth pertained to employment. In May 1991 the Planning Commission adopted a resolution establishing a nonprofit corporation called the Central Employment Brokerage Association (CEBA). Marcia Rosen, an attorney who helped draft the resolution, called it "a landmark step in an over-six-year struggle to have private downtown developers have some responsibility for creating jobs for low-income San Francisco residents." The board of directors of the new employment agency would be equally divided between representatives of community-based employment agencies and downtown developers. The agency would be a central clearinghouse providing accurate information on what kinds of jobs are being created by the downtown office buildings and what people are getting the new jobs; moreover, the agency would require that developers of commercial office buildings work with employment agencies to ensure that San Francisco residents would, in fact, be hired.[8]

As with the other linkage policies, the legal authority for this program was rooted in the mitigation provisions of the California Environmental Quality Act. That statute requires that a developer mitigate the negative environmental impacts of its project, *unless* the developer can demonstrate the existence of an overriding societal benefit. In almost all cases developers have findings in their EIRs that their proposed projects will create job opportunities for local residents and that this benefit outweighs all other negative impacts. Growth-control activists generally concede that new jobs are created, but then point out that the societal benefit is limited by the fact that most of the new jobs go to upper-middle-class people who live in the suburbs and whose commuting to and from work exacerbates air pollution.

The Board of Supervisors had actually enacted a weak version of employment linkage in 1985 as an amendment to the Downtown Plan. But the 1985 measure permitted developers to establish and operate their own employment brokerage service for each project. Activists discovered that monitoring the developers' implementation of the employment outreach placement and training services was an impossible task. Rosen explained: "What we found was developers really resisted this, and it was a very big job for the community to monitor compliance when the developer had this individual responsibility, and no one was looking at the overall picture. So we came to the conclusion that . . . forming this new nonprofit would be a way of empowering the community organizations and giving them a centralized view of the big picture. And this we think is a significant step."[9]

City officials were well aware of the controversial nature of an employment linkage program that pressured developers of new commercial office buildings to hire local residents. Apart from ideological objections about government interfering in employment decisions, Planning Director Macris said that "[new developers were] very conscious of putting their buildings at a disadvantage because they're having to compete with renting space with a building that doesn't have those kinds of requirements. So their argument was, 'You'll destroy our marketability for this building if you impose something that we in turn impose on the tenant, the user of the building.' They just didn't want to do that and the [Planning] Commission listened to that." To obviate expected hostility from developers, the city tried to present the CEBA as an attractive employment service, not as an intrusive and coercive public policy. Planning Commissioner Doug Engmann, himself a business person, explained:

> My point . . . is to create CEBA as an attractive alternative to tenants who might hire through employment agencies, and the whole concept was for [developers] to actually provide a real service to employers who want to hire. If you can provide a source of people to be hired and not have to pay the employment agency fees, you've created a real service for the tenants of your building. And to the extent that the CEBA was able to provide that kind of pool of candidates, it would be accepted and the whole concept of hiring locally would be implemented a lot easier than trying to jawbone tenants into hiring because they don't happen to meet certain kinds of criteria.

Yet while city officials were eager to "sell" jobs linkage as a worthwhile service to developers, they were at the same time willing to apply pressure to ensure that downtown development would, in fact, create jobs for San Francisco residents. Although Planning Commissioner Doug Engmann conceded that enforcement is "very, very difficult" in the event of noncompliance, he believed the city could resort to "jawboning" developers, especially those that have permit applications for another project pending. For instance, city planner Paul Lord, who supervised the CEBA program, noted that the Planning Department could delay the tenant improvement permit process if developers failed to comply.[10]

Thus, city officials and activists hoped to obligate new developers to participate in the CEBA and then, once the value of the program had been established with this select group, market the program to existing commercial property owners as a useful service. But the collapse of the real estate market in the early 1990s hampered efforts to get the CEBA off the ground.[11] Nevertheless, growth-control activists believe that when the real estate market recovers, the institutional machinery will be in place to hold developers accountable for their promises to provide employment opportunities to local residents.

In sum, after the passage of Proposition M in 1986, a host of policies implemented at the end of the Feinstein administration and throughout the Agnos administration helped to validate such progressive goals as broad popular participation in the planning process and an equitable development of the city. Downtown development was now guided by a healthy mix of developmental, regulatory, and redistributive policies, something that would have been inconceivable when a privatist vision dominated the local political culture prior to the 1980s.

Development Politics in the 1990s

To appreciate the extent to which a progressive political culture had taken hold in San Francisco, it will be illuminating to look at the city's handling of the largest development project in the city's history, the Mission Bay development, as well as more routine downtown projects. This examination illustrates how land use politics in San Francisco became a routinely progressive phenomenon.

The proposed site for the massive Mission Bay project is a 315-acre expanse of abandoned railroad yards and warehouses in the China Basin district along San Francisco Bay just south of downtown. Underutilized since the 1940s when the Southern Pacific Railroad moved its operations to Oakland, the value of the site soared in the 1970s because of its attractive location. Hoping to cash in on its suddenly lucrative property, Southern Pacific submitted several development proposals in the late 1970s and early 1980s ranging from "a suburb in the city," featuring garden apartments, ranch-style houses, and spacious lawns, to a grandiose plan for, in effect, a second downtown for San Francisco.[12] With growth-control activism heating up, neither plan moved forward. Still, negotiating over the Mission Bay project continued sporadically during the next few years.

It was not until Proposition M passed in 1986 that real progress was made. The new owner of the development site, the Catellus Development Corporation, decided that, given the power of the growth-control movement, a novel approach would be necessary if Mission Bay were ever to be built. To overcome the climate of suspicion toward developers and large-scale development projects, Catellus decided to open up the planning process and encourage widespread community participation. Pamela Duffy, the lead attorney for Catellus in the Mission Bay project, described the post–Proposition M thinking:

> The whole notion of the plan was that a project of this scale and magnitude was never going to get approved . . . if there wasn't very good communication about what it was all about and what the constraints were and what was totally unfeasible. . . . So that was the process of beginning to build consensus. The notion was that if people are informed and they feel like their opinions are going to have an influence, they're more likely to have some confidence that what you say is truthful and begin to work with you rather than shutting them out and saying this is what we're going to do and you're an idiot. So that was really the point was to pull the

> public into the process . . . give them access to information and data and not what some developers have a tendency to do . . . y'know, assume that . . . they don't understand and won't understand and if they do understand that their agenda is just no-growth and so they'll use the information you've given against you.

Duffy also noted that with its new project director for Mission Bay, a long-time San Francisco resident named James Augustino, "Catellus brought perhaps a little fuller understanding of those issues . . . certainly more than their predecessors did, who had a series of disastrous planning proposals that were just phenomenally insensitive to the community."[13]

Growth-control activists were gratified by Catellus's novel commitment to citizen participation but nevertheless remained skeptical, wondering whether the developer had simply adopted an appealing facade to obscure its business-as-usual approach. That skepticism deepened when the Feinstein administration refused to allow any neighborhood-based organizations to participate in the initial round of negotiations set to begin in 1987. City officials insisted they could be more effective in dealing with Catellus if they took the first crack at negotiating a development plan before opening up the process to all concerned groups.[14] That policy remained in place even after the new Agnos administration took over following the 1987 mayoral election. Growth-control activists were stunned that an avowedly progressive mayor had decided to limit citizen participation at such an important stage of the development process.[15]

In general, both the Feinstein and the Agnos administrations wanted to see a large, mixed-use development consisting of low-rise office buildings and a range of housing, retail businesses, community buildings, and parks. In January 1990 the Agnos administration released the plan that it had negotiated with Catellus. The key elements were:

- 4.8 million square feet of office space
- 8,000 housing units, 3,000 of which would be affordable
- Over 23,000 jobs, with preference given to San Francisco residents
- Job training programs for women, minorities and locally-owned businesses
- Maximum building height of eight stories
- Clean-up of toxics
- 67 acres of public parks and open space
- Public facilities, including child care and senior centers, a school, fire and police station, theater and community center
- $217 million in surplus revenue to the city during the first 30 years (offset by $100 million the city would spend on housing subsidies during the same period)

Commenting on the plan in January 1990, Mayor Agnos said, "This is the best package I can put together prior to public review. It will become even better when more public input has been heard." Catellus expressed confidence that the deal, loaded with public amenities, would gain wide support from San Francisco voters, who would have to approve the project as an exemption from Proposition M's annual limit of 475,000 square feet of office space. James Augustino, Catellus's project director for Mission Bay, declared, "We're very comfortable that this project will stand the test of public scrutiny. We feel we've got something that is do-able, and we feel the city has done a good job in protecting and enhancing the city's interests."[16] Walter Keiser, a Berkeley economist advising the city, remarked, "Anybody who can oppose a project that takes an industrial wasteland inundated with toxics and turns it into a viable neighborhood with 3,000 affordable housing units and 70 acres of parks is out of their mind."[17]

But opposition to the Mission Bay project did develop. Growth-control activists were incensed that they had been ignored by the mayor during the previous two years of negotiations. In their view Agnos had betrayed his promise of open government and extensive citizen participation. Although Agnos had promised adequate time for public review and comment, many activists feared that it would be difficult to amend the plan in any significant way. When the mayor appeared at a community meeting in Potrero Hill, a neighborhood adjacent to Mission Bay, he heard stern criticism from disgruntled activists for shutting community groups out of the process. One told him, "The Art Agnos we knew as a candidate is not the same Art Agnos we know as mayor."[18]

The Planning Commission, which had won praise from activists for opening its business to the public during the Agnos years, scheduled informational workshops in March and April to address substantive points of controversy. Perhaps the most often heard complaint concerned the jobs-housing imbalance. Put simply, activists argued that the plan would create several thousand more jobs than housing units, thus aggravating the city's housing crunch. Others expressed concern that the three thousand units of affordable housing were not sufficiently affordable. Jim Morales, the president of the Planning Commission, asserted, "A certain number of people working in Mission Bay will not be able to afford housing. Until we can provide housing for these lower-income employees, the plan is unacceptable." Still others focused on the toxic waste cleanup. After lengthy negotiations, Catellus had agreed to pay for the cleanup of toxic residues on the site and complete the job before any future residents would move in. Activists, however, insisted on the right to oversee the cleanup process. Environmentalists also wanted more open space to make up for the high density of residential and commercial buildings and the creation of a 12.5-acre wetland park on the Bay. Finally, African American activists viewed the jobs linkage provisions with skepticism. They had often heard developers make generous commitments for minority hiring, only to see those commitments go unrealized. This time, activists demanded that the affirmative action programs be offered in the context of a legally enforceable contract.[19]

In short, the Mission Bay proposal was subjected to a level of scrutiny at the Planning Commission rarely seen in urban development politics. One Catellus official remembers that "the Planning Commission literally read every single page of that document.... They went through it with just a toothpick. It was just unbelievable."[20] Public participation also intensified during the summer of 1990; two dozen hearings, each one ranging from four to ten hours, were held to examine the development agreement. The planning department's project director for Mission Bay, Alec Bash, estimated that as many as fifty civic groups participated in the planning process.[21]

The Planning Commission's review produced a number of changes intended to satisfy the activists. First, to help mitigate the increased housing demand generated by the project, the developer promised to extend its linkage obligation by contributing another $4 million to build 250 residential hotels in nearby neighborhoods. Second, the new plan deepened the city's housing subsidies to ensure that one-third of Mission Bay's 3,000 below-market units would be affordable to singles earning less than $16,000 a year and families earning less than $24,000 a year. Thus, under the new plan, Catellus and the city would jointly build 8,250 units of housing, 3,250 of which would be affordable. The city's share of affordable housing would be 2,300 units, of which 1,000 would be affordable to very-low-income residents. Catellus's share would be 925, of which 250 would be affordable to very-low-income residents. Third, to satisfy the environmentalists, Catellus agreed to create an eleven-acre wetlands near the mouth of Mission Creek.[22]

With respect to affirmative action provisions, Catellus had reason to reach an agreement that would be acceptable to the African American community. Knowing that San Francisco voters would have to approve the Mission Bay project as an exemption from Proposition M's annual limit on office construction, Catellus was mindful of the need to court black citizens. They were widely seen as a pivotal constituency in what would probably be a close election. Therefore, Catellus proposed an attractive four-part plan. First, it put together an economic development package that included clearly established goals for a small-business participation program, an employment program, and a minority business program for *all* aspects of the project. Second, cognizant of mounting distrust of developers in the African American community, Catellus accepted the necessity of putting its promises into contractual form and backed up with strict financial penalties in the event of noncompliance. Third, the contract was drafted to give legal standing to any group of citizens, not just personally aggrieved individuals, as a third-party beneficiary to the contract, to file a lawsuit to force Catellus to abide by the contract's terms. Finally, to make the affirmative action goals more achievable, Catellus agreed to put up $12.5 million to provide working capital for new minority businesses. African American activists were satisfied that this time they had reached an agreement with a developer whose promises would be carried out.[23]

In August the Planning Commission voted seven to zero to approve the amended five-hundred-page development agreement. The progressive weekly the *Bay Guardian* praised the new agreement in an editorial as "a vast improvement over previous proposals." It went on to declare:

> The Agnos-appointed commissioners squeezed far more concessions out of the developer, Catellus Corp., than previous commissioners ever would have. The project isn't anywhere near as bad as when Southern Pacific first put plans on the table in 1983. It isn't as bad as when Agnos and Santa Fe Pacific Realty . . . passed it on to the commission earlier this year. . . . The Planning Commission did its best to promote public input, open discussion and reasonable changes in the project. The process was a far cry from the Feinstein days, when something like this might well have been rammed through with little debate and less public input.[24]

Catellus was also pleased. It believed that it had devoted a great deal of time and energy to soliciting the views of a wide range of community groups and trying to accommodate those views. As the Proposition I campaign began in the fall of 1990, Catellus felt optimistic that San Franciscans would vote to exempt the Mission Bay project from Proposition M's annual restriction on commercial office development.

Yet many neighborhood activists retained doubts about even the modified agreement. Calvin Welch remarked, "There's no question the Planning Commission helped make some changes to the plan. But you have to consider how lopsided the agreement was when it first came into the public arena. It was flawed by nature, and still is." One problem was the continuing jobs-housing imbalance. Although the Planning Commission had succeeded in increasing the number of below-market housing units for low-income residents, activists charged it had done little to alter the fundamental problem of allotting only 8,250 dwellings to accommodate an expected workforce of 23,000; that imbalance would aggravate San Francisco's housing crunch. Second, the new agreement required the city to raise $150 million to subsidize affordable housing but did not specify how the city would raise the revenue. If future administrations were unable to find the money, the majority of low-cost housing intended to mitigate the impact of the jobs/housing imbalance would never be built. Third, although Catellus promised to provide an array of public amenities, activists were concerned about the lack of enforcement mechanisms to ensure compliance. For instance, Catellus had agreed to remove toxic residue from the project site, but the agreement did not specify who would monitor the clean-up.[25]

Growth-control activists ran an aggressive campaign on the theme that the city could still negotiate a better deal with Catellus. But for the first time, there was a serious rupture in the progressive coalition. Progressive black activists concluded that Catellus had satisfied their demands regarding their primary concern, employment opportunities for lower-income citizens, and thus broke ranks with their old allies. Yet the loss of progressive blacks was partly compensated for by support from an unlikely source. Walter Shorenstein, the city's biggest developer, decided to oppose the exemption for Mission Bay because he feared it would generate competition for the many commercial office buildings that he owned downtown. Shorenstein donated eighty thousand dollars to the campaign against Mission Bay.[26]

On election day the initiative to exempt Mission Bay was defeated by a margin of only 554 votes. Planning Commission president James Morales, who had supported the initiative, soon announced that city planners and Catellus would resume negotiations to devise a new plan for Mission Bay. Officials at Catellus publicly expressed a willingness to make additional changes to win over the city's influential progressive activists.[27]

In the weeks after the election, Catellus took steps to ensure that the affordable housing would be truly affordable to low-income residents. Affordable units would range in price from $37,000 to $147,000 and would be available to individuals and families earning between $15,400 and $56,000 a year. The revised scheme would also add another 250 affordable housing units, thus raising the total to 3,500 affordable units.[28]

In addition, housing activists restructured the timing of the housing/office construction so as to give Catellus an economic vested interest in the city's performance of its promise to build affordable housing. The development agreement provided that Catellus could not build at a rate in excess of 712 square feet of commercial office space for each housing unit developed. Attorney Marcia Rosen explained the significance: "We can now hold up . . . their office developments if the city does not produce its share of affordable housing, and that is really significant, that we now have political pressure on the city that the housing is the necessary antecedent to future commercial development. . . . It's not unusual to tell a developer you can't go forward unless you've met your obligations, but now we're telling Catellus you can't go forward unless the *city* has met the obligations. Catellus in a way becomes an informal guarantor of the city meeting its responsibilities."[29] The changes satisfied the activists. The Board of Supervisors voted ten to one to approve the revised plan for Mission Bay.

The uniqueness of the Mission Bay development agreement was emphasized by practically everyone who had been involved in the process. Substantively, the deal offered an "extraordinary number of linkages" in housing, employment, transportation, recreation, child care, and public art. Catellus thus set a remarkable precedent regarding the extent to which it accepted responsibility as a large-scale developer to mitigate the adverse effects of its project and give something back to the community. Procedurally, the planning process during the final year was marked by extensive public participation, which reflected Catellus's willingness to embrace the concept of working with neighborhood groups from the start. Jim Jefferson observed: "Most developers spend all of their time and resources trying to fight the community as opposed to sitting down [with community groups]. Although I'm sure many developers thought that the Catellus people were crazy to be sitting down negotiating with neighborhood groups, but that's the way business gets done in San Francisco."[30]

Unfortunately, reaching a landmark development agreement is one thing; making that agreement a reality is another. The sharp downturn in the real estate market in 1991 meant that Catellus could not proceed with plans to construct the first cluster of commercial office buildings. Prospective tenants were no longer available and wary lenders pulled back. Hence, the driving force for the rest of the Mission Bay development had been wiped out. The project was put on hold and the development agreement expired after five years in 1996.[31]

But momentum picked up again when Catellus learned that the University of California at San Francisco wanted to expand its medical school facilities and was considering various sites throughout the Bay Area. An aggressive lobbying campaign ended successfully when Catellus announced in May 1997 that UCSF had agreed to build an $800 million biomedical center on forty-three acres at Mission Bay. With such an attractive tenant as an anchor, the developer planned a new business park that would surround the campus and serve primarily biomedical-compatible companies. Catellus anticipated that this would yield 5 million square feet of commercial office space and eight thousand jobs.[32] Progress on the commercial front enabled the developer to move forward with other aspects of the project and in July 1997 the city and Catellus declared that they had agreed on yet another blueprint for Mission Bay. The highlights of the plan are:

Six thousand units of housing (approximately one-third would be "affordable")

UCSF campus, consisting of three buildings of 125, 000 square feet each, providing a total of eight thousand jobs
Five million square feet of commercial and industrial space around the campus and serving biotech firms
Two hundred fifty thousand square feet of retail space
At least thirty-eight acres of open space
Land donated by Catellus for a school and fire and police stations[33]

The proposed deal resembles the 1991 development agreement in a number of ways, but there are some notable departures too. For instance, it allows for the possibility of a five-hundred-room waterfront hotel and a number of fifteen-story residential towers and details about the affordable housing component remain fuzzy. At the time of this writing, growth-control activists have not yet had an opportunity to respond to the latest plan, but given the progressive norms of citizen control over land use decision making and activist government to assure orderly and equitable growth there is little doubt that Mission Bay will undergo additional modifications prior to the scheduled start of construction in late 1998.

In the years since the passage of Proposition M, a progressive politics has also characterized more routine development projects in downtown San Francisco. The confluence of strict limits on annual commercial office construction and the proliferation of linkage policies continued to advance the goal of equitable growth. When in 1985 the Board of Supervisors passed the Downtown Plan, which included an annual cap on office development, it was forced to establish a competition to determine which developers would be entitled to proceed with their projects. The yearly competition came to be known as the "beauty contest" and, as the name suggests, city planners at the time felt that architectural and design features should be the most important factor in choosing among the many applicants.[34]

But perceptions of downtown development were evolving quickly during the mid-1980s. By 1987 the *Chronicle*'s architecture critic, Allan Temko, noted that the winners of that year's beauty contest mainly benefited from the *economic* amenities they offered: "The three projects almost certainly will be approved when they come before the planning commission later this month because economic attractiveness is an even more important criterion in the beauty contest than architectural quality." Planning Director Macris confirmed that "the criterion of architectural merit has diminished in importance considerably from the first round." Instead, he noted that the Agnos Planning Commission has prompted it to be more concerned with questions like "How is this building going to be used? Who's going to use it? What kind of jobs are going to be in it?" For their part, developers were quick to catch on to the shift in expectations. For example, in 1989 one entrant in the beauty contest frequently reminded the Planning Commission that its thirty-four-story highrise offered sufficiently large floor space to accommodate back office jobs that had been moving to lower-cost sites in the suburbs.[35]

Thus, the annual growth limits contained first in the Downtown Plan and then in the more restrictive Proposition M have allowed the city to be selective, choosing what kinds of buildings and what kinds of uses it wants. Andy Nash of San Francisco Tomorrow described how Proposition M has worked to the city's advantage:

> I had lunch with Don Fisher from The Gap because he's been talking about Proposition M. . . . I said to him his building will have no trouble through the process because he's a local business; we like the kind of stuff they do, that's a great company to have located in your city. . . . He would contribute to the social good of the city. He would contribute to making sure there was better MUNI service, making sure there was affordable housing. He would do it because that's the kind of company it is. And that's the kind of company we want.[36]

But the advantages of having a development cap have exceeded even the expectations of growth-control activists. Developers realized that a five-hundred-thousand-square-foot cap on downtown office growth allows for only a small number of projects each year. For their proposed projects to be selected, developers understood that it was no longer sufficient simply to comply with existing provisions in the Planning Code, even though those provisions already included the most demanding linkage exactions in the nation. Developers now recognized that it was necessary to compete with other developers by offering public amenities *above and beyond* those mandated by law. City planner Larry Badiner pointed out that the Agnos Planning Commission came to expect such a competition. "The [Planning] Commission can . . . demand, because it's a competition for space, can demand things above and beyond what the code requirements are. And it's really a question of whether you go above and beyond the code requirements. . . . The Agnos Commission clearly wanted to see a number of things beyond the strict code requirements."[37]

In the 1991 beauty contest, the Bechtel Corporation was competing against a developer that offered an impressive employment and training program for minority residents. Marcia Rosen, who was involved in the negotiations, said that Bechtel was initially reluctant to do anything other than comply with the law. As a multinational developer, Bechtel was "used to calling the shots wherever they go and for awhile they played hardball," threatening to bring legal action and to embarrass the mayor in an election year. But Bechtel eventually changed its stance at the negotiating table, and its project was later approved after Bechtel agreed to provide a minority and women's business program, participate in the CEBA program for local residents, and in general "do a lot more than they initially said they were going to do."[38]

Attorneys for the development community confirmed that Proposition M's annual growth limit engendered a situation in which developers tried to outbid each other in terms of public amenities as a way of winning development rights. Bob Thompson described what has become a familiar scenario:

> We represented Crocker Land Co. in their attempts to get [development rights to the site at] 3rd and Mission.... It wasn't a beauty contest situation, but it was certainly a competition because the Redevelopment Agency basically put the site up for bid. Y'know, come and make us your best offer. That included preservation of the Jesse St. substation; a couple of other amenities were insisted upon. But then it just kept escalating between the parties. Y'know, more and more money for housing, more and more money for this.... And I think the same clearly existed [with the beauty contest].

From his perspective as a member of the Planning Commission, Doug Engmann added, "Many of [the developers] in the competition have aggressively promoted their ability to meet those linkages. I think they understood from '87 on they have to do that, particularly in the Agnos administration where you had a commission that was looking for those kinds of linkages." And, of course, the activists are pleased with the competition generated by Proposition M's annual cap. Andy Nash remarked, "I think it's a great idea.... I think every city should do it. We should be auctioning off development rights. If you want to build in our city, y'know, you pay for these parcels and we control it in a very—I'm probably a socialist or something—in a very organized and logical way."[39]

Populist Mayor/Progressive Politics

A peculiar thing happened in 1991. Just as a progressive political culture came to dominate the politics of downtown development in San Francisco, voters decided to reject the avowedly progressive mayor, Art Agnos, and elect instead a moderate populist,[40] Frank Jordan. This apparently puzzling event had ramifications for the city's land use politics.

Mayor Agnos was defeated in large measure because he had alienated his progressive base. It was not just his endorsement of projects such as a downtown baseball stadium and hotels on the waterfront that angered progressives. What most bothered his former supporters was the manner in which he conducted his administration. After assembling a powerful grassroots coalition that got him elected mayor in the first place, Agnos promptly turned his back on community organizations and largely excluded them from meaningful involvement in key decisions. Regarding the ballpark, Andy Nash of SFT commented, "We had questions about the process the mayor went through. . . . I quite frankly felt that if he had brought more people in so that they could have worked with him . . . and toned down some things and improved some things, we could have been for it. . . . A lot of [SFT] Board members were in favor of it."[41] His barring of growth-control activists and neighborhood-based groups from the negotiations with the developer of the Mission Bay project was another example. Because Agnos had campaigned as a progressive and promised open government, the sense of betrayal was intense.

Agnos compounded problems within his electoral base by playing one group off against another. For instance, he would tell affordable housing activists that the city was broke because it was funding AIDS research and treatment and vice-versa. If any group crossed the mayor, Agnos was capable of being extremely vindictive. Calvin Welch declared, "By the end of his term, there was not . . . an electoral political entity that was not weakened by internal divisions. The divisions ran along the lines of, do we support this asshole or don't we? I mean that's what it came down to." But consternation with Agnos's performance in office did not generate any progressive alternatives. Welch said, "There was a real failure . . . of community political leadership to overcome . . . the animosities that Art unleashed."[42] Without a candidate to rally around, many progressives lost interest in the 1991 election.

The situation created a vacuum that a former police chief, Frank Jordan, was able to fill. Jordan ran his campaign as a moderate populist reaching out to people who felt they had been ignored in city politics ever since the Alioto administration in the 1960s. He charged that neither the downtown business elites who had always backed Dianne Feinstein nor the progressive groups who had originally supported George Moscone and later Art Agnos had ever paid much attention to the problems of rising crime, dirty streets, and the increase in homeless people soliciting pedestrians. Homeowners in the more conventional southern and western neighborhoods of San Francisco believed that they finally had a candidate who could relate to their interests and champion their causes. Feeling empowered for the first time in decades, they rallied around Frank Jordan's mayoral campaign. By September Agnos realized that he was in trouble. He apologized profusely at campaign rallies for "losing touch" with his constituents and promised a renewed commitment to open government in his second term.[43] But it was not enough. On election day, Jordan, capitalizing on the anti-incumbent mood sweeping throughout the country, pulled off a stunning upset and defeated Agnos.

Jordan's victory reflected the empowerment of older and more conservative homeowners in the neighborhoods that had been revitalized politically by the growth-control movement. Although they had traditionally identified with the views of the downtown growth coalition, by the early 1990s they had become ardent defenders of Proposition M. The homeowners liked the measure of control over downtown that the citizens initiative had given them. The Jordan campaign further politicized areas of the city that had largely opted out of city politics for over two decades. Political commentator Tim Redmond described the unusual scene on election night: "The strangest thing about the Jordan victory party was the number of strangers in the room: I've been covering these things for 10 years now, and I didn't recognize more than three or four people. . . . There weren't many big-business types, or social climbers, and hardly anyone seemed to have the vaguest interest in becoming a commissioner. The Jordan faithful were almost exclusively white, mostly middle-aged, and invariably dressed for an old-fashioned working-class house party: lots of polyester, no blue jeans."[44] In many ways, therefore, the growth-control movement's success in promoting the progressive ideal of popular empowerment helped make the Jordan phenomenon possible. As ordinary citizens were politicized in response to growth-control activism, they became a potent force in mayoral politics. But when progressives balked in getting behind Agnos, and with the downtown growth coalition in disarray, an opportunity opened up for long-neglected homeowners in the more conservative neighborhoods to flex their muscle and elect one of their own.

Although Frank Jordan's constituency shared with the progressives a commitment to popular empowerment, populists do not evince the same enthusiasm for an activist public sphere. Instead, government is viewed with suspicion, as an institution that, notwithstanding America's democratic creed, inevitably comes under the sway of groups whose interests are antithetical to those of the average person in the neighborhood struggling to make a decent living. In San Francisco, Jordan's populist supporters believed that city government had long been controlled by either downtown elites or left-wing activists from neighborhoods they rarely had reason to visit. No matter which group controlled city government, the Jordan constituency felt that the government was inherently incapable of acknowledging its needs and aspirations. That being the case, the Jordan populists preferred to minimize the scope of the public sphere in order to maximize the opportunity of ordinary people to fulfill their potential. In their minds limited government offered the most promising path to popular empowerment. Frank Jordan's populism thus represented a new vision of politics in San Francisco, one that was distinct from the privatist vision of the downtown growth coalition and the progressive vision of the growth- control movement. It would not last long.

When the new mayor took office in 1992, he immediately encountered one problem after another related to his inexperience with governing a major U.S. city. Moreover, his populist determination to bring fresh faces into his administration and thus empower a previously disempowered constituency only added to his difficulties in mastering the art of governance. Jordan quickly developed an image as a well-meaning neophyte, even a bumbler. As San Franciscans began to lose confidence in his administration, the mayor reached out for help. Given his populist predilection for the private market and his distrust of government, he turned not to the progressive neighborhood groups, but to the business community. Several well-known downtown elites were offered important positions in the still young Jordan administration. This turn to the downtown growth coalition certainly worried growth-control activists, who feared that the achievements of the growth-control movement—growth limits, linkage policies, broad public participation in the development process—might be in jeopardy.

But two decades of growth-control activism had resulted in fundamental changes in the city's political culture. Not only would a return to the old ways be difficult to carry out; it was not clear that downtown business leaders really wanted to head in that direction anyway. The principles of Proposition M had antagonized downtown elites for years, but few people in the first year of the Jordan administration called for its repeal; few even criticized it. And although Jordan appointed an entirely new Planning Commission and replaced Dean Macris as the head of the Planning Department, the appointees seemed content to follow land use policies set during the preceding administration. Former Commissioner Doug Engmann commented, "I don't see the Planning Commission that's been appointed as [being] that different than the Planning Commissions that have existed in the Feinstein or Agnos years. Maybe a little more conservative, a little bit more development-oriented and having their own ideas about how things ought to be run, but I don't see significant shifts in policy." Engmann observed that any attempt to "throw out all the work that's gone into" particular policies would show a "real naïveté about what you can and can't do in the city." For one, "it belies the power of neighborhood organizations" to seek such a reversal. But just as importantly, perceptions about development have changed in fundamental ways. "I know the people who are on the Planning Commission. I know they believe in housing, affordable housing.... you can't sit in that position, know what the residence element of the Master

Plan is, know what our housing problems are, and not try to take advantage of opportunities . . . that have already been established. I mean you have part of your responsibility to try and develop that housing. So when a developer comes forward, and [linkage has already been established], you push."[45] Likewise, Calvin Welch was cautiously optimistic about the Jordan Planning Commission. He noted, "They are fairly cognizant of the relationship . . . between affordable housing and economic development"; they had affirmed their support for the city's inclusionary housing program and the policy of restricting the conversion of residential hotels to tourist hotels.[46]

In some ways the Jordan administration even extended progressive land use policies. A discount retailer sought permission to build a giant outlet store in the South of Market area in early 1992. Although the housing linkage ordinance applied only to *commercial office* development, the Jordan Planning Commission prodded the retail company into abiding by the linkage ordinance anyway and making a substantial contribution to the affordable housing fund. Marcia Rosen remarked, "The new president of the Planning Commission . . . whose name is Sidney Unobsky, apparently he is one of the major shopping center developers in the country. And I had never seen him as a visible player in any kind of San Francisco land use politics before. But he's the one who ended up apparently putting the muscle on [the retailer], which shocked the hell out of the community people." Moreover, the new Planning Commission also demonstrated a commitment to citizen participation, thus continuing the practice of the Agnos commission and improving upon the practice of the former mayor. By law there is an annual review process to consider compliance with the Mission Bay development agreement. In 1992 activists testified that Catellus was not cooperating satisfactorily in providing affordable housing: "When [Planning Commission President Sidney Unobsky] heard Calvin [Welch] testify about [how] they were nowhere on the affordable housing and there still was no financing plan, there was still no advisory committee, he called a meeting between him and Calvin and said what can we do, y'know, to push Catellus and the city into complying? And we were all blown away that, y'know, this is not who we thought Jordan would be appointing."[47]

What accounts for the willingness of a nonprogressive administration to nevertheless continue pursuing progressive policies regarding downtown development is the transformation of the local political culture engendered by the growth-control movement. The new appointees, regardless of their ideological inclinations, were now operating within an environment that was culturally predisposed toward progressive practices. Such practices had become reasonable and desirable in the context of a progressive political culture that was now hegemonic.

Conclusion

Perhaps the strongest testament to the extent of cultural/political change in San Francisco with respect to the politics of downtown development involved the behavior of the Jordan administration, which was widely considered to be a moderate or conservative administration on most issues. Progressive ideas, values, beliefs, and practices regarding downtown development had so deeply saturated the local political culture that even Frank Jordan and his top appointees approached land use policy in ways that were perfectly acceptable to the growth-control activists. Cultural change had yielded enduring political change.

In 1995 San Franciscans voted the moderate populist Frank Jordan out of the mayor's office and replaced him with the flamboyant Willie Brown, former speaker of the state assembly. Growth-control activisits were not sure what to expect from the new mayor. On one hand, Brown had often taken liberal positions on many social and economic issues; on the other hand, he also had a long history of cooperating with major real estate developers. But just like his predecessor, Brown was moving into a new political culture, one that he was reluctant to combat. Rather, he soon began to appoint prominent growth-control advocates to high-level posts in city government. Marcia Rosen was named head of the Mayor's Office of Housing; Jim Morales took over as chief of the Redevelopment Agency; and, perhaps most significantly, Mayor Brown began to meet with the influential activist Calvin Welch every Friday morning at City Hall.[48]

Such access to power has further cemented a progressive politics of urban development. For example, the Brown administration prepared a $100 million bond issue to fund affordable housing production during the next decade. Although property taxes would be raised to pay off the bonds, 67.6 percent of all voters in the November 1996 election supported the measure, just barely enough to clear the two-thirds majority needed for approval. Of the total $100 million, 85 percent would enable the city's housing providers to renovate at least three thousand rental units, and the remaining 15 percent would go to a loan program to assist first-time home owners with down payments. Moreover, the public money generated from the bond issue was then used to leverage an additional $300 million from Wells Fargo Bank and $50 million from the AFL-CIO Housing Trust for affordable housing. This only reinforced San Francisco's reputation as one of the nation's leaders in the area of housing and community development.[49]

A powerful argument can thus be made that the progressive reforms initiated by the growth-control movement during the 1980s have endured over the years.[50] The key to the longevity has been the entrenchment of a progressive political culture that has significantly altered how both ordinary citizens and elites view their interests and options. It follows that progressive policy making is likely to last for as long as that political culture remains hegemonic in San Francisco. For that to happen, the activisits reponsible for cultural/political change in the city (as well as their successors) must continue to be active in pressing their vision of politics. And therein lies the danger of some kind of cultural/political backsliding. Since the collapse of the downtown real estate market, growth-control activisits have lost their primary motivation for mobilizing. Although some have moved into positions of governance and others are still active in neighborhood affairs, many have withdrawn from the political sphere. The lack of ongoing political activity increases the possibility of a cultural vacuum opening up, thereby creating space for a revival of privatist ideas, values, beliefs, and practices, which are alive and well in myriad locales beyond San Francisco.

Of course, even the smallest spark might be enough to rally a seemingly dormant activist community committed to a progressive vision. With respect to downtown development, after over six years of virtually no new construction, the demand for commercial office space has recently increased. As of July 1996, San Francisco had the third lowest office vacancy rate in the United States at 6.3 percent.[51] As the amount of available office space continues to decline and rents rise, another round of downtown development is almost inevitable. When that occurs, the growth-control activists can be expected to organize once again to ensure that any new development is both orderly and equitable. Only this time they will wage their battles within a cultural milieu already slanted in favor of progressive politics and policy making.

Part 3
Washington, D.C.

✦

✦9

The Hegemony of Privatism (2)

As in San Francisco, rapid downtown expansion in Washington, D.C., during the 1970s and 1980s sparked neighborhood-based opposition to the growth coalition's policies. Activists advocated an alternative vision of politics emphasizing popular control over decision making and a more activist government to ensure a more equitable distribution of the costs and benefits of downtown development. But ultimately they failed to engender the sweeping changes that occurred in San Francisco.

The inability of the Washington growth-control movement to transform the local political culture proved decisive. Whereas growth-control activists in San Francisco offered a coherent oppositional vision and engaged in practices that were consistent with that vision, Washington activists could not muster the same counterhegemonic force. The two principal contingents of the growth-control movement, although purportedly committed to a progressive vision of politics, actually offered a brand of grassroots activism that was more consistent with a managerial and populist vision respectively (see chaps. 10 and 11). This detracted from the counterhegemonic potential of the neighborhood activists and rendered their movement vulnerable to divisive and co-optive strategies. The failure to transform the local political culture meant that Washingtonians would continue to evaluate their interests and options through a cultural prism that privileged privatist ideas, values, beliefs, and practices. In such a cultural environment, the policy preferences of the downtown growth coalition always appeared to be the more compelling path to downtown development.

Early Development of the Federal City

Any study of urban development in Washington, D.C., must begin with the original plan for the city prepared by the French engineer Pierre Charles L'Enfant. Chosen in 1791 to design a capital on the swampy banks of the Potomac and

Anacostia Rivers, L'Enfant imagined a grand city of majestic buildings, glorious monuments, and inspiring vistas—an awesome symbol to the world of America's noble experiment with democracy. The central element of his plan was a triangle formed by the Capitol, the "President's House," and a monument to George Washington. Each structure would be on high ground, thus assuring visibility from afar, and each would be linked to the other by broad, tree-lined boulevards. Other public buildings and foreign embassies would arise in the immediate vicinity. Beyond this monumental core, L'Enfant foresaw the development of a large and bustling city with a full panoply of commercial, cultural, civic, and residential uses, all of which would be functionally and visually integrated with the governmental center. It would be a capital city worthy of a great republic. And indeed, in the history of American urban planning, the L'Enfant plan would be regarded as a remarkable achievement.[1]

Unfortunately, L'Enfant never saw his plan realized. Although construction of the Capitol and what came to be known as the White House began promptly, the young nation lacked resources to do very much else. As a result the federal mall degenerated into an unsightly sheep pasture, and Washington remained a small and sleepy town for decades. That changed rather abruptly when the Civil War brought a massive influx of Union soldiers to protect the capital, civil servants to administer the war effort, and more than forty thousand former slaves who had escaped from bondage in the South. The population boom, together with the establishment of a streetcar system in the District, pushed the boundaries of urban life well beyond the area surrounding the mall. Commercial activity shifted several blocks to the north away from Pennsylvania Avenue as F Street became the center of the city's new business district. Luxurious mansions and ornate townhouses for the affluent were built farther to the north and west.[2]

But the city was not growing into the grand and inspiring place that L'Enfant had envisioned. Physical expansion proceeded in a piecemeal, pell-mell manner that translated into anything but the harmonious order promised by the original plan. As new residents continued to stream into the city, conditions in Washington's already congested and impoverished neighborhoods deteriorated. At this point Alexander "Boss" Shepherd, the flamboyant head of the Board of Public Works, initiated an ambitious campaign to improve and extend the District's infrastructure. In two short years he supervised the installment of hundreds of miles of sewers, water mains, gas lines, and sidewalks; the planting of tens of thousands of trees; and the construction of markets, schools, and other civic buildings. But Shepherd's aggressive effort to accommodate the District's growth came at a heavy price. He had executed his vast public works program in an arrogant manner and in the process alienated many prominent citizens and business leaders. Furthermore, critics charged that the unprecedented cost of Shepherd's campaign threatened to bankrupt the District; others questioned whether Shepherd and his underlings had enriched themselves at the city's expense. In any event, Congress lost confidence in the ability of the municipal government to handle its own affairs and in 1874 took the extraordinary step of assuming direct control over the District. A full century passed before home rule was restored.[3]

Washington's experience with rapid growth was not unlike that of many other U.S. cities of the era. As the myriad social and economic ills associated with rampant urbanization in late-nineteenth-century America became increasingly evident, the profession of city planning emerged with a solution. City planners insisted that cities could avoid or at least minimize many of their problems if they would simply engage in careful, long-term, comprehensive planning. In particular, city planners of the day embraced the principles of the City Beautiful movement: controlled and orderly development, natural beauty, monumental form, wide boulevards, and civic spirit. And nowhere was the City Beautiful movement embraced more enthusiastically than in the nation's capital. With its palatial public buildings and stirring monuments to America's past glory, Washington was a perfect fit. Pierre L'Enfant had anticipated the ideals of the City Beautiful movement by over a hundred years, and city planners now relished the opportunity to revive his plan. Beautification would be the answer to the mounting urban crisis.[4]

In 1901 a commission of highly respected planners and architects assembled by Senator James McMillan of Michigan, the chair of the Senate Committee for the District of Columbia, issued its bold plan. The McMillan plan recommended an extension and improvement of the mall; a memorial to Abraham Lincoln near the Potomac River; a series of immense, classically designed buildings lining the mall and filling in the area between the Capitol and the White House; a huge railroad station just north of the Capitol (and elimination of the existing rail station in the middle of the mall); acquisition of park land along the Potomac and Anacostia Rivers; and creation of a large park in Rock Creek Valley as well as smaller parks throughout the District. City planners believed that the numerous physical improvements and the protection of nature in an otherwise dirty and overcrowded city would boost the public's morale, promote civic pride, and encourage the masses to lead virtuous lives. The McMillan plan would guide development in the District for years to come.[5]

But given its emphasis on the ceremonial core and its heavy slant toward physical rather than social planning, the McMillan plan did little to address directly the poverty and congestion that afflicted many of the city's residential neighborhoods. The situation was particularly bad for the District's African American community. After hopes were raised during the first decade of

Reconstruction that race relations might improve, progress on civil rights ground to a sudden halt, and the city lapsed into its old ways. Then came the ignominious era of Jim Crow and a further deepening of the racial gulf as white racism intensified first in the Deep South and then spread throughout much of the country. In Washington employment discrimination in both the public and the private sectors was pervasive, and extensive use of racially restrictive covenants barred even the city's proud black middle class from moving into white neighborhoods.[6] Unwelcomed by white Washingtonians, black Washingtonians banded together and built their own communities with vibrant institutions and strong social, economic, and political bonds.

The next wave of urban development in the District of Columbia occurred in the 1930s and 1940s when the federal government swelled first in response to FDR's New Deal and later to fight a world war. In a twenty-year period, the District's population nearly doubled, going from 486,869 to 802,178. The population explosion put enormous pressure on the city's housing stock. Although there was some new construction, supply never kept pace with demand, and long-time residents, many of whom were black, were displaced. Perhaps the most notorious case of black displacement, and one of the nation's earliest experiences with gentrification, took place in colonial Georgetown. Once a thriving port city on the Potomac that predated Washington, by the early twentieth century Georgetown had become a quiet, predominantly black neighborhood. With the housing crunch of the 1930s, however, young white civil servants flocked to Georgetown, attracted by its quaint townhouses and relative proximity to government jobs. Gentrification soon spread to other black neighborhoods such as Foggy Bottom and the West End. Thousands of African Americans were forced to seek shelter in the city's back alleys, in small, overcrowded dwellings that often lacked modern plumbing and electricity.[7]

Growth pressures brought on by the federal government's expansion thus heightened the competition for affordable housing and employment. On both scores the city's African American community suffered. Pervasive racial discrimination had always meant that black citizens would be given lowest priority, but unprecedented population growth during the 1930s seriously exacerbated an already grim situation. Accordingly, the 1930s also witnessed an upsurge in black protest in Washington. Black civic associations became increasingly active in pressing for more affordable housing in the wake of mounting displacement pressures in Georgetown and other near-downtown neighborhoods. Also, the New Negro Alliance was formed to fight for an end to job discrimination by white businesses operating in black neighborhoods. Its use of consumer boycotts proved to be an effective weapon in compelling business owners to change their ways.[8] But with the outbreak of World War II, debates over housing, employment, and urban development subsided as the city, along with the rest of the nation, turned its collective attention to fighting the war.

Two features, then, distinguish Washington's development from that of other U.S. cities. First, as the nation's capital Washington has from the beginning accorded a prominent role to its core of federal government buildings, monuments, and landmarks. Second, largely because of the federal presence, urban growth has often proceeded under a managerial political culture characterized by broad state involvement in city planning by professional planners, architects, and engineers. L'Enfant's managerial approach to guiding the growth and development of the District proved to be enduring, and that legacy has given Washington's political culture a unique twist.

But not that unique. After all, beyond the ceremonial core, Washington has always been a fairly typical city with ordinary citizens going about their routine business.[9] Moreover, L'Enfant's plan was all but forgotten for most of the nineteenth century, when Washington expanded much like any other American city during the era of mass urbanization. Privatism prevailed for decades as city elites did their best to follow and react to powerful societal forces acting upon the national landscape. And after a renewed flurry with managerialism during the ascendancy of city planning in the early years of the twentieth century, Washington joined the rest of urban America in fully embracing the ideas, values, beliefs, and practices of privatism following World War II.

The Downtown Building Boom

Americans returned from the battlefields in Europe and Asia to a nation that was much like it had been before the war and yet at the same time was a nation on the verge of an unprecedented transformation. On one hand Washington still confronted many of the same old problems: a congested city, a desperate shortage of affordable housing, an aging downtown business district, and chronic poverty in residential neighborhoods just a stone's throw from the mall. On the other hand, changes in the global economy portended dramatic changes for life in the District. Throughout the United States, urban manufacturing was already on the decline as factories were moving out of the cities and relocating to areas with lower production costs—the suburbs, the Sunbelt, and eventually developing nations overseas. In its place a postindustrial economy based on corporate services, information, and advanced technology was emerging, and its nerve center was the downtown business districts of large U.S. cities. This transformation was fortuitous for Washington; since the city had never been an industrial power, the downside of economic restructuring was minimal, but the upside of an ascendant postindustrial economy looked very promising.[10]

The other major societal trend affecting urban America during the postwar years also seemed attractive to Washington's leaders, at least at first. Suburbanization was perceived as a welcome phenomenon because it would relieve pressure on the overly crowded urban core, alleviate the housing shortage, and defuse racial tensions. Thus, civic and business leaders in the years following World War II concluded that all they had to do was to go along with the natural forces already at work throughout America and many of the District's most intractable problems would diminish. The primary role of the public sector would be to facilitate positive trends in the private sector, and government would rely on skilled professionals to make sure the job was executed efficiently. In short, a privatist vision of politics would guide the growth and development of the city in the postwar era.

In 1950 the National Capital Planning Commission (NCPC) released a comprehensive plan for the metropolitan area that was consistent with the decentralizing impulses of the day. It recommended construction of a series of spoke highways connecting the downtown core with a couple of belt highways, one around the business district and the other around the entire District. This conformed to Americans' growing infatuation with the automobile and their desire to move quickly, conveniently, and independently in commuting between their new homes in the suburbs and their jobs in the city. The NCPC also advised dispersing some federal government agencies throughout the metropolitan area to relieve congestion around the mall.[11]

At the same time, city planners were eager to encourage the expansion of a postindustrial economy linked to the heart of the District. But the focal point of new commercial office development would no longer be the old downtown business district just a few blocks east of the White House. Although businesses in that area had prospered during the 1930s and 1940s because of the federal government's rapid growth, after the war developers looked to the west, where land values were lower. In effect, a second business district emerged along the K Street and Connecticut Avenue corridors as law firms, trade associations, and lobbying groups rushed in to sign leases in the new buildings.

To ensure that private investment in the District would remain strong, city planners felt it was necessary to do something about the decaying residential neighborhoods that surrounded the mall and the business district. In their view these neighborhoods with their dilapidated homes and stores were a deterrent to future downtown development. Congress's enactment of the Housing Act of 1949 gave cities a mechanism with which to revive blighted areas by providing generous federal subsidies to underwrite the cost of land assembly and clearance. In exchange, cities would then be obligated to construct affordable housing for the residents who had been displaced. The 1949 law was later amended, however, to give cities more options concerning how to redevelop the land, and developers took full advantage to build much more lucrative office buildings and market-rate housing for middle- and upper-middle class people who would want to work in the nearby offices. When this happened, former residents were forced to relocate to other sections of the city, often in public housing projects with limited access to jobs, shopping, and transportation.[12] This is exactly the scenario that unfolded when District leaders selected a poor black neighborhood in the southwest quadrant of the city just below the mall as their first major redevelopment site and one of the first urban renewal projects in the nation.

The public backlash against certain aspects of the District's redevelopment plans, namely urban renewal and the proposed highway system, was substantial. First, African Americans attacked the city's designation of southwest Washington as a blighted area when the Redevelopment Land Agency's own study had found a high degree of residential stability in the neighborhood. Second, they criticized the decision to raze an entire neighborhood when rehabilitation would have revitalized the area but at a greatly reduced cost to local residents. And third, they denounced a redevelopment strategy that had caused the forced displacement of thousands of people and destroyed what had been a stable, albeit poor, community. Outraged black citizens soon picked up significant support from white citizens in the District who were anxious about highway plans that threatened to displace thousands of residents near Rock Creek Park. With public opposition building, District leaders were compelled to reevaluate the 1950 comprehensive plan.[13]

By the early 1960s, city leaders had made a number of important adjustments. First, urban renewal efforts in residential neighborhoods would now emphasize rehabilitation instead of demolition and reconstruction; also, redevelopment programs would be implemented so as to minimize the displacement of residents. Second, a new planning document issued by the National Capital Planning Commission moved away from automobile-centric transportation planning by eliminating proposed highways that would have run through existing neighborhoods and instead declared its intention to build a state-of-the-art rail transit system to serve the metropolitan area.[14] Each of these changes was expected to reduce significantly the volume of popular protest emanating from the neighborhoods in reaction to the city's earlier development plans.

At the same time, the city expedited its efforts to reinvigorate the old downtown district. While the K Street/Connecticut Avenue corridors continued to flourish to the west, the traditional business district had stagnated. The area was beginning to look seedy, notwithstanding its desirable location between the White House and the Capitol. One strategy was to place the center of the planned metro rail system in the heart of the downtown district; the influx of commuters would surely boost business activity and investment interest. Another was the formation in 1960 of an organization called Downtown Progress to promote downtown development. The organization established a planning staff, hired consultants, and obtained congressional authority to utilize urban renewal powers in the downtown core.

Despite these efforts, most developers continued to build office buildings and hotels in the new business district throughout the 1960s. Whatever private investment interest had existed in the old business district suddenly vanished following the 1968 riots triggered by Martin Luther King's assassination. Much of the devastation took place only a few short blocks north of the old downtown core, and the lingering blight postponed substantial development activity for nearly another decade.

Public investment, however, increased. Most prominently, construction finally got under way in 1969 on the downtown-centered metrorail system. The city also acquired large tracts of downtown property as urban renewal sites and announced plans for a new downtown convention center. Finally, the federal government created a development corporation to revitalize the deteriorating Pennsylvania Avenue corridor, which connects the Capitol with the White House; the Pennsylvania Development Corporation assembled large tracts of land and began promoting a number of ambitious, multiuse developments such as the renovation of the Old Post Office. These actions were instrumental in prompting private investors to reconsider the east end of the business district as a potential growth area just as commercial office space was becoming increasingly scarce in the K Street/Connecticut Avenue district.[15]

At this point important changes in local politics were taking place. The civil rights movement had reignited popular demands for the restoration of home rule in the District, and by the early 1970s most high-ranking officials in the federal government, including President Richard Nixon, had declared their support for such a measure. The last obstacle fell away in 1972 when the chair of the House District Affairs Committee, John L. McMillan, was defeated in a reelection bid. McMillan, a southern conservative and segregationist, had long opposed granting home rule powers to a city with a majority of blacks. His removal from the scene paved the way for Washingtonians to finally regain the right to elect their own representatives in 1974. Congress did retain several important controls over District affairs, most notably oversight of the city's budget and judicial system and a veto power over all local legislation. But as the historian Howard Gillette observed, home rule gave Washington its first opportunity to take the initiative in setting its own policy agenda. The city seized that opportunity, and with few exceptions Congress showed restraint in not interfering in local issues, especially regarding downtown development, during the next two decades.[16]

Although Walter Washington served as the first mayor of the District of the Columbia, the one individual who has been at the center of local politics since the adoption of home rule has been Marion Barry. His rise to power was swift. Born into rural poverty in the Deep South, Barry was the first in his family to attend college and later studied chemistry as a graduate student at Fisk University. He then joined the civil rights movement and became a founding member of the Student Non-Violent Coordinating Committee (SNCC). In 1965 Barry moved to Washington to start up a branch office of SNCC, where he attracted considerable publicity advocating civil rights and pressing for home rule in the District. In 1971 he won his first campaign, getting elected president of the District School Board. Shortly thereafter he captured an at-large seat on the District Council, and by 1978 Barry was ready to run for mayor.

In doing so, Barry took on the incumbent mayor, Walter Washington, and the chair of the District Council, Sterling Tucker, both established political leaders with strong ties to the city's black middle class. Barry decided early on that his best hope for victory was to secure the backing of the downtown business community and white voters in the northwest quadrant of the city. His opposition to a series of tax measures condemned by the Metropolitan Washington Board of Trade earned him some support from business leaders. Still, the downtown establishment remained cool to the former militant civil rights activist; although the Board of Trade declined to endorse any mayoral candidate, most of its campaign contributions went to Sterling Tucker. Barry proved to be more successful courting middle-class, white voters, who perceived the candidate as a reformer.[17] The strategy worked. Although the three candidates divided the black vote, Barry seized an impressive 53 percent of the white vote, enough to give him a narrow victory over his veteran rivals.

The new mayor immediately set out to bolster the confidence of downtown business elites in his administration by doing two things. First, he responded to the sizable budget deficit he had inherited from his predecessor and an unexpected $25 million reduction in the annual federal appropriation to the District by carrying out a number of austerity measures, including laying off four thousand of the city's sixty thousand employees.[18] Second, Barry enthusiastically endorsed the policy of aggressive downtown development as the city's primary urban revitalization plan. Along with opposing new taxes on business, the mayor sought to foster a favorable investment climate by trimming red tape and expediting the permit process for new developments. Barry also backed plans for several high-profile projects such as a large-scale, mixed-use complex on the Georgetown waterfront, as well as a multitude of proposed office buildings, hotels, and retail facilities. The timing was perfect. Just as Barry had moved into city hall, the downtown building boom accelerated into a higher gear with commercial office construction leading the way (see table 9.1).

As downtown construction increased, demand kept up with supply. The occupancy rate of office buildings in the District was 98.9 percent in 1980 and 99.5 percent in 1981. With developable properties fast disappearing in the K Street/Connecticut Avenue area, private developers finally heeded the wishes of city planners and turned back to the old downtown business district. Property values in the East End tripled from roughly $200 per square foot in 1976 to over $600 in 1981 as developers scrambled to purchase real estate and construct office buildings. In April 1981 a block-long stretch of seedy pornography shops was sold to a Canadian developer for $615 per square foot. Local developer Oliver T. Carr succinctly summed up the booming downtown office market: "The word is delirious."[19] The immediate motivation was easy to discern; rental rates for new, first-class, downtown office space were shooting upward (see table 9.2). Office rents were rising all over the country, especially in cities with unique amenities. As the home of the federal government, Washington was clearly attractive to investors. Trade associations and prestigious law firms needed to be close to the center of political power. Furthermore, the urban atmosphere appealed to business leaders contemplating relocation. Downtown Washington, with its human-scale architecture, open spaces, sunlight, pedestrian-friendly environment, and proximity to restaurants, museums, and landmarks, offered an inviting setting. City officials were well aware of their advantages; when the city planning director was asked why businesses did not bypass the high office rents in the District and move to Maryland and Virginia in greater numbers, he replied:

> Well, that's a good one. And the reason they can't say that is because downtown Washington, D.C., is not Virginia or Maryland. Look around. You can walk around here and you go out to any one of them suburbs and ask where would I rather be? You ask the corporate president. . . . Ask my employees where would they want to be. They'd want to be right here. The metro stops here. . . . The central city is back . . . because you want to be able to walk around the block. You want to be able to feel it. You want to be able to see people. You want to be able to go to the dentist right down the street like I do.

And veteran city planner Nate Gross added, "There's nothing like the prestige or the location of being in downtown Washington. And what we have left to develop is not only between the White House and the Congress, but it's near some other interesting areas as well: Chinatown, our emerging arts district, and Pennsylvania Avenue, which you can see is looking pretty grand these days.

Table 9.1. Commercial Office Construction in Central Business District, Washington, D.C., 1972-1983 (in millions of square feet)

Year	New Office Space
1972	0.4
1973	0.7
1974	0.2
1975	1.1
1976	0.6
1977	0.5
1978	1.7
1979	1.0
1980	2.1
1981	1.5
1982	3.5
1983	3.9

SOURCE: *Development Review and Outlook, 1984-1985,* 70

So it has a lot going for it in comparison with other office locations around the region."[20] The combination of convenience and ambience proved to be a powerful formula for new economic investment. By the mid-1980s downtown Washington had become one of the nation's hottest real estate markets (see table 9.3).

Finally, the downtown building boom was not confined to commercial office development. The retail industry also flourished during this period. In a striking reversal from postwar patterns, Washington witnessed the construction of the only full-sized, free-standing department store in the downtown business district of a major U.S. city since 1945. The opening of that Hecht's department store complemented the renovation of two others in the Metro Center area, which helped to revitalize smaller retail establishments along F Street, the city's traditional shopping corridor. Other retail centers at Georgetown Park (220,000 square feet), the Old Post Office (50,000 square feet), and the National Place (126,000 square feet) opened during the early 1980s. Also, a jump in hotel construction brought two new luxury hotels to the West End and four new hotels clustered around the downtown convention center, offering a total of 2,468 rooms for tourists, conventioneers, and others with business in the nation's capital.[21] Downtown development in Washington was booming, and the Barry administration and the downtown business community were pleased. And by and large, so were most citizens. Home rule had been restored and the District seemed to be thriving.

Table 9.2. Standard Lease Rates for New Class A Office Space in Downtown Washington, D.C., 1980-1984 (dollars per square foot)

Year	Range
1980	$18.00-22.00
1981	$20.00-35.00
1982	$21.00-37.00
1983	$23.00-42.00

SOURCE: *Urban Land Institute Market Profiles, 1986* (Washington, D.C.: Urban Land Institute, 1986), 206

Evaluating Downtown Development

Washington's downtown boom appeared to fulfill the expectations of progrowth advocates and reaffirm the values and assumptions of a privatist vision of politics. Commercial office growth generated a substantial increase in property tax revenue from $230 million in 1981 to $780 million in 1991,[22] revenue that presumably could be used to fund affordable housing programs and improve public services in the city's neighborhoods. Also, Mayor Barry asserted that downtown growth created a plethora of construction jobs, many of which went to residents of the District. The mayor instituted a minority partnership program to ensure that black citizens would reap some of the financial rewards of the building boom by being included as partners in major development projects. Aside from materially benefiting District residents, the city's development policies helped to reinvigorate a decaying downtown core. The Urban Land Institute observed in 1987 that the Franklin Square section of downtown Washington, "once the home of pornography shops and bars, has now become a respectable and established office node."[23] Indeed, the newest wave of construction sweeping through the East End showcased the latest in postmodern architecture—stylish and decorative office buildings and hotels that enhanced the human scale and pedestrian-friendly environment of downtown Washington. Even growth-control activists who were mainly concerned with community development agreed that downtown had come a long way: "Washington, D.C., is very proud of what took place in downtown. I remember I came to this city nine years ago.... Downtown looked like hell. There were lots of old, decaying buildings, blackened buildings, boarded-up buildings. It looked like hell. And I said, 'Is this the nation's capital?' And today I can't say that. It's a big difference today. I'm proud I live in a city with such a beautiful downtown."[24] The retail district around Metro Center was flourishing, and lively new festival marketplaces on the periphery of downtown in Georgetown and at the renovated Union Station added to the general sense that Washingtonians were prosper-

Table 9.3. Rental Rates for Class A Office Space in Downtown Business Districts of U.S. Cities, 1984 (dollars per square foot)

City	Average	Range
New York City	$42.17	$24.75-75.75
San Francisco	$34.00	$29.00-39.00
Los Angeles	$28.50	$19.00-38.00
Washington	$26.20	$13.50-36.00
Miami	$26.00	$22.00-30.00
Denver	$25.00	$22.00-28.00
Houston	$24.00	$12.00-30.50
Boston	$22.76	$18.00-30.00
San Diego	$21.60	$16.80-35.40
Hartford	$21.00	$13.50-24.00

SOURCE: *Development Review and Outlook, 1984-1985,* 73.

ing and enjoying themselves. Finally, the downtown building boom had helped to rejuvenate nearby residential neighborhoods by encouraging an influx of young white-collar workers who wanted to be a pleasant walk or a short Metro ride away from their downtown jobs.[25] There seemed to be plenty of evidence to support the position of the downtown growth coalition that downtown development in Washington was improving the material well-being and overall quality of life for District residents.

Some observers, however, were unimpressed with the purported benefits of downtown development. Although commercial office growth undeniably raised tax revenues, many wondered what the city had done with the money. Some of it was used to reduce the budget deficit that the Barry administration had inherited from its predecessor, and some of it was used to replace lost federal funds for social welfare programs. But the chair of the District Council, David Clarke, accused Mayor Barry of squandering the bulk of it by expanding the city's already large bureaucracy: "The building boom in the city ran the city's treasury for years. Barry didn't come back for tax increases because he would just take the increased commercial property tax base and spend it. And he would know what it was before we would. Wouldn't tell us. . . . Then about three years ago, we started really facing the problem. Well, what had he done with the money? He had gone and hired people. And he had put all the money into personnel and so it made it very difficult to cut back."[26] A *Washington Post* report that the District government had ballooned from thirty-nine thousand employees in 1982 to over forty-eight thousand just eight years later supported Clarke's charges. With the bureaucracy swallowing up so much of the revenue surplus, little was left over for programs to revitalize the city's struggling neighborhoods. John

Wilson, who later replaced David Clarke as chair of the District Council, observed, "It wasn't trickling down anywhere. Now we don't have the money to deal with the social problems."[27]

With respect to the employment opportunities that downtown development was supposed to create, again, many were disappointed. One problem was that a significant percentage of the new jobs in downtown office buildings required education levels that many District residents did not possess. Also, with a large labor pool available in the suburbs, employers had no special reason to give hiring priority to city dwellers. Causton Toney of the D.C. Chamber of Commerce was quite frank: "I would probably say, y'know, as long as employers don't have that incentive to hire D.C. residents that they don't really care. They don't care. I mean they simply don't care." As a result a senior official at the city's Office of Planning declared, "I guess the bad news is that consistently about two-thirds of the [downtown office] jobs are held by suburbanites."[28] With fewer city residents securing jobs downtown than had been expected and with less downtown-generated tax revenue finding its way to neighborhoods in need, some began to question just how beneficial downtown development had been.

Others began to express concern about the costs of rapid downtown development. To start, some were not entirely pleased with the appearance of the revitalized downtown business district. Urban design specialists criticized many of the development projects of the 1970s and 1980s for their lack of streetscape amenities and their unwelcoming feel: "By and large, the buildings have crowded out the old scales and overwhelmed it and there isn't much left of the grain of the old downtown that people used to find intimate, familiar, and friendly. They're somewhat intimidated by the new scale and the sleekness and the inaccessibility of the new spaces." Some long-time residents simply did not see the old downtown district as a national embarrassment desperately in need of revitalization. The area had been for decades the home to dozens of small businesses and in the minds of loyal patrons had a distinctive charm. A recent book on the city put it this way: "Before 1980 [downtown] was a neighborhood of townhouse storefronts: millinaries; pawnshops and printshops; hometown restaurants, such as Reeves Coffee Shop, which served up the best strawberry shortcake in the city, and Whitlow's Diner, which did the same with meatloaf. It was the only remaining part of downtown that had character and a sense of tradition."[29] Downtown development posed a serious threat to this way of life.

As construction accelerated, so did the displacement of small businesses in the downtown core. Commercial office development drove up the value of land so that only office buildings, hotels, and high-priced retail facilities could afford the escalating rents and property taxes. In his study of downtown expansion in Washington, social scientist Dennis E. Gale noted, "As competition for property in the CBD has increased, other types of businesses have felt the pressure. For example, traditional enterprises such as movie theaters and gas stations—dwindling in numbers even prior to the recent surge of reinvestment in the old downtown—have suffered the loss of leases, rising rents, or climbing property tax liabilities." Small-business owners joined together and formed the Downtown Retail Merchants Association in 1983 to fight a trend that threatened their existence. One store owner commented, "No matter how much empty space there is, developers just keep building. Washington needs special care, and it's not getting it. The developers are going to build Washington the way they want to."[30] One of the founders of the Downtown Retail Merchants Association contended that the city had decided to replace existing small businesses with more upscale boutiques and expensive restaurants. As a result, he concluded, downtown is no longer "a place for the middle class to shop."[31]

More broadly, downtown development threatened entire communities within the downtown district. For instance, the city initially wanted to build its new convention center in the middle of Chinatown, a neighborhood of about six hundred residents and forty restaurants. Community protests forced the city to move the proposed site two blocks west, but that solution proved inadequate. The convention center, which opened in 1983, sparked the further development of hotels and office complexes in the immediate area and a renewed cycle of real estate speculation that put considerable pressure on residents and businesses. A local physician who grew up in Chinatown said, "The people who are staying are struggling very hard. . . . The taxes are so great, it's driving people out." The city expressed an interest in building affordable housing to alleviate some of the pressure but then sought to steer new residential development several blocks north, where land values remained lower. As an alternative strategy for preserving the neighborhood, the city prepared a set of voluntary guidelines for office developers to use Asian design elements in their projects to maintain Chinatown's cultural heritage. But local residents doubted whether attention to architectural and design features would have much of an impact on the ability of Chinatown to survive as a neighborhood.[32]

The boom in commercial office development also had an adverse effect upon the city's stock of affordable housing. The most obvious problem occurred in residential areas within the downtown area, where real estate speculation encouraged landlords to convert their properties from residential use to more lucrative commercial uses. Some landlords would clear out all of their tenants in apartment buildings, demolish the structures, and use the land as parking facilities until a commercial office developer appeared with an offer to purchase the property at a greatly inflated price. Veteran city planner Nate Gross recalled: "In the Judiciary Square area downtown, that was close enough to the office market in the '70s that some land speculators did go ahead and clear the housing and operate it as surface parking lots. That was a real problem over there for many years. And, of course, the result was it prematurely depopulated the area. . . . The people who did that early speculation, a lot of them became parking lot operators, and they did a lot of displacement but without any government involvement or any obligation or any relocation payments." Gross estimated that in the Judiciary Square neighborhood about three hundred row houses were demolished, causing the displacement of between two thousand and three thousand residents.[33]

More housing was lost when small businesses that were displaced from the downtown business district because of rising property values relocated in nearby residential neighborhoods and in the process took over what had been residential buildings. Dupont Circle activist Ed Grandis commented, "You'll find law firms that can't afford the commercial space downtown but want to service those clients are going to turn the townhouses into law firms. . . . This is . . . not the way to protect the residential stock in a city."[34]

Downtown development also contributed to the gentrification of surrounding residential neighborhoods. Observers of the city's demographic shifts first became aware of the trend in the 1970s when office growth in the K Street/Connecticut Avenue corridors helped spark a "back-to-the-city" movement among young, upwardly mobile professionals. After two decades of unprecedented middle-class flight to the suburbs, this apparent reversal caught some observers by surprise. But the back-to-the-city movement is not hard to understand, particularly in a city like Washington with a burgeoning supply of high-status, white-collar jobs and a growing population of singles and childless couples. Many individuals who had been raised in the suburbs had become dissatisfied with what they felt was a sterile existence and now looked to the city as an exciting alternative. An urban lifestyle promised something new: social diversity, a cosmopolitan atmosphere, architecturally distinctive housing, neighborhoods with character, and good access to jobs in downtown office buildings. All of these amenities were available in such near-downtown neighborhoods as Foggy Bottom, Dupont Circle, Adams Morgan, Mount Pleasant, Logan Circle, Shaw, and Capitol Hill. All of these areas attracted back-to-the-city baby boomers. One scholar wrote in 1980, "Washington, D.C. has become the national leader in private neighborhood revitalization." A year later, a study by the U.S. Census Bureau confirmed that the gentrification of inner-city neighborhoods was occurring faster in Washington than in any other major American city.[35]

Gentrification has a number of positive features: it reenergizes what may have been a transitional or declining neighborhood, bolsters local businesses, and generates tax revenue for revenue-starved cities. But the downside is that

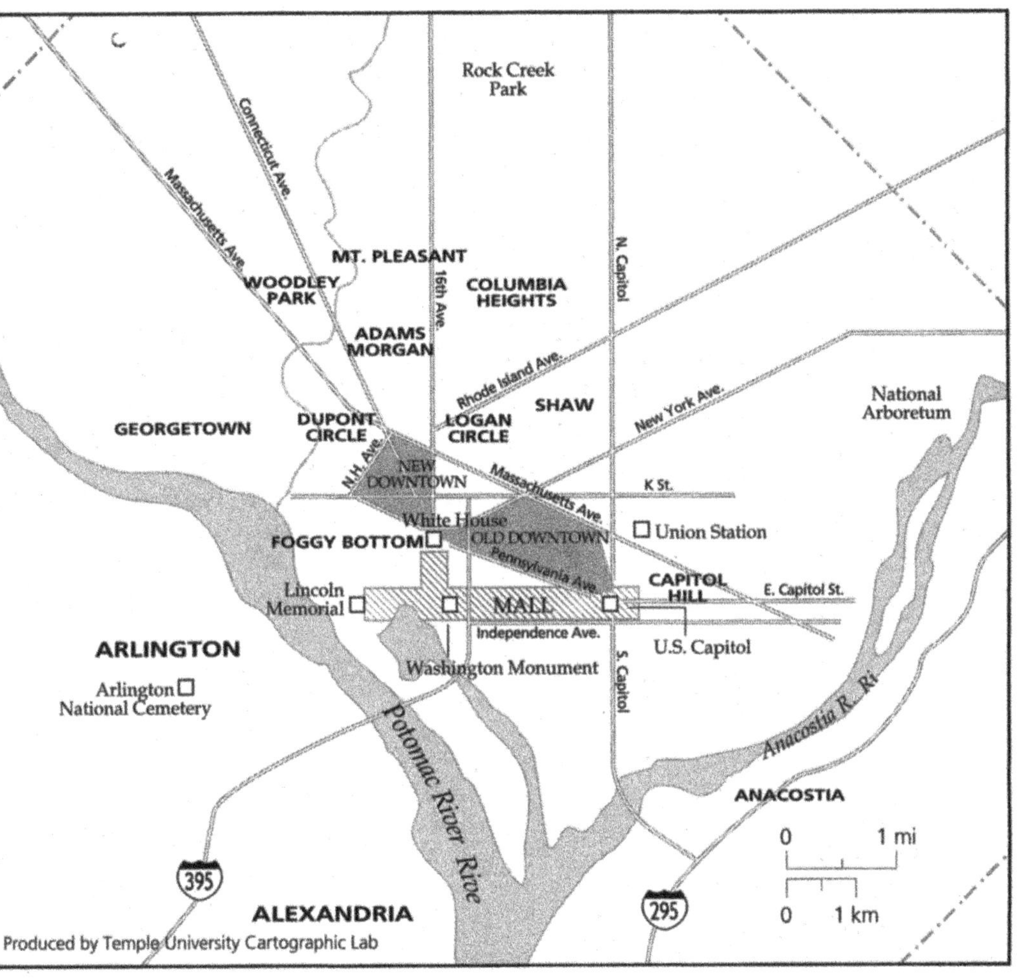

residents may be displaced when rapidly rising property values translate into steep increases in rents and property tax assessments. The shady practices of real estate speculators only add to the displacement pressures. A 1979 study issued by the Washington Urban League found that two-thirds of all homeowners in close-in neighborhoods had been approached by real estate interests about the possibility of selling their homes.[36] If residents were unwilling to sell at the proffered price, many found themselves subjected to visits from housing inspectors searching for code violations; if they lacked the means to undertake whatever repairs were ordered, some homeowners were then forced to sell their homes to the speculators. Once the speculators obtained title, they would turn around and sell the property, often realizing an exorbitant profit in the process. "Flipping" was a common practice in Washington's gentrifying neighborhoods. One researcher reported that "between October 1972 and September 1974 . . . one out of every five sales of homes in the District involved two or more sales of the same property, 80% within 10 months of each other."[37]

A study by the District of Columbia Advisory Committee to the U.S. Commission on Civil Rights in 1981 determined that displacement of black and Latino families in Dupont Circle and Capitol Hill was "nearly complete" and that displacement was "substantially under way" in a number of other close-in neighborhoods.[38] Even one of the city's more historically renowned black neighborhoods could not avoid the problems caused by gentrification because of its proximity to the downtown business district. During much of the twentieth century, the area around the busy commercial corridors of U Street and 14th Street had been the African American community's economic and cultural center. But that neighborhood, which later came to be known as Shaw, was the scene of the 1968 riots and had fallen on hard times. As the downtown building boom gathered steam, Shaw residents felt the same displacement pressures that lower-income groups had experienced in other close-in neighborhoods. Community activist Ibrahim Mumin observed, "You can see them scoping out the area in their Mercedes and BMWs. There are tremendous external pressures we can't control in our neighborhood."[39]

Gentrification of the District's inner-ring neighborhoods thus resulted in considerable displacement of working-class and lower-income residents, and especially black residents. A 1985 study of demographic trends stated: "In contrast to the slight gains in percent black registered by the adjacent and peripheral areas of Washington, the representation of blacks in the revitalizing core declined sharply, from 69.7 percent to 55.6 percent of the core population. This decline was the consequence of a net loss of 37,000 black residents and an increase of 4,600 white or, more precisely, nonblack residents during the decade. Elsewhere in the city, the population became proportionally blacker because the number of blacks decreased at a slower rate than that of white." Finally, scholar Dennis Gale, who had been tracking demographic patterns in the District during the 1970s and 1980s, offered this assessment of gentrification's impact on the city's affordable housing stock: "Because much of today's inner ring of revitalizing neighborhoods surrounding the central business district once encompassed a significant share of the city's supply of low- and moderate-income housing, reductions in the housing supply in those areas connote reductions in the city's overall stock of nonsubsidized housing for people of limited means. In short, gentrification has doubtless been responsible for much of the decrease in Washington's stock of affordable housing to needy households."[40]

Progrowth advocates questioned the connection between commercial office development and displacement pressures felt by lower-income citizens living near downtown, insisting instead that other societal trends were responsible. But Georgetown law professor Robert Stumberg, who specialized in local housing issues, disagreed: "It's like the glaciers that moved all the way down into roughly the area now bounded by the Missouri River. Folks don't think of that as land shaped by glaciers. It still happened. It just happened very slowly and receded very slowly. My unscientific impression is that housing values in Mt. Pleasant and Columbia Heights are directly affected by downtown development. Why else would those neighborhoods be targets of speculators or developers or . . . white, middle-class people who would be looking to buy in those neighborhoods? It's because of the proximity to downtown." Although no study exists that conclusively establishes a direct link between downtown growth and rising housing costs in nearby neighborhoods, some progrowth advocates conceded that there is a causal relationship. Causton Toney, an official with the D.C. Chamber of Commerce, believed that while commercial office development raised downtown property values and thus expanded the city's tax base, there was also a cost: "On the negative side, what it's done is priced a lot of areas out of the reach of low- and moderate-income persons. . . . I'm not sure it's resulted in gentrification, at least not in the '80s as much, but I think it has resulted in certain low- and moderate-income populations just being priced out of its housing on the fringes of the downtown commercial district."[41]

A final way in which the downtown building boom adversely affected the city's affordable housing situation involved not displacement, but deteriorating living conditions. City planner Nate Gross explained why real estate speculation driven by office construction may have prompted some landlords to neglect their residential properties: "If you're an owner of, let's say, a row of row houses, you probably disinvest in those row houses, keep rents low; you're just carrying the ground for the future possible redevelopment, rezoning, or redevelopment. Because if you put more of the value into the land and less into the structure, effectively that's what happens. Then it doesn't make sense to put a lot of money into improving their structure. Just carry the ground."[42] In short, many lower-income residents were driven from their neighborhoods because their homes were demolished to make room for new office buildings, because the building boom sparked real estate speculation and gentrification, or because landlords failed to maintain their properties while waiting to cash in on spreading downtown development.

For many Washingtonians, another alarming aspect of vigorous commercial office development was its direct encroachment into adjoining residential neighborhoods. In the 1970s, as developable real estate in the K Street/Connecticut

Avenue area diminished, developers set their sights on such stable residential neighborhoods as Dupont Circle, Foggy Bottom, and the West End. The city responded by adopting new zoning regulations in 1974 that would allow commercial office development in the West End as long as it was coupled with residential development. The idea was to accommodate commercial developers anxiously searching for new real estate while preserving the residential character of the neighborhood. However, the city's attempt to save a neighborhood and simultaneously promote office development did not please West End residents. One problem was that the zoning change allowed developers to build luxury hotels to meet the residential requirement; although this was consistent with the planners' goal of keeping people on the streets past working hours, thus enhancing the nighttime vitality of an increasingly commercial area, the transient hotel population did not contribute to neighborhood stability. Moreover, with property values rising because of office and hotel development, many small businesses serving the neighborhood were forced to surrender their leases and move elsewhere. Some long-time residents decided to stay, but development in the neighborhood seriously disrupted a way of life. The *Washington Post* concluded a 1984 study of land use changes in the area by stating, "There is no sense of neighborhood and not a whole lot of appealing urban texture in the new West End."[43]

In the late 1970s developers discovered a mechanism that would allow them to follow the precedent set in the West End elsewhere in the city. Washington's planned unit development (PUD) law, which had been used sparingly since it was incorporated into the zoning code in 1958, was initially intended to stimulate the production of housing in conjunction with large-scale, mixed-use development projects. But as land costs escalated during the 1970s, developers sought ways to build PUDs that were more heavily geared toward lucrative commercial uses. The city encouraged this trend by amending the PUD ordinance in 1977 and again in 1979 to facilitate office development. Increasingly, developers were allowed to build a higher concentration of offices within a PUD if they would provide added public amenities such as pedestrian malls and more landscaping. The number of applications for permission to construct PUDs beyond downtown began to soar.[44]

Neighborhood groups that worried about commercial encroachment into residential neighborhoods came to believe that the city was more inclined to side with the developers in zoning disputes. For instance, in 1983 the city proposed establishing a special buffer district between Dupont Circle and the downtown office district to the south that would allow both commercial and residential uses. When neighborhood activists complained that the buffer district would encourage further encroachment instead of discouraging it, city officials were not sympathetic. City Planning Director John McKoy lectured neighborhood residents about the local political economy: "The city can't be in a position to say [to business entities seeking affordable office space], 'If you can't pay rent downtown forget it.' That's not realistic looking at population projections and the way the town functions economically."[45]

As the risk of commercial office encroachment into residential neighborhoods mounted in the 1970s and 1980s, and as popular awareness of land use matters increased, community activists came to believe that downtown real estate interests wielded immense power with the cooperation of city government. The Barry administration seemed eager to do everything it could to promote the boom in commercial office development regardless of adverse impacts to the city's neighborhoods. As noted above, one example of the city's willingness to accommodate developers concerned changes in zoning laws to permit commercial office development in residential areas as a matter of right or as part of a planned unit development providing certain public amenities. Another common practice was the sale of city-owned downtown property at prices far below market value to spur redevelopment. For instance, in December 1980 the District's redevelopment agency sold a prime parcel of downtown land for $130 per square foot, or about one-fourth of the market rate. At one point the U.S. General Accounting Office intervened to examine the city's habit of selling downtown properties at bargain basement prices. The GAO criticized the city for setting sale prices based on outdated appraisals and for failing to establish a competitive bidding process for the sale of property. The city also seemed unduly generous in providing other public incentives for development projects, such as density bonuses, investment tax credits, tax abatements, differential tax assessments for historical sites, and greater use of industrial revenue bonds.[46]

A 1984 *Washington Post* study of business-government relations during the first decade of home rule supported the suspicions of neighborhood activists that developers enjoyed an advantageous position in local politics. It noted "a consensus in the business community that home rule has improved relations between the local government and business. . . . There is also general agreement in the private sector that the D.C. government is more responsive to business than it was 10, or even five years ago." In particular, the *Post* study reported that "commercial developers . . . say publicly and privately that they have found the city much easier to deal with in recent years" and that corporate attorneys who represent them "say they detect a genuine desire to be helpful on the part of the mayor and the council."[47]

The comfortable relationship between the city government and the downtown business community only seemed to grow stronger with the passage of time. In 1986, as Marion Barry campaigned for a third consecutive term as mayor, he emphasized his unflinching support for aggressive downtown growth: "This administration is pro-jobs and pro-business. That's why we work hard with businesses of all kinds to come to Washington. . . . I have a bias towards businesses doing business in Washington."[48] The Board of Trade rewarded the mayor's stance by endorsing his candidacy for the first time, and business leaders backed up their endorsement with hefty campaign contributions. The real estate industry was particularly active around election time, and its influence over local politics was apparent, as city planner Nate Gross recalled: "See, one thing about the political dynamics in Washington is that real estate money is the big political money. We don't have home-grown corporations and . . . so downtown real estate is where the council and mayoral candidates have always gotten their big campaign contributions. And that's a lot of it right there."[49]

As the downtown building boom accelerated in the late 1970s and early 1980s, neighborhood activists had reason to be concerned. The city's enthusiastic support of aggressive growth policies seemed to ignore certain social and economic costs such as the displacement of small businesses downtown and the gentrification of close-in residential neighborhoods. Furthermore, the Barry administration appeared to be oblivious to the direct encroachment of commercial office development in residential neighborhoods throughout the city. Activists felt that the West End had been ruined, and many feared that the same fate awaited their communities unless some kind of preventive action were taken. But perhaps the most serious source of anxiety for community activists was the growing conviction that land use politics in the District was fundamentally skewed in favor of real estate interests. The increasingly cozy relationship between the city government and the development community seemed to constitute evidence of a structural flaw in local politics. Such suspicions were strengthened when activists sought a more substantial voice in land use policy making but were often frustrated by an unsympathetic coalition of public and private elites. In 1982, for example, the Board of Zoning Adjustment (BZA) proposed rules to limit the participation of representatives of the city's Advisory Neighborhood Commissions (ANC) in zoning hearings. Under the new rules, ANC representatives' involvement at public hearings would be limited to reading previously submitted written statements or responding to questions from the BZA; they would also be barred from examining or cross-examining zoning applicants.[50] It was within this political environment that the level of citizen activism around issues of downtown development escalated in the early 1980s.

Conclusion

American cities generally developed within a privatist political culture that privileged market-oriented, elite-dominated approaches to policy making. The growth of Philadelphia is a classic case, as shown by Samuel Bass Warner's *The Private City.* Cities would sometimes depart from the privatist path, usually during those periods when state-directed city planning was in vogue. For example, Chicago, Cleveland, San Francisco, and even Philadelphia adopted a "managerial mood"[51] during the era of the City Beautiful movement.

Washington also experienced long stretches of development guided by privatist ideas, values, beliefs, and practices. But the District's deviations from the privatist norm were more frequent and substantial. The practice of extensive state intervention by city planners was established at the outset with Pierre L'Enfant and his grand plan for the federal city. The revival of the L'Enfant plan over a century later helped make Washington a center of city planning, and that managerial respect for planning by trained professionals has lingered in the city's political culture.

After World War II, however, a privatist worldview reassumed its hegemonic status in Washington, just as it did in all major U.S. cities. Urban development would be driven by sweeping market forces that would make the downtown business districts of urban America the hub of the ascending postindustrial economy. It was assumed that downtown development would create jobs, expand tax revenues, and enhance the quality of life for people who worked in the area and lived in surrounding neighborhoods. The city government's role in developing downtown was accordingly confined to inducing growth by offering tax breaks or easing zoning regulations. Business leaders acknowledged the need for some planning controls, but only as a vehicle for promoting development, not discouraging it. With the privatist vision guiding policy making, downtown Washington grew and prospered. Other cities looked on with envy. District leaders and citizens expressed satisfaction and pride.

It was not until the building boom shifted into an even higher gear in the late 1970s and 1980s that some neighborhood groups began to grumble about the negative impacts of rapid growth. Other citizens raised questions about the long-promised benefits that were supposed to flow to the surrounding neighborhoods. As in San Francisco, public discontent with the adverse effects and limited gains of downtown development converged to spark the formation of a neighborhood-based movement in Washington to challenge the downtown growth coalition's power over land use policy making.

This is not to suggest that growth-control activism in Washington was a monolithic phenomenon. Like growth-control movements in San Francisco and other U.S. cities, it was composed of various neighborhood groups with distinct interests and priorities. Two groups within the Washington movement were particularly prominent. The first consisted of neighborhood activists who were mainly dissatisfied with the negative consequences of downtown expansion. This group believed that the market-driven approach to downtown development favored by the growth coalition had run amok. Development pressures were threatening the quality of life in the nation's capital, and only a series of strong regulatory and redistributive policies could possibly straighten out the mess. In particular, this group of activists put its faith in comprehensive planning to ensure that Washington would be not just a livable city, but a dynamic and cosmopolitan center of politics and culture. This wing of the growth-control movement will be referred to as the planning advocates.

The second key group within the Washington growth-control movement also consisted of neighborhood activists, but neighborhood activists who were primarily concerned about ensuring that downtown development produced meaningful improvements in the material well-being of the city's residential neighborhoods. These activists were generally associated with community development corporations, nonprofit housing organizations, and other neighborhood-related groups; they were preoccupied with issues of affordable housing production and local economic development. This wing of the growth-control movement will be referred to as the community development advocates.

Despite having somewhat different priorities, both contingents of the Washington growth-control movement seemed to have the same general orientation in taking on the downtown growth coalition. Both voiced support for the central elements of a progressive vision of politics. Planning advocates and community development advocates alike sharply criticized a policy-making process that had become the exclusive domain of high-ranking city officials and influential real estate interests; they insisted that the development decision-making process be opened up to broader citizen participation. Furthermore, both groups within the growth-control movement called for public policies that would better control downtown development and more fairly distribute the costs and benefits of vigorous growth. Hence, citizen empowerment and an energetic public realm committed to equitable growth seemed to characterize growth-control activism in Washington.

The discourse and conduct of the Washington growth- control movement reveals marked deviations regarding the issues of who should govern and the proper role of government. Planning advocates exhibited a managerial approach to politics, characterized by a clear attachment to the public sphere to correct market-generated inequities but a lack of confidence in ordinary people to devise and implement appropriate regulatory and redistributive policies. Community development advocates demonstrated a populist world-view, characterized by a faith in popular empowerment but a distrust of the public sphere. In each case, the deviations from a progresive vision of politics would undermine the counter-hegemonic potential of growth-control activism.

✦10

Managerial Activism

As downtown development in Washington gathered momentum in the 1970s, neighborhood activists became increasingly anxious about the unanticipated problems of vigorous growth. Higher housing costs, small-business displacement, and aggravating traffic congestion were harming the District's neighborhoods. Moreover, as the supply of developable properties decreased in the downtown core, and as developers began to look elsewhere for expansion, the threat of commercial encroachment into close-in residential neighborhoods intensified.

When neighborhood activists began to voice their concerns about downtown development in the public arena, progrowth advocates explained that Washington, like all American cities, was caught up in a sweeping transformation of the global economy. Manufacturing was on the decline in the United States, but a service- and information-based economy centered in downtown business districts was on the rise. This market-led transformation was good news for Washington, according to the downtown growth coalition. As the nation's center of government, Washington, and downtown in particular, was well positioned to take advantage of a postindustrial economy. All the city had to do was ride the wave of free market trends and capitalize on the prosperity that downtown growth was sure to bring.

Activists in the neighborhoods remained skeptical. They contended that government still needed to play a prominent role to correct the flaws in market-driven policies. Accordingly, the vehicle that one wing of the Washington growth-control movement seized upon to reorder downtown development policy was comprehensive planning. These activists believed that government regulation through long-term, prudent planning offered the best hope for minimizing the negative impacts of aggressive growth while maximizing the opportunities for using the building boom to fashion a more desirable city in which to work and live. Inspired by the cosmopolitan capitals of Europe, many of the planning advocates believed that Washington too could become a lively center of culture, commerce, and politics—if only the city's development could be guided by a reasonable plan.

The Promise of Planning

The Home Rule Charter of 1973 obligated the mayor's office to present a comprehensive plan for the future development of the city by 1978. But progress toward that goal was slow in coming. The city's first mayor, Walter Washington, failed to comply with the planning mandate, and this failure became an issue in the 1978 mayoral campaign. Encouraged by neighborhood activists concerned about the adverse effects and lost opportunities of the downtown building boom, mayoral candidate Marion Barry criticized the Washington administration for its delay in completing a plan and promised that his administration would "not tolerate a government where city departments operate without goals."[1]

At the same time a group of about sixty individuals concerned about urban development in Washington banded together and formed the Citizens Planning Coalition (CPC) to lobby for a comprehensive plan. Heartened by Barry's promises to prepare such a plan, the CPC endorsed his candidacy for mayor. After Barry's victory, the CPC sent a letter to the new mayor reminding him of the need for sound planning. The coalition warned that the lack of a plan "at a time when development pressures are greater than ever in the city's history [might result in] the disruption of our neighborhoods, still greater traffic congestion, increasing pollution, inadequate water supply and sewage capacity, shrinking open spaces, higher taxes, and just plain ugliness." Moreover, without adequate guidelines, the CPC asserted that "we exist in a planning vacuum in which zoning decisions are made without any underlying logic of land use arrangement based on agreed citizen objectives." The letter went on to criticize the structure of land use decision making, labeling the Zoning Commission "a developer-oriented body" and calling for a tightening of conflict-of-interest regulations to curb the "revolving door problem between city planning offices and law firms that represent developers." Finally, insisting that "the zoning process must be responsive to the citizens," the CPC urged Mayor Barry to request the resignations of all mayorally appointed members of both the Zoning Commission and the Board of Zoning Adjustment.[2] The CPC's commitment to prudent planning, neighborhood preservation, environmental protection, and responsive government thus was apparent from the start.

One other important goal sought by the planning advocates through a new comprehensive plan was the promotion of a "living downtown." The idea had been floated for years, at least as far back as 1962 when the civic organization Downtown Progress published a report outlining its plan for revitalizing downtown Washington.[3] As a general matter, the notion of developing a downtown business district that would be lively past regular working hours, and thus avoiding the "ghost town" effect that plagued many other urban business districts, attracted broad support. But exactly what a "living downtown" meant to different groups varied. Mayor Barry, for instance, anticipated hotels, restaurants, theaters, and expanded retail facilities.[4] The planning advocates, however, wanted all that and more; in particular, they sought to encourage residential use downtown. In their view only a large number of full-time residents could transform downtown Washington into a truly "living downtown," much like the vibrant capitals of many European countries. Comprehensive planning would be the vehicle for advancing this vision of the city.

Yet, despite pressure from the Citizens Planning Coalition, the Barry administration appeared to be in no hurry to complete a comprehensive plan for the city. By the time of the next mayoral election in 1982, the Barry administration still had not delivered on its promise of submitting a comprehensive plan to the District Council. Carol Currie, chair of the CPC, remarked, "One of the promises Marion made when he was running . . . was that he would get the Comprehensive Plan done right away. He wasn't going to sit on it like Walter Washington. But it's been the same thing. I think he's happy to see development done on an ad hoc basis, lot by lot."[5] It was not until the election campaign heated up in October 1982 that Barry finally responded by releasing a 332-page draft comprehensive plan to guide future development.

But the planning advocates remained dissatisfied. They criticized the administration for having excluded them from the planning process. Currie commented, "There are people in different parts of town who have worked on plans for ages but haven't gotten the city's attention or respect. . . . I have to wonder whether the city is serious about listening to its citizens."[6] Another neighborhood activist, Peggy Robin, charged that the process followed by the city planning office in preparing the draft comprehensive plan was "backwards." She explained that "if the citizens had been consulted first, they wouldn't now have the feeling that they must bring their comments to a body with its mind essentially made up." On substantive grounds activists faulted the plan for being "vague and sometimes inconsistent." Activists from the Dupont Circle neighborhood contended, for example, "The draft plan fails to propose and map the kinds of specifics that would assure both the survival of Dupont Circle as a residential neighborhood and the preservation of its unique character."[7] Activist Dorn McGrath of the Committee of 100, a planning watchdog organization, called the draft plan "a completely vacuous set of policies . . . which meant nothing to anyone. It was all motherhood. Pages and pages and pages of 'There shall be birds in every tree; all trees shall be healthy; people shall have access to all necessary services at reasonable cost.' . . . Utter hogwash."[8]

The city's response to such criticism did little to encourage the planning advocates. With regard to the limited citizen participation, planning chief John H. McKoy answered that the draft plan was intended to be only the first phase of a far-reaching comprehensive plan. Whereas the first phase outlined long-range policies to guide development throughout the District, the second phase called for the preparation of specific, small-area plans; it was at this second phase that city officials deemed citizen involvement to be "proper." As for the substantive charge that the comprehensive plan was so vague as to be practically useless as a zoning document, city planners replied simply that they needed flexibility in dealing with developers. The District Council's stance on the comprehensive plan was ambivalent. In light of the planning advocates' complaints, the District Council first postponed considering the land use plan in January 1984, but by the end of the year the city's lawmakers voted to approve it.[9]

Despite the plan's vagueness and inconsistencies,[10] the activists believed they now had a legal mechanism with which to block the march of commercial office development into residential neighborhoods. Richard Nettler, a land use attorney who represented neighborhood organizations, recalled that proposed development projects along the Wisconsin Avenue corridor in the mid-1980s sparked "the first big battle over the comprehensive plan and what it meant and how it could be enforced."[11] Although the Wisconsin Avenue corridor was removed from the downtown district, developers were eager to build in the area to take advantage of existing commercial and retail uses and busy Metro stations. The planning advocates feared that a burst of office building construction would further detract from the primarily residential character of the neighborhood. Vowing to fight any additional commercial encroachment, they filed a lawsuit to block new development along Wisconsin Avenue.

Although the developers prevailed in the initial legal battles, which enabled them to proceed with their proposed projects, Nettler believed that the experience "changed significantly how the community dealt with development, how politics was going to be played in the District, and the type of success that the community was able to have later on." More than ever, neighborhood activists were determined to use the vehicle of comprehensive planning to shape development patterns in the city. Where the comprehensive plan itself proved too vague to control unwanted development, the planning advocates would push for concrete changes. In 1986 they drew upon their experience with the Wisconsin Avenue confrontation to mount a series of campaigns to pressure the Zoning Commission to downzone residential neighborhoods in order to deter large-scale development. At last, neighborhood activists felt they had the means to take on the downtown growth coalition.[12]

Taking Stock of Planning Advocacy

The prudent planning wing of the Washington growth-control movement undoubtedly prompted some changes in urban development in the District. Particularly in white, middle-class neighborhoods, activists raised popular consciousness about the threats posed by downtown expansion. Suspicions of developers were prevalent in some black neighborhoods too, especially neighborhoods close to the downtown business district. Council member Charlene Drew Jarvis commented: "When you talk about old neighborhoods that are gutted and business districts left vacant and fallow, you're talking about white developers. And there's a tremendous resentment among black families when they're pushed out and reap none of the benefits." Dupont Circle activist Dennis Bass remarked, "Speaking of this area, I think people have become much more conscious of the fragility [of] in-close, in-town neighborhoods and how easily they can be destroyed or significantly altered. . . . And if you just look at what's happened, ten years ago there was no Dupont Circle Historic District. . . . There was no overlay. . . . I've just seen people become very conscious of the impact of development and I've seen that spread."[13] That heightened level of concern about rapid growth motivated the Barry administration to finally submit to the District Council a comprehensive plan for all aspects of future development in the city. Activists hoped that a careful elaboration of planning goals by trained professionals would bring some order to a process that had run out of control.

Activists also gained ground with respect to historic preservation. Along with saving many historically significant buildings from demolition, including the famed Old Post Office and Willard Hotel, activists made historic preservation a vital attribute of downtown planning. Scholar Dennis Gale writes: "One of the surest indicators of the saliency of historic preservation in Washington's CBD is the frequency with which it is now discussed in local government planning, as well as in business circles. Little more than an afterthought [for city planners] in the 1960s, it has been much more extensively discussed in plans and proposals of the late 1970s and 1980s. For example, an entire volume of the seven-volume Comprehensive Plan recently adopted by the District of Columbia government was devoted to historic preservation." Nearly four thousand structures in the District have received historic designation status, and a city law that allows activists to delay demolition of certain types of older buildings is one of the strictest in the nation.[14]

Perhaps the most impressive victory of the planning wing of the Washington growth-control movement came when activists became more assertive in city electoral politics. In 1982 about forty residents of the Dupont Circle area established the Dupont Circle Political Action Committee to combat the spread of commercial office development, a trend they claimed had contributed to housing and small-business displacement. Faced with such a threat to their neighborhood, the organization warned, "We join together to use the political process to reward leaders who respect a neighborhood that cares for its residents

. . . and to vote out those who oppose us."[15] Other neighborhoods in Ward 3 concerned about commercial encroachment also began to mount campaign efforts in preparation for local elections in the mid-1980s. Citizens along the Wisconsin and Connecticut Avenue corridors were especially determined to hold politicians accountable for their prodevelopment votes.

An astute politician, Mayor Marion Barry was not slow to recognize the potential dangers posed by growth-control activism to his own political future. With a mayoral election approaching in 1986, Barry acted to defuse tension in Ward 3 caused by fears of commercial development along Wisconsin Avenue. Although the Barry administration had consistently favored prodevelopment interests in the past, the mayor reversed his stand soon after he lost Ward 3 in the Democratic Party primary to a relatively weak challenger. In late September Barry announced that he would back a permanent downzoning of the Wisconsin Avenue corridor under dispute.[16] Growth-control activist Joel Odum remarked, "The primary result must have hit Barry. . . . This sure will take the edge off [the growth issue] in the general election." A few months later the Zoning Commission accepted the mayor's recommendation and officially approved a measure to downzone the area. The planning advocates hailed the commission's decision to follow the comprehensive plan rather than outdated zoning maps adopted in 1958. Developers denounced the action, stating that it unfairly lowered the investment value of their land.[17]

Pressure from the planning advocates prompted Mayor Barry to follow a similar course of action with respect to development along another busy corridor in a primarily residential area. Citing the need to protect neighborhood retail establishments from large-scale commercial growth, Barry called for a downzoning along upper Connecticut Avenue in the Woodley Park and Cleveland Park communities. Developers condemned the move for restricting the rights of property owners and expressed dismay over Barry's newfound tendency to engage in "zoning by plebiscite." Whayne S. Quin, a leading land use attorney who represented developers, declared that the mayor's support for downzoning Wisconsin and Connecticut Avenues reflected "a trend toward taking action according to the number of votes" rather than according to rational planning principles.[18]

Thus, by the mid-1980s neighborhood activists could point to a number of accomplishments in their battle with the downtown growth coalition. They had raised popular consciousness about the downside of downtown development. Many Washingtonians, as a result, no longer subscribed to the conventional wisdom that the city had a unitary interest in pursuing aggressive growth. The shift in thinking compelled the Barry administration to present a comprehensive plan that would enable the city to better control the negative effects of downtown development. This had been the highest priority of the planning advocates, and it was achieved in 1984. The comprehensive plan helped to advance specific goals of the growth-control movement, most notably with respect to historic preservation. It was also used effectively to block commercial office expansion into residential neighborhoods. The neighborhood downzonings along Wisconsin and Connecticut Avenues had been a clear victory over the growth coalition. Attorney Richard Nettler asserted that these positive experiences had "energized a lot of people around the city" as to how they could employ the comprehensive plan to oppose unwanted development projects. Other neighborhood downzonings were later pursued successfully all over the city. Also, the planning advocates no longer hesitated to appeal unfavorable decisions of the Zoning Commission to the Court of Appeals if they believed that the letter and spirit of the comprehensive plan had been breached. And finally, electoral pressure by the planning advocates during the 1986 campaign prompted the mayor to appoint new members to the Zoning Commission and other city agencies who were more sensitive to the costs of rapid growth.[19]

On the other hand, these achievements did not transform the politics of downtown development in Washington. This becomes apparent if one takes a closer look at the story behind the comprehensive plan. It is important to understand that the downtown growth coalition did not resist the adoption of a comprehensive plan. As the building boom quickened in the late 1970s and early 1980s, even business leaders acquiesced to some controls on downtown development. A report issued by the Board of Trade after a year-long study advised Mayor Marion Barry to appoint a "downtown coordinator" to ensure reasonable planning. Board of Trade president Pat Galloway commented: "Our concern is not whether development will occur. . . . Our concern is with the quality of that development." The board wanted to avoid the kind of development that had turned the K Street/Connecticut Avenue area into a sterile district of dreary office buildings. Moreover, to guarantee that downtown would offer not just commercial offices for a metropolitan workforce but an array of cultural and recreational attractions as well, the Board of Trade report endorsed the notion of a "living downtown" by recommending that the city provide incentives to developers to subsidize the preservation of historic buildings and the construction of theaters, restaurants, and hotels.[20] Significantly, business leaders did not back the activists' call for expanded residential use in the downtown core, and the Barry administration sided with the real estate industry on this pivotal issue. Thus, the growth coalition did not oppose citizen demands for comprehensive planning, provided planning was undertaken for the proper purpose.

The Board of Trade's support for "reasonable" planning should not be seen as any kind of general consent by the growth coalition to broad government regulation of the private sector. Progrowth advocates would go along with the practice of planning only on the understanding that it would *encourage* further downtown development. If government had to play any role at all, it would be a facilitative, and not an obstructionist, one—hence the Board of Trade's support for public inducements such as density bonuses and tax abatements to steer private investment in desirable ways. And, finally, comprehensive planning was instituted in the District in a way that had little adverse impact on the growth coalition's vision for *downtown* Washington. Although the planning advocates had inhibited commercial office expansion into residential neighborhoods, the downtown building boom roared along. For the most part, whatever regulatory and redistributive policies were imposed regarding downtown development came about at the behest of progrowth elites.

The key point is that the growth coalition backed the notion of comprehensive planning only so long as it retained power over the planning process. As the years passed, downtown business leaders never sensed that they were in danger of losing control over that process to pesky activists in the neighborhoods, and for good reason. Most obviously, the Barry administration excluded neighborhood groups from participating in the preparation of the comprehensive plan, even though many neighborhood groups had been in the forefront of calling for such a plan ever since the adoption of home rule in 1974. When growth-control activists objected over being shut out of that process, they were assured that they would have ample opportunity to assist in the preparation of individual ward plans for the District. They were told that the ward plans would be more important anyway because they would be considered the specific embodiments of the much more general comprehensive plan.

At first it appeared that city officials would honor their promise. In March 1985 the District Council approved an ambitious planning process emphasizing broad citizen participation to transform the general goals of the comprehensive plan into specific land use policies for the eight wards that comprise the city. Each ward plan would be prepared by a citizen advisory committee (CAC) consisting of 40 to 50 members. Of the total 350 CAC members, 60 percent would come from advisory neighborhood commissions or civic associations, 25 percent from the business community, and the remainder from various institutions such as universities, hospitals, and churches.[21]

Notwithstanding the proposed format, some activists began to wonder whether the Barry administration was genuinely committed to popular participation in the land use planning process. First, the Office of Planning dragged its feet for seven months in appointing the CAC members. This led District

Council Chair David Clarke to comment, "I have serious questions as to what extent the Office of Planning is serious about the development of ward plans that reflect citizen participation." Activists also criticized the administration for neglecting to hire consultants or provide technical support to the citizen advisory committees. Most ominously, Planning Director Fred Greene cautioned that the Office of Planning would revise the ward plans before sending them on to the District Council for final review; he declared, "The CACs serve as advisory to me."[22] Greene's warning proved prophetic. The CACs spent the next three years drafting individual ward plans for the District, which were then sent to the Office of Planning for review. The planning advocates were dismayed, however, when the Barry administration dropped many of the explicit policy requirements in favor of general language that was no better than the vaguely worded comprehensive plan. Activists condemned the revised plans as "a useless document." Council member John Wilson agreed: "After [planning officials] went through the whole process, they ignored the desires of the people in the neighborhoods." Many felt that the ambiguous language would allow the downtown growth coalition to exercise decisive influence over individual development projects. Activist planner Dorn McGrath concluded, "It's a license to cut deals wherever one comes up."[23]

In the wake of this defeat, District Council Chair David Clarke tried to enhance the ability of citizens to use the comprehensive plan to influence land use decisions. In 1989 he submitted a bill that would have enabled citizens to block any development project that failed to conform to the comprehensive plan. Developers and the Barry administration attacked the measure and warned of dire consequences. Real estate attorney Whayne S. Quin said implementation of the bill would be "absolutely disastrous" and added: "I just cannot imagine that the business community would want to contribute" to any politician backing it. Developer Sam Rose criticized Clarke's entire approach: "His [Clarke's] way of solving the problem is to give a sword to the citizens, to say you can stick this sword in every project."[24] Under intense lobbying from the downtown growth coalition, Clarke's bill was never adopted. On another vote shortly thereafter, the council caved in to pressure from progrowth forces again when it weakened a bill that would have strengthened the specificity of land use restrictions in the comprehensive plan.[25]

Thus, though "reasonable" planning had become customary practice in Washington, the planning process remained under the control of progrowth forces. After years of growth-control activism, the planning advocates had made little headway in breaking into the decision-making process. Even Planning Director Fred Greene acknowledged a lack of citizen participation in land use policy making: "If I could put my finger on something that was missing throughout the process, it was the involvement of the populace, y'know, it was the involvement of the people who are really in need."[26]

The downtown growth coalition's suspicion of citizen participation in development policy making is revealed in its attitudes toward Washington's Advisory Neighborhood Commission (ANC) system. That system is composed of popularly elected neighborhood commissions that advise the city on issues that affect the neighborhood. Hence, the ANC system offers at least some potential for the exercise of grassroots power. Causton Toney of the D.C. Chamber of Commerce explained his discomfort with the ANCs:

> I just don't think that an ANC commissioner is necessarily at the hub or the pulse of that particular individual's community. . . . They can probably be a focal point for communicating issues that a community may have about a project. . . . But I think the member of the City Council who represents the ward is probably a better focal point for that kind of input and dialogue. I think when you start throwing ANC commissioners in there . . . civic associations in there, when you start throwing those kinds of players into the process, you make the process more time-consuming, more costly, and probably less efficient.

Toney elaborated on why he felt public officials at the city level are better positioned to represent popular views than are neighborhood leaders: "[Neighborhood leaders] don't really have a way of working into the process, getting a consensus, getting an approval that is uniform and that is agreed to [by] everyone in the community. They just don't have that kind of broad-based support in the community. A council member, I think, probably is politically bright enough, astute enough, to penetrate that local community and get a sense of what might be the appropriate response to a development project." Toney's preference for institutions of representative democracy over participatory democracy was further evidenced in this concluding remark: "My view is the District is small and it doesn't need a situation as cumbersome as the ANC commissioner process. It doesn't need people who don't really have any power, but have the power to get a microphone and say I'm so and so and that is what I think. I just don't think it needs that kind of gumming of the works when we have ward council members, we have at-large council members, we have a mayor. . . . All those I think obviate the need for something like an ANC commissioner."[27] The lack of respect for popular participation in politics was a common perspective among members of the downtown growth coalition, as indicated by the limited opportunities available to neighborhood activists to participate directly in land use policy making.

As a result the capacity of downtown elites to shape land use policy remained impressive through the 1980s and into the 1990s. Downtown development continued at a feverish pace throughout this period despite the opposition of planning advocates concerned about the negative impacts of rapid growth. Public policy continued to be aimed at inducing even more growth. In the late 1980s, developers were still reaping the benefits of generous land sales and financing arrangements, tax abatements, zoning variances, and a host of other government incentives. There was little doubt as to who was in charge. Although Chamber of Commerce officials such as Causton Toney disputed the conventional wisdom that city government and business leaders enjoyed a comfortable working relationship, Toney's own words pointed to a different conclusion: "The business community could lobby, could raise money, could make a political difference in the outcome by simply taking a proposal, reacting to it, supporting those financially who agreed with their view, and not supporting those who did not. As a direct result, the business community, once it flexed its muscle through the Greater Washington Board of Trade, flexed its financial muscle, was able to get what it wanted in many, many instances in terms of what was approved and what was not approved, OK? It was able to get what it wanted for the most part."[28]

The Cultural Ramifications of Managerial Activism

The mostly disappointing results of planning advocacy require an explanation of what went wrong with this wing of the Washington growth-control movement. Much can be gleaned from a careful analysis of the planning advocates' brand of grassroots activism, an examination of their discourse and conduct in taking on the downtown growth coalition. In this regard, a quick comparison with the San Francisco growth-control movement would be instructive.

The empowerment of ordinary citizens such that they are able to exercise significant influence over the decisions that affect their lives represents a core principle of a progressive vision of politics. But exactly what does citizen empowerment mean? In San Francisco neighborhood activists held a strong faith in the virtues of participatory democracy. They had come of age in the midst of the civil rights and antiwar movements of the 1960s, when grassroots challenges to governmental authority were the norm. In the 1970s they turned from national and international issues to local matters, but in doing so they reaffirmed their commitment to community-based activism. Through classic grassroots organizing, activists campaigned for changes in neighborhood zoning and for structural changes in how local elections were conducted. They canvassed door-to-door, and as one activist put it, conducted civics lessons on street corners about municipal government.[29]

When these neighborhood activists focused their attention on the problems caused by downtown development, their commitment to the value of citizen empowerment was manifested in their practices. Their chief strategy for fighting the downtown growth coalition was the citizens initiative. That alone indicated two important characteristics of the mindset of the San Francisco growth-control movement: a profound distrust of the "regular" institutions of city government, which they viewed as structurally biased in favor of prodevelopment interests; and an unswerving confidence in the capacity of ordinary people to govern directly. That San Francisco activists turned to the initiative process again and again during their sixteen-year campaign against the downtown growth coalition helped to steadily erode the public's habit of deferring to the presumed expertise of trained professionals downtown and delegating control over land use policy making to city planners. Instead, citizens became more likely to regard the growth coalition's claim to expertise with suspicion. As they became accustomed to the progressive value of popular empowerment, they began to evaluate the activists' proposals for policy reforms in a new light. By the end of the 1980s, San Franciscans had experienced a thorough transformation in their perceptions about who ought to decide the future of downtown development.

Washington's growth-control activists also voiced enthusiasm for the progressive goal of popular control over downtown development, but their actual discourse and behavior suggest a starkly different interpretation of citizen empowerment. A useful place to start would be with the activists' attitudes toward the main strategy of the San Francisco grassroots movement, the citizens initiative. One activist from Dupont Circle, Ed Grandis, who considered himself a long-time progressive advocate, explained why it was never used in Washington:

> I think that in this area you come from a tradition of elitism or aristocracy. And there's an educated class and a working class. . . . in the establishment, there's a real queasiness to letting the public decide on things. . . . There's a real skepticism to mob decision making that I think in areas like Arizona and in California . . . you tend almost, people relish getting into massive decision making. I think in, y'know, some of the New England states where they have town meetings, they have the most sophistication in understanding how it works and how to frame things that are in the public interest. . . . I just don't think a mob—and that's to me where the minority and majority thing comes into conflict—I think in the west, my sense is that there has been a history of . . . these initiatives. . . . You don't have that here. It's almost a new concept.[30]

Grandis makes an important point in trying to explain why citizens initiatives were used by growth-control activists in San Francisco but not in Washington. There has been a longer and more extensive tradition of participatory democracy in the west through the use of the citizens initiative, referendum, and recall.[31] However, Grandis's language reveals his own discomfort—not just that of "the establishment"—with allocating too much responsibility for governing to "the mob." At another point Grandis acknowledged that Washington actually did have a history of citizen activism through its civic associations.[32] But his explanation for how the civic associations differed from the grassroots activism associated with initiative campaigns illuminates much about how the Washington movement conceived of citizen empowerment:

> I think the civic associations tend to be people who learn the issues in their neighborhood and work on those issues. They're volunteers, but they really become experts. They're knowledgeable about their issues. . . .
>
> I'm not saying initiatives aren't good. We just don't use them properly. [Explains that initiatives in Washington tend to be poorly drafted and marketed]. And I think there's a skepticism by our establishment in that they tend to become mob rule instead of a collective wisdom. But I think civic groups tend to become a collective wisdom. You may disagree with them, but they come up with facts and figures. They can tell you how many homes in their neighborhood have been burglarized, how many homes have been changed from a housing stock to a business stock. They go out and do research. Y'know, that to me is the distinction. And I don't oppose initiatives. I just think the way they're presented here . . . that they're very poor.[33]

Grandis suggested that popular participation in politics produces a "collective wisdom" only when citizens possess sufficient skills to do research and compile the kinds of "facts and figures" that would make them "experts" on neighborhood issues. This is what made the old civic associations such an effective force in Washington politics prior to home rule. At the same time Grandis implied that grassroots efforts to shape policy making that are not driven by citizens with suitable skills and expertise tend to degenerate into "mob rule." According to this perspective, a broad-based citizens initiative campaign would be ineffectual, maybe even counterproductive, in Washington because most citizens simply lack the requisite tools with which to make a worthwhile contribution.

Grandis's doubts about the capacity of certain kinds of citizens to participate in grassroots politics were by no means unrepresentative of the Washington activists, which points to another subtle but crucial difference in how the San Francisco and Washington growth-control movements conceived of citizen empowerment. Not only did San Francisco activists have faith in ordinary people to govern themselves, but they had faith in *all* ordinary people to do so. The San Francisco movement was characterized by an overriding commitment to inclusion.

As chapter 4 indicates, that was not always the case. In the early 1970s, the growth-control movement in San Francisco was run by white, upper-middle-class professionals, and their postmaterial concerns about the aesthetic and environmental impacts of downtown development dominated the first two initiative campaigns to limit new highrises. It was only later in the decade, when a fresh group of activists with a much more inclusive conception of citizen empowerment ascended within the movement, that grassroots activism became a potent political force. These new activists were themselves a diverse bunch in terms of race, ethnicity, gender, sexual orientation, and class. They consciously sought to maintain that diversity as they expanded the movement.

The commitment to an inclusive movement enabled San Francisco growth-control activists to establish contacts with diverse groups around the city. The resulting communication facilitated a fuller understanding of how those groups perceived downtown development and thus allowed activists to tailor their agenda more carefully to take into account their needs and desires. The drafting and marketing of the initiatives themselves became a collaborative process, with individuals and groups from all over the city participating. By the end of the 1970s, the San Francisco growth-control movement had shifted its priorities from such postmaterial preoccupations as architectural design and historic preservation to material issues that struck closer to home for most citizens—housing costs, public transit, and jobs. That, in turn, further widened the composition of the growth-control movement, making it an even more serious threat to the downtown growth coalition.

Given the somewhat elitist slant on how the planning advocates in Washington conceived of citizen empowerment, it is not surprising that their attachment to inclusion was much more limited. Indeed, they tended to be quite open about drawing class-based distinctions regarding the political abilities of District residents. They maintained that grassroots activism around land use issues in less privileged sections of the city was minimal in the 1980s because lower-income people were forced to contend with more urgent matters such as saving enough money to feed their families and avoiding the pervasive violence spawned by crack addicts hanging out on street corners. But although San Francisco growth-control activists also recognized how poverty and crime tend to sap the energies of lower-income people and thus discourage them from becoming engaged in local politics, they plunged in anyway, still hoping to win their political support and perhaps active participation.[34]

By contrast, Washington's predominantly white, middle-class planning advocates seemed to think that organizing in lower-income neighborhoods was a hopeless endeavor. Terry Lynch, who got his start in politics by helping local churches set up homeless shelters before becoming one of the city's most visible growth-control activists, contended that because lower-income people are forced to deal with more pressing concerns, they tend not to be sufficiently educated about city politics or land use matters; hence, appeals from activists like himself were not likely to attract much attention.[35] Other Washington activists have expressed similar views: "My sense is that for a lot of African Americans in Washington life is so stressful that to do anything more than try to survive is a very difficult proposition. I truly think that . . . I mean how do you expect these people to get together and go down to City Hall." In trying to explain why mandatory linkage policies like those in San Francisco never caught on in Washington, a nonprofit housing provider commented, "We have a very different population here. We have an extremely poor city. You don't have a voting population that understands these issues and will vote it. You have a very small number of people that would force the politicians into that kind of position."[36]

Such assessments, however, say more about the perspectives of the planning advocates than they do about the reality of socioeconomic conditions in the District of Columbia. Washington is not "an extremely poor city" compared to San Francisco. Among the twenty-five largest U.S. cities, San Francisco has the fourth lowest poverty rate at 12.4 percent, but Washington is not far behind in ninth place at 16.9 percent. With respect to educational attainment and household income, the two cities rank two and three with respect to the former category and one and two with respect to the latter. Furthermore, this profile of relative economic security cuts across racial boundaries. One study of socioeconomic conditions in the District found that median black family income in Washington in 1987 was higher than in any other large U.S. city.[37] And yet the common perception among the planning advocates was that their city is overwhelmingly populated with poor black people who lack the resources to acquaint themselves with land use issues. Two important consequences flow from that perception. First, the planning advocates tended to overlook middle-income blacks as potential allies in fighting the downtown growth coalition. Second, they avoided engaging in grassroots activism in lower-income black communities, assuming that any efforts to mobilize residents there would be exceedingly difficult and probably futile.

Some of the planning advocates were extremely pessimistic about the potential of building bridges between diverse groups on development issues. Paul Aebersold believed that his Logan Circle neighborhood, one of the most diverse in the city, was marked by irreconcilable differences along racial and class lines:

> When you have ghetto dwellers who basically do not hold the same values of life and family and work as I do, I mean where's the common ground? I'm not going to their ground! No way. The United States of America is not going to that ground

> unless it's going to hell. And you tell me, y'know, when is the country going to recognize that that's an intolerable situation and really make some fundamental changes? . . . Certainly a small community group like this which [has] a very different view of what community should be from what the folks on the other side of 9th Street and certainly on the other side of North Capitol, y'know, there's no way we're going to resolve differences which are really a fundamental problem for the United States of America today and have been for 125 years.[38]

To Aebersold, the notion of building an inclusive, broad-based movement to challenge the downtown growth coalition was a quixotic dream.

Given their elitist conception of citizen empowerment, the planning advocates confined their efforts to reform land use policy to organizing within their own neighborhoods. Accordingly, the hub of planning advocacy became the mainly white, middle-class neighborhoods of northwest Washington. To the planning advocates, it made sense that this would be the focal point of grassroots opposition against the downtown growth coalition. After all, in their minds, the most effective way to fight a powerful opponent was to rely on individuals and groups with access to ample resources, and nowhere in the District was there a more impressive stockpile of resources than in the middle-class neighborhoods of the northwest. There was no question that residents there were well endowed in terms of income, education, political experience, and technical and professional skills—all of which would be vital in a protracted struggle with downtown interests.

More specifically, the planning advocates followed a three-pronged strategy in trying to regulate downtown development through the mechanism of comprehensive planning: grassroots organizing within middle-class neighborhoods, lobbying public officials, and filing lawsuits to stop development projects. In the view of the planning advocates, each of these three tactics would weaken the growth coalition's grip on downtown development.

Because of their lack of confidence in the efficacy of trying to mobilize lower- and working-class residents around development issues, the planning advocates were content to organize within their own ranks. They encouraged residents, especially in predominantly white, middle-class neighborhoods, to attend community meetings, sign petitions, write letters, and even congregate at development sites to block bulldozers. During local election years, sustained efforts were undertaken to educate voters on how candidates stood on land use issues. Those efforts soon paid off; politicians who had habitually supported the downtown growth coalition were vulnerable in such white, middle-class enclaves of growth-control activism as Dupont Circle, Foggy Bottom, and Capitol Hill.

Lobbying public officials in between general elections was also an important element in the planning advocates' arsenal of growth-control tactics. The city had had a long history of citizen activism through its system of civic associations. After home rule was adopted in 1974, the civic associations functioned as neighborhood associations and were a persistent presence at meetings of the District Council and the Zoning Commission. But the primary vehicle in fighting for community interests on development issues was the Advisory Neighborhood Commission (ANC). With the advent of home rule, the city established an extensive network of neighborhood commissions that would be able to maintain more personal contact with citizens than the District Council or the mayor. Based on those contacts, neighborhood commissioners would serve in an advisory capacity to other city government institutions. Significantly, the Home Rule Act invested the advisory neighborhood commissions with meaningful power on land use matters; by law, the Zoning Commission was obligated to give "great weight" to the recommendation of any ANC whose district was affected by a proposed development project. Thus, lobbying through the ANC became a major weapon of the growth-control movement in preventing commercial encroachment into middle-class, residential areas.

But Washington's planning advocates had broader concerns about downtown development than just neighborhood preservation. They also had a keen interest in seeing the city develop according to a set of clear principles that would be established, not by the downtown growth coalition behind closed doors, but as the result of a public process to prepare and implement a comprehensive plan to guide development in the District during the ensuing years. The most influential organization devoted to proper planning was the Committee of 100 on the Federal City, which was established in 1923 to preserve the traditions and goals of the L'Enfant plan. The organization became increasingly active during the 1970s and 1980s in response to the perceived threats that spreading commercial office development posed to L'Enfant's vision for the city. Its president, Dorn McGrath, described the composition of the Committee of 100 as "largely professionals; some are not, but some are leaders who were elected to . . . advisory neighborhood commissions . . . and some educators, but lots of planners, architects, lawyers, engineers, business leaders, lot of them, maybe two hundred of them."[39] A second organization, the Citizens Planning Coalition, consisted of neighborhood groups concerned about local zoning issues. Both of these organizations endeavored to prepare their own planning studies of individual neighborhoods as well as of the overall city and advocate planning proposals before such public bodies as the District Council, the Zoning Commission, the Office of Planning, and the mayor's office.

The third tactic for combating the downtown growth coalition was to file lawsuits to block individual projects that failed to conform to the comprehensive plan. Although the planning advocates would rarely win such suits outright, they could force developers to expend considerable resources in litigation and delay completion of their projects, and thus the inflow of profits, for months or years at a time. Anxious to avoid such costly delays, developers would sometimes agree to concessions demanded by the planning advocates. Attorneys also argued before the Zoning Commission in support of petitions to downzone residential neighborhoods to safeguard against commercial encroachment. This proved to be quite successful in the middle and late 1980s, as one residential community after another persuaded the Zoning Commission to downzone its neighborhood with the assistance of land use attorneys.[40]

The overall political impact of the planning advocates' elite-oriented tactics, however, proved to be rather limited. With respect to advancing the progressive value of citizen empowerment, the activists achieved mixed results at best. Although planning advocacy increased popular engagement in development politics in white, middle-class neighborhoods, it had little effect in the majority of Washington neighborhoods. The prudent planning wing of the growth-control movement simply failed to promote citizen empowerment by fostering contacts across racial, ethnic, and class lines. The cultural ramifications of that failure were far-reaching.

To start, the planning advocates continued to be consumed with their own interpretation of downtown development. In their view the main cost of downtown growth was the encroachment of commercial office buildings into residential neighborhoods; but even if that could be prevented through amendments to the zoning code, downtown development still contributed to unpleasant spillover effects like traffic congestion, worsening pollution, fewer parking spaces, displacement of neighborhood shops because of rising property values, and other undesirable changes in the quality of life. The planning advocates sought to use the tool of comprehensive planning to control what they felt were the most harmful impacts of the downtown building boom.

But in doing so, the planning advocates never developed much awareness of the kinds of concerns that mattered most to people living in other neighborhoods in the city. Consequently, they never appreciated the extent to which they shared common grievances with other groups. Downtown development posed a threat to the quality of life in black, working-class neighborhoods like Shaw. That neighborhood was close enough to the downtown business district to be affected by development-induced real estate speculation, and therefore residential and commercial displacement was a serious problem there too. And yet the planning advocates from white, middle-class neighborhoods acted as though they were the only victims of downtown development policies. A Dupont Circle activist said, "In Dupont Circle, we're kind of parochial. We are parochial. There's just no doubt about it. Occasionally, we get drawn into some larger issues but at the invitation of someone else. But basically we're here to protect . . . the interests of Dupont Circle."[41]

By neglecting to reach out to other groups in the city, the planning advocates missed an opportunity to learn about other people's grievances regarding downtown development. They might have discovered that working-class blacks would have gladly joined a neighborhood-based movement against the downtown growth coalition if the activists had proposed strategies to link downtown development with neighborhood revitalization and employment opportunities. For instance, Shaw residents could only watch in dismay the ever mounting prosperity of the adjoining downtown district while their neighborhood stagnated. Had the planning advocates devoted more time and energy to communicating with citizens in Shaw, they might have tapped into the growing disappointment that smoldered beneath the surface of so many other black, working-class neighborhoods. Instead, they remained oblivious to the sense of injustice felt by numerous Washingtonians arising from the unfulfilled promises of city leaders. The current president of the Dupont Circle Citizens Association, Dennis Bass, conceded as much: "I don't really know anybody over there. I really don't, which just goes to show you the gulf." And when a former president of the same neighborhood organization was asked whether downtown development had been "a positive or negative thing for the African American community," he replied: "That's really something I haven't looked at. I mean that's not really my field. It's not something I looked at that closely."[42]

As a result, working-class African Americans, who also felt victimized by the policies of the downtown growth coalition, experienced isolation, alienation, and apathy. Ignored by the planning advocates, most working-class blacks felt a mixture of dim hope that Mayor Barry would eventually deliver on his promise that downtown development would stimulate economic development in the city's neighborhoods and a deflating suspicion that conditions were not likely to change soon. A sense of resignation set in. One resident of Shaw described her thoughts about downtown development before she became active in land use politics, thoughts that she said were "typical of everybody" in her neighborhood: "I would just see buildings go up and say 'Oh, there's a new building.' . . . I didn't know the community really had a say-so. I just thought buildings went up and it would go through my mind that pretty soon I won't even be able to recognize downtown. But it never occurred to me that I as a citizen of D.C. and a resident of a neighborhood close to downtown would be able to have some input on it."[43] This feeling of powerlessness, of course, turned the planning advocates' preconceived notions about the capacity of most Washingtonians to participate effectively in grassroots activism into a self-fulfilling prophecy and reaffirmed their inclination to channel their energies toward organizing only in resource-rich neighborhoods.

As the racial and class schism that separated Washington neighborhoods widened, opportunities for communication, empathy, and cooperation grew more remote. Planning advocacy fixated on land use issues that resonated in white, middle-class neighborhoods, but not so much in black, working-class neighborhoods. The goals and strategies of planning advocacy seemed irrelevant to most Washingtonians.

But the problems associated with the planning wing of the Washington growth-control movement ran deeper than just irrelevance to the majority of citizens. The discourse and conduct of the planning advocates also generated a good deal of resentment in many quarters of the District. When a prominent growth-control activist such as Terry Lynch attempted to explain why Washington activists have achieved fewer successes than their counterparts in San Francisco by stating, "We're short on a middle-class here," working-class people were understandably troubled. When Lynch added that because middle-class activists have access to resources they are not as likely to be "bought off" by the real estate industry, that further alienated working-class citizens. Many Washingtonians were even more offended by the tendency of some planning advocates to lump them into the same category as welfare cheats and drug addicts. When asked about the possibility of nurturing a political relationship with working-class blacks in his Logan Circle neighborhood, white activist Paul Aebersold replied: "The law-abiding citizens who raise families, by and large, if they ever had a reasonable job, they leave Washington. The black flight from Washington is well documented. . . . What you've got left is the prosperous middle class, the blacks who live from all over the city, but the obvious nice areas are up along 16th Street. I guess there are some nice areas in Takoma Park, some nice areas in Ward 7. . . . [So] you've got left that element of the black community, and then the other element would be the hard-core ghetto. Very little in between."[44] According to this view, virtually all of the thousands of black residents of the Logan Circle/Shaw area are part of the "hard-core ghetto." This suggests one more compelling reason why African Americans, especially in the near-downtown neighborhoods of Logan Circle and Shaw, felt alienated from the planning advocates.

Such talk raises the thorny question of racism. To what extent did planning advocacy evince a racist character that alienated citizens in a city with a majority of blacks? There is clear evidence that the comments of a small number of individuals connected with the planning wing of the growth-control movement smacked of racism. For most of the planning advocates, however, the more damaging problem was elitism. Because they focused narrowly on their own postmaterial concerns, it was almost inevitable, as the political scientist Ronald Inglehart would argue, that the planning wing of the growth-control movement would attract a middle-class base of support. As that base expanded, and as the postmaterial values and goals of the activists solidified, the likelihood of organizing in working-class neighborhoods—black or white—would diminish because popular concerns in these neighborhoods would be strongly material in nature. Planning advocacy in Washington thus had a decisive middle-class bias. This was confirmed by Dennis Gale in his study of Washington's downtown revival. He found that "land use conflicts in the city's core have increasingly become the province of middle- and upper-middle class participants."[45] In this regard Washington's planning advocates were reminiscent of the first wave of growth-control activists in San Francisco in the early 1970s; those activists had emphasized the environmental and aesthetic impacts of downtown development, ignoring the fact that most citizens saw downtown development as an engine of economic prosperity.

In both cases, the Achilles' heel of grassroots protest was the elitism inherent in the managerial vision of the activists. Despite a rhetorical attachment to the progressive value of popular control, activists did not feel comfortable allowing the majority of ordinary people to wield power. They believed that a protest movement against such an imposing foe as the downtown growth coalition required leaders who possessed sufficient skills and expertise to navigate the turbulent waters of development politics. By and large those leaders came from white, middle-class neighborhoods where familiarity with the intricacies of comprehensive planning was at its peak. The managerial impulse of the planning advocates led them to eschew inclusive practices such as a citizens initiative and instead rely on such exclusionary, elite-oriented tactics as the preparation and advocacy of comprehensive plans and litigation to enforce the plans. Managerial activism thus reinforced the parochial mentality that pervaded white, middle-class neighborhoods and exacerbated feelings of isolation and resentment that increasingly characterized black, working-class neighborhoods. The political consequences for the growth-control movement were disastrous.

Whether one interprets the discourse and conduct of the Washington planning advocates as mainly elitist or racist almost becomes irrelevant in the racially charged context of Washington, D.C. Regardless of the actual mindset of white growth-control activists, their practices often were interpreted as racist by black citizens. And the leaders of the downtown growth coalition, anxious to subvert any neighborhood-based opposition to its policies, did everything possible to ensure that elitist practices would be interpreted as racist behavior. Mayor Marion Barry was especially clever at exploiting racial divisions by pointing out how the planning advocates had systematically ignored the economic aspects of downtown development that mattered so much to most of the city's African American community.

Popular resentment among black Washingtonians against the planning advocates was manifested in two ways. First, the genuine expertise that the planning advocates possessed regarding downtown development was often shunned. For example, activist Dorn McGrath, a professional planner and university professor, remarked, "All those well-educated, white faces around town could say whatever they want and it may not matter too much in the big picture. Because sometimes . . . people in the government seek out the educated, white faces and people with concerns and civic motivations and all that for help, but more often than not they resent your putting your nose into it. And that's just reality." Logan Circle activists experienced a similar repudiation of an offer to "do good." They tried to arrange a linkage deal that would enable them to produce forty units of affordable housing in the community. But to their surprise the Logan Circle Citizens Association had "real trouble getting anything accomplished because we're white." Logan Circle's Leslie Steen noted that as the gulf between the planning advocates and the community development advocates widened, it became increasingly difficult for white activists associated with the former who genuinely wanted to build bridges to do so.[46]

The second way in which popular resentment against the growth-control movement was manifested was the tendency for working-class blacks to look to city officials for guidance on development issues. With animosity toward the planning advocates running high, the turn toward the downtown growth coalition seemed to reflect the old adage "The enemy of your enemy must be your friend." Thus, the elitism (often interpreted as racism) of the planning advocates had the effect of prompting black residents in working-class neighborhoods to maintain their allegiance to the growth coalition despite the negative impacts and unfulfilled promises of its development policies. Any hope for a unified, neighborhood-based movement to challenge the power of downtown elites over downtown development simply evaporated.

Conclusion

The planning wing of the growth-control movement had high hopes of reordering the politics of downtown development in Washington. The combination of strict regulation through comprehensive planning and expanded citizen control over the policy-making process would reign in the building boom and ensure a proper development of the city. But although the planning advocates purported to support the progressive value of popular empowerment as a key element in their battle against the downtown growth coalition, analysis of their

Washington, D.C.

(*Left*)A new day and a new era in Washington, D.C.: Mayor Marion Barry and his wife, Effie, relishing the joy of inauguration day. (Copyright *Washington Post;* reprinted by permission of D.C. Public Library)

(*Below*) Mayor Barry addresses his staff for the first time in January 1979. (Copyright *Washington Post;* reprinted by permission of D.C. Public Library)

(*Left*) A priority of the Barry administration was to build upon the downtown development initiatives of the 1970s, including the restoration of the Old Post Office Building and the renewal of Pennsylvania Avenue between the White House and the Capitol. (*Below*) The focal point of commercial office growth during the 1970s had been the K Street and Connecticut Avenue district. Urban design specialists criticized the boxy, undistinguished architecture of the "new" downtown business district.

Early in his administration, the mayor confers with a group of local bankers eager to finance the accelerating downtown building boom. (Copyright *Washington Post;* reprinted by permission of D.C. Public Library)

Mayor Barry appoints one of the city's leading land-use attorneys, Robert Linowes, to head the Committee to Promote D.C. in April 1981. (Copyright *Washington Post;* reprinted by permission of D.C. Public Library)

During the 1980s, commercial office construction shifted eastward into what had been the "old" downtown business district. Franklin Square was rejuvenated with large, new office buildings and lunchtime concerts in the park.

The Washington Convention Center opened in 1982 at 9th Street and New York Avenue. Within a decade, however, industry analysts determined that the facility was too small to accommodate most large conventions.

(*Right*) The building boom's impact on retail business was mixed. Hecht's built the first downtown department store in a major U.S. city since World War II. But two other department stores in Metro Center closed, including Woodward & Lothrop, which will be converted into an opera house.(*Below*) Small businesses in the heart of the old downtown along F Street continue to struggle.

Hotel construction also fueled downtown development. The Westin Hotel, developed by the Oliver T. Carr Corporation, was one of several new luxury hotels constructed in the West End.

To make room for new hotels and office buildings in the West End, townhouses resembling these two-story homes in lower Dupont Circle were demolished.

Dupont Circle, just north of the expanding downtown business district, was a hotbed of growth-control activism. Citizens mobilized to block the encroachment of office buildings into their neighborhood. Shops and restaurants line busy Connecticut Avenue.

Local residents congregate at Dupont Circle on a pleasant spring afternoon.

(*Right*) Oliver Carr, the city's most prominent developer and a past president of the Greater Washington Board of Trade, was a champion of downtown revitalization years before it became fashionable. (Copyright *Washington Post;* reprinted by permission of D.C. Public Library)

Mayor Marion Barry meets business leaders at a Board of Trade gathering. (Copyright *Washington Post;* reprinted by permission of D.C. Public Library)

discourse and their conduct reveals a different story. Although they voiced a desire to open up the development decision-making process to expanded citizen control, their practice of relying so heavily on planners, attorneys, and other professionals indicated that they had certain citizens in mind for the job. The planning advocates preferred responsible citizens who did their homework, mastered the "facts and figures," and demonstrated a sophistication fit for governing. Planning advocacy turned out to be much more consistent with a managerial vision of politics—that is, a strong faith in government to correct market imperfections, but a government that is ultimately controlled by trained experts with the knowledge to get things done right. As such, the counterhegemonic potential of the planning advocates' brand of activism was diminished.

It is important to underscore that grassroots activism that includes elite-oriented practices is not necessarily inconsistent with a fully counterhegemonic progressive vision, provided those practices are conducted within a broader framework that genuinely emphasizes popular empowerment. For example, San Francisco's progressive activists used planning and litigation as vital components in their attack on the downtown growth coalition too, but only as a complement to a grassroots strategy that relied primarily on a series of citizens initiative campaigns. In the San Francisco case there was no confusion about the growth-control activists' unwavering commitment to popular control over downtown development. In Washington, by contrast, the elitist leanings of the planning advocates were unmistakable.

The ramifications of managerial activism for the local political culture were significant. The white, middle-class professionals who mainly constituted the planning wing of the growth-control movement were motivated by postmaterial concerns that held little interest for most Washington residents. Even worse, the exclusionary character of the movement breeded resentment among black, working-class citizens, which only widened existing racial and class divisions within the city. Leaders of the downtown growth coalition were quick to employ their vast resources to exploit such divisions in attempting to undermine the legitimacy of the planning advocates as representatives of the neighborhoods' interests regarding downtown development.

Finally, the planning advocates unwittingly reinforced through their managerial discourse and conduct the tendency of ordinary citizens to look to skilled experts for guidance in assessing their own interests and options regarding downtown development. Given a choice between the predominantly black professionals in the Barry administration and the predominantly white professionals who made up the prudent planning movement, African Americans in Washington were inclined to take their cues from the former. Therefore, planning advocacy had not only failed to promote cultural/political change; it had actually reaffirmed the practice of elite control, a key component of a privatist political culture. This only strengthened the capacity of the downtown growth coalition to make authoritative claims about downtown development based on its experience and expertise, and to repudiate the policy proposals of the growth-control movement as naive and impractical. Downtown development policy, consequently, changed very little in Washington.

✦11

Populist Activism

The planning advocates represented one important component of the Washington growth-control movement. The other key component of the grassroots movement that challenged the downtown growth coalition consisted of neighborhood-based activists typically associated with community development corporations and nonprofit housing organizations. Like the planning advocates, the community development advocates were disturbed by some of the negative impacts of downtown expansion on the quality of neighborhood life. Residential and small-business displacement caused by rising property values in close-in neighborhoods were seen as particularly problematic. But unlike the planning advocates, the community development advocates were primarily concerned about the unfulfilled promises made by downtown elites. For years neighborhood activists had heard all about how inexorable forces in the global economy were operating to revitalize the District. The expanding post-industrial economy was transforming the downtown business district into a mighty engine capable of generating jobs and tax revenue that would reinvigorate not just the downtown business community, but all of Washington's neighborhoods. The underlying logic for encouraging rapid downtown development seemed to make sense, even to the advocates of community development.

But as the building boom moved into the 1980s, the community development advocates began to lose patience. Downtown development was not producing noticeable improvements in the city's residential neighborhoods; if anything, some neighborhoods near downtown were being harmed. Community development advocates concluded that the problem was with the downtown growth coalition. The firm hold that downtown elites maintained over land use policy was somehow working against the interests of the neighborhoods. The answer was to loosen that hold by opening up the policy-making process to those groups that best represented the needs and interests of ordinary people. Community development advocates felt that from their base in the District's predominantly black neighborhoods they were in a better position than either the downtown growth coalition or the planning advocates to express the wishes of most Washingtonians. If they could just break into the decision-making process, the community development advocates offered the best hope of empowering ordinary citizens and ensuring that downtown development really would enhance neighborhood revitalization.

Rumblings of Discontent

As the most visible leader of the growth coalition, Mayor Marion Barry had assured Washingtonians that downtown development would enrich not just citizens with close ties to downtown but citizens in all of the city's neighborhoods. One way he proposed to carry out that promise was to establish a program requiring minority equity partnerships in new development projects, and Barry did, in fact, launch such a program soon after he was first elected as mayor. Within a few years, however, many business leaders, activists, and public officials pointed to the program as evidence of cronyism and corruption within the administration. Developers found themselves competing among themselves to enlist as partners a relatively small circle of friends of the mayor or other top city officials. District Council member John Wilson said, "I call them the chosen ones.... What started out to benefit the minority community at large" has turned into a program enabling some well-connected blacks to "move out to McLean or Potomac."[1] Many neighborhood activists soon concluded that the mayor's minority equity partnership program would not be a satisfactory mechanism for securing equitable growth.

Occasionally, criticism of inequities produced by the city's development policies was more sweeping. *Washington Post* columnist Dorothy Gilliam targeted "the building barons of the private sector" as "a small, exclusive group of those with chunks of money and good connections . . . that is remaking the skyline of the nation's capital, effectively deciding what this town will look like over the next several decades." She then proceeded to contest the privatist assumption that what was good for the development community was good for the city. Noting that developers were becoming wealthy, Gilliam queried whether "the Club is really getting out more than they are putting in." But, interestingly, in 1981 there were limits as to how far critics of existing policies would go in calling for structural reforms to promote a wider distribution of the benefits generated by downtown growth. Although Gilliam favored "imposing a policy of social responsibility on the private developers," the only concrete program that she could suggest was expanding the minority equity partnership program.[2] This inability to articulate alternative policies illustrates the hegemonic power of the privatist political culture.

Still, Gilliam's critique reflected a budding suspicion among activists based in lower-income neighborhoods that downtown interests were interfering with a process that should be leading to more meaningful improvements in the residential neighborhoods. Instead, elite control over downtown development was resulting in the enrichment of developers, corporate attorneys, and other groups connected to the real estate industry. Moreover, most of the new jobs in the gleaming downtown office buildings were going to suburban commuters. The majority of Washingtonians did not seem to be sharing in the fruits of the downtown building boom.

The earliest attempt to alter development policies to ensure that downtown growth would, in fact, benefit the neighborhoods came in 1983. District Council member Charlene Drew Jarvis responded to the simmering disgruntlement among neighborhood activists by proposing the city's first linkage bill. Influenced by San Francisco's housing linkage policy, the Jarvis bill required developers of commercial office buildings costing in excess of $20 million to spend an amount equal to 10 percent of their costs to build or renovate housing; as in San Francisco, developers would have the option of constructing the housing themselves, contracting the work out, or contributing money into a special city fund. However, the bill quickly came under a barrage of attacks from the downtown growth coalition. Years later, Jarvis recalled that the Barry administration "went ballistic" when it learned about the bill. The linkage measure was allowed to die in committee. During the ensuing months, a few members of the District Council would periodically chastise the Barry administration for neglecting less privileged areas of the city in favor of its program to revitalize downtown.[3] But without a strong constituency pushing for policy reforms such as linkage, the council rarely proposed its own initiatives.

Such a constituency did begin to take shape in the mid-1980s when community development advocates finally started to make some political noise. Their immediate motivation for doing so was not so much dissatisfaction with downtown development but the devastating impact of federal budget cuts provoked by the Reagan administration. With federal funds for affordable housing production and neighborhood development drying up, local activists began to search for alternative sources of revenue. Aware of other cities' experiences with linkage policies, Washington's community development advocates set their sights on finding ways to tap into the wealth being created by downtown expansion. With the general public growing more suspicious about who was really benefiting from the city's land use policies, the timing seemed ideal for an aggressive campaign in support of linked development.[4]

Linkage in Washington

Although the community development advocates did not realize it, by the mid-1980s progrowth interests had become receptive to some form of linked development. The reason for this surprising openness to a redistributive policy that had been bitterly opposed by the downtown growth coalitions in other cities is that the other wing of the Washington growth-control movement had been pushing hard for serious changes in land use policy. The city had responded to the planning advocates' call for more restrictive zoning regulations to clamp down on the downtown building spree by adopting a comprehensive plan. Next, city officials, including the mayor, began to express sympathy for community groups demanding a downzoning of residential neighborhoods to guard against new office development. On top of these discouraging events, community development advocates were suddenly voicing complaints about the growing gap between the downtown core and the neighborhoods. The trend was alarming to the growth coalition.

It was at this point that progrowth advocates found a way to dodge the bullets being fired by the two wings of the growth-control movement. Linkage offered a strategy for avoiding the restrictive zoning controls demanded by the planning advocates while at the same time appeasing the community development advocates. In the eyes of downtown elites, the beauty of the strategy was that not only would the Washington version of linkage weaken the growth-control movement, but the cost to the real estate industry would be minimal. Washington-style linkage would be a far cry from the burdensome set of exactions imposed on developers in San Francisco.

The origins of the Washington version of linkage can be traced to the city's planned unit development (PUD) law. That law had long allowed the Zoning Commission to grant zoning variances if developers of large-scale, mixed-use projects would provide certain on-site public amenities such as improved architectural designs, pedestrian plazas, and scenic landscaping. In the mid-1980s, office developers suggested an extension of the PUD practice. Developers would offer not only on-site public amenities but *off-site* public amenities as well. It was hoped that amenities such as affordable housing in lower-income neighborhoods might induce the city to allow developers to construct downtown office buildings in excess of existing zoning limits. It was really just an extension of a tried and true practice. Activist Robert Stumberg saw it coming: "The developers and particularly their attorneys have become very skilled at manipulating a planned unit development law, and they had established a tradition and a track record of offering public amenities in exchange for density bonuses. That was their style. And housing linkage was simply one more way of playing that game. So they were used to offering street furniture or open space." The Barry administration seemed to consent to this extended form of bargained linkage when the Office of Planning proposed amending the zoning ordinance to allow such linkage arrangements.[5]

The first linkage deal in Washington occurred in 1986. A developer, the

John Akridge Company, offered to donate $750,000 to a nonprofit housing developer to provide affordable housing in the District in exchange for a 50 percent increase in building density for a proposed commercial office building in a section of downtown that allowed a mix of residential and commercial land uses. The offer would enable the nonprofit developer to build seventy-five units of low-income housing or renovate about fifty units. But city planners recommended rejecting the offer because it provided no assurances that the housing would actually be built, or that it would be built downtown, the preferred site of the Barry administration.[6]

After several more weeks of negotiations, the Zoning Commission voted to approve what the *Washington Post* termed "the city's first housing linkage project." The agreement allowed the Akridge Company to construct an office building at a downtown site that would exceed zoning restrictions by ninety thousand square feet. In exchange for the extra four floors that the developer would now be able to build, the Akridge Company agreed to pay $1.5 million to two nonprofit housing developers to rehabilitate 150 low-income housing units. The developer's counsel, Whayne S. Quin, expressed satisfaction with the linkage agreement. He estimated that the extra zoning density would bring his client as much as $25 million in additional gross rents in the next decade. Community development advocates were also pleased to have tapped a new revenue source that would enable them to produce desperately needed affordable housing.[7]

On the other hand, the planning advocates who had fought for the comprehensive plan were disturbed with the Zoning Commission's decision. In earlier testimony before the commission, Anne Hughes Hargrove of the Committee of 100 and the Citizens Planning Coalition asserted, "This kind of program will be a boon for developers because they will no longer have to argue that a project is appropriate for its site. Instead, they can just offer to build a housing project somewhere else and they will get their rezoning." Moreover, one member of the Zoning Commission, John Parsons, opposed the practice of linkage because he feared that such deals would contribute to the "erosion" of the "promise to bring housing into the downtown."[8]

Despite such criticism, the city's approval of the Akridge Company project encouraged additional linkage proposals. In September 1987 the Hadid Development Company sought permission to build a twelve-story, 369,000-square-foot office building downtown that was 72,000 square feet beyond the existing zoning limit. Zoning regulations for the site also called for a mix of commercial and residential uses. In exchange for the added density and an exemption from the on-site housing requirement, the developer proposed donating $1.4 million to the Shaw Coalition Redevelopment Corporation to build affordable housing on a site a little more than a block away. The developer pointed out that the offer was consistent with the city's goal of promoting housing downtown and providing amenities close to the proposed development site.[9]

After several public hearings, the Zoning Commission asked the D.C. Department of Housing and Community Development to evaluate the developer's offer. Based on the Hadid Company's intent to charge thirty dollars per square foot in rent for the proposed office building, the Housing Department calculated that the developer would retrieve its $1.4 million linkage offer within seven years; during the next fourteen years the developer would earn approximately $6.4 million. The Housing Department concluded, "We believe it would be reasonable to ask the developer to share these long-range benefits with the city by requiring the developer to contribute 50 percent of the net cash flow increase generated" by the additional seventy thousand square feet of office space. It went on to suggest that a contribution of $4.6 million would be more appropriate. The Hadid Company called the Housing Department's estimations of its future profits "extremely exorbitant" and insisted that rejection of the linkage offer "would have a chilling effect on the whole housing linkage concept."[10] The developer threatened to revoke its offer altogether and simply comply with the zoning code.[11]

One week later, the Zoning Commission decided to ignore the Housing Department's recommendation to seek a more substantial contribution for affordable housing and accept the Hadid Company's proposal. Mohamed Hadid, president of the development firm, commented, "We are pleased . . . housing linkage is here to stay." City Planning Director Fred Greene added that the Hadid case "sends a message that housing linkage is something we encourage and will work for developers. The District is committed to housing linkage."[12]

Another highly visible linkage proposal surfaced in the summer of 1987 when a Boston-based developer, Mortimer B. Zuckerman, sought to build an eight-story office building on a parcel of property in the West End zoned exclusively for residential use. To overcome zoning restrictions, Zuckerman offered to contribute $2.2 million to the People's Involvement Corporation (PIC), a nonprofit organization that purchases and renovates affordable housing. In keeping with the city's policy of promoting housing production in the West End, Planning Director Fred Greene said he would prefer that the donation be used to build housing within one-quarter mile of the proposed office building. However, PIC's development director Ernestine Jackson replied that this was unlikely given the high cost of land in the area: "PIC's perspective is to make the most of the [donation]. We'd like not to see it get lost in an expensive neighborhood like Foggy Bottom or the West End. . . . There should not be concern where [the housing] will be but if it will be." Jackson predicted that the housing would probably be located in Shaw, "where there is a greater need for low-cost housing."[13]

At this point the planning advocates, who had viewed the earlier linkage deals with serious concern, spoke out strongly in opposition. Many of them condemned a practice that they viewed as nothing less than "zoning for dollars." They wondered why they and the city had invested so much time, money, and energy into devising a comprehensive plan if the Zoning Commission was so willing to abandon the law for cash contributions from developers. One activist said, "I don't believe in selling zoning. I believe that zoning exists for a purpose, and while I don't believe that it is static—I do believe that it must be fluid and dynamic and responsive to changes in the marketplace—I don't think you should be able to *buy* it."[14] Other planning advocates worried that linkage would be used to hasten the encroachment of commercial office buildings into residential neighborhoods. Con Hitchcock, the president of the Dupont Circle Citizens Association, asserted, "Housing linkage can erode the protections that zoning laws provide from unwanted uses coming into a neighborhood. . . . If developers can buy their way around zoning restrictions, then the whole zoning map may be up for grabs." Finally, some local residents decried the lack of any public amenity that would benefit the West End. Activist Ralph Rosenbaum commented, "I don't want to seem unsympathetic to the Shaw neighborhood because they have needs. But so do we, and one of our needs is housing. Where are the benefits to this community?"[15]

With the anxiety level of community activists rising in many neighborhoods in response to the proliferation of linkage proposals, the city decided to switch gears. The Zoning Commission for the first time rejected a linkage proposal. Although Zuckerman had revised his linkage offer to provide housing close to the planned office building in addition to donating three hundred thousand dollars to a nonprofit group in Shaw, the Zoning Commission determined that the package still did not adequately compensate residents in the West End.[16]

The downtown growth coalition was not discouraged by the Zoning Commission's action. Private developers, knowing they had the support of the Barry administration, hurried to assemble new development proposals with substantial linkage components. The planning advocates responded by intensifying their criticism as linkage soon became the most inflammatory land use issue in city politics in many years.

The planning advocates opposed the Washington version of linkage on several grounds. First, as already noted, they denounced the whole concept that land use regulations could be circumvented if developers simply paid the city enough money. This turned the zoning code into a farce and left residential neighborhoods highly vulnerable to commercial encroachment.

Second, the planning advocates rejected the substance of the bargain in the typical linkage deal. They asked why it was necessary to give office developers *any* inducements at all as a condition for providing amenities such as new housing. Many of them were aware of the mandatory programs in San Francisco and Boston in which developers received *nothing* in exchange for sizable linkage fees except official permission to proceed with their projects. They went on to point out that the city had already provided the real estate community with ample incentives to build through such major public investments as the construction of a modern, state-of-the-art metro system that happened to be centered downtown.[17] Any additional incentives in the form of density bonuses would only further enrich the developers at the taxpayers' expense. The planning advocates dismissed claims by real estate interests that linkage without additional incentives would discourage future investment and perhaps "kill the goose that laid the golden egg." They asserted that because Washington was the site of the federal government, it would always be a desirable location for businesses, law firms, and lobbyists with or without a modest linkage program. The sentiments of activist Dorn McGrath, a professor of urban planning, are typical: "I think in a city like this [business inducements are] a joke. Because this is the nation's capital and the land is very, very scarce, it's very special. And I don't think you need to give away. People ought to be delighted to have a chance to build something big in the nation's capital."[18]

The planning advocates argued that if the city was going to engage in linkage deals, then it should be extracting much better exactions for the public. After all, developers were obtaining extremely valuable density bonuses that would translate into millions of dollars in future office rental profits in exchange for comparatively paltry sums for housing production. One activist put it bluntly: "If you're going to be a whore, don't be a cheap whore."[19]

Finally, the planning advocates objected to how the money raised through linkage was being used. Although mindful of the need for affordable housing in lower-income neighborhoods, they maintained that the city should be committed to carrying out the mandates established in the comprehensive plan. A mandate that was particularly important to the activists was the nurturing of a "living downtown." They saw linkage as an appropriate vehicle for preserving the "sanctity" of the comprehensive plan by channeling some of the wealth generated by the commercial office boom into the production of housing in the downtown district.[20] Indeed, this was the brightest hope for transforming downtown Washington from simply a place of work to a place of work, residence, and leisure. The planning advocates dreamed of a Paris by the Potomac.

The District Council attempted to respond to the mounting criticism of linkage by proposing new approaches to link downtown development with neighborhood development. Council member Charlene Drew Jarvis offered a bill in June 1987 that would have established a purely voluntary housing linkage program. But activists charged that such a program would be practically useless since no developer would voluntarily contribute funds for affordable housing. Jarvis answered that a mandatory policy like San Francisco's would drive development out of the city and into the suburbs.[21]

District Council Chair David Clarke then submitted his own linkage bill. He contended that the downtown building boom had contributed to the city's shortage of affordable housing and that this alone justified the establishment of a mandatory linkage policy to mitigate that adverse impact. But although such rhetoric and rationale were reminiscent of those employed by San Francisco activists earlier in the decade, Clarke's "mandatory" policy stopped considerably short of the San Francisco program. The Clarke bill obligated commercial office developers to provide new housing, but only if they received special dispensation from the city in the form of a density bonus or an alley closing.[22] Although developers disputed Clarke's contention that downtown development had exacerbated the city's housing crisis, they had no quarrel with his proposed remedy.

Meanwhile, Washington's planning advocates, who were troubled by the whole concept of trading "zoning for dollars," continued to lobby for an alternative strategy for linking downtown development with affordable housing production. After retreating from her original voluntary linkage proposal, council member Jarvis tried a fresh approach. She submitted a bill in February 1989 calling for an annual surtax of ten cents for every square foot of existing office space in the District. She explained: "The objections to the use of zoning bonuses to produce housing were loud and clear, so I wanted to move away from the zoning process." Jarvis said the tax would raise $7 million a year and would be imposed for three years.[23] Developers approved of levying a small tax on a much wider class of property, but the rest of the business community remained cool to the idea of any kind of tax increase. The District Council was never able to arrive at a politically acceptable compromise to the linkage debate.

With the District Council bogged down, attention shifted to the Zoning Commission, which had continued to consider ad hoc linkage deals proposed by commercial office developers. Under pressure to establish a consistent policy for considering such linkage proposals, the Zoning Commission began to hold public hearings in the spring of 1990 on what the *Washington Post* called "the District's biggest zoning debate in 30 years."[24]

After delaying a decision through the summer, the Zoning Commission voted three to two in September to give preliminary approval to a plan that made overtures to both sides of the linkage debate. Under the plan, developers would be required to produce housing or contribute to a housing fund in exchange for added rights to develop commercial offices downtown. Hence, the Zoning Commission retained the most distinctive feature of Washington's version of linkage—the exchange of public amenities for zoning variances. But in a break from past practice, the Zoning Commission insisted that the new linkage policy be consistent with the comprehensive plan's goal of creating a "living downtown." It therefore directed that the bulk of the new housing generated through the linkage program, a projected six thousand units, be located in the downtown area.[25]

This was a serious setback for the real estate industry, which had always claimed that any mandate to develop housing downtown, even market-rate housing, instead of much more lucrative commercial office buildings, would discourage economic investment. Community development advocates also expressed disappointment with the mandate since in their view valuable linkage resources would now be expended on expensive market-rate housing downtown instead of on affordable housing in lower-income neighborhoods. Activist Jim Dickerson stressed the equity issue:

> Everybody that I know of, including myself, thinks that housing is great to have downtown. The only issue is the money, and if it was in the early '80s I bet you that nobody would be complaining that money created by public policy would be going to subsidize luxury housing. The problem is [now] everyone's at the well. And who's the priority? And that's basically it—who gets that money? And if it's a choice between low- and moderate-income [housing] throughout the city as opposed to upper-income, building a new neighborhood down in the city, . . . we're saying let the market bear that downtown. Those folks are able to pay; they can live anywhere they want to.

Activist Clarene Martin echoed Dickerson's point by noting that the idea of a living downtown "sounds fine and dandy if you live in a nice little house with heat and you can pay your mortgage," but it does not excite "the people who were being displaced" by the city's development policies. Other community development advocates argued that the downtown business district had already become a "living downtown" with the addition of the convention center and numerous shops, restaurants, theaters, and hotels.[26]

To soften the blow for both groups, the Zoning Commission permitted developers to fulfill 30 percent of their housing requirement by funding production in other parts of the city; those contributions were expected to add another four thousand units of housing beyond the downtown core. The Zoning Commission postponed the difficult task of adopting a formula to determine the precise link between office space and housing units. Despite continuing attacks from real estate interests and community development advocates during the next two months, the Zoning Commission stuck with its original position and voted in December to reaffirm the plan it had tentatively approved in

September.[27] Ironically, just as the Zoning Commission finally acted to resolve the thorniest issues regarding linkage, the downtown building boom fizzled to a halt. As in most U.S. cities, years of aggressive expansion had led to a glut in commercial office space by the early 1990s. The resulting sharp decline in downtown development meant a sharp decline in linked development as well.

The upshot is that the Washington growth-control movement had only limited success in promoting government policies that would ensure a more equitable distribution of the costs and benefits of downtown development. The version of linkage that was pursued in Washington bore only minimal resemblance to linkage in San Francisco. In the latter city, activists succeeded in getting a series of ordinances enacted imposing mandatory fees on all new commercial office buildings in the downtown district exceeding twenty-five thousand square feet. Developers got nothing in return except permission to proceed with their projects. Moreover, the benefits that San Francisco derived from linkage exceeded what was explicitly mandated by statute. Because the city had adopted through a citizens initiative in 1986 an annual cap on office construction of only five hundred thousand square feet, developers soon found themselves competing with each other for the right to develop a sharply constricted supply of office space. To secure development rights in the post–Proposition M era, developers promised to provide amenities above and beyond what was officially required in the linkage ordinances. In this way linkage in San Francisco generated a steady stream of revenue throughout the 1980s for affordable housing, mass transit, child care, public art, open space, and job creation for local residents.

Linkage in Washington was much more limited. Both as an ad hoc practice and as an established policy of the Zoning Commission, linkage took the form of a deal. Developers would make donations to housing providers based on the amount of commercial office space they planned to build; in exchange for the donations, the city would give the developers some bonus—permission to build office space in excess of existing zoning regulations or perhaps an alley closing. In a sense developers would give to the city with one hand while taking from the city with the other, and the terms of the bargain were always slanted decisively in favor of the developer. Moreover, linkage in Washington was generally confined to housing. No attempts were made to link downtown development with other issue areas such as mass transit, child care, or employment as a matter of law. Finally, even within the one issue area of housing, linkage did not assure the production of much *affordable* housing in residential neighborhoods; a substantial proportion was diverted to help fund market-rate housing in the downtown business district. District Council Chair David Clarke lamented several missed opportunities: "We didn't use our linkage money when it was an opportune time to use it. And we were all late in suggesting something. And then, finally, we came up with something, and there was such a political bind, not only in the council, but in terms of the constituencies." Another city official concluded, "If [linkage] had been in effect at the beginning of the '80s, we would have capitalized a tremendous amount of money."[28] In short, the use of linkage to advance equitable growth was hardly a success.

The Cultural Ramifications of Populist Activism

To explain the disappointing outcome of the battle for equitable growth in Washington, it is necessary to scrutinize how exactly that battle was fought. The bottom line is that notwithstanding their purported commitment to a progressive vision of urban politics, the community development advocates engaged in a brand of activism that helped to solidify the privatist political culture that legitimated the preferred policy positions of the downtown growth coalition. Although the activists remained true to the counterhegemonic principle of popular empowerment, they deviated noticeably from the progressive goal of a robust public sphere devoted to securing a fairer distribution of the costs and benefits of rapid downtown growth.

To start, although the community development advocates obviously supported linkage, they were always intent on not doing anything that might discourage capital investment in the District. Indeed, their zeal for aggressive downtown expansion paralleled that of any commercial office developer. Jim Dickerson's view was representative: "My philosophy is that [downtown] is an economic engine. Let's crank that thing up and get as much money out of that as we can reasonably within the guidelines of what's good zoning and planning and make sure that that money gets distributed equitably throughout the city to those who need it the most. And that's basically where I'm coming from."[29]

One difficulty with Dickerson's well-intentioned position is that it overlooked the negative impacts of rapid development, impacts that hit lower-income neighborhoods as hard as higher-income neighborhoods. Such talk reaffirmed the privatist view that downtown development is an inherently positive approach to urban regeneration that should be encouraged, even if that policy required substantial public subsidies in the form of tax abatements and density bonuses.

The lack of sensitivity to the costs of rapid growth may be attributable to an underlying assumption that market forces are powerful phenomena that simply can not be redirected in any substantial way. Speaking of the problem of residential displacement in near-downtown neighborhoods caused by commercial office expansion in the downtown core, activist Clarene Martin commented, "The black community basically thinks that there's nothing that can be done. . . . The black community sees themselves as 'Eventually I'm gonna be pushed out of my neighborhood.' The white community sees it as 'There's nothing we can do about black people being pushed out.' It's progress. Y'know, this is the way things are moving. That's the flow and we have to go with the flow." The pessimism in this deterministic view is balanced somewhat by the assumption that market forces may bring positive changes too. Community development advocate Deirdre Williams reflected on her expectations about how downtown growth would affect the District's residential neighborhoods:

> I think there were some good assumptions made at the beginning. And they were good assumptions. They were based on the goodness of man and he doing the right thing, giving, y'know, ample incentives, and I believe that's what Reagan believed that, y'know, you just lay off, don't regulate people too much and they'll do the right thing. Not that they'll take the money and run. They will make it trickle down to the little man. And the same assumption, I believe, happened here, that if we just do the downtown core, that'll expand the tax base, we'll have more revenue to do all the programs we need to do in the neighborhoods.[30]

Such attitudes toward the positive and negative aspects of private-sector forces were, of course, consistent with the privatist vision of politics propagated by the downtown growth coalition.

The community development advocates also tended to follow privatist assumptions about the role of government interfering with the private sector. They were always wary of the impact of regulatory and redistributive policies. For example, Jim Dickerson criticized a proposal by the planning advocates to impose a surcharge on all existing commercial office space in the District as a way to raise revenue for affordable housing; he called it a "punitive" measure that would create an antibusiness climate and deter future investment. Clarene Martin agreed, predicting that such a move would cause developers to shift their investment sights from the city to the suburbs, a warning that issued from the D.C. Chamber of Commerce almost on a daily basis. Martin asserted: "I have problems with this taxing the square footage of office space. . . . I think it's very important for D.C.'s office space to remain competitive with that in the suburban areas, because the suburban areas are probably more desirable because you don't have the parking problem, you don't have the crime problem, you don't have the congestion." Dickerson concluded with this observation: "Developers per se are not my enemy. I don't want to see neighborhoods destroyed, residential characters destroyed. But at the same time, I don't want to see that economic engine shut down. That's a goose that laid a golden egg for the whole city economically. So I want to see how we can get the most out of it. So that's how I view it."[31]

The community development advocates' distrust of government was also manifested in their preferred strategy for generating revenue for affordable housing production. They rejected the planning advocates' proposal for a surtax on all commercial office space to fund affordable housing production, not just because of concerns about capital disinvestment, but because they feared that the money from a broad-based tax would go into the city government's general fund and simply disappear. By contrast, revenue from linkage deals would be deposited in a special fund earmarked for specific affordable housing projects to be built by specified affordable housing providers. Linkage money was money that could be depended on, whereas general tax revenue was at risk. Community development advocate Jim Dickerson made clear which approach he preferred when he opined that most people in city agencies today "don't know their ass from a hole in the ground!"[32]

Significantly, the lack of confidence in government extended to some of the highest officials in city government. Activist Robert Stumberg tried to explain why District Council Chair David Clarke had decided to support the Washington style of linkage:

> He was passionate about his concern that the city couldn't be trusted to spend the money. It was much better to create a system of chits in the private sector, so that the private-sector developers and the private-sector nonprofits would work deals out and housing would be sparked by that public policy. I mean government wouldn't have to put its dirty hands in the process. I mean that's a credible position. I tried to argue with him on the grounds that it was also a default on the part of the council to make public agencies do their job . . . but he preferred not to get the government involved.[33]

Clarke's preference for linkage anchored in the private sector was in keeping with his concern about government infringing on the private property rights of developers. He questioned, for instance, the constitutionality of the linkage programs in San Francisco and Boston that exacted mitigation fees for "matter-of-right" office development projects. Clarke believed that a city government should impose a linkage exaction only when developers are given some special treatment such as an alley closing or a zoning variance. His reasoning is rooted in a privatist conception of property rights that stresses the value of limiting government interference in private activity:

> I pledged in my campaign not to go with . . . mandatory linkage . . . where [developers] had a right to build. My sense is [if] you've got a piece of private property, you have the right to build on your piece of private property. But if you want to do something beyond what you're allowed to do, then you're demanding some-

> thing from the people and then you should have to pay for it. It just works on that basic sense that you have a definite piece of property with a definite right associated with it. But if you want to go beyond that, if you want something exceptional, you want the city to bend the rules, not to ignore the rules, but to change the rules a bit . . . [then developers must] pay for it.

In emphasizing the *rights* that accrue to property ownership, it could be argued that Clarke overlooked the *responsibilities* that also attach to property owners. When told that San Francisco's legal rationale for subjecting all downtown developers of commercial office buildings to a linkage ordinance was that such buildings create negative impacts for the surrounding community that need to be mitigated, Clarke maintained that such mitigation should be funded through the city's property tax and not a special exaction on new commercial office development.[34] It is indicative of the strength of Washington's privatist political culture that Clarke, one of the city's most visible advocates of disadvantaged groups, would hold views on linkage that were compatible with those of the downtown growth coalition.

These views on the public/private dichotomy would seem to indicate that the community development advocates adopted a privatist vision of politics, but not quite. This is because, unlike the downtown growth coalition, they coupled their suspicions about government with a demand for popular empowerment. The community development advocates insisted on having influence over development decision making, and they felt that their partnership with the commercial office developers gave them that influence. They had broken through the wall of government that normally excludes ordinary people from participating meaningfully in policy making and wielded genuine power.

And yet, despite their populist commitment to empowering the citizenry, the community development advocates' queasiness about the public sector inhibited their inclination to mobilize ordinary citizens. Jim Dickerson, the executive director of one of the city's leading nonprofit housing organizations, contended that housing activists are first and foremost "providers" of housing. He emphasized: "We're producers. We're practitioners. We have been drawn into the political realm by necessity because someone else was taking off with some resources and not consulting us. But we don't have time to do all that [political work]." Other community development advocates were quite open about their disdain for political activism. One commented, "We're new to this. We are not politically sophisticated or sophisticated in the area of press relations and what have you. We're community folks, and we have built on a community level for the longest time. . . . We have not in the past seen it as important for us to run to the media and tell them our side of the story and have a media person hang on. It may get to that point where we may have to." Later on, she added, "We shy away from politics as *much* as we possibly can." The only community-based organization active in downtown development issues that did engage in grassroots organizing was Project WISH. A Project WISH activist noted that "the rest of the nonprofit housing community doesn't know how to organize people. It's not part of their mission."[35]

Clearly, the community development advocates did not relish the idea of going into the neighborhoods and building popular support for housing linkage. Their partnership with the commercial office developers afforded them a convenient excuse not to do so. That partnership ensured a steady stream of revenue for affordable housing production; all the community development advocates had to do was take the money from each individually negotiated linkage project and do what they did best—construct and rehabilitate affordable housing. Occasionally, some political work needed to be done, but that tended to be confined to lobbying city officials or testifying before the Zoning Commission or the District Council. Little or no effort was expended on grassroots organizing.

The cost of the community development advocates' reluctance to do political organizing soon became apparent. Citizens who would most benefit from policies intended to promote equitable growth never knew about linkage. Activist Clarene Martin asserted: "The only black groups that support linkage are those groups that are directly involved. For the most part, the black community has not yet been involved with linkage. I mean most of the black community doesn't even know about linkage." As a result no constituency ever arose to push the city for anything like the programs adopted in San Francisco. Robert Moore, the director of housing and community development during Mayor Barry's first term in office, recalled that in 1983 when council member Charlene Drew Jarvis introduced a mandatory linkage bill patterned after the one in San Francisco, no grassroots support surfaced to counter the opposition of the business community and the mayor:

> I don't think the proposal was developed in a way where there was a constituency for it.... There [were] no people in the neighborhoods coming out in favor of linkage. And even if they came out, OK you're talkin' about something, but what are you talkin' about? We don't know what you're talkin' about. So I don't think [council member Jarvis] . . . built a constituency for it, the linkage program. . . . I just remember her coming out with a legislative proposal that was pretty much her proposal that didn't get a lot of support from members of the council, and didn't get a lot of support from members of the community. I don't think they understood it. And it got a negative reaction, a real negative reaction from the administration, from the executive.

Because the community development advocates neglected to engage in grassroots organizing that would build popular awareness of and support for linkage, redistributive policies that were being debated and implemented in San Francisco remained off the public agenda in Washington. Some progressive proposals did not even occur to certain activists and public officials who had always considered themselves to be progressive. For example, when former Housing and Community Development Director Robert Moore was asked whether the city had ever tried to establish a program linking downtown development with employment opportunities in new office buildings for local residents, he replied: "I never thought about it until you brought it up." Others admitted being aware of progressive initiatives in other cities and yet somehow failed to follow through in Washington. District Council Chair David Clarke struggled to explain his initial inaction regarding linkage: "Boston and San Francisco had started doing [linkage]. Don't know. I mean obviously had I looked at it and thought more about it I would have moved quicker. So I didn't sit down and say no I can't do this now. It wasn't like a decided choice not to do it at a certain point, and that caused the lateness. . . . I do know that Boston and San Francisco [had] established good programs by the time we got into it."[36]

In sum, the campaign to promote equitable growth through linkage policies was hindered by the populist consciousness of the community development advocates. Despite their rhetorical support for the progressive notion of equitable growth through government intervention, their discourse and conduct were characterized by fears of an expansive public sector. They worried about imposing excessive burdens on business. They doubted the legal and ethical propriety of restricting property owners. And for the most part, they trusted the private market to distribute the costs and benefits of downtown development fairly. Market-driven downtown growth together with relatively mild linkage policies would be sufficient to revitalize the District's neighborhoods.

The community development advocates suspected that an activist government inevitably comes under the control of groups whose interests are hostile to those of ordinary citizens. Therefore, the best strategy is to limit the scope of government while doing whatever is necessary to ensure that the interests of neighborhood residents are well represented. In their view no group represented the interests of ordinary Washingtonians better than the community development advocates. They could be entrusted to empower people in the neighborhoods.

However, the community development advocates' populist discomfort with a vibrant public realm undermined their attempt to play a significant role in the policy-making process. They would exercise influence only if they succeeded in building a power base in the neighborhoods. But their reluctance to participate in political activity proved to be an obstacle. Most community development advocates readily acknowledged their disdain for politics and thus their avoidance of the task of grassroots organizing. They saw themselves as policy implementers, as "builders." Organizing in the neighborhoods was dismissed as someone else's responsibility. The idea of conducting civics lessons on street corners, as the San Francisco growth-control activists had done, never occurred to most of the Washington activists.

As a result the community development advocates' brand of populist activism had the unintended effect of reaffirming the privatist ideas, values, beliefs, and practices of the downtown growth coalition. They never insisted on strong mandatory exactions as in San Francisco, and linkage was always limited to one issue—housing. At times activists would lobby to apply linkage to child care or education, but such moments were sporadic and half-hearted. No consistent effort was ever undertaken to implement alternative linkage policies as formal statutes. Moreover, the downtown growth coalition never relinquished its firm command over decision making. Even when the community development advocates had a direct stake in some particular project, their role in the negotiating process was limited. One activist recalled, "[City officials and the developers] were not very welcoming of our [input]. I mean we weren't a part of the process even once. It was a closed-door kind of process."[37] In short, populist activism reinforced the privatist faith in market-driven policy making while failing to promote popular empowerment.

Friction within the Growth-Control Movement

Neighborhood-based activism around the issue of linkage not only had the unintended effect of solidifying the privatist political culture and thus further strengthening the downtown growth coalition's control over urban development; it also fractured the growth-control movement. The planning advocates and the community development advocates adhered to very different visions of politics. The resulting tension between the two groups foreclosed any hope of a united neighborhood front against downtown power.

As discussed in chapter 10, the planning advocates' managerial preference for elite control had the effect of limiting how they would use the public sphere to alter downtown development policy. They sought to harness the power of government to advance their narrow constituency's postmaterial goals. Comprehensive planning was the preferred vehicle for improving the quality of life in the District, and one of the principal mandates of the comprehensive plan, in the eyes of the planning advocates, was the nurturing of a "living downtown" by expanding residential land use in the business district. The planning advocates saw linkage as a mechanism to compel commercial office developers to work toward a living downtown. They reasoned that if developers were willing to donate money for housing in the neighborhoods in exchange for zoning variances and alley closings, then they should be willing to make similar donations for downtown housing. With this approach, linkage would be used to subsidize market-rate housing downtown. Although the immediate beneficiaries of such a linkage policy would be middle- and upper-middle-income citizens attracted by the social and cultural amenities of an increasingly vibrant downtown core, the benefits would eventually spread throughout the city. One planning advocate explained the link: "We think part of a long-term, smart downtown strategy is getting people to live down there. And probably most of those people, if they make good money, it'll make good sense for a long-term tax strategy because D.C. has . . . income taxes plus the sales tax. So you have high-income people, particularly those who spend pretty freely, living downtown. That's a good tax return for the city."[38]

That this view of linkage did not sit well with the community development advocates is hardly a surprise. Their populist worldview caused them to bristle at the specter of limiting the fruits of downtown development to upper-income groups. According to the community development advocates, all District residents should have the opportunity to share in the wealth emanating from downtown. A linkage policy that settled for anything less was prima facie evidence that the people's voice was not being heard at City Hall.

Moreover, the community development advocates' suspicion of government reinforced their inclination to respect the market. They tended to side with the commercial office developers who warned that any linkage policy mandating downtown housing would stifle economic investment in Washington and risk snuffing out the downtown building boom altogether. The planning advocates scoffed at the marketism of the community development advocates by insisting that investment demand for real estate in the District was so strong that few developers would be deterred by the implementation of a linkage policy designed to enhance the vitality of the downtown business district; indeed, such a policy, they predicted, would more likely heighten investor demand over the long term.

The visionary split between the planning advocates and the community development advocates over the issue of linkage grew increasingly heated as the two positions hardened. The former came to see the latter as being "ideologically driven" and motivated by a "class war" mentality. Terry Lynch declared, "It's their religion, their ethic, to be opposed to middle- and upper-income people." Others criticized the community development advocates for entering into an alliance with the developers. Land use attorney Richard Nettler contended: "The nonprofits were co-opted by the developers. . . . It would have been more natural for them to have worked with Terry [Lynch] to create some kind of proposal downtown that would have thrown off money for them as well. And instead they allowed the developers' attorneys to represent their interests. And the developers had no interest in protecting their interests, but only the developers' own interests." Activist Ed Grandis added: "I truly think that we have this bizarre situation where people who had set up these wonderful housing programs have now almost aligned themselves with the developers. And the people who are policy people, and who are left-of-center policy people, distrust the developers and so now have come to distrust the housing activists because the housing activists don't want to negotiate. What they want to do is support the developers' interests in reducing [the] housing stock in our core downtown." Given the poor opinion that most planning advocates had of commercial office developers, it followed that many would come to have a low regard for the community development advocates as well. Planning advocate George Colyer questioned the integrity of the community development advocates: "[Developers'attorney] Whayne Quin has got them sort of hooked. They're like heroin addicts. They've gotten a little taste of this zoning money through mostly PUDs . . . and so of course they think any let's-cut-a-deal arrangement is just peachy-dandy because they get the money." With such doubts about their integrity, Colyer proceeded to wonder about the wisdom of turning over large sums of money to nonprofit organizations: "We throw $10 million a year to MANNA and WISH. What are they gonna do? . . . I've seen a lot of money just go down the toilet. . . . Why should we give these people [more money]? Are they producing? Who oversees what they are doing? What's the framework? What's the public policy framework? Who elected Jim Dickerson to be God? But you tell them things like that and their eyes glaze over."[39]

For their part, the community development advocates came to hold a similarly negative view of the neighborhood activists. Jim Dickerson claimed that Terry Lynch resorted to frequent public castigations of commercial office developers "as a political tool to gain a constituency of support to get himself elected to the City Council and be a political force in the city." Speaking of one of the primary bastions of planning advocacy, Martha Davis of Project WISH referred to activists in Dupont Circle as "elitists" and "awful people." Another veteran participant in Washington land use politics, activist Laura Richards of the Citizens Planning Coalition, saw merit in how both sides of the movement perceived each other. On one hand, she believed that many of the nonprofit housing developers were essentially business people motivated by a desire to make contacts in the business world and obtain an equity share in the next major office project downtown; on the other hand, Richards criticized the planning advocates as "just about the most elitist bunch going."[40]

Some individuals have tried to bring the two groups together in an attempt to work out a compromise, but as activist Robert Stumberg observed, "there's a lot of tunnel vision to go around." Although he was more closely associated with the planning advocates, Stumberg tended to be critical of their outlook: "Some of these folks are just talking about what's best for their beautiful city. Very middle-class, exclusive concept of innovative housing with commercial use downtown. They're not thinking creatively or thinking at all about how to link their political interests with those of the nonprofit housing developers." Activist Paul Aebersold's fears about affordable housing illustrate Stumberg's point: "The affordable housing people would turn this city into something that looked like, y'know, Poland under the Russian occupation. Y'know, block after block of faceless, cheap, low-cost housing that falls apart after fifteen years, if that. I mean, who wants to live in a city like that? I don't want to be poor. I don't want to live in affordable housing. I have different aspirations." Community development advocates responded by insisting that affordable housing did not have to be "faceless" and "cheap" and that much of it would be built in behalf of police officers, firefighters, and other civil servants who had been priced out of the District's expensive housing market.[41]

The climate of suspicion and animosity that developed between the two groups dashed any hopes for a reconciliation. Activist Clarene Martin, who ran for District Council in 1990, was viewed in middle-class neighborhoods as "the developers' candidate" because of her consistent support for linkage projects. Jim Dickerson recalled the hostility demonstrated by middle-class residents toward Martin during her campaign: "I was at a meeting one night over in Dupont Circle where there was a candidate's forum and they almost hooted [Clarene Martin] out of the room 'cause she had voted for these linkage deals. So I'm saying after an experience like that and some others . . . we write 'em off in a way and say . . . I don't have enough time to go convince these folks about this." Antagonism between the two groups thus led to a breakdown in communication. Community development advocate Robert Moore admitted that "we don't have tentacles" into the middle-class neighborhoods that tend to oppose linkage, and that consequently "we live in a very divided community." Likewise, Dennis Bass, the chair of the Dupont Circle Citizens Association, conceded that he is completely unfamiliar with the leaders of the community development corporations. He observed, "Neighborhood empowerment almost always favors affluent, well-educated neighborhoods. And so we get attention that people in Shaw just don't get because they're not as articulate; they don't have as much money. . . . So I can see why some people are angry because they may feel like the Ward 3 neighborhoods of Dupont Circle and Georgetown get their way a lot." But although Bass acknowledged the severity of the problems faced by citizens in lower-income neighborhoods, saying they are "light years" apart from the problems that arise in Dupont Circle, he still maintained that it is up to the community development advocates to take the initiative and approach activists in middle-income neighborhoods like Dupont Circle for solutions to problems.[42]

On the other hand, the community development advocates could make a compelling case for why planning advocates should take the first step toward reaching a compromise. Robert Stumberg contended: "My position has been, you've got the privileged position of not having to manage a heavy caseload and not having to struggle for your survival. And you're coming from a political constituency that meets with more politicians, so if you care about affordable housing, why don't you guys lay something out? A peace offering if nothing else."[43]

With respect to land use politics in Washington, the crucial point about linkage was how divisive the issue turned out to be. Linkage split the growth-control movement. On one side were planning advocates mainly concerned about the costs of rapid downtown development incurred by surrounding residential neighborhoods; on the other side were community development advocates primarily interested in seeing a more equitable distribution of the benefits generated by the building boom. To the former group, linkage, as it was implemented in Washington, enabled progrowth interests to continue runaway development and further exacerbate the resulting social and economic problems. To the latter group, linkage was a device that helped to ensure that less privileged sectors in the District benefited from downtown expansion. The two groups could have joined in a common assault on the downtown growth coalition, which is precisely what happened in San Francisco. Instead, linkage divided potential partners and emasculated the growth-control movement as a force in city politics.

The split between the planning advocates and the community development advocates played into the hands of the downtown growth coalition. Conflicting visions of politics prevented the two groups from working together and establishing the kind of regular contacts that would have facilitated social learning and respect for other people's viewpoints. All of that might have led to alternative, and more aggressively progressive, strategies for linking downtown development with neighborhood development. But the practices of Washington activists in advocating equitable growth ended up reaffirming the elitism and marketism of the privatist political culture. As a result proposals to replicate the San Francisco linkage policies were never seriously considered. The growth coalition's approach to downtown development continued to dominate the policy agenda.

The Emergence of Counterhegemonic Activism?

As the downtown building boom skidded to a halt at the beginning of the 1990s, many Washingtonians began to reevaluate the privatist values and assumptions associated with downtown development. Community development advocates, in particular, began to wonder whether downtown expansion was as positive a phenomenon as the growth coalition had always presumed. Some questioned whether the benefits of urban growth actually filtered down to all citizens or were disproportionately enjoyed by developers and other privileged groups such as suburban commuters. Activist Deirdre Williams asked:

> Did we really do what was best for all involved? Did we get the biggest bang out of the buck? There were a lot of expectations, and a lot of assumptions went into it. We build the downtown core, it will just naturally, I guess everybody in the '80s thought, trickle-down [laughs]. Y'know that if we just do this, everyone else is going to get taken care of. And it just didn't happen.... The tax base increased . . . but did that . . . directly translate into infrastructure improvements in the neighborhoods? Did it directly impact businesses being able to get loans? . . . It didn't happen. None of that happened.

Activist Laura Richards speculated that most Washingtonians have only recently come to the realization that the building boom did not improve their lives much. She commented, "I think people were still doing a lot of waiting and expecting.... The buildings have only been completed in the last five years. What you got [during most of the 1980s] were a lot of cranes, a lot of disruption. All of a sudden, when it finished and you had this new downtown and where was anything else happening elsewhere? It was like surprise."[44]

District Council Chair David Clarke came to believe that much of the property tax revenue raised through downtown development was squandered by the Barry administration. He blamed Mayor Barry for putting "all the money into personnel," which made it difficult for the council to find alternative uses for the revenue because cutting back on the city's bloated bureaucracy was practically impossible. In their recent book on Washington politics, Harry S. Jaffe and Tom Sherwood support Clarke's position. They contend that Marion Barry used revenue generated through downtown development to build upon his own political power base by offering government jobs to loyal backers: "Barry had been on a hiring binge since 1982 when he bought labor peace—and votes—by packing and then mollifying the city work force with raises. . . . The 1988 census and an independent commission on budget and financial priorities put the count at forty-eight thousand—one worker for every thirteen residents—more government workers per capita than any other city or state government, including New York, Chicago, Houston, Philadelphia and Detroit. Barry's work force soaked up half the city's budget, which had grown from $1.2 billion to $3.2 billion under Barry's regime."[45]

In one sense, then, Mayor Barry delivered on his promise that downtown growth would generate employment opportunities for local residents. But the expansion of the city bureaucracy was hardly the most efficient jobs program. Also, knowledgeable observers doubt that many Washingtonians found jobs in downtown office buildings. The former director of housing and community development under Mayor Barry, Robert Moore, said, "There were a lot of good job opportunities, but not for D.C. residents. I haven't seen any study, but my sense is that much of the increase in employment benefited non-D.C. residents." Moore's suspicions were confirmed by one investigator who reported: "Despite the creation of forty thousand new jobs in the District between 1980 and 1986, one thousand fewer District residents were employed, as new positions routinely went to suburban commuters."[46]

Given the rising sensitivity to the costs of downtown growth such as the displacement of lower-income residents in nearby neighborhoods,[47] many activists began to ask whether the costs of downtown development outweighed the benefits. With such doubts about the privatist vision of downtown development, activists became more open to an activist role for government to *ensure* a more equitable distribution of the costs and benefits of urban growth through mechanisms like mandatory linkage.

At the same time, however, the activists' faith in city government had been shaken by the disappointments of the building boom. Lillian Wiggins, a columnist for one of the city's African American newspapers and a long-time supporter of Mayor Barry, found herself asking critical questions about Barry's legacy almost a year after he left office. She faulted the mayor for failing to do more to spread the wealth created by downtown development:

> During the administration of Mayor Marion Barry, money was spent and contracts were let, but very little of this booming business came back—in terms of financial and rehabilitative gain—to the African-American community. Downtown got a face-lift, Chinatown got a face-lift and the most important services went to Georgetown and Ward 3.
>
> What meaningful rehabilitation was given to residents in Anacostia and the inner city? What major African-American contractors were involved in the building of the many office and commercial buildings in downtown Washington? . . . Do you realize that we lost most of the African-American business district during the Barry administration? I can't blame all of this on former Mayor Barry, but he takes the lion's share, while many other African-American politicians and community leaders must eat up the rest of the pie.

Wiggins and many community development advocates came to see Mayor Barry as an eager partner in a downtown growth coalition dominated by the views of commercial office developers. *Washington Post* columnist Juan Williams was also critical of the mayor: "Barry did more for his people when he was working in the civil rights movement to gain power than he did after he had that power. The constant bouts with petty corruption have diverted attention from Barry's policy failures and from the larger agenda of reforms that black voters might demand of the practically white development firms, real estate companies, banks and utilities. Consequently, the promise of black political power in Washington and the change it could bring for the city's black residents, particularly the poorest, has gone down the drain."[48] Given that negative perspective of city government in the 1980s, why would activists in the 1990s believe that government offered the promise of a more equitable approach to urban development in the future?

The answer involves a cardinal tenet of the progressive vision of politics—popular control over government decision making. Acknowledging the structural biases in local politics that motivate public officials to seek alliances with resource-rich interests such as the real estate community, some activists began to believe that the same public officials can be reined in if induced to cooperate with concerned citizens. Popular pressure can serve as an antidote to the pressures exerted by developers and their progrowth allies.

But this kind of popular pressure requires a substantial change in popular consciousness. In order to change popular expectations of public officials and exert greater influence over development policy making, community development advocates gradually warmed to the idea of grassroots organizing. The turning point came in 1990 when the Zoning Commission adopted a housing linkage policy that channeled 60 percent of the revenue raised through exactions on downtown office development to the production of market-rate housing downtown and only 40 percent to affordable housing in lower-income neighborhoods. Jim Dickerson explained: "When we lost at the Zoning Commission, we realized that . . . to get [a bill linking downtown development with community development] through the council, you have to have a constituency of people, of voters from the District. So, y'know, we organized . . . forums, one of [which attracted] four hundred or five hundred people . . . which was unheard of for affordable housing in the city." Dickerson added that he and other activists organized three different coalitions of housing providers and community development advocates, which then branched out to solicit support in every ward in the District. He estimated that two thousand people have been mobilized to write letters and attend public hearings since 1990.[49]

Activist Marcia Glenn, who had once expressed reluctance to engage in any kind of political activity during the course of her work in providing affordable housing, later acknowledged a need for grassroots organizing: "In February of this year, the Coalition had a town meeting at the Carnegie Library, and we had a little over four hundred people show up to air their concerns on the housing crisis in the city. We had folks of all kinds of income groups, all kinds of educational backgrounds. . . . A lot of them said we had no idea of what was going on until, y'know, we got this invitation to come and air our concerns." As community development advocates began to discover the political potential of grassroots activism, one organization, Project WISH, actually demonstrated a level of organizing sophistication reminiscent of the kind of community-based activism that became routine in San Francisco. Although Project WISH's emphasis was on tenant organizing, it has also mobilized around development issues. One activist, Martha Davis, described how the organization tried to empower citizens:

> We have three people on staff who are organizers, so they knock on doors initially, and what they hope to do is get a core of leaders in a building. . . . Maybe six people would come [to a first meeting], and they'd try to form a leadership core among those people, and try to meet with those people on a regular basis, probably every week or two . . . and then try to have them become door-knockers in the future. But meet with them and help plan an agenda. Depending on what is going on, maybe have a formal organization formed legally and set up by-laws. Even if not, get a little bit of structure there so people have to start to go through a process of figuring out what they're going to need to do to solve their problem. We just try to facilitate that.[50]

In addition to a growing appreciation for the benefits of organizing *within* neighborhoods, some community development activists have come to appreciate the value of organizing *across* neighborhoods. For many years the two wings of the growth-control movement ignored each other despite occasional attempts to encourage contact. Law professor Robert Stumberg asserted, "I've always argued to both sides of this argument that they had a lot to gain by joining forces with each other as opposed to just the nonprofits joining forces with the development attorneys. Because if they could play political football on that broader scale, their long-run gains and sustainability of [a stronger] form of linkage would be much bigger." Recently, community development advocates have begun to see merit in such a strategy. Robert Moore agreed that it would be wise for his organization to establish "tentacles" into middle-class neighborhoods that had previously looked at linkage policies with considerable skepticism. And Jim Dickerson confirmed that he has already made some overtures: "I go down and talk to some of these neighborhood groups that are *yuppies* and whatnot in this area, and, y'know, we can discourse now the pros and cons. It's less emotionally and rhetorically charged now." Robert Moore notes "the common ground" that exists between the two wings of the growth-control movement: "We don't want the intrusion of office buildings in our neighborhoods either. We have a commonality or an agreement with a lot of common ground available to both of us.... These developers don't care. They'd build over their mother's house. They have no scruples on these issues. . . . There are many more things I think we can agree on."[51]

At the same time, community development advocates have moved to distance themselves somewhat from the commercial office developers. This began when they finally recognized the image problem that had arisen after many Washingtonians perceived that the "nonprofits are in bed . . . with for-profit developers." But even apart from the influence of outside perceptions, the community development advocates came to regard the commercial office developers in a new light. There was a fresh understanding of differing agendas. Activist Robert Moore recalled that the nonprofits told their linkage partners: "You guys have your interests. We have our interests. Sometimes they coincide; other times they do not. So we need to go alone. And don't think you've got us in your back pocket because we're not. We're not."[52] Jim Dickerson echoed the point: "We better see that our interests separate at certain points, and that we are not used by them in that sense of preventing them [from] cough[ing] up the maximum amount that they ought to cough up."[53] When the District Council held hearings to consider the latest linkage bill in April 1992, the community development advocates made a symbolic statement by refusing for the first time to testify jointly with the commercial developers.

Since 1992, then, community development advocates have demonstrated a new approach to the politics of downtown development. They have backed away from values and assumptions associated with a privatist political culture and embraced a worldview more attuned to a progressive political culture. The best indication of this evolution is their apparent determination to engage in grassroots organizing within and across the city's neighborhoods in order to achieve stronger linkage policies. Their activities reflect a more progressive conception of citizen empowerment when compared to their behavior in the 1980s.

But if the practices of community development advocates suggest a change of consciousness and conduct in recent years, it is not clear whether the same can be said for the planning advocates. There is little indication that their brand of grassroots activism has become increasingly counterhegemonic. Although they continue to organize effectively within middle-class neighborhoods, minimal effort has been made to reach out to other communities in the city to consider their interests regarding downtown development. The practice that best enabled activists in San Francisco to promote citywide contacts and understanding was the citizens initiative. In Washington some activists have actually tried to draft an initiative that would establish a 10 percent surcharge on all existing commercial property in the District in excess of fifty thousand square feet to fund the production of affordable housing. Attorney Con Hitchcock said he first heard about the idea when Robert Stumberg proposed it at a Committee of 100 meeting in the late 1980s: "His idea initially is why should we go through these bloody battles pitching one neighborhood against the other where you exacerbate tensions, where you call everyone else names. . . . Why not try and get a situation where we avoid these conflicts and we put everybody working on the same side? And to do that you simply impose a tax on the group you want to target and use the money accordingly rather than to tie it into changes in the zoning." At first glance, the surtax proposal would seem to diminish conflicts between different communities over the "zoning for dollars" version of linkage, and thus offer some potential for uniting the two wings of the Washington growth-control movement. But Washington's attempt to promote a citizens initiative had little in common with the San Francisco movement's practices. Washington activists made no attempt to include a broad range of activists from other communities in preparing the language; instead, a handful of attorneys and planners from the middle-class neighborhoods drafted the initiative. Once that task was completed, they neglected to meet with community development advocates to try to persuade them of the initiative's utility; they simply moved to have it placed on the ballot. At no time did anyone consider how a large-scale, inclusive campaign might be conducted so as to promote widespread support. The predominant attitude seemed to be "Let's have a vote on it. Let's see what people say."[54]

As it turned out, the initiative effort got bogged down in litigation over a technical issue about the propriety of appropriating revenue to a specific fund. But even if activists manage to redraft the initiative to avoid legal complications, the planning advocates' approach to grassroots organizing does not bode well for building popular support. Without a commitment to an inclusive grassroots campaign, they stand little chance of effecting the kind of cultural and political transformation that San Francisco activists were able to engender through their multiple citizens initiative campaigns. Nor does it seem likely that any significant change of heart among the planning advocates is forthcoming. Typical is the view of Dupont Circle activist Dennis Bass. Although he sympathized with the problems facing activists from lower-income neighborhoods in the city, he maintained: "I guess my feeling [is that] it's kind of incumbent [on them] to come to us."[55]

Part 4
Conclusion

✦

✦12

Counterhegemonic Activism in American Cities

Political Culture as a Catalyst for Political Change

Political culture matters in local politics because individuals' thinking about their interests and options is shaped by the prevailing ideas, values, beliefs, and practices of the society. This is important because the political culture tends to slant popular impressions and judgments in ways that reaffirm the policy preferences of groups that wield power. This is not to suggest that those without power always share in the general political orientation of those with power. As Gramsci recognized, the consciousness of subordinate groups is better characterized as a mixture of feelings of discontent arising out of their immediate experience in daily life but tempered by a worldview that tends to legitimate existing social, economic, and political relations. The result of such a contradictory consciousness is that alternative ways of ordering society are dismissed as impractical or unattainable; sometimes they are simply unthinkable. Public policies that have been in place for years and years come to be regarded as the only game in town. In the realm of urban politics, the hegemony of a privatist political culture is such that market-driven, elite-directed downtown development is widely viewed as the only rational strategy to revitalize American cities. Alternative approaches just do not make sense.

Any possibility for political change is thus intertwined with the potential for cultural change. If there is a basic shift in the prevailing ideas, values, beliefs, and practices of a polity, the likelihood of individuals perceiving their interests and options in novel ways increases. New policies may be seen as reasonable and desirable. Such a transformation in consciousness is crucial for enduring political reform.

Recently the most influential theorist of cultural/political change in American political science has been Ronald Inglehart, who emphasizes the constitutive impact of political culture by arguing that advanced industrial nations have witnessed a proliferation of postmaterial values during the preceding decades that has, in turn, prompted a noticeable shift in political behavior. A growing number of citizens have moved away from their traditional preoccupation with material concerns such as economic growth and job security and toward such postmaterial issues as environmental protection and civil rights. Furthermore, the manner in which citizens act on their concerns has changed from a relatively passive form of political participation (for example, voting in periodic elections) to a much more activist engagement in politics (for example, joining a social movement).

One of the more striking aspects of Inglehart's theory of political culture as a catalyst for political change is its deterministic nature. The political culture of advanced industrial nations has evolved because broad social and economic forces have been under way for generations. Any role for human agency in expediting the process of cultural/political change is limited. In Inglehart's scheme the leaders of new social movements are seen as *exploiting* preexisting shifts in the political culture and not as *initiating* changes in the political culture. Moreover, Inglehart exaggerates the extent to which a postmaterial culture pervades contemporary society; it is therefore not surprising that when activists actually attempt to mobilize people around postmaterial issues they often find a small audience receptive to their appeals. Hence, political change proceeds slowly.

This study contends, as the Italian theorist Antonio Gramsci believed, that individuals can play a more direct role in promoting changes in political culture as a vehicle for political change. Counterhegemonic activism is activism that subverts the cultural hegemony of the dominant groups in a society and simultaneously advances an alternative view of the world that facilitates a very different set of political practices and policies. Such activism transforms the political culture and thus how individuals perceive their interests and options. The shift in mass consciousness paves the way for fundamental political change.

The two elements of counterhegemonic activism are a coherent vision of politics that offers subordinate groups a genuine alternative to the vision preferred by the dominant groups and a congruence between that vision and the discourse and conduct of the oppositional movement. That congruence is necessary to overcome the typically contradictory consciousness of most individuals and promote a clear alternative conception of what is possible, reasonable, and desirable.

In the context of the politics of downtown development, the growth-control movement in San Francisco represents a model of cultural/political change through counterhegemonic activism. That movement formulated an oppositional vision of politics based on the progressive values of popular control over development policy making and an expansive public realm dedicated to equitable growth. Growth-control activists offered a coherent alternative to the downtown growth coalition's vision of politics built around the privatist respect for market forces and skilled expertise. But what truly enhanced the counterhegemonic potential of the San Francisco growth-control movement was that it practiced what it preached. The discourse and conduct of the activists over the course of many years conformed to the progressive vision. As a result their activism steadily chipped away at the hegemonic privatist culture, prompting both ordinary citizens and elites to begin to question long-held values and assumptions while giving increasing credence to a progressive approach to downtown development policy making.

Grassroots activism in San Francisco was consistent with the two central tenets of a progressive vision of politics: popular empowerment and a vigorous public sphere. The growth-control movement's commitment to broad popular control over development decision making was best manifested by the movement's reliance on citizens initiatives to shape the pace and character of downtown development. Five times during a fifteen-year period, the growth-control movement turned away from the institutions of representative government in favor of a vital institution of participatory democracy. There was never any hesitation about the wisdom of entrusting major land use decisions to the general population; activists always believed that ordinary citizens were in the best position to determine the future of the city. Moreover, the way San Francisco activists ran the initiative campaigns provides further evidence of their commitment to the principle of popular empowerment. After the first two initiatives in the early 1970s, all of the campaigns functioned as miniature models of participatory democracy. Most impressive was their inclusive nature. Activists from the African American, Latino, Asian, and gay and lesbian communities were all well represented, along with white, middle-class activists. The diversity of the growth-control movement was apparent in the makeup of the subcommittees established to operate the campaigns on a day-to-day basis and as hundreds of activists fanned out into the neighborhoods to do door-to-door canvassing as election day approached. The initiative campaigns were, in short, genuine grassroots efforts that politicized tens of thousands of San Franciscans with respect to downtown development.

Furthermore, there was never any doubt about the growth-control movement's commitment to an expansive public sphere to promote equitable growth. San Francisco activists consistently pushed for the adoption of regulatory and redistributive policies that would encourage a fairer distribution of the costs and benefits of downtown development. They believed, for example, that a strict cap on annual commercial office growth would go far to minimize the negative impacts on housing, transit, and other public services that were disproportionately felt in certain neighborhoods. Linkage policies would obligate developers to shoulder more of the responsibility for mitigating the costs of their projects on the broader community while ensuring that at least some of their promises would be fulfilled. But it was the *combination* of growth limits and linkage that proved particularly effective in advancing the progressive goal of equity through government activism. Developers were compelled to compete among themselves for the privilege of building a restricted number of projects by offering linkage amenities above and beyond those mandated by law.

As all of these progressive practices became increasingly routine, there was an evolution in how people—both elites and nonelites—viewed the politics of downtown development. New practices came to be accepted, institutionalized, and legitimated. As the principle of popular empowerment took root in the city's political culture, the very notion of citizen participation took on new meaning. Provisions assuring citizen input at public hearings were no longer considered an adequate expression of popular involvement in land use policy making. Counterhegemonic activism had raised expectations. Citizens now expected an even more direct role, not just at the deliberation stage, but at the decision-making stage as well. Frequent use of the initiative process solidified the norm that the citizens were the ultimate arbiters of major land use decisions. The practice of citizen empowerment expanded into unprecedented areas such as the inclusion of neighborhood activists in direct negotiations with the developers of a massive development project. In the new political culture, empowerment meant more than passive participation; it meant active engagement and control.

Likewise, popular perceptions of the state changed as a result of the counterhegemonic practices of the city's growth-control activists. The privatist faith that market forces would bring about a fair distribution of the costs and benefits of downtown development gave way to an insistence that government action guarantee a more equitable outcome. Whereas city government's role in the privatist political culture had been limited to offering incentives to businesses contemplating investment in San Francisco, in a progressive culture government now sought exactions from business so that the impacts of rapid growth would be more evenly distributed. Under pressure from progressive growth-control activists, San Francisco enacted the strongest linkage policies in the nation.

As the progressive political culture became hegemonic, it became harder for downtown interests to even consider returning to the old approach to downtown development. Even the election of a moderate-conservative to the mayor's office could not undo what years of counterhegemonic activism had accomplished. And when a more left-leaning politician was elected mayor in 1995, the achievements of the growth-control activisits became even more securely entrenched.

On first impression, growth-control activists in Washington seemed to follow their counterparts in San Francisco by embracing a progressive vision of politics in their clash with the downtown growth coalition. But close scrutiny of their discourse and conduct indicates that the Washington activists were themselves unable to extricate themselves from the hegemonic privatist culture and advance a genuinely counterhegemonic vision of cultural/political change. At best they offered a conflicted vision that did little to counteract the contradictory consciousness of the citizenry; at worst their brand of activism reaffirmed key aspects of the hegemonic political culture, thus rendering their struggle against the downtown growth coalition even more arduous, frustrating, and ultimately, ineffective.

One wing of the Washington growth-control movement, the planning advocates, avowed their support for popular control over downtown development, but it shunned the principal tactic of the San Francisco growth-control movement—the citizens initiative. Suggesting that most citizens lack the requisite skill and expertise to decide complicated land use issues, and fearing that an initiative process would degenerate into "mob rule," the planning advocates opted for more traditional, elite-driven tactics with which to combat the downtown growth coalition. Lobbying, litigation, and comprehensive planning carried out by knowledgeable professionals constituted the key elements of their protest activities. Minimal effort was expended to reach out to diverse communities and include them in a broad-based coalition against downtown power. Thus, the planning advocates' managerial activism reinforced a core feature of the privatist political culture—the notion that only skilled elites should govern. This simultaneously discouraged widespread citizen engagement in local politics, deepened misunderstandings among diverse neighborhood groups, exacerbated preexisting social and economic cleavages, and afforded the growth coalition an opportunity to emasculate further an already fragmented grassroots movement.

The community development advocates, who made up the other wing of Washington's growth-control movement, also deviated from their purported attachment to a progressive agenda. Although eager to make downtown development more equitable for District residents, they shied away from aggressive government intervention for fear of upsetting the market. Their discomfort with a vigorous public sphere was also evident in their reluctance to do the nuts-and-bolts work of grassroots organizing to build a neighborhood-based constituency for more equitable land use policies. The community development advocates' brand of populist activism thus bolstered the privatist political culture's reverence for the private sphere. Consequently, the linkage policies that emerged in Washington were an anemic version of those pioneered in San

Francisco and had only a negligible impact in spreading the costs and benefits of downtown growth more fairly.

In short, the managerial activism of the planning advocates had the effect of reaffirming the value of skilled expertise in policy making, which undermined the development of a broad-based grassroots movement seeking extensive popular control over policy making. At the same time, the populist activism of the community development advocates had the effect of reaffirming the practice of allowing market forces to set policy priorities, which undermined popular faith in the public sector as an instrument to secure a more equitable development of the city. In other words, growth-control activism in Washington had the unintended consequence of reinforcing the privatist political culture that favored the downtown growth coalition. To the extent that growth-control activists challenged downtown elites' power over downtown development by advocating various regulatory and redistributive policies, those policies ended up being either greatly watered-down versions of the policies adopted in San Francisco or they were viewed by most Washington residents as utopian, risky, and impractical. When Washingtonians evaluated their interests and options through their privatist lenses, they inevitably sided with the more "reasonable" agenda of the downtown growth coalition.

Growth-control activism in Washington had another consequence, besides unwittingly strengthening the hegemonic political culture. Because there were two distinct wings of the growth-control movement in Washington, offering clashing visions of politics, the potential for conflict within the movement was significantly heightened. And in fact there was considerable friction between the planning advocates and the community development advocates, arising from their diametrically opposed views on the core political issues of who should rule and what is the proper role of the state. That friction gave downtown elites a golden opportunity to pursue a divide-and-conquer strategy. Mayor Marion Barry, in particular, was adept at exacerbating latent racial tensions within the District to drive a wedge between the primarily white planning advocates and the more racially diverse community development advocates. When the planning advocates attacked Barry's development policies, the mayor's appeals to racial pride and solidarity gave the community development advocates reason to pause. As racial pressures intensified, the likelihood of diverse neighborhood groups coming together and cooperating in a unified coalition against downtown interests diminished.

An important question then becomes whether any other outcome was ever possible in such a racially polarized city as Washington. Perhaps racial conflict will always be an overwhelming obstacle to grassroots challenges to downtown power. Before leaping to such a conclusion, it should be noted that black and white neighborhood groups have cooperated in Washington before on land use issues, and in ways that are reminiscent of the San Francisco growth-control movement. For example, biracial cooperation was crucial in the fight to save a historic landmark from being demolished to make way for a large office and retail project proposed by the District's most prominent developer. The landmark was Rhodes Tavern, the oldest commercial building in downtown Washington, which had also served as the first unofficial city hall. When city officials announced that they were going to back the developer and allow Rhodes Tavern to be destroyed, a local lawyer with an interest in historic preservation decided to appeal directly to the people of Washington through a citizens initiative to make saving Rhodes Tavern a matter of public policy. After getting the initiative placed on the ballot, he organized an extensive network of community groups concerned with preserving historically significant buildings, and especially those that had come to symbolize cherished home rule in the District. All of the grassroots organizing throughout the city paid off. On election day the initiative was approved by 60 percent of the voters despite strong opposition from the downtown growth coalition. Significantly, the measure carried in 91 percent of the District's 137 precincts, demonstrating the potential for biracial cooperation on land use issues even in a city long characterized by racial division.[1]

The Rhodes Tavern initiative campaign illustrates what might have been in Washington had the planning advocates and the community development advocates found a way to join forces. Racial tension was not an insurmountable obstacle. What was necessary, however, was for the two wings of the growth-control movement to adhere to a common vision of politics and promote a counterhegemonic political culture. The activists who organized the citizens initiative campaign to preserve Rhodes Tavern did just that; they adopted a progressive vision of politics that attracted citizens from all over the District. For a brief period the Washington growth-control movement posed a genuine counterhegemonic challenge to the downtown growth coalition.

That is not to say that fundamental political change was right around the corner in Washington. Although a citizens initiative, when used properly,[2] represented a potent counterhegemonic device for bringing diverse groups together, one initiative campaign does not make for a successful grassroots movement. The downtown growth coalition can always be expected to fight back with all of its imposing weapons. Growth-control activists in San Francisco had to resort to running citizens initiative campaigns five times over a fifteen-year period before they began to see meaningful changes in development policy. And throughout that period, they had to "work like hell" to maintain the allegiance of various urban groups who were not always sure which side to take. Crucial to their ultimate success was their adherence to a progressive vision that served both as a magnet for neighborhood groups all over the city *and* as a shield against the unceasing efforts of the downtown growth coalition to co-opt and divide the grassroots challenge to its power.

It is safe to assume that even if the Washington activists had continued on the path they followed in 1983, they too would have faced a long and difficult struggle. Still, the Rhodes Tavern initiative campaign does suggest that progressive activism provided a vehicle for racially diverse groups to work together against the downtown growth coalition. By the same token, the remainder of the Washington case study shows what happens when growth-control activists deviate from the progressive model and pursue conflicting visions of cultural/political change. Not only will their activism unintentionally strengthen the hegemonic political culture, but their opposing views of politics will inevitably lead to fissures within the movement. That, in turn, will give politically shrewd leaders of the growth coalition a chance to foment further discord by playing on preexisting cleavages based on race, class, or ethnicity.

One more issue should be addressed in this context. The argument that activists seeking fundamental cultural/political change must offer a coherent oppositional vision to overcome the contradictory consciousness of the public raises the question, Just how oppositional? In the context of the politics of downtown development, is it necessary for growth-control activists to *always* engage in practices that are fully consistent with a progressive vision and diametrically opposed to a privatist vision? Common sense as well as the actual experience of the San Francisco growth-control movement suggests that such a high standard need not (nor probably could) be maintained. For instance, San Francisco activists scored many points against the downtown growth coalition through a litigation campaign, even though litigation is essentially an elitist strategy that inhibits popular participation in the policy-making process. Yet, the lawsuits filed by the activist organization San Franciscans for Reasonable Growth (SFRG) and their lead attorney Sue Hestor were extraordinarily effective at exposing what appeared to be a lack of expertise among city planners who failed to identify negative impacts of commercial office expansion on the environment and compel adequate mitigation measures as required under state law. SFRG's practice of suing developers for not complying with the law and then extracting sizable sums for mitigation, most of which were then turned over to the city's affordable housing and public transit funds, embarrassed the Feinstein administration and undermined its claim to authoritative expertise in managing downtown development. At one point in the mid-1980s, an exasperated Mayor Feinstein cried out to a group of reporters: "Who's the mayor of this city, anyway? Me or Sue Hestor?"[3]

Thus, while the use of litigation to promote equitable growth more closely responds to a managerial than a progressive vision, the primary effect in this case was to weaken the privatist confidence in elite rule. The key reason for this progressive outcome is that the San Francisco litigation campaign took place in conjunction with growth-control activism that very clearly affirmed the activists' commitment to the progressive principle of popular empowerment. As Sue Hestor herself readily acknowledged, SFRG was able to successfully sue wealthy developers represented by the most prestigious law firms in the city because neighborhood groups from all over the city were running intensive citizens initiative campaigns every few years. That kind of overwhelming popular pressure from the grassroots strengthened the litigation campaign and left no doubt about the progressive nature of the growth-control movement. The San Francisco case study indicates, therefore, that practices with a managerial or populist bent can be effective in furthering cultural/political change, provided they take place within a larger context in which the progressive vision of the oppositional movement remains clear.

But is even this claiming too much? The Gramscian logic would assume that only a fully counterhegemonic, progressive approach[4] to grassroots activism would suffice to transform the contradictory consciousness of the masses. The San Francisco case in this comparative case study provides strong confirming evidence. However, the Washington case may leave the door open to alternative paths to cultural/political change. What crippled the Washington growth-control movement was not just that it deviated from the fully counterhegemonic progressive model but that the two wings of the movement deviated in sharply conflicting ways. One wing pursued a managerial model of activism and the other a populist model. By taking antithetical stances on the core issues of who should govern and what is the role of the state, Washington activists were working at cross purposes. In effect, they canceled each other out. As a result mass consciousness was bound to remain conflicted and the privatist political culture was likely to remain hegemonic.

But suppose Washington activists had all agreed on *either* a managerial vision *or* a populist vision as an alternative to the downtown growth coalition's privatist preferences? Although each vision of politics shares a key element with the privatist vision, in another way there is a decisive break. The question then becomes whether a partially counterhegemonic assault on the hegemonic political culture would bring fundamental change. Or would managerial or populist activism necessarily be doomed to fail? The Washington case does not supply a conclusive answer. It simply suggests that when different contingents of activists pursue opposing visions of politics, the potential for transforming the hegemonic political culture shrinks. This leaves open the question of whether a consistently managerial or populist grassroots movement may pose an effective counterhegemonic challenge.

Replicating the San Francisco Experience?

This comparative case study provides empirical support for the proposition that counterhegemonic activism is the key to bringing about fundamental changes in the politics of downtown development. But how generalizable is this finding? Whereas the focus of this research has been on the cultural and political determinants of effective grassroots activism, some scholars have stressed the economic preconditions for progressive land use policies. In his study of linkage, for example, Douglas R. Porter concludes that such redistributive policies "are feasible only in a handful of cities that can boast a vigorous downtown development market capable of overriding suburban competition."[5] Recent events seem to confirm this. Since the nationwide slump in commercial real estate commenced in the early 1990s, few cities have enacted strong regulatory or redistributive policies for fear of deterring what little investment potential remained. But if a vibrant downtown market really is an essential precondition for counterhegemonic activism, how many American cities during the 1970s and 1980s could have even hoped to follow the San Francisco model of cultural/political change? Perhaps Paul Peterson is right after all in asserting that the vast majority of cities are limited to adopting developmental policies. Perhaps San Francisco is the exception that proves the rule.[6]

I suggest that although the underlying economic condition of cities may impose some limits on the ultimate gains of a counterhegemonic campaign against downtown growth coalitions, the argument is typically overstated. To start, it should be emphasized that a significant number of U.S. cities offer abundant or unusual amenities that will tend to ensure relatively strong investment interest, subject to the normal ups and downs of economic cycles, in the use of their downtown property. A good example is Washington, D.C. As the nation's capital, downtown Washington will always benefit from a high demand from law firms, trade associations, and lobbyists who need to be close to the hub of the federal government. This, of course, gives downtown Washington a competitive advantage over other cities and surrounding suburbs that District officials are well aware of, as evidenced in the following observation from the city's planning director during most of the 1980s: "This is not Sioux City, Iowa. . . . This is Washington, D.C., the nation's capital, the capital of the free world. . . . [As a result] I can play the [linkage] game. I can get away with murder here. . . . I can get away with a number of things that a suburban community, or a community without the flair and flavor and the right connections as a Washington, a Chicago, or a San Francisco. You know, we can get away with things that some other places can't."[7] Yet, despite recognition of its privileged position, public officials in Washington failed to take advantage of that position during the boom years of the 1980s by pursuing more aggressively progressive land use policies such as mandatory linkage. That failure, in turn, is attributable to the inability of grassroots activists in Washington to transform the local political culture through counterhegemonic activism. The point is that, as in San Francisco, the economic preconditions for a progressive politics of downtown development clearly existed in Washington.

The same argument could be extended to many other cities in the United States. New York City qualifies as a privileged city because it is the financial and commercial capital of the nation. Therefore, a large number of corporations and their vast supporting network of law firms, banks, insurance companies, advertising agencies, and accounting firms need to maintain offices in one of the city's two central business districts. Other cities can count on relatively steady demand for downtown office space because they are regional centers of commerce; these include Atlanta, Chicago, Los Angeles, and Boston. Still other cities combine some of the above-mentioned attractions with natural beauty, charm, or a desirable climate; consequently, San Francisco, San Diego, and Seattle enjoyed comparatively vigorous downtown markets that at least afforded them the opportunity to pursue progressive development policies. Whether they actually acted on that opportunity depended on the success of grassroots activists in transforming the local political culture.

Some cities did follow the San Francisco model. Boston's experience in the politics of downtown development deserves special attention if for no other reason than to demonstrate that what happened in San Francisco was not a unique aberration. The grassroots campaign waged by community-based activists against Boston's downtown growth coalition has been described elsewhere.[8] For the purposes of this book, it is enough to say that that grassroots movement was, as in San Francisco, counterhegemonic. Activists sought to subvert the prevailing privatist political culture by advocating a progressive agenda centered around popular control over decision making and a more equitable distribution of the costs and benefits of downtown development. The influence of grassroots activism was apparent in 1983 when the top two candidates to emerge from the Democratic primary election for mayor, Ray Flynn and Mel King, both strongly endorsed the progressive development agenda; the candidate favored by the growth coalition finished well behind.

Flynn was later elected mayor and remained an unswerving supporter of citizen participation and equitable growth through the duration of his administration. He often made his commitment to linkage very clear: "We have a city that is growing and thriving, but . . . there are a number of people who are not benefiting from that economic growth. . . . We want to see that it's shared with the people in the neighborhoods. Linkage has strong political support. The only people who are opposed to it are a very few greedy developers."[9] By the end of the 1980s, the city had extracted $76 million through its housing linkage program and produced twenty-nine hundred units of low- and moderate-income housing. The city had also worked to promote equitable growth by steering commercial office development into less-privileged neighborhoods and by encouraging industrial development as a way of increasing skilled manufacturing jobs for blue-collar residents.[10]

The Flynn administration, moreover, consistently promoted citizen participation in the planning process. One scholarly report observed: "Community groups, acting through local neighborhood councils or other officially recognized citizen advisory groups, have been involved directly in the review of major development projects. Although these groups rarely have enough power to stop a project, they have been able to influence the scale and density of most developments and have succeeded in negotiating additional contributions from developers. In addition to the mandatory linkage fees, community groups have insisted on . . . supplementary affordable housing, jobs or financial contributions for other community services." And the city's planning director during most of the 1980s, Stephen Coyle, whom the *Boston Globe* called "perhaps the most influential figure in city government after Mayor Flynn," believed that the administration's efforts to promote citizen participation was its most valuable accomplishment:

> What I looked upon and learned the most from and felt changed the city the most was the planning process, more than the architecture or the linkage itself, more than the projects, more than getting investment in the black community, rebuilding the waterfront. More important was that a thousand or more citizens would take time out of their lives every month, and frequently go down and meet with their neighbors to discuss where the road should be and whether this variance should be granted, what kind of economy the city should have and who works in that economy and how do you train your kids. How do you make what the school system does fit what the development planners do? And that level of dialogue at the end of seven years produced a ton of involvement, and more importantly, it just allowed a lot of people to become engaged.[11]

Such widespread citizen engagement democratized the planning process and helped to bring about a more equitable development of the city during the 1980s.

Counterhegemonic activism challenging the downtown growth coalition produced progressive reforms in a few other American cities as well. In Seattle, citizens mobilized in opposition to rapid commercial office growth in the downtown business district. Concerned that development was putting upward pressure on housing costs, activists put a citizens initiative on the ballot in 1980 to regulate rental housing. Although the initiative was defeated, the campaign raised public awareness about the costs of office growth and motivated the city to prepare a downtown plan to better control those costs. As a part of that plan, Seattle adopted a version of linkage that provided density bonuses to developers in exchange for affordable housing, public transit improvements, and child care. But growth-control activists attacked the linkage arrangement as a giveaway to developers that did little to mitigate the negative impacts of commercial office expansion. Impatient with city officials, activists proposed their own plan to control downtown development, the Citizens Alternative Plan (CAP). The CAP strengthened height and density limits and imposed an annual cap on commercial office space of five hundred thousand square feet per year for the next five years and one million square feet for the following five years. The CAP was put on the ballot as a citizens initiative in 1989, and although it was opposed by the mayor, the city council, and the rest of the downtown growth coalition, the initiative was approved by a wide margin, 62 percent to 38 percent.[12]

The possibilities for promoting a progressive politics of urban development through counterhegemonic activism are not confined to major cities. A phenomenon that has recently attracted the attention of land use specialists has been the proliferation of so-called edge cities.[13] They are mainly new developments of commercial office buildings and retail facilities that have sprouted on the periphery of large cities, providing an alternative place for work and shopping for suburban residents reluctant to commute downtown. Some metropolitan areas have only one or two edge cities; a few have more than a dozen.

The development of edge cities during the past two decades provided additional opportunities for counterhegemonic activism. Area residents unhappy with the adverse impacts of vigorous growth such as traffic congestion, pollution, burdens on infrastructure, and rising housing costs could have pushed for greater citizen control over decision making and for linkage policies designed to mitigate those impacts. And occasionally this did happen. For example, in Montgomery County, which is adjacent to Washington, D.C., citizens managed to convince the county council to levy a tax on all new development to moderate the costs of sprawling growth. Significantly, the tax was not just an antigrowth measure; the ordinance required that the first $5 million in revenue from the tax be used to build affordable housing in the county.[14] A public official remarked, "Here, politicians who don't insist that developers satisfy public concerns are at risk of getting voted out of office and replaced by people who'll say no to a development that isn't what people will want."[15]

Another real estate market that experienced high demand and therefore might have been conducive to San Francisco–style counterhegemonic activism around growth issues involved some of the boom towns in the Sun Belt and in the Northwest. Fed up with the costs of overcrowding—traffic congestion, air pollution, and extremely high housing costs—many residents of large metropolitan areas such as Los Angeles County fled to smaller towns and cities in California's vast central valley. During the 1980s San Bernardino, Fresno, and Bakersfield were some of the fastest-growing cities in the United States.[16] Other city-dwellers in California, Oregon, and Washington sought refuge from urban ills by moving to tranquil rural areas in eastern Washington and Idaho. Although residents of these boom towns were at first pleased with the economic prosperity stimulated by the migratory influx, they soon discovered the costs of rapid growth as well.[17] Grassroots activism in support of restrictions on new development and linkage policies might have been an appropriate response. In particular, economic conditions were such that the San Francisco growth-control movement could have served as a model for such an organizing effort.

Returning to the primary focus of this study, downtown centers of large cities, it is important to consider to what extent counterhegemonic activism around issues of downtown development would be appropriate in cities that might not be considered "privileged." For instance, is San Francisco's experience in transforming the politics of downtown development at all relevant to the older Rustbelt cities in the eastern half of the country? Here it might be easier to concede to the privatist logic that such cities should simply do whatever is necessary to attract development and avoid the kinds of regulatory and redistributive policies that presumably deter business investment so that progrowth elites can do their job without unwarranted government interference.

But even in "less privileged" cities experiencing only a moderate demand for downtown investment, the privatist logic unnecessarily limits the policy options of city officials. There are many examples in the literature. Todd Swanstrom's study of growth politics in Cleveland in the 1970s demonstrates that even struggling Rustbelt cities are capable of significantly scaling back policies to induce business investment through the generous provision of tax abatements and pursuing a host of regulatory and redistributive policies. As time passed, Cleveland proved unable to sustain the progressive policies of the Kucinich administration, but Swanstrom attributes this not to the *economic* conditions of the city but to the *political* failure of the mayor himself in neglecting to build a solid constituency in the neighborhoods for his progressive agenda. Pierre Clavel's *The Progressive City* documents several cases of U.S. cities rejecting a privatist vision by emphasizing popular empowerment and an activist government promoting equitable growth; one of his progressive cities was Hartford, Connecticut, which could hardly boast of a booming local economy at the time. Finally, Edward Goetz's surveys of policy making in American cities disclose a surprisingly widespread use of redistributive policies even among cities with less than favorable economic amenities. Such findings have led him to conclude that the whole question of market demand in determining urban policy is misplaced: "To ask, then, whether San Francisco, by virtue of its economic position, has more latitude than, say, Buffalo on development and redistributive matters is not really the primary question. One needs to examine the political capacities of competing land-based interests within the two cities, the distribution of political power locally, and the composition of the local governing elite (or regime) in order to understand the political lens through which external economic factors are defined and interpreted."[18]

In sum, numerous studies during the past decade have shown that even cities presumed to be relatively vulnerable to threats of capital disinvestment are capable of pursuing progressive policies, provided the proper political environment is in place. Unfortunately, those same studies have been rather sketchy in detailing the nature of that political environment. All too often, scholars have simply stressed the need for extensive grassroots activism to put pressure on city officials who are inclined to bend to the will of the downtown growth coalition. But as this study points out, extensive grassroots activism is not enough to ensure meaningful changes in public policy. The grassroots activism must also transform the ideas, values, beliefs, and practices that shape how individuals think about downtown development. Only counterhegemonic activism that transforms the local political culture will engender fundamental changes in public policy that will endure.

Conclusion

This study began with a review of the conventional interpretation of the politics of downtown development. According to that perspective, any city has a powerful incentive to pursue policies aimed at inducing development through a host of government incentives, while avoiding measures that impose restrictions on capital or seek to redistribute the costs and benefits of market-propelled growth. Such a policy agenda is presumed to ensure a favorable business climate, generate jobs and tax revenue, and maximize the general prosperity. With the city's interest so clear, local politics is simplified. The need for public debate over urban development virtually vanishes. All that is needed are trained professionals to administer a set of policies that have garnered broad consensus.[19]

But the first lesson of this study is that perceptions of interests are shaped by the prevailing political culture. This alone renders the assumption of an "objective" or "unitary" interest in market-driven, elite-dominated downtown development problematic. The better way to interpret the conventional perspective is that such an approach to urban growth enjoys widespread support because the political culture that is hegemonic in most American cities slants perceptions of interests in ways that reinforce the policy preferences of downtown growth coalitions. In an alternative political culture, what once appeared to be a "rational" course of public action may seem utterly irrational. A whole new set of downtown development policies may come to make sense.

Even terms like "a good business climate" take on a very different meaning in an alternative political culture. Instead of signifying a limited governmental role in the private sector (except for public inducements to encourage economic investment), a good business climate may describe a situation in which a vigorous government characterized by extensive citizen engagement moves aggressively to correct market flaws in ways that enhance the quality of urban life and the material well-being of the public. This constructivist approach to thinking about the politics of downtown development might explain why business investment is so strong in a number of U.S. cities where progressive policy making is pervasive. Table 12.1 is a ranking by a market analyst of the central business districts of U.S. cities based on their investment return potential for commercial office development in 1995. (Note that cities like Houston that boast of their laissez-faire approach to urban affairs are not included on the list.) Given the extent of progressive policy making in Portland, Boston, San Francisco, Minneapolis, Seattle, and perhaps even Charlotte, it is possible that a progressive political culture has taken hold in each of these locales and that this has altered how citizens, including business leaders, think about how the city ought to deal with downtown development. Rather than discouraging capital investment, as the conventional wisdom would predict, the existence of an activist government under popular control has actually strengthened business demand in the downtown office market of these progressive cities. In short, this study's analysis of the role of political culture reveals serious flaws in the Petersonian conception of "objective" interests in city politics.

The focus on political culture as a vehicle for political change also has implications for regime theory, which tends to be unduly pessimistic about the prospects for an enduring progressive politics at the local level. Scholars such as Stephen L. Elkin and Clarence N. Stone have provided valuable insights into the systemic bias that privileges the business perspective in urban political economy.[20] They contend that the arrangement of political institutions and the distribution of material resources are so tilted in favor of business interests that whenever oppositional movements do emerge from the grassroots, they are unable to sustain sufficient pressure on city hall to pursue a progressive

Table 12.1. Highest Potential Return on Investment for CBD Office Markets

City	Score
Columbus	93
Salt Lake City	93
Charlotte	92
Portland	92
Boston	91
San Francisco	90
Minneapolis	89
Seattle	89
Orlando	88
Raleigh	88

SOURCE: Sobolik and Rice, "A Tale of Recovery," 34.

agenda. Instead, city officials inevitably gravitate into the powerful orbit of progrowth forces.

But the structural approach of regime theory, like Peterson's analysis of city politics, overlooks the constitutive impact of the local political culture. In a progressive culture, the role of institutions and resources may change. To cite one simple example, whereas in a privatist political culture a newspaper editorial warning that a proposed linkage policy will "kill the goose that laid the golden egg" might sway public opinion to the growth coalition's position, in a progressive political culture the same editorial might be widely dismissed as the same old song and dance. Similarly, in a progressive political culture, new institutions such as the citizens initiative might play a much more prominent role in maintaining pressure on city officials who might otherwise slip back into their former habits. Moreover, in a transformed political culture, even downtown business leaders might perceive their interests in novel ways so that governing regimes guided by a different vision of politics would emerge and flourish.

If it is assumed that political culture is crucial to understanding local politics, the inquiry then shifts to the question of transformation. How can cities that have always functioned according to the conventional logic of urban politics go about pursuing alternative approaches to executing the public business? This was, of course, the principal question of this study. The case of the San Francisco growth-control movement stands as a model of political change in local politics. In accounting for the success of the political transformation that took place in San Francisco, this study departs from the research of the leading contemporary theorist of political culture, Ronald Inglehart. Rather than emphasizing underlying social and historical forces as the principal engine of cultural/

political change, this study highlights the role of human agency. It was ordinary citizens engaging in sustained and deliberate collective action that led to a reconstruction of the politics of downtown development. And what made collective action so effective in San Francisco was its counterhegemonic character. Fundamental political change occurred because the proponents of political change also succeeded in effecting a fundamental change in the local political culture. The transformation of the prevailing ideas, values, beliefs, and practices of the polity is what made political change so thorough and enduring.

Notes

Preface

1. Peterson, *City Limits,* 25.
2. Elkin, *City and Regime,* 156.

1. Interpreting Downtown Development

1. See Teaford, *The Twentieth-Century American City;* Kantor, *The Dependent City.*

2. The logic underlying the physical transformation of cities following World War II is elucidated in Beauregard, *Atop the Urban Hierarchy.*

3. Teaford, *The Rough Road to Renaissance.*

4. For an excellent analysis of urban renewal policies and politics, see Mollenkopf, *The Contested City.*

5. For a thorough catalog of traditional economic development policies, along with an examination of more innovative policies, see Eisinger, *The Rise of the Entrepreneurial State.*

6. Peterson, *City Limits.*

7. Ibid., 129; cf. Stoker, "Baltimore."

8. There is a vast literature on growth coalitions. Cf. Molotch, "The City as Growth Machine"; Logan and Molotch, *Urban Fortunes;* Cummings, *Business Elites and Urban Development.*

9. For a sympathetic review of Pittsburgh's redevelopment efforts, see Lowe, "The New Coalition: Pittsburgh's Action Formula Saves a City," in *Cities in a Race with Time.* For a more critical account, see Sbragia, "The Pittsburgh Model of Economic Development." For a positive assessment of downtown development as an urban revitalization strategy, see Frieden and Sagalyn, *Downtown, Inc.*; Catlin, *Racial Politics and Urban Planning.*

10. Again, Peterson's *City Limits* offers the best expression in the academic literature of market-driven policy making at the local level. For studies on the widespread influence of this perspective on urban development policy making among city officials, see McGovern, "Mayoral Leadership and Economic Development Policy"; Longoria, "Empirical Analysis of the *City Limits* Typology."

11. The classic analysis of the interconnectedness of the public and private sectors is Polanyi, *The Great Transformation.*

12. Many scholarly studies have contended that downtown development has exacerbated inequities throughout the city as a whole. Cf. Levine, "Downtown Redevelopment as an Urban Growth Strategy"; Bartelt, "Renewing Center City Philadelphia."

13. DeLeon, *Left Coast City;* Dreier and Ehrlich, "Downtown Development and Urban Reform"; Keating and Krumholz, "Downtown Plans of the 1980s."

14. Henig, "Collective Responses to the Urban Crisis," 221-22, 243, 222. See also Fainstein and Fainstein, "Economic Restructuring," in which the authors follow Henig in emphasizing how the ability of conservatives to promote "a coherent ideology in which individuals are seen as the victims of clumsy and misguided governmental programs, to be saved by private-sector individuals" was crucial to undermining urban activism in the 1980s (203).

15. M.P. Smith, *The City, State, and Market,* 79, 80-81. One recent book does respond to Smith's call for research on how culture shapes local politics: Ramsay, *Community, Culture, and Economic Development.* Ramsay's study of two rural communities demonstrates how local cultures influence "rational" decisions about economic development strategies.

2. Political Culture and Political Change

1. Ronald Inglehart has published numerous articles and two key books on the rise and significance of a postmaterial culture in advanced industrial nations: Cf. "The Silent Revolution in Europe," *The Silent Revolution,* and *Culture Shift.*

2. Inglehart, *Culture Shift,* 5, 11.

3. Ibid., 3.

4. Ibid., 339; see chap. 10.

5. Inglehart, *The Silent Revolution,* 321; Inglehart, *Culture Shift,* 295.

6. See Buechler, "New Social Movement Theories," for a useful theoretical analysis. See Larana, Johnston, and Gusfield, *New Social Movements,* for a good collection of empirical case studies.

7. Cf. Dalton and Keuchler, *Challenging the Political Order;* Savage, "Postmaterialism of the Left and Right"; and Barnes et al., *Political Action.*

8. Rosdil, "The Context of Radical Populism in U.S. Cities"; Kann, *Middle Class Radicalism in Santa Monica;* Clavel, *The Progressive City.*

9. Brooks and Manza, "Do Changing Values Explain the New Politics?"

10. Bluestone and Harrison, *The Deindustrialization of America.*

11. Inglehart, *Culture Shift,* 103, 19.

12. Golding, *Gramsci's Democratic Theory;* Sassoon, *Gramsci's Politics;* Mouffe, *Gramsci and Marxist Theory;* Femia, *Gramsci's Political Thought,* 55-56.

13. Gramsci, *Selections from the Prison Notebooks,* 12; Boggs, *The Two Revolutions,* 160-61.

14. Gramsci, *Selections from the Prison Notebooks,* 419, 327, 333.

15. Femia, *Gramsci's Political Thought,* 43-44; Gramsci, *Selections from the Prison Notebooks,* 333.

16. Femia, *Gramsci's Political Thought,* 52; quoted in ibid., 54. Antonio Gramsci, *Il Risorgimento,* Turin: Einaudi, 1949, 70.

17. Gramsci defined the term "intellectual" expansively to include not just scholars or writers, but anyone holding a position facilitating the transmission of ideas within civil society. Thus, teachers, politicians, journalists, clerics, lawyers, government clerks, business managers, and technicians might all be considered intellectuals (*Selections from the Prison Notebooks,* 97).

18. Gramsci contrasted such "organic" intellectuals with "traditional" intellectuals who did not arise from the subordinate classes. He felt that although traditional intellectuals may support radical change, their disconnectedness means that they may be ignorant of or even antagonistic to the actual needs and interests of subordinate classes. Ibid., 328-30. Mindful of the elitism in a situation in which intellectuals were expected to provide "moral leadership" to subordinate groups, Gramsci emphasized the dialectical nature of the intellectual/mass relationship; each group would cooperate with and learn from the other in developing an oppositional worldview. The Sardinian felt that the mutuality of the relationship would afford some safeguards against the pitfalls of the Leninist model of an elite vanguard imposing its values and goals on the masses (418). See also Femia, *Gramsci's Political Thought,* 158.

19. Gramsci, *Selections from the Prison Notebooks,* 126-30. Gramsci often referred to the revolutionary party as a "modern prince," a collective version of Machiavelli's mythical leader.

20. Ibid., 133.

21. Of course, some scholars would hotly dispute the notion that relaxing adherence to some Gramscian themes could still produce meaningful reform. Carl Boggs, for example, maintains that a full-scale transformation of civil society is a prerequisite to real political change (Boggs, *Social Movements and Political Power,* chap. 4).

22. Gramsci, *Selections from the Prison Notebooks,* 78.

23. Almond and Verba, *The Civic Culture,* 13; cf. Pye, "Political Culture and Political Development"; Kavanagh, *Political Culture.*

24. Fagen, *The Transformation of Political Culture in Cuba,* 5. For a critique of combining attitudes and behavior, see Brown, "Ideology and Political Culture"; Tucker, *Political Culture and Leadership in Soviet Russia,* 3. See also White, *Political Culture and Soviet Politics:* "Political culture may be defined as the attitudinal and behavioural matrix within which the political system is located" (1). Fetterman, *Ethnography,* 27. See also Agnew, Mercer, and Sopher, *The City in Cultural Context.*

25. Political scientist Lucian Pye makes the same point: "Not all the political attitudes and sentiments of a people are necessarily relevant in defining their political culture, for many are too ephemeral and lightly held to affect fundamental development" ("Political Culture and Political Development," 8).

26. Elazar, *American Federalism.* See also Kincaid, *Political Culture, Public Policy, and the American States.* Hartz, *The Liberal Tradition in America.*

27. Ellis, *American Political Cultures,* 169.

28. Wildavsky, "Choosing Preferences by Constructing Institutions"; see also Thompson, Ellis, and Wildavsky, *Cultural Theory,* 21.

29. Thompson, Ellis, and Wildavsky, *Cultural Theory*, 6-11.

30. See John Stuart Mill for a classical treatment of representative democracy. Analyses that follow in that tradition include Schumpeter, *Capitalism, Socialism and Democracy;* and Lipset, *Political Man, The Social Bases of Politics.* Theories of direct democracy can be found in the works of Jean-Jacques Rousseau and in Barber, *Strong Democracy.* For an overview of the different strands of democratic theory, see Arblaster, *Democracy.*

31. Cf. the works of classical liberal philosophers Thomas Hobbes and John Locke. The most penetrating analysis of the public/private dichotomy in political philosophy is Wolin, *Politics and Vision.*

32. The best expression of Hamilton's privatist worldview can be found in his *Report on the Subject of Manufactures* (1791), a remarkably prescient blueprint for the nation's economic growth. See also Miller, *Alexander Hamilton.* Warner, *The Private City;* Logan and Molotch, *Urban Fortunes;* Cummings, *Business Elites and Urban Development;* cf. Barnekov, Boyle, and Rich, *Privatism and Urban Policy.*

33. Shearer, "In Search of Equal Partnerships." Shearer actually uses the term "populist" interchangeably with "progressive." This is common practice among urbanists. Cf. Rosdil, "The Context of Radical Populism in U.S. Cities." But in this work "populism" has a very different meaning from "progressivism." Clavel, *The Progressive City;* Nickel, "The Progressive City?" Goetz, *Shelter Burden.*

34. Finegold, *Experts and Politicians;* Caro, *The Power Broker;* Hartman, *Yerba Buena.*

35. There are exceptions, however: cf. Henry, *In Defense of Elitism.*

36. The term "managerial mood" comes from Steinberger, *Ideology and the Urban Crisis;* cf. Neil MacFarquhar, "New Jersey Sends Team to Manage Newark Schools," *New York Times,* July 6, 1995, A1.

37. Swanstrom, *The Crisis of Growth Politics.* On the other hand, Swanstrom's study of Kucinich's behavior as mayor casts doubt on the sincerity of his commitment to popular empowerment. At times one suspects that Kucinich's only quarrel with his downtown opponents over who should rule was which *elites* should exercise power. If one adopts this reading of the Kucinich phenomenon, one might then characterize Kucinich as a managerialist.

38. Paolantonio, *Frank Rizzo.*

39. Savas, *Privatization;* Donahue, *The Privatization Decision.* As of late 1994, there were thirty-three business improvement districts in New York City and over a thousand in the United States (Thomas J. Lueck, "Business Districts Grow at Price of Accountability," *New York Times,* Nov. 20, 1994, A1).

3. The Empirical Framework

1. Jaffe and Sherwood, *Dream City.*

2. Agronsky, *Marion Barry.*

3. Kantor and Savitch, "Can Politicians Bargain with Business?" Goetz, "'Type II Policy.'"

4. For an interesting application of grievance theory, see Walsh, "Resource Mobilization and Citizen Protest."

5. McCarthy and Zald, "Resource Mobilization and Social Movements"; Jenkins, "Resource Mobilization Theory"; cf. Barnes et al., *Political Action;* Milbrath and Goel, *Political Participation.* One commentator observed, "What distinguishes Washington from other large American cities is not the rash of drugs or the ordeals of its demoralized underclass, but the vitality of its large black middle class" (Spitzer, "A Secret City," 107).

6. Note that San Francisco ranks sixth and Washington ranks twelfth in percentage of citizens with at least a high-school education, out of a total of twenty-five cities.

7. Gillette, *Between Justice and Beauty.*

8. Tarrow, *Power in Movement,* 18, 81; Doug McAdam, *The Political Process;* Costain, *Inviting Women's Rebellion;* Meyer, *A Winter's Discontent.*

9. Barone and Ujifusa, *The Almanac of American Politics, 1992,* 242.

10. The most comprehensive analysis of federal-local tensions in the District is Harris, *Congress and the Governance of the Nation's Capital;* Eugene Robinson, "Home Rule in Rhodes' Debris," *Washington Post,* Sept. 16, 1984, B5.

11. Cf. Hippler, *Hunter's Point;* Lortie, *San Francisco's Black Community.*

12. Broussard, *Black San Francisco.* The black-white segregation index for the San Francisco area in 1970 and 1980 was 80.1 and 71.7, respectively; for the Washington area in 1970 and 1980, it was 81.1 and 70.1, respectively. The authors define the black-white segregation index as "the percentage of all blacks who would have to move to achieve an even, or 'integrated,' residential configuration—one where each census tract replicates the racial composition of the metropolitan area as a whole" (Massey and Denton, *American Aparteid,* 63-64).

13. DeLeon, *Left Coast City,* 2-3.

14. A particularly influential approach to the study of culture in the social sciences has been Clifford Geertz's notion of "thick description." See *The Interpretation of Cultures,* 5.

4. The Hegemony of Privatism (1)

1. Wirt, *The Power in the City;* Hartman, *Yerba Buena;* Mollenkopf, *The Contested City.*

2. Jackson, *The Crabgrass Frontier;* Teaford, *The Twentieth Century American City;* Fogelson, *The Fragmented Metropolis;* Abbott, *The New Urban America.*

3. Another factor motivating San Francisco's leaders to redevelop the city's downtown business district was their recognition of the need to respond to the challenge posed by rapidly growing Los Angeles to San Francisco's reputation as the nation's western capital of business and finance.

4. Richard Reinhardt, "Downtown Could Become a Ghost Town," *San Francisco Chronicle,* March 18, 1954, 1.

5. "It's Time for San Francisco to Wake Up," *San Francisco Chronicle,* March 22, 1954, 1.

6. Walter H. Blum, *Benjamin H. Swig: The Measure of Man* (1968), quoted in Brugmann and Sletteland, *The Ultimate Highrise,* 14.

7. Aaron Levine, "The Urban Renewal of San Francisco," report to the Blyth-Zellerbach Committee, March 20, 1959, quoted in Mollenkopf, *The Contested City,* 162.

8. M. Justin Herman had supervised urban renewal programs throughout the western United States from his position as head of the Housing and Home Finance Agency's regional office in San Francisco from 1951 to 1959 (the HHFA was the predecessor of the Department of Housing and Urban Development). At the time of his death in 1971, he was called "the last of the Robert Moses autocrats . . . a flamboyant, autocratic wheeler-dealer." William Lilley III, "Herman Death Ends an Era," *National Journal*, Sept. 18, 1971, 1939. quoted in Mollenkopf, *The Contested City*, 167).

9. Hartman, *Yerba Buena*, 37-38. In 1960 Mayor George Christopher designated SPUR the city's official "citizens group" for urban renewal (38).

10. Temko, "San Francisco Rebuilds Again," 55.

11. The most thorough account of urban renewal in the South of Market area is Chester Hartman's book, *Yerba Buena: Land Grab and Community Resistance in San Francisco.*

12. Wirt, *The Power in the City*, 213; Bierman, interview; Emerson, interview.

13. Wirt, *The Power in the City*, 197.

14. Ibid., 183.

15. Mollenkopf, *The Contested City*, 160.

16. "Lapham Fails in Plea for Building Plan," *San Francisco Chronicle*, Dec. 28, 1957, 1.

17. "Chamber's Position on Height Limit," *San Francisco Chronicle*, Oct. 10, 1963, 4; A.B. Jacobs, *Making City Planning Work*, 10.

18. "Lapham Fails," 2; A.B. Jacobs, *Making City Planning Work*, 55; see also 148.

19. "How Business Spurs a City's Revival," *Business Week*, Sept. 9, 1961, 87-92. quoted in Hartman, *Yerba Buena*, 36.

20. A.B. Jacobs, *Making City Planning Work*, 13-14.

21. Ibid., 68, 132. Jacobs recalled that the Planning Department issued negative recommendations on five major projects: the Transamerica Pyramid, the U.S. Steel Building, Sutro Tower, the Holiday Inn on Van Ness Street, and the Haas Russian Hill apartments. Although the Planning Commission decided to approve each of these projects anyway, two of them—the U.S. Steel Building and the Haas apartments—were never built (141). Ibid., 179.

22. See Mollenkopf, *The Contested City*, and Hartman, *Yerba Buena*, for a thorough analysis of urban renewal policies and the neighborhood opposition they provoked.

23. In October 1971 the influential columnist Herb Caen lamented the changing character of the city: "Only 15 or so years ago, the city was still comparatively uncluttered and open. The skyline had a decent proportion—graceful and light. When you look at photos of the skyline of 1957 and compare it with today's it is hard to believe you are looking at the same city, which of course you aren't. The old city grew beautiful by accident, the new one is growing ugly by design" (quoted in Brugmann and Sletteland, *The Ultimate Highrise*, 14).

24. Welch, interview, May 29, 1991.

25. A.B. Jacobs, *Making City Planning Work*, 179.

26. Duskin first became a prominent figure in city politics in the fall of 1969 when

the Board of Supervisors approved a plan to convert Alcatraz Island into a miniaturized recreation of Victorian San Francisco combined with a monument to the Apollo 8 mission to the moon. Duskin paid five thousand dollars of his own money to run an advertisement in the *Chronicle* and the *Examiner* attacking the proposal. The advertisement ignited considerable public protest, and the city was forced to abandon its plan. In October 1970 Duskin helped to spark the controversy over the spread of high-rises by again running an influential advertisement in the local press, with the headline "Skyscrapers Are Economically Necessary, but Only If You Own One." It was in the *San Francisco Chronicle,* Oct. 17, 1970, 17. Duskin, interview.

27. Duskin, interview.

28. Starbuck, interview.

29. Allan Jacobs observed that the Chamber of Commerce "wanted as few controls and as little city planning as possible, because that only hindered private development" (*Making City Planning Work,* 145).

30. Ralph Craib, "Highrise Vote May End Boom," *San Francisco Chronicle,* Nov. 4, 1971, 1; Duskin, interview.

31. Welch, interview, May 29, 1991. Although Alvin Duskin ran a strongly hierarchical campaign, his attachment to democratic values was evident in other ways. For example, Duskin continues to take pride in the fact that he gave activists such as Hestor and Starbuck their start in San Francisco politics and then stepped back to allow them to assume greater responsibility in the growth-control movement. Duskin's commitment to recruiting new adherents and to periodic turnovers in leadership was not always followed by subsequent leaders of the movement who claimed to be stronger disciples of participatory democracy (Duskin, interview).

32. Wirt, *The Power in the City,* 204; quoted in Dick Meister, "Labor Power," *San Francisco Bay Guardian,* Dec. 23, 1970, 25, quoted in Wirt, *The Power in the City,* 183.

33. Duskin, interview; Wirt, *The Power in the City,* 206.

34. George Murphy, "Moscone Names the New City Planning Commission," *San Francisco Chronicle,* Jan. 17, 1976, 2. The most prominent issue to preoccupy local activists was the campaign to change the city's method of electing officials to the Board of Supervisors from an at-large system to a district election system, a reform that activists believed would make local politicians more accountable to neighborhood constituents.

35. Starbuck, interview; Bruce B. Brugmann, "Mayor Moscone's 'Dear Dick' Letter to the *Chronicle* Publisher," *San Francisco Bay Guardian,* Feb. 8, 1979, 3 (emphasis in original); Robin Evans, "Neighborhood Groups Get Bigger, Better Organized," *San Francisco Progress,* Jan. 27, 1988, B1.

36. The vacancy rate for office buildings in downtown San Francisco was 2.3 percent in 1980 and only 1.0 percent in 1981 (*Urban Land Institute Market Profiles, 1986).* This, in turn, exerted powerful upward pressure on office rental rates commanded by commercial office developers. Rental rates for downtown office space in 1977 ranged between ten and fourteen dollars per square foot; by 1982 they had soared to twenty-five to forty-two dollars per square foot (*Development Review and Outlook, 1984-1985,* 253). Mayor Feinstein decided to retain Sue Bierman despite her growth-control leanings in

part because the two had had a long-standing friendship dating back to the 1950s when, ironically, Feinstein first encouraged Bierman to get involved in city politics to stop a proposed development project in the neighborhood where they both lived. Moreover, with six reliable votes in favor of aggressive growth, Bierman's lone dissenting vote was tolerable; in fact, thanks to Bierman's presence, Feinstein could claim that her Planning Commission represented both sides of the issue.

37. Gerald Adams, "The Perpetual Crisis," *San Francisco Chronicle and Examiner,* Aug. 28, 1983, California Living sec., 8.

38. "What Goes Up," documentary produced by Bob Calo and John Roszak, KQED-TV, aired Dec. 22 and 26, 1982, quoted in Hartman, *The Transformation of San Francisco,* 228; Henrikson, "No Place to Grow," 8.

39. Starbuck, interview.

40. Brugmann, interview.

41. One campaign organizer commented: "It's phenomenal that we were able to get at least one volunteer working in every precinct in San Francisco." Another estimated that "we had 6,000 walkers and 2,000 telephoners in Northern California" (Maitland Zane, "How McGovern Did It in San Francisco," *San Francisco Chronicle,* June 7, 1972, 6). Welch, interview, May 29, 1991.

42. Welch, interview, May 29, 1991.

43. Ibid.

44. Ibid.; Welch believed that most people were "appalled" by the "third-rate people" making planning policy who had "functioned for twenty years out of public view" and who continued to engage in "open . . . manipulation of land use laws to benefit certain property owners" (ibid.).

45. Downtown groups perceived district elections as a major threat to their interests and mounted a sustained drive to repeal the 1976 initiative. That effort eventually succeeded in 1980 as a repeal initiative was approved by San Francisco voters by a 51 percent to 49 percent vote in an August ballot and by a 52 percent to 48 percent vote in a November ballot. The city has operated under an at-large system ever since.

46. Welch, interview, May 29, 1991.

47. Ibid.; Chester Hartman found that evictions in San Francisco increased from approximately two thousand in 1971 to almost six thousand in 1983 (Hartman, *The Transformation of San Francisco,* 232); Welch, interview, May 31, 1991.

48. Welch, interview, May 29, 1991.

5. Progressive Activism: Expanding the Public Sphere

1. One SFT activist declared, "The Planning Commission has approved every downtown office building and the supervisors have never overruled them. We fear what may come in the future, and it's already coming" ("Group Trying to Halt 'New Yorking' of S.F.," *San Francisco Chronicle,* Jan. 25, 1979, 4).

2. Gerald Adams, "A Hard Look/The Battle of the Skyscrapers," *San Francisco Examiner,* Jan. 28, 1979, A1.

3. Welch, interview, May 29, 1991; Prowler, interview.

4. David Johnston, "How Tough Will the Anti-Highrise Measure Be?" *San Francisco Bay Guardian,* Feb. 1, 1979, 4; see also David Johnston, "The Anti-Highrise Initiative Is Rolling," *San Francisco Bay Guardian,* March 1, 1979, 4.

5. D. Johnston, "How Tough Will the Highrise Measure Be?" 4; Marshall Kilduff, "Two Proposals for Highrise Controls," *San Francisco Chronicle,* Jan. 24, 1979, 4.

6. D. Johnston, "How Tough Will the Anti-Highrise Measure Be?" 4.

7. D. Johnston, "The Anti-Highrise Initiative," 3-4.

8. Proposition O, San Francisco Registrar of Voters, "Elections, Propositions, and Candidates," Nov.-Dec. 1979, 82, 112; see also D. Johnston, "The Anti-Highrise Initiative," 4.

9. Welch, interview, May 29, 1991; D. Johnston, "The Anti-Highrise Initiative," 4.

10. David Johnston, "Grandfathering Out SP, Crocker, Itel and the New Highrises," *San Francisco Bay Guardian,* May 17, 1979, 5.

11. Hestor, interview.

12. Proposition 13 was a statewide initiative on the June 1978 ballot. It proposed limiting future increases in local property taxes and was approved by California voters by a two-to-one margin. The anti-tax fever sparked by Proposition 13 soon spread throughout the United States and contributed to Ronald Reagan's success in the 1980 presidential election.

13. William Ristow, "The Vicious Spiral of Highrise Economics," *San Francisco Bay Guardian,* Oct. 18, 1979, 7.

14. City Assessor Sam Duca reported that in 1979 "75 percent of the property tax burden [in San Francisco] is now borne by residential properties" (Adams, "A Hard Look," A6).

15. David Johnston, "The Highrise Watch," *San Francisco Bay Guardian,* Sept. 20, 1979, 3.

16. Adams, "A Hard Look," A6. Within a few years that stance would emerge as the central feature of the Feinstein administration's downtown development program.

17. Larry Liebert, "Feinstein's Balancing Act on the Highrise Issue," *San Francisco Chronicle,* Feb. 5, 1979, 2. Days before the election in November, Feinstein finally gave a weak endorsement to the growth-control initiative; however, the mayor's impact on the Proposition O campaign from beginning to end was negligible (Larry Liebert, "Mayor Backs Anti-Highrise Prop. O," *San Francisco Chronicle,* Nov. 1, 1979, 6).

18. D. Johnston, "The Highrise Watch," 3.

19. Morten, "Can San Francisco Afford the Anti-Highrise Initiative?" 23-24, 23.

20. Marshall Kilduff, "SF Chamber's Plan for Highrise Limits," *San Francisco Chronicle,* Sept. 28, 1979, 5.

21. Bruce B. Brugmann, "Memo to the Mayor, Supervisors and Planning Commission," *San Francisco Bay Guardian,* Nov. 22, 1979, 3; "Planners Approve Highrise Limits," *San Francisco Chronicle,* Feb. 1, 1980, 2; Don Wegars, "Mayor Says Hire San Francisco People First," *San Francisco Chronicle,* Jan. 17, 1980, 1. Although the mayor may have been swayed by community activists, the Chamber of Commerce was not; its response

to Feinstein's plea was a polite but swift rejection ("Feinstein's Plea to Hire San Francisco Workers is Rejected," *San Francisco Chronicle,* Jan. 18, 1980, 2).

22. Marshall Kilduff, "A Compromise in Downtown Highrise Battle," *San Francisco Chronicle,* Sept. 23, 1980, 2.

23. For an overview of developer exactions in land use law, see Alterman, *Private Supply of Public Services;* Collin and Lytton, "Linkage," 413; Taub, "Exactions, Linkages, and Regulatory Takings," 515.

24. National Environmental Policy Act, 42 U.S.C.A. 4320 et seq., sec. 4332(2)(c)(i), (iii); California Environmental Quality Act, Pub. Resources Code, sec. 21000 et seq. (1970), sec. 21061.

25. California Environmental Quality Act, sec. 21002; California Administrative Code, title 14, sec. 15093(a).

26. Hestor, interview.

27. Bash, interview; Blazej, interview. Approximately one year after this interview was conducted, Blazej succeeded Dean Macris as San Francisco's director of city planning.

28. Susan Milstein, "Judge Upholds Muni Highrise Fee," *San Francisco Chronicle,* Aug. 6, 1985, 2.

29. Blazej, interview.

30. Okamoto, interview.

31. T. Robinson, "Gentrification and Grassroots Resistance," 494-95.

32. Mayor Feinstein told sponsors of the Ramada project that she was ready to "turn cartwheels . . . I am so proud and grateful" for the planned development in the Tenderloin (quoted in Hartman, *The Transformation of San Francisco,* 256).

33. David Johnston, "The Battle of the Tenderloin," *San Francisco Bay Guardian,* Dec. 10, 1980, 11.

34. Ibid.

35. Robinson points out that the Planning Department had some leverage in "suggesting" mitigation measures because each hotel was required to apply for a conditional use permit. Since each hotel proposal exceeded existing zoning limits on height and density, the hotels could not build "by-right" ("Gentrification and Grassroots Resistance," 497 n. 7).

36. David Johnston, "Two Tenderloin Hotel Developers Offer Concessions," *San Francisco Bay Guardian,* Feb. 4, 1981, 5.

37. Sanger, interview. The leading California case is *Associated Home Builders v. City of Walnut Creek,* 94 Cal. Rptr. 633, 484 P. 2d 606 (1971); see also *Grupe v. California Coastal Commission,* 166 Cal. App. 3d 148, 212 Cal. Rptr. 578 (1985). Sanger, interview.

38. Sanger, interview.

39. "Feinstein and the Undeserving Poor," *San Francisco Bay Guardian,* Feb. 28, 1980, 3.

40. David Johnston and David Israels, "The Downtown-Backed Feinstein Plan to Raise Muni Fares Runs into Trouble," *San Francisco Bay Guardian,* March 20, 1980, 5.

41. PUC commissioner John Sanger recalled that he and other linkage proponents had initially persuaded top Chamber of Commerce officials of the policy's benefits to

the city: "In 1979 or '80, interestingly enough, we got the Chamber of Commerce to support the transit fee, which I thought was one of the great accomplishments of all time." But when some of San Francisco's most powerful developers caught wind of the Chamber's stance, they repudiated it in forceful terms (Sanger, interview).

42. David Johnston, "The Aftermath of the City Election: The City Winds Up with a Big Shortfall, and the Residents and Neighbors Foot the Bill," *San Francisco Bay Guardian*, June 12, 1980, 7.

43. Lazarus, interview (Lazarus had previously served as a deputy mayor in the Feinstein administration); Lewis Leader and Larry Hatfield, "War Declared on MUNI Tax," *San Francisco Examiner*, April 21, 1981, A1. The idea of a special assessment district was intended to respond to the business community's objection that the one-time linkage fee payment was too steep and that it unfairly penalized new developers. An assessment district would spread the burden more broadly by requiring all downtown businesses to pay for increased transit services, though the annual payments would be much smaller.

44. Leader and Hatfield, "War Declared on MUNI Tax," A14.

45. Larry Liebert, "2 Sides Try to Reconcile on Fees," *San Francisco Chronicle*, May 26, 1981, 2.

46. Feinstein believed that although the assessment district was attractive in theory, it would be difficult to build a political constituency for it. The measure would provoke the opposition of too many property owners in the financial district. By contrast, imposing a transit fee only on the developers of new commercial office buildings would generate much less opposition. John Sanger observed, "[The transit fee] was much more politically appealing.... Passing on the costs to another generation, if you will, to outsiders . . . It's always politically more appealing to hit the new guy" (Sanger, interview). Cf. a letter written in January 1982 by Mayor Feinstein to *San Francisco Business*, the monthly periodical of the Chamber of Commerce, forcefully defending the city's housing and transit linkage policies in response to an earlier, critical commentary (Feinstein, "Commentary").

47. Blazej, interview. Blazej was uncertain whether the best efforts promises were ever carried out; he believed that city planners made little effort to enforce those promises.

48. Marshall Kilduff, "S.F. Planners Act to Trade Highrises for New Housing," *San Francisco Chronicle*, Dec. 12, 1980, 7; see also Marshall Kilduff, "New Offices Tied to Housing," *San Francisco Chronicle*, March 13, 1981, 5. The nonbinding nature of these early linkage deals was underscored by the comment of one developer who promised to "try very hard to meet this [housing linkage] goal. But we all know there are a lot of variables" (Kilduff, "New Offices Tied to Housing," 5).

49. Macris, interview.

50. Not everyone went along with that leap in logic. For example, PUC commissioner John Sanger, who had fought for a transit linkage policy, questioned whether the same "rational nexus" existed to sustain a housing linkage policy (Sanger, interview).

51. Marshall Kilduff, "How Planners Get Housing from Highrises," *San Francisco Chronicle*, April 10, 1981, 7.

52. Gresham, interview.

53. Heller, interview. Indeed, office vacancy rates in downtown San Francisco hovered as low as 1 percent in 1980 (Cushman and Wakefield, *Downtown Plan Monitoring Report, 1985-89,* 10).

54. Duffy, interview; Gresham, interview.

55. Heller, interview; see also J. Jacobs, "The Delicate Balance."

56. Henrikson, "No Place to Grow," 9; Blazej, interview; Bash, interview.

57. Blazej, interview; Carlson, interview.

58. Gresham, interview.

59. On this point, planner Lu Blazej commented, "If you look at the history of [early linkage] you can see it was kind of an up the ante. . . . The next guy had to do a little more, the language was a little stricter. . . . I think [the business community] supported [formalizing linkage by having the Board of Supervisors enact an ordinance] just because at least they knew what the bottom line is" (Blazej, interview).

60. Welch, interview, May 31, 1991.

61. Kilduff, "How Planners Get Housing from Highrises," 7. The rationale for this provision in the original linkage policy was that building *any* kind of housing would contribute to alleviating the housing shortage caused by downtown growth (Blazej, interview).

62. "Planning Commission OKs 'Pioneer' Highrise," *San Francisco Chronicle,* Jan. 29, 1982, 5; Hestor, interview.

63. Gerald Adams, "Utilities Chief Hits High-Rise Plan: Too Much Strain on MUNI," *San Francisco Examiner,* June 20, 1982, B1; Marshall Kilduff, "Skyscraper OKd—Sklar Blasts Panel," *San Francisco Chronicle,* July 23, 1982, 4.

64. Sue Hestor expressed concern that the city had used the linkage fees as "palliatives . . . to neutralize opposition to runaway growth. The fees are used to tell people that the problems are all being solved" (Marshall Kilduff, "Downtown Levies Collect More Critics," *San Francisco Chronicle,* Aug. 6, 1985, 2). Welch, interview, May 31, 1991. Welch and most activists felt that since San Francisco, with its forty-nine square miles, was such a land-scarce city, it simply lacked the space to allow aggressive downtown development even if such development were made more equitable through linkage.

65. Alan Ramo, "Remember Prop. O?" *San Francisco Bay Guardian,* Feb. 9, 1983, 5.

66. Welch, interview, May 29, 1991.

67. Tim Redmond, "April 30th Kickoff," *San Francisco Bay Guardian,* April 13, 1983, 5; Tim Redmond, "Anti-Highrise Initiative Looms on the Horizon," *San Francisco Bay Guardian,* March 9, 1983, 7.

68. Looman, interview. Looman was the chair of the Proposition M campaign of 1983.

69. San Francisco Registrar of Voters, "Elections, Propositions and Candidates," 1983, 92.

70. Looman, interview.

71. San Francisco Registrar of Voters, "Elections, Propositions and Candidates," 1983, 92.

72. Looman, interview.

73. Welch, interview, May 31, 1991.

74. Looman, interview; Emerson, interview.

75. "What the Neighbors Are Saying," *San Francisco Business,* June 1982, 21.

76. Tim Redmond, "The No on M Campaign Falters," *San Francisco Bay Guardian,* Oct. 19, 1983, 9; Looman and Welch, interviews, May 31, 1991.

77. "The Right Vision for Downtown," *San Francisco Examiner and Chronicle,* Aug. 28, 1983, B10; Tim Redmond, "The Downtown Plan—A Highrise Developer's Dream," *San Francisco Bay Guardian,* Aug. 31, 1983, 7, 9.

78. Gerald Adams, "Plan: Halt Building Downtown," *San Francisco Examiner,* Aug. 25, 1983, A1.

79. Ibid. A subheadline of this story announced: "Proposal Would Cut Growth 50%." Redmond, "The Downtown Plan," 9.

80. Tim Redmond, "Anti-M Forces Keep Their Fundraising Simple: $10,000 a Head from Developers," *San Francisco Bay Guardian,* Sept. 21, 1983, 8; Hartman, *The Transformation of San Francisco,* 277.

81. Morten, "Warning," 26.

82. Ibid., 29.

83. J. Jacobs, "Power in America's Cities"; see also Evelyn Hsu, "Prop. M—The Debate over Growth Returns," *San Francisco Chronicle,* Nov. 3, 1983, 6; Grosboll, interview.

84. Tim Redmond, "The Chron's No on M Editorial: The Old Tune's Familiar; Now Even the Words Are the Same," *San Francisco Bay Guardian,* Nov. 2, 1983, 12; Cazenave, interview, May 31, 1991; see also Bruce B. Brugmann, "The News Is Still No News at the Chron . . . ," *San Francisco Bay Guardian,* March 16, 1983, 5.

85. Evelyn Hsu, "What the Close Vote on Prop. M Means," *San Francisco Chronicle,* Nov. 10, 1983, 28.

86. In Bayview/Hunters Point, only 42 percent of the voters backed Proposition M; in Ingleside, only 44 percent voted for Proposition M (Tim Redmond and Alan Kay, "Is San Francisco Still a Liberal City?" *San Francisco Bay Guardian,* Nov. 16, 1983, 10).

87. Looman, interview.

88. Hsu, "What the Close Vote on Prop. M Means," 28.

6. Progressive Activism: Promoting Popular Empowerment

1. Pettit, interview.

2. *San Franciscans for Reasonable Growth v. City and County of San Francisco,* 151 Cal. App. 3d 61, 198 Cal. Rptr. 634 (1984).

3. William Carlsen, "Court Scolds S.F. on Planning Policy," *San Francisco Chronicle,* Jan. 25, 1984, 1, 18.

4. "Downtown Highrise Foe Sue Hestor," *San Francisco Chronicle,* Aug. 22, 1983, 10.

5. Tim Redmond, "SFRG: What the *Chronicle* Did—and Didn't—Chronicle," *San Francisco Bay Guardian,* March 13, 1985, 7; Welch, interview, May 29, 1991.

6. Marshall Kilduff, "Highrise Foe Gets $450,000 Settling Suits with Developers," *San Francisco Chronicle,* March 11, 1985, 16.

7. Ibid.

8. Carlson, interview. As for the potential profit to be gained by switching from condominiums to a hotel, Doug Engmann, then a member of the Board of Permit Appeals, estimated the conversion to be worth $25 million to $50 million to the developer (John Jacobs, "Highrise Dispute Settled," *San Francisco Examiner,* July 6, 1986, A12).

9. J. Jacobs, "Highrise Dispute Settled," A12.

10. Tim Redmond, "Who's Afraid of Big, Bad SFRG?" *San Francisco Bay Guardian,* Feb. 13, 1985, 13; Tim Redmond, "Feinstein Joins the Dirty Tricks Campaign to Discredit the Highrise Fighters," *San Francisco Bay Guardian,* April 10, 1985, 7. For her part, Sue Hestor asked a state court judge to rescind an order requiring SFRG to seek pretrial settlements with developers of environmentally suspect projects. She requested permission to take her complaints directly to trial, instead ("Anti-Highrise Group Wants to Fight Its Cases in Court," *San Francisco Chronicle,* April 16, 1985, 2).

11. Carol Pogash, "Sue Hestor's Private War for the Public Good," *San Francisco Examiner,* Oct. 27, 1985, Image sec., 18.

12. Duffy, interview; Hestor, interview.

13. Hestor, interview.

14. San Francisco Planning Code, sec. 313.4 (7), 313.5 (1).

15. The elitist dimension of litigation as an oppositional strategy is illustrated by the fact that an individual cannot simply march into court and file a lawsuit blocking a large-scale development project unless that individual has been licensed to practice law by the state bar association and has the ability to articulate a viable legal theory for halting construction.

16. Elberling, "Community Origins of the Downtown Plan," 4-5.

17. Sedway-Cooke, "Downtown San Francisco Conservation and Development Planning Program." 56-57, 58.

18. Paul, "San Francisco's Growth Management," 7.

19. Ibid., 7-8.

20. Ibid., 8-9, 9.

21. Chin, interview.

22. William Ristow, "After the Fall," *San Francisco Bay Guardian,* March 15, 1979, 8.

23. Chin, interview.

24. Ibid.; Prowler, interview.

25. Chin, interview.

26. Ibid.

27. Cf. T. Robinson, "Gentrification and Grassroots Resistance." In particular, see the section entitled "Downzoning the Tenderloin" (pp. 497-500), which reviews actions taken by the North of Market Planning Coalition to rezone the Tenderloin to ward off commercial office development.

28. Chin, interview.

29. Rosen, interview, June 3, 1992.

30. Evelyn Hsu, "San Francisco Downtown Plan Roundly Criticized," *San Francisco Chronicle,* April 27, 1984, 23.

31. A third new linkage policy was also proposed in the Downtown Plan—child care linkage. But this redistributive policy had been pushed primarily by progressive activists and not the Feinstein administration (Hestor, interview).

32. Larry Liebert, "Inside the Politics of the San Francisco Downtown Issue," *San Francisco Chronicle,* May 15, 1985, 4.

33. Reginald Smith, "San Francisco Builders Make Final Pitch against Downtown Plan," *San Francisco Chronicle,* May 22, 1985, 2.

34. Marshall Kilduff, "Feinstein Praises the Downtown Plan," *San Francisco Chronicle,* July 3, 1985, 1.

35. "Downtown Plan Merits Approval," *San Francisco Chronicle,* May 28, 1985, 44.

36. Calvin Welch cited in particular the movement's ability to draw in leaders from the Mission District, the city's principal Hispanic district, and "develop some trust" and "include that indigenous leadership in designing the timing and content" of Proposition M as being crucial to broadening the movement's support (Welch, interview, June 23, 1992).

37. Nash, interview.

38. SFT activist Tony Kilroy explained that he and other activists had learned from previous campaigns the value of having a few concise policy objectives that would catch the eye of voters instead of forcing voters to pore over a long and complicated initiative (Kilroy, interview).

39. Larry Liebert, "Foes of Controls Split over How to Fight Them," *San Francisco Chronicle,* May 15, 1985, 4. In responding to his critics, the executive director of the Chamber, John Jacobs, revealed how political power relations surrounding downtown development had evolved by 1986: "The worst thing one can do is to attempt to exercise power when you don't have it. Let's be realistic" (ibid.).

40. Marshall Kilduff, "Business May Ignore Highrise Fight," *San Francisco Chronicle,* July 7, 1986, 2.

41. Cushman and Wakefield, "Downtown Plan Monitoring Report, 1985-89," 10.

42. Heller, interview.

43. The argument that the split within the business community paved the way for Proposition M's victory is advanced in DeLeon and Powell, "Growth Control and Electoral Politics."

44. That O'Donoghue was no friend of the downtown growth coalition is reflected in the following comment: "There needed to be constraints on [downtown development], and I have no problem with that because [high-rise developers] don't give a crap about the city, and including the Chamber of Commerce today. They live in the suburbs, they're here to rape the city if possible, and they should pay for some of the social inequities that the projects do create. No doubt about it." Such comments from a housing developer who had previously taken a libertarian view of government involvement in land use matters also suggest the broadening transformation in consciousness that growth-control activists were effecting in San Francisco.

The Planning Department actually had some cause to apply the policy strictly with respect to the RBA members. They had acquired a reputation for demolishing existing single-family homes and replacing them with cheap, multi-unit apartments that were often denounced as eyesores by neighbors. Even O'Donoghue acknowledged that the building designs "left a lot to be desired. They were schmuck designs." Aggrieved neighborhood groups thus pushed for a planning policy that required RBA members, before demolishing any home, to submit plans demonstrating that the replacement building would be consistent with the character of the neighborhood. O'Donoghue feared that an overzealous implementation of such a policy would result in myriad bureaucratic hurdles and a crippling slowdown in construction (O'Donoghue, interview).

45. Ibid.; Warren Hinckle, "Big Rigs and Pickups at City Hall to Fight Proposition M," *San Francisco Examiner,* Oct. 30, 1986, B3.

46. Emerson, interview.

47. John Wildermuth, "Anti-Growth Fight Heats Up in San Francisco," *San Francisco Chronicle,* Sept. 18, 1986, 32.

48. Jack Davis, the "No on M" campaign manager, confirmed that "Mayor Feinstein was definitely the catalyst in explaining what Proposition M would do to [various interest] groups" (ibid., 29).

49. Marshall Kilduff, "Foes Fight Growth Measure," *San Francisco Chronicle,* Sept. 25, 1986, 44.

50. John Jacobs of the Chamber of Commerce asserted, "Proposition M is one more signal to business about how unwelcome they are" (Marshall Kilduff, "6th Time May be the Charm for San Francisco Highrise Initiative," *San Francisco Chronicle,* Oct. 31, 1986, 8).

51. "Dangers in City Prop. M," *San Francisco Chronicle,* Sept. 21, 1986, A10.

52. Phillip Matier, "How to Spell SF's Prop. M? Try M-O-N-E-Y," *San Francisco Chronicle,* Nov. 2, 1986, B1.

53. Wildermuth, "Anti-Growth Fight Heats Up," 29.

54. Tim Redmond, "Behind the Black Split over Prop. M," *San Francisco Bay Guardian,* Oct. 1, 1986, 11.

55. Black leaders who opposed Proposition M continued to maintain that a high-rise limit would deter economic development in the African American community. Rev. Amos Brown contended that anger over the shortcomings of past developments was misplaced: "We can't blame our problems on the developers. . . . Problems in the Black community are due to problems in the school, the family and the church. We need increased development so that we can enact more joint ventures with developers" (Greg Brooks, "Reverend Brown Denounces High-Rise Control Initiative," *The Sun-Reporter,* Oct. 22, 1986).

56. Greg Brooks, "Proposition M Supported by Religious Leaders: High Rise Initiative Limits Development," *The Sun Reporter,* Oct. 1, 1986, 1.

57. Ibid.; Tim Redmond, "Behind the Black Split over Prop. M," 11.

58. Cox, interview; Welch, interview, June 23, 1992; Johnson, interview. The vote was almost dead even in Bayview/Hunter's Point (51% yes, 49% no) and the Ingleside (49% yes, 51% no) and overwhelmingly supportive in the Fillmore (60% yes, 40% no) (*The Pettit Report,* Nov. 29, 1986, 5-6).

59. Campaign literature was provided by Dick Grosboll, member of the executive committee overseeing the Proposition M campaign.

60. Welch, interview, May 31, 1991.

61. Welch, interview, June 23, 1992.

62. Kilroy, interview.

7. Cultural Change

1. Rosen, interview, June 4, 1991; Cazenave, interview, May 31, 1991; Binder, "Public Opinion Survey of City of San Francisco," 1. Binder's survey was commissioned by the Catellus Development Corporation.

2. Binder, "Public Opinion Survey of City of San Francisco," 2.

3. Hestor, interview.

4. Wachob, interview.

5. McCarthy, interview.

6. Grosboll, interview; Nash, interview; Rosen, interview, June 3, 1992.

7. Hestor, interview.

8. DeLeon, *Left Coast City,* 28. The Redevelopment Agency had required each new business to sign a land disposition agreement that it would make a "good faith effort" to hire at least half its new workers from within the Hunters Point community (Jim DuPont, "Manhattanization Comes to Hunters Point," *San Francisco Bay Guardian,* Sept. 26, 1984, 11).

9. Johnson, interview; Bell, interview.

10. Bell, interview; Cox, interview; Bell, interview.

11. Johnson, interview.

12. Ibid.

13. Ibid.; Cox, interview.

14. Johnson, interview.

15. Macris, interview.

16. Bash, interview.

17. Blazej, interview; Nash, interview.

18. Okamoto, interview; Lord, interview.

19. Rosen, interview, June 3, 1992; Hestor, interview.

20. See A.B. Jacobs, *Making City Planning Work.*

21. Evans, "Neighborhood Groups Get Bigger, Better Organized," B3.

22. Heller, interview.

23. DeLuca, interview; Bradley Inman, "Business Community Still Split on Prop. M," *San Francisco Examiner,* Nov. 27, 1988, D5.

24. Heller, interview; Carlson, interview. San Francisco's office vacancy rate stood at about 13 percent in 1991, compared to rates in excess of 20 percent in Denver, Houston, and many other municipalities. Many business people believe that an 8 percent to 10 percent vacancy rate is optimal. If the rate drops much below this, office rents start to rise, thus deterring businesses from locating in the city.

25. Inman, "Business Community Still Split on Prop. M," D5.

26. Lazarus, interview. Lazarus's position may not reflect that of the typical business person because he had earlier served as one of Dianne Feinstein's deputy mayors and thus played an active role in attempting to build support for linkage. Nevertheless, the fact that the vice president of the Chamber of Commerce took such a firm position in favor of linkage is a significant indicator of how far the city's political culture had evolved. Other business leaders also acknowledged a rational nexus between downtown development and increased pressure on public transit and the city's affordable housing supply, and thus accepted the constitutionality of linkage (DeLuca, interview).

27. Thompson, interview.

28. Gresham, interview.

29. Gonzales-Burns, interview; Thompson, interview.

30. Cohen, "San Francisco Commercial Real Estate Industry," 20; Rosen, interview, June 4, 1991.

31. Heller, interview.

32. DeLuca, interview.

33. Heller, interview.

34. Duffy, interview. She was chief legal counsel to the Catellus Development Corporation on the Mission Bay Project. Duffy noted that Catellus even agreed to pay for the outreach program as a demonstration of its commitment to public participation in the planning process. Jefferson, interview.

8. Political Change

1. Welch, interview, May 31, 1991.

2. Jim Balderston, "Counting the Closed Doors," *San Francisco Bay Guardian*, March 21, 1990, 19; "South of Market," *CitiReport*, March 26, 1990, 3.

3. Steve Massey, "South of Market Rezoning Approved," *San Francisco Chronicle*, March 13, 1990, A4. Agnos-appointed Planning Commissioner Doug Engmann said that one of his highest priorities was to "try and preserve the light industrial, small business base that exists in South of Market and limit creeping office development" (interview). "South of Market," 3.

4. Section 313, San Francisco Planning Code, amended by ordinance 105-90, approved March 23, 1990; Jones, interview.

5. Cushman and Wakefield, "Downtown Plan Monitoring Report, 1985-89," 38-39. In the summer of 1991, the Planning Commission held hearings to consider expanding application of the housing and transit linkage ordinances to hotels, along with commercial office buildings, but the downturn in the real estate market prompted the city to delay such a move (Blazej, interview).

6. Bradley Inman, "Inclusionary Zoning Stages a Comeback," *San Francisco Examiner*, Feb. 26, 1989, F4. Under this policy, "affordable" was deemed to be 100 percent of the city's median income (Blazej, interview).

7. Steve Massey, "San Francisco Agency Moves to Ensure More Lower-Cost Hous-

ing," *San Francisco Chronicle*, April 11, 1990, A2. Under the new policy, low and moderate income were defined as $44,000 a year for a family of four if it buys and $26,4000 if it rents. San Francisco had been building six hundred to one thousand units of housing each year in renewal areas, but most of that had been at market rates and thus was far beyond the means of lower-income people. (ibid.).

8. Rosen, interview, June 4, 1991.

9. The initial inspiration for the policy came from the 1983 growth-control initiative Proposition M. One of the proposed linkage ordinances in that initiative involved the establishment of a job training and placement program for local residents. The Downtown Plan's program was a watered-down version of the Proposition M proposal. Planning Director Dean Macris credited the Agnos Planning Commission, and particularly Commissioner Jim Morales, for giving jobs linkage sufficient support to make it a workable program. He admitted that the Feinstein administration "didn't give it a lot of priority because we sort of ran out of gas, steam, and staff until Morales wanted to put it up higher on the agenda" (Macris, interview). Rosen, interview, June 4, 1991.

10. Macris, interview; Engmann, interview; Lord, interview. But Lord stressed that the mindset of city officials in promoting the CEBA was one of cooperation rather than confrontation. For instance, Lord encouraged developers to keep the employment agencies constantly updated on their hiring needs so that local training agencies could be responsive. He also urged developers to post job notices with local employment agencies before placing advertisements in newspapers with a metropolitan-wide circulation to give San Francisco residents a competitive advantage.

11. Rosen, interview, June 3, 1992; Lord, interview.

12. The latter plan, drafted by architect I.M. Pei, included skyscrapers as high as forty-two stories, commercial office space totaling 11.4 million square feet, 7,000 housing units, 2,000 hotel rooms, 18,000 enclosed parking spaces, and a series of canals, lagoons, and islands. The projected cost was $4 billion. Although consistent with the Feinstein administration's progrowth leanings, the proposal sharply conflicted with the views of the increasingly powerful growth-control movement (Tim Redmond and Alan Kay, "Mission Bay: Will the Deal Hold?" *San Francisco Bay Guardian*, Aug. 8, 1984, 9).

13. Southern Pacific Railroad had earlier merged with the Chicago-based Santa Fe Pacific Realty Corporation; its real estate subsidiary then legally changed its name to the Catellus Development Corporation. Duffy, interview.

14. Bash, interview; Macris, interview. Planning Director Macris elaborated: "There had to be a decision about when are the activists going to be most effective. . . . I always saw them as a critical component in getting what we wanted and when to unleash all of that was important. . . . I think we got more in this process than we would have if we had let them in too early. . . . The more steps you have to go through the more you're likely to get in the process. So the negotiating strategy as I saw it was create more hoops and not play all your cards at the same time." The Planning Director proceeded to give another reason for keeping activists out of the early negotiations, one which may have been even more compelling to him: "I would have been perfectly willing to talk to . . . the activists, but they were always too confrontational with me to allow them in. So I

just had to develop it on my own terms. . . . They're much more into ideology than I am; I'm much more into the process." Note that the last comment is squarely in tune with a managerial vision that places a premium on objective planning by professionals.

15. In response, growth-control activists negotiated with Catellus and the city in 1988 to include in whatever development agreement was eventually signed an assortment of public particiaption provisions requiring public hearings, public access to documents, and public reports on any private negotiations. The development agreement thus gave the activists "a retrospective view of the back room negotiations" and ensured extensive public review of the plan released by Mayor Agnos in early 1990.

16. Steve Massey, "Who Pays for the Project: Financial Details of the City's Deal on Mission Bay," *San Francisco Chronicle,* Jan. 13, 1990, A4.

17. Kathy Bodovitz and Steve Massey, "Mission Bay Planner Ready to Show Off New Neighborhood," *San Francisco Chronicle,* Jan. 26, 1990, A2.

18. Jim Balderston, "The C-Minus Mayor," *San Francisco Bay Guardian,* Feb. 21, 1990, 16; Thomas G. Keane, "Agnos Hears Complaints from Neighborhoods," *San Francisco Chronicle,* Feb. 20, 1990, A1.

19. Balderston, "Counting the Closed Doors," 19; Carter Harris, "Mr. Agnos's Neighborhood," *San Francisco Bay Guardian,* June 27, 1990, 23. According to the development agreement, "affordable" houses would sell for between $105,000 and $150,000, with an average unit going for $125,000. Housing activists estimated that a family would have to earn at least $30,000 in order to buy a home at the low end of the scale. They further estimated that almost half of the anticipated twenty-three thousand jobs would not pay salaries high enough for employees to afford any of the subsidized housing. Those new workers would then have to find housing elsewhere in the city, thereby putting an additional strain on San Francisco's tight housing market, or move to the suburbs, thus exacerbating the transit and pollution problems (Harris, "Mr. Agnos's Neighborhood," 23). "Issues of Contention at Mission Bay Project," *San Francisco Chronicle,* Jan. 31, 1990, A4; Cox, interview.

20. Gonzales-Burns, interview.

21. Porter, "Mission (Almost) Impossible," 29, 30.

22. To pay for the housing subsidies, the city agreed to raise $5 million annually for the next thirty years, a jump of $50 million over the January plan. Deputy Mayor for Housing Brad Paul said the money could be raised by doubling the city's real estate transfer tax or by issuing bonds backed by tax revenues produced by the development project. Steve Massey, "San Francisco Planners Back Mission Bay," *San Francisco Chronicle,* Aug. 24, 1990, A2.

23. Jefferson, interview. For example, the goal of minority-business participation is 20 percent. If Catellus fails to achieve that, it is obligated to pay one dollar per square foot for every square foot of commercial office space it builds until it attains the agreed upon 20 percent goal (ibid.). Gonzales-Burns, interview.

24. "Entrepreneur Art and Mission Bay," *San Francisco Bay Guardian,* Aug. 29, 1990, 6.

25. Carter Harris, "The Other Side of Mission Bay," *San Francisco Bay Guardian,* Aug. 29, 1990, 23.

26. Johnson, interview; Welch, interview, May 31, 1991. Shorenstein's unexpected support for the growth-control movement was not representative of the downtown business community's position in general. Most business leaders did not view Mission Bay as serious competition for the downtown district since much of the new office space was intended for back office uses.

27. Voters also approved a citizens initiative that would require the city to prepare a master plan for development of its waterfront, thus delaying construction of two waterfront hotels. Kathy Bodovitz, "Mission Bay Developers Offer Modifications to Woo Critics," *San Francisco Chronicle*, Dec. 6, 1990, A1.

28. Ingfei Chen, "Still Some Hurdles for Mission Bay," *San Francisco Chronicle*, Feb. 27, 1991, A2.

29. Porter, "Mission (Almost) Impossible," 31; Rosen, interview, June 4, 1991.

30. Duffy, interview. Catellus was obligated to pay the city's transit linkage fee, fund a $13.4 million affirmative action and job training program for city residents, clean up toxic wastes that may remain on the property, provide affordable housing, and fund a $5.3 million public arts program (Porter, "Mission [Almost] Impossible," 32). Jefferson, interview.

31. John King, "Major Shift in Mission Bay Plan," *San Francisco Chronicle*, September 30, 1996, A17.

32. Rachel Gordon, "SF Picked for Second UC Campus," *San Francisco Examiner*, May 17, 1997, A1.

33. John King, "Hotel, Highrises Part of Mission Bay Plan," *San Francisco Chronicle*, July 10, 1997, A17; Gerald D. Adams, "Developer Given Public Grilling on Mission Bay Plan," *San Francisco Examiner*, October 2, 1996, A6.

34. Macris, interview.

35. Allan Temko, "3 S.F. Highrise Projects Pass a Beauty Test," *San Francisco Chronicle*, June 2, 1987, 8; Macris, interview; Steve Massey, "4 Entrants in Skyscraper 'Beauty Contest,'" *San Francisco Chronicle*, April 7, 1989, A25.

36. Nash, interview.

37. Badiner, interview.

38. Rosen, interview, June 3, 1992.

39. Thompson, interview; Engmann, interview; Nash, interview. It should be noted that, with the collapse of the commercial real estate market in the early 1990s, most of the projects selected as winners of the beauty contest were never built. "Highrise Projects Drop Out," *San Francisco Examiner*, July 9, 1995, E9. Still, when the market does revive, activists believe they have a structure in place that rewards developers conscious of equity issues.

40. Note that I use the term "populist" in accordance with the typology of cultures set forth in chapter 2.

41. Nash, interview.

42. Welch, interview, June 23, 1992.

43. A typical Agnos campaign speech would include the following apology and promise: "I haven't, in three and a half years, I haven't been able to get with you, to talk as much and I'm sorry, I'm sorry about that. And I'm going to do better in the next four

years because I do better when I have this kind of communication. So my pledge to you tonight is to maintain regular communication, every two months at least if not more, in the next four years" (Jerry Roberts, "Agnos Gets Humble, Jordan Gets Help," *San Francisco Chronicle,* Sept. 14, 1991, A14).

44. Welch, interview, June 23, 1992; Tim Redmond, "Lighten Up, Francis," *San Francisco Bay Guardian,* Nov. 13, 1991, 12. A Firefighters Union leader attending the Jordan election party observed: "There are a lot of very disenfranchised San Franciscans here tonight. . . . For a long time, they haven't felt like there was anyone in politics they really wanted to work for" (12).

45. Engmann, interview.

46. Welch, interview, June 23, 1992.

47. Rosen, interview, June 3, 1992.

48. John King, "Brown Names Matrix Foe to Head SF Agency for Affordable Housing," *San Francisco Chronicle,* April 11, 1996, A18; Gerald D. Adams, "Redevelopment About-Face: Agency's New Boss to Concentrate First on Kids, Housing" *San Francisco Examiner,* March 7, 1997, A12; John King, "SF Redevelopment Pick Stalls on Taking Job," *San Francisco Chronicle,* February 7, 1997, A22.

49. Venise Wagner, "Affordable Housing Gets SF Affirmation," *San Francisco Examiner,* November 6, 1996, A27; Gerald D. Adams, SF on Cutting Edge for Affordable Housing," *San Francisco Examiner,* May 12, 1997, A4.

50. For an opposing view, see Richard E. DeLeon, *Left Coast City: Progressive Politics in San Francisco, 1975-1991* (Lawrence: Univ. Press of Kansas, 1992). DeLeon contends that although community based activists succeeded in dismantling the former downtown regime, they were unable to consolidate their power to erect a new governing regime.

51. David Armstrong, "Office Space Hard to Locate in SF," *San Francisco Examiner,* July 25, 1996, E1.

9. The Hegemony of Privatism (2)

1. Reps, *The Making of Urban America;* National Capital Planning Commission, *Worthy of the Nation.*

2. Gutheim, *The Federal City.*

3. Lessof, *The Nation and Its City;* Diner, "From Jim Crow to Home Rule"; Schmeckebier, *The District of Columbia.*

4. Scott, *American City Planning since 1890.*

5. Reps, *Monumental Washington.*

6. A. Johnston, *Surviving Freedom;* Johnson, "The City on the Hill"; Gatewood, *Aristocrats of Color* (see chap. 2, "Washington: Capital of the Colored Aristocracy").

7. U.S. Bureau of the Census, *1990 Census of Population and Housing: District of Columbia* (Washington, D.C.: Government Printing Office, 1992), 1; Lesko, Babb, and Gibbs, *Black Georgetown Remembered;* Gillette, *Between Justice and Beauty,* 141-42; Borchert, *Alley Life in Washington.*

8. Gillette, *Between Justice and Beauty,* 141-47; Pacifico, "'Don't Buy Where You Can't Work.'"

9. Cf. "Washington, D.C. Is a City As Well As a Capital . . . ," *Architectural Record* (April 1981): 100-103.

10. Knox, "The Restless Urban Landscape."

11. *Washington Present and Future: A General Summary of the Comprehensive Plan for the National Capital and Its Environs* (Washington, D.C.: National Capital Park and Planning Commission, 1950).

12. Teaford, *The Rough Road to Renaissance.*

13. Gillette, *Between Justice and Beauty,* 163-66.

14. *A Policies Plan for the Year 2000: The Nation's Capital* (Washington, D.C.: National Capital Planning Commission, 1961).

15. See Oliver T. Carr Jr., "It's Time to Renew Old Downtown," *Washington Post,* Feb. 2, 1982, A15.

16. Gillette, *Between Justice and Beauty,* 190; E. Robinson, "Home Rule in Rhodes' Debris." The strongest case against federal government interference in District affairs is presented in Harris, *Congress and the Governance of the Nation's Capital.*

17. Kenneth Bredemeier, "Board of Trade: No Mayor Endorsement," *Washington Post,* Aug. 18, 1978, C1; Henig, "Race and Voting."

18. Gillette, *Between Justice and Beauty,* 195.

19. *Development Review and Outlook, 1984-1985,* 343; Eugene Robinson, "Downtown: Newest Boom Area," *Washington Post,* April 26, 1981, A1, A31.

20. Greene, interview; Gross, interview.

21. Knox, "The Restless Urban Landscape," 190; *Development Review and Outlook, 1984-1985,* 340; *Urban Land Institute Market Profiles, 1987,* 176.

22. Michael Abramowitz, "The Urban Boom: Who Benefits?" *Washington Post,* May 10, 1992, H1.

23. *Urban Land Institute Market Profiles, 1987,* 177.

24. Knox, "The Restless Urban Landscape," 190-93. Virtually all observers agreed that the new architecture in the "old" downtown was a dramatic improvement over the old architecture in the "new" downtown around K Street and Connecticut Avenue, which was characterized by mind-numbing rows of box-like, drab buildings. Glenn, interview.

25. Gale, "Neighborhood Resettlement."

26. Clarke, interview.

27. Abramowitz, "The Urban Boom: Who Benefits?" The same report also faulted the District Council for approving "sizeable" pay hikes for city workers.

28. Toney, interview; Gross, interview.

29. McGrath, interview; Jaffe and Sherwood, *Dream City,* 148.

30. Gale, *Washington, D.C.,* 47; Rudolph A. Pyatt Jr., "Historic District Heightens Firms' Fears," *Washington Post,* Oct. 16, 1984, E1, E12. See also Rudolph A. Pyatt Jr., "Small Store Owners in Relocation Dilemma," *Washington Post,* Dec. 21, 1983, D1; and Judy Mann, "Death of a Restaurant: A Neighborhood Loss," *Washington Post,* Nov. 5, 1980, B1.

31. Rudolph A. Pyatt Jr., "D.C.'s Retail Neglect," *Washington Post,* Jan. 9, 1987, D2.

32. John Mintz, "Chinatown Fights to Survive amid Building Boom," *Washington Post,* Jan. 3, 1988, D1, D5; James A. Wu, "Chinatown Divided," *Washington Post,* Jan. 10, 1988, C8.

33. Gross, interview.

34. Grandis, interview.

35. Goldfield, "Private Neighborhood Redevelopment and Displacement," 453; Lawrence Feinberg, "Revival: D.C. Leads Country in Renovation of Inner-City Housing," *Washington Post,* Dec. 11, 1981, B1.

36. Lewis M. Simons, "Washington Nomads: The Poorest Are Victims of Renewal," *Washington Post,* Feb. 1, 1979, A1, A12.

37. Goldfield, "Private Neighborhood Redevelopment and Displacement," 457. Dupont Circle activist Ed Grandis commented, "What I do think is a big problem is there are people who have been buying residential stock to flip it, and when they buy it they'll pay almost any price because . . . they're doing it as an economic investment and they're going to flip it, subdivide it, turn it into condos, or find some wealthy couple to purchase it. . . . I think that's what has really hurt the near-downtown neighborhoods is the speculation" (interview).

38. Sandra Evans Teeley, "The Nether Side of District Renewal," *Washington Post,* July 11, 1981, E1.

39. Michael Andrew Fitzpatrick, "'A Great Agitation for Business'"; John Mintz, "Investors Reclaiming Riot Corridors," *Washington Post,* April 7, 1988, A1.

40. Lee, Spain, and Umberson, "Neighborhood Revitalization and Racial Change," 587. The authors proceeded to note that the only other American city to exhibit such a striking shift in racial composition because of gentrification was San Francisco (596). Gale, *Washington, D.C.,* 81. Although it is safe to say that the stock of affordable housing was diminishing in neighborhoods near the downtown core, it should be pointed out that high suburbanization rates among whites and blacks meant that housing opportunities were available in other sections of the city, especially in Wards 4 and 5. Still, forced displacement from one's neighborhood was an undesirable outcome of downtown development.

41. Stumberg, interview; Toney, interview. Toney proceeded to discuss the displacement problem in the close-in Shaw neighborhood: "The pricing of housing there is beyond the reach of a low- and moderate-income person. You have a real change going on in that segment, where the homes are dilapidated, rat-infested, etcetera. [They] are being bought up by developers. They're being cleaned up, refurbished, and now they're trying to get middle-class people to come in there and take a risk until things turn over."

42. Gross, interview.

43. Benjamin Forgey, "West End Story: Striving for a Sense of Neighborhood amid the Pains of Building," *Washington Post,* Jan. 21, 1984, B5.

44. The most famous example of a PUD in Washington is the Watergate, a complex consisting of residential apartments, commercial offices, and retail facilities. Andrich, "Planned Unit Development in the District of Columbia, 1958-1990."

45. Joe Pichirallo, "Neighborhood Groups Object to Land-Use Plan," *Washington Post,* March 26, 1983, B3.

46. Thomas W. Lippman, "Urban Renewal Policies Lower Selling Price of City-Owned Land," *Washington Post,* May 18, 1981, B1. See also LaBarbara Bowman, "New Deal Cuts Price of Metro Center," *Washington Post,* March 23, 1983, A1. LaBarbara Bowman, "Renewal Agency Criticized for Sale Procedures," *Washington Post,* March 10, 1982, C1; Eric Pianin, "Board of Trade Backs Downtown Development Plan," *Washington Post,* April 5, 1983, B5.

47. Rudolph A. Pyatt Jr., "Business, Government Ties Strong Under Home Rule," *Washington Post,* Dec. 31, 1984, Washington Business sec., 12; Albert B. Crenshaw, "Firms Score Legislative Coups in City," *Washington Post,* Dec. 31, 1984, Washington Business sec., 15.

48. John Mintz, "Barry and the Developers: A New Alliance," *Washington Post,* Aug. 31, 1986, A1.

49. Arthur S. Brisbane, "Business Giving Big to Barry Bid," *Washington Post,* June 13, 1986, B6; Gross, interview.

50. Tom Sherwood, "ANCs Blast Zoning Hearing Proposals: Ask Council's Help," *Washington Post,* March 31, 1982, D.C.7.

51. Warner, *The Private City.* The term "managerial mood" comes from Steinberger, *Ideology and the Urban Crisis.*

10. Managerial Activism

1. Juan Williams, "City Plan: Still a Distant Goal," *Washington Post,* March 31, 1982, D.C.1.

2. Anne H. Oman, "Citizen Coalition Asks Barry to Adopt Land-Use Plan," *Washington Post,* Feb. 8, 1979, D.C.3.

3. National Capital Downtown Committee, *A Report and Sketch Plan.*

4. Moore, interview.

5. J. Williams, "City Plan: Still a Distant Goal," D.C.5.

6. Eric Pianin, "Shaping the Future of the D.C. Area: D.C. Plan Would Restrict Growth," *Washington Post,* Oct. 7, 1982, A22.

7. Eric Pianin, "Many Groups Criticize Barry's Land-Use Plan," *Washington Post,* Feb. 13, 1983, B6.

8. McGrath, interview.

9. John H. McKoy, "D.C.'s Plan: It Does What It's Supposed to," *Washington Post,* Dec. 14, 1983, A23; Marcia Slacum Greene, "D.C. Council Backs Land-Use Plan Incorporating Citizens' Ideas," *Washington Post,* Dec. 6, 1984, C3.

10. Council member John Wilson observed, "The text is so soft . . . that you can make it anything you want. It's open to all kinds of interpretations" (Kenneth Bredemeier, "Land Use Plan Assailed," *Washington Post,* Nov. 2, 1984, B3).

11. Nettler, interview.

12. Ibid.

13. Marilyn W. Thompson and Sue Anne Pressley, "Developers Turn into a Drawback," *Washington Post,* Sept. 9, 1990, B1. See also Thomas Bell, "Builders Targeted in Races," *Washington Post,* Aug. 2, 1990, DC1. Bass, interview.

14. Gale, *Washington, D.C.*, 40-41; Knox, "The Restless Urban Landscape," 193, 198; Marcia A. Slacum, "D.C. Protects 200 Buildings in Downtown Historic Areas," *Washington Post*, March 25, 1984, B1.

15. Rich Zahradnik, "And Now, DuPAC—Lobby for a Neighborhood," *Washington Post*, April 21, 1982, DC4.

16. See series of letters to the editor from a community activist, a developer, and a city planner, in "The Fight for Wisconsin Avenue," *Washington Post*, June 22, 1986, C8. Mayor Barry captured 71 percent of the citywide vote in the primary, but lost to a former school board member 40 percent to 29 percent in Ward 3. Arthur S. Brisbane and Tom Sherwood, "Barry Toughens Opposition to NW Development," *Washington Post*, Sept. 25, 1986, C3.

17. John Mintz, "Barry Asks NW Building Slowdown," *Washington Post*, Sept. 20, 1986, B2; Tom Sherwood, "Wisconsin Avenue Downzoning Hailed," *Washington Post*, March 4, 1987, C6.

18. John Mintz, "Barry Backs Limit on Connecticut Avenue Growth," *Washington Post*, Sept. 30, 1987, B1. For further evidence of Mayor Barry's post-1986 support for the downzoning of predominantly residential neighborhoods, see David S. Hilzenrath, "Barry Backs Plan to Limit Growth," *Washington Post*, April 30, 1988, F3, which describes tactics employed by grassroots activists in Ward 3 to persuade the Barry administration and the Zoning Commission that downzoning was necessary to preserve their community's way of life from disruptive commercial encroachment.

19. Nettler, interview.

20. Jerry Knight, "Business Leaders Urge Downtown Management," *Washington Post*, Jan. 27, 1981, D6, D7.

21. Tom Precious, "Arduous D.C. Planning Effort Begins," *Washington Post*, Jan. 11, 1986, F1.

22. Ibid., F11.

23. David S. Hilzenrath, "D.C. Council, Citizens Assail Ward Proposals," *Washington Post*, Oct. 8, 1988, E1, E19.

24. David S. Hilzenrath, "Dissension Builds over District Plan," *Washington Post*, Sept. 30, 1989, E1, E16.

25. McGrath, interview; Nathan McCall, "D.C. Council Switches Gears on Development," *Washington Post*, Oct. 12, 1989, B4.

26. Greene, interview.

27. Toney, interview.

28. For instance, the city agreed to sell a parcel of downtown property for $16.7 million less than the city's assessment of the property. Some real estate brokers said the property was worth significantly more than even the assessed value. Moreover, the city offered to loan the developers $28 million at a reduced interest rate (David S. Hilzenrath and John Mintz, "D.C. Agrees to Sale of Prime Tract," *Washington Post*, Feb. 8, 1989, D1; D4). Toney, interview.

29. Welch, interview, May 29, 1991.

30. Grandis, interview.

31. But note that Washington, D.C., has also had considerable experience with

direct democracy. In 1938 a citizens group sponsored a drive resulting in a District-wide plebiscite on popular elections for governmental officials (Green, *Washington,* 432-33). And since home rule there have been numerous initiatives and referenda on issues such as gun control, homelessness, bottle deposits, and term limits.

32. Grandis commented, "D.C. has very strong civic neighborhood associations. . . . I think in D.C. because there wasn't home rule, I think that a lot of the leadership came from the civic associations, and I think they had a lot of influence with the government that was overseeing D.C. and with Congress. So I think there was a lot of activism" (interview).

33. Grandis, interview.

34. For example, San Francisco activist Geraldine Johnson acknowledged that in her community "African Americans have been . . . so caught up in the day-to-day issues, the day-to-day struggles, that questions of planning could never supplant the immediacy of those . . . needs." She nevertheless maintained her practice of visiting thirty homes in the neighborhood to alert citizens whenever a major development issue was at stake (interview).

35. Lynch, interview.

36. Grandis, interview; Steen, interview.

37. See 1990 U.S. census data on Washington and San Francisco presented in chap. 3; Diner, "From Jim Crow to Home Rule," 101.

38. Aebersold, interview.

39. McGrath, interview.

40. Nettler, interview.

41. Martin, interview; Bass, interview.

42. Bass, interview; Hitchcock, interview.

43. Martin, interview.

44. Lynch, interview; Aebersold, interview.

45. Gale, *Washington, D.C.,* 43.

46. McGrath, interview; Steen, interview. Although this observation is accurate enough, it is also crucial to understand that despite the difficulty of nurturing ties across racial lines, some white planning advocates were successful, including Steen herself. Moreover, some of the most influential community development advocates were white, including Jim Dickerson, Martha Davis, and Rick Eisen, a testament to the possibility of biracial cooperation provided the activists are motivated by a similar vision of politics.

11. Populist Activism

1. Mintz, "Barry and the Developers," A46. Corporate attorney Robert Linowes added, "Some developers and bidders look for influential [black] participants and not those who can pay their share. . . . The desire to provide equity [to blacks] has been perverted" (LaBarbara Bowman, "Fear of 'Cash Calls' Gnaws Minority Partners in Big Projects," *Washington Post,* Aug. 5, 1982, B6). For further evidence of misuse of the minority equity program, see David S. Hilzenrath, "District Approves Western's Portal Project," *Washington Post,* April 7, 1989, F1.

2. Dorothy Gilliam, "Club," *Washington Post,* Oct. 17, 1981, B1.

3. Councilmember Jarvis made the comment during hearings before the District Council on proposals for a new linkage bill on April 8, 1992. John Perrotta, "Office Developers Hit D.C. Plan to Make Them Provide Housing," *Washington Post,* June 11, 1983, F1, F20; cf. Marcia Slacum Greene, "D.C. Officials: Poor Areas Slighted," *Washington Post,* Feb. 14, 1985, B1.

4. Eisen, interview; Dickerson, interview.

5. Stumberg, interview; Wendy Swallow, "D.C. Rejects Offer for Housing Funds," *Washington Post,* Sept. 20, 1986, E1.

6. Swallow, "D.C. Rejects Offer for Housing Funds," E1, E9.

7. Wendy Swallow, "D.C. Panel Approves Linkage," *Washington Post,* Dec. 20, 1986, E1, E4; Dickerson, interview.

8. Wendy Swallow, "D.C. Zoning Panel Favors City's First 'Linkage' Project," *Washington Post,* Oct. 11, 1986, E7; Swallow, "D.C. Panel Approves Linkage," E4.

9. Tom Precious, "District Developers Trading Donations for Bigger Projects," *Washington Post,* Sept. 26, 1987, E1, E23.

10. Tom Precious, "D.C. Seeks to Raise Hadid 'Linkage' Fee," *Washington Post,* Nov. 14, 1987, E4.

11. Tom Precious, "D.C. Zoning Board Approves Second 'Linkage' Project," *Washington Post,* Nov. 21, 1987, E1.

12. The Zoning Commission increased the number of units of low-income housing that would be renovated from forty-four to sixty but did not specifically raise the developers' initial monetary offer of $1.4 million (ibid., E18).

13. Tom Precious, "Developer Wants to Trade Cash for Zoning," *Washington Post,* Aug. 22, 1987, E8.

14. Blakeslee, interview. She was the Advisory Neighborhood Commission member for Downtown.

15. Precious, "District Developers Trading Donations for Bigger Projects," E23.

16. David S. Hilzenrath, "D.C. Zoning Panel Rejects 'Linkage' Deal," *Washington Post,* April 16, 1988, E1.

17. Referring to downtown office developers, planning advocate Terry Lynch remarked: "The metro made these guys rich" (interview).

18. McGrath, interview.

19. Stumberg, interview; Blakeslee, interview. Even housing advocate Jim Dickerson conceded that the first linkage deal with the Akridge Company had been disappointing in retrospect, but he maintained that the exactions for affordable housing improved thereafter (interview). City planning director Fred Greene responded to criticism of the amount of exactions from developers this way: "You enter into a business negotiation and you have the right folks around the table to help you. They're going to have, obviously, their attorneys . . . and you try to strike a deal. And it was all about deal making, stacking the deal and getting the maximum you can for the public. And then this whole thing about did you get enough? Well, shit, y'know, who can answer that question? . . . I would say this: we got something, and something is better than nothing" (Greene, interview).

20. Bass, interview. Many planning advocates blamed linkage for subverting the living downtown mandate: "It's totally ruined the plan for Franklin Square, which was supposed to [have] a residential component all around Franklin Square, which is now totally commercial" (Aebersold, interview).

21. Precious, "District Developers Trading Donations for Bigger Projects," E24. Jarvis argued, "Establishing a mandatory policy . . . would not only make adjacent suburban markets more attractive, it would also subject the District to the kinds of lawsuits faced by other cities that have adopted a mandatory linked development policy" (Charlene Drew Jarvis, "D.C.'s Housing Bill Will Not Lead to 'Zoning Abuse,'" *Washington Post,* March 13, 1988, C8).

22. David S. Hilzenrath, "Housing 'Linkage' Bill near D.C. Council Test," *Washington Post,* Nov. 19, 1988, E1, E27.

23. David S. Hilzenrath, "D.C. Weighs Office Tax to Fund New Housing," *Washington Post,* Feb. 4, 1989, F2.

24. David S. Hilzenrath, "Clarke Criticizes Mayor's Housing Plan," *Washington Post,* May 17, 1990, DC7.

25. David S. Hilzenrath, "D.C. Panel Links Housing, Offices," *Washington Post,* Sept. 18, 1990, D1.

26. Dickerson, interview; Martin, interview; Glenn, interview. Glenn stressed the impact of the new hotels: "We have thousands of hotel units downtown. Every night at least 50 percent of them are occupied. . . . If we're asking for a living downtown, we already have as many people as we want running around downtown. It is there" (Glenn, interview).

27. Michael Abramowitz, "Downtown Zoning Plan Attacked," *Washington Post,* Oct. 6, 1990, B1. The only modifications to the original plan were (1) a slight increase in the percentage of the housing requirement that developers could satisfy by funding housing production beyond the downtown district and (2) an increase in the allowable density of some downtown office space (David S. Hilzenrath and Michael Abramowitz, "Downtown Housing Plan Voted," *Washington Post,* Dec. 18, 1990, A1, A7).

28. Clarke, interview; Hayes, interview.

29. Dickerson, interview.

30. Martin, interview; D. Williams, interview.

31. Dickerson, interview; Martin, interview; Dickerson, interview.

32. Dickerson, interview.

33. Stumberg, interview.

34. Clarke, interview.

35. Dickerson, interview; Glenn, interview; Davis, interview. However, Project WISH tended to limit its organizing efforts to landlord-tenant disputes as opposed to land use issues.

36. Martin, interview; Moore, interview; Clarke, interview.

37. Davis, interview.

38. The planning advocates did acknowledge the disparity in land values between downtown and residential neighborhoods and thus recognized that similar donations would result in fewer housing units downtown than in the neighborhoods. Colyer,

interview. Note the parallel between this rationale for downtown *residential* development and the growth coalition's rationale for downtown *commercial* development.

39. Lynch, interview; Nettler, interview; Grandis, interview; Colyer, interview.

40. Dickerson, interview; Davis, interview; Richards, interview.

41. At one point, District Council Chair David Clarke brought the two groups together in hopes of brokering a compromise, but the talks degenerated into a shouting match before the planning advocates walked out of the room (Clarke, interview). Stumberg, interview; Aebersold, interview; Martin and D. Williams, interviews.

42. Dickerson, interview; Moore, interview; Bass, interview.

43. Stumberg, interview.

44. D. Williams, interview; Richards, interview.

45. Clarke, interview; Jaffe and Sherwood, *Dream City,* 186.

46. Moore, interview; Sam Smith, *Progressive Review* (March 1989), quoted in Gillette, *Between Justice and Beauty,* 198.

47. Martin and Stumberg, interviews.

48. Lillian Wiggins, "Barry Put a Noose around Our Necks," *Washington Informer,* Aug. 8, 1991, 12; J. Williams, "A Dream Deferred." 39.

49. Wiggins, "Barry Put a Noose around Our Necks," 12; Dickerson, interview.

50. Glenn, interview; Davis, interview.

51. Stumberg, interview; Dickerson, interview; Moore, interview.

52. Eisen, interview; Moore, interview.

53. Dickerson, interview.

54. Hitchcock, interview.

55. Bass, interview.

12. Counterhegemonic Activism in American Cities

1. Joe Picharallo, "Rhodes Tavern Initiative Carries 91 Percent of City's 137 Precincts," *Washington Post,* Nov. 10, 1983, B4. To the dismay of the preservationists, the citizens initiative did not save Rhodes Tavern. Three months after the election, the city declared that the wording of the initiative "merely authorizes negotiations, information-gathering and advice" and therefore did not prevent the city from ultimately permitting the building's demolition. Activists filed a lawsuit to block the city's apparent intention to ignore the initiative, but a D.C. Superior Court ruled in August 1984 that the initiative had improperly singled out Rhodes Tavern for special treatment and thus violated the developer's constitutional rights to due process and protection from unlawful seizure of private property. The landmark was demolished three weeks later (Al Kamen, "Rhodes Tavern Razing Not Ruled Out," *Washington Post,* Feb. 8, 1984, B1; Ed Bruske, "Ruling Backs Demolition of Tavern," *Washington Post,* Aug. 21, 1984, B1).

2. This study indicates that mechanisms of direct democracy such as a citizens initiative have considerable potential as instruments of progressive cultural/political change. This assumes that the initiative campaigns are executed in a genuinely grassroots manner. When they are carried out in a more autocratic manner, as in the early years of the San Francisco growth-control movement, the counterhegemonic potential is greatly

reduced. Moreover, the possibilities for abusing the true wishes of the people increase when the initiative process is commandeered by entities with disproportionate amounts of political power and wealth. Cf. Cronin, *Direct Democracy.*

3. Welch, interview, May 31, 1991.

4. Again, this means that managerial and populist elements would be permissible provided they take place in an overall context that is clearly progressive.

5. Porter, "The Linkage Issue," 16.

6. Peterson, *The New Federalism,* 28-29.

7. Greene, interview. This assessment of Washington's attractiveness to business is supported by a contemporaneous report prepared by the real estate brokerage firm of Cushman and Wakefield, Inc., which listed downtown Washington as having the highest office rents in the United States (Kirsten Downey, "Study: Office Rents in Downtown D.C. Highest in the Nation," *Washington Post,* May 7, 1992, B13).

8. Cf. Jennings and King, *From Access to Power.*

9. Ann Mariano, "Boston Trying 'Linkage' to Bring Neighborhoods into Building Boom," *Washington Post,* April 12, 1986, E1.

10. Dreier and Ehrlich, "Downtown Development and Urban Reform." For example, the city announced plans to build a large office and retail complex in the lower-income neighborhood of Roxbury. Efforts to encourage industrial development included renovation of the Charlestown Navy Yard and persuading a biotechnology corporation to construct a $75 million manufacturing plant in Allston (Michael Rezendes and Don Aucoin, "BRA Chief Coyle to End 7-Year Role," *Boston Globe,* Dec. 20, 1991, 1, 28).

11. Dreier and Ehrlich, "Downtown Development and Urban Reform," 369; Rezendes and Aucoin, "BRA Chief Coyle to End 7-Year Role," 1; Coyle, interview.

12. Roger W. Caves, "Seattle, Washington: Capping Downtown Growth"; Keating and Krumholz, "Downtown Plans of the 1980s," 141-42.

13. Garreau, *Edge City.*

14. Bruce Adams, "Montgomery Must Tax Developers," *Washington Post,* Jan. 5, 1992, C8.

15. Deakin, "The Politics of Exactions," 106.

16. The 1990 Census shows rapid growth in many California cities over the past decade:

City	1980	1990
Bakersfield	105,611	174,820
Fresno	218,202	354,202
Riverside	170,876	226,505
Sacramento	275,741	369,365
San Bernardino	117,490	164,164
Stockton	149,779	210,943

Source: U.S. Bureau of the Census, "Population, Social, and Economic Characteristics, Summary of Social Characteristics," 1-10. (Washington, D.C.: Government Printing Office, 1992).

17. Andree Brooks, "Idaho Panhandle: 'Paradise' Seekers Drive Up House Prices," *New York Times,* Nov. 29, 1992, sec. X, 3.

18. Cf. Stone and Sanders, *The Politics of Urban Development.* The main purpose of this collection of case studies was to contest the Petersonian conception of limited cities by underscoring the variation in urban development strategies pursued by a wide range of cities, including less privileged cities. Swanstrom, *The Crisis of Growth Politics.* An alternative explanation for Cleveland's inability to sustain a progressive agenda would focus less on the shortcomings of elected officials such as the mayor and more on the absence of counterhegemonic activism at the grassroots level; Clavel, *The Progressive City;* Goetz, "'Type II Policy'"; Goetz, *Shelter Burden,* 195.

19. Peterson, *City Limits.*

20. Elkin, *City and Regime;* Stone, *Regime Politics.*

Bibliography

Books, Scholarly Articles, and Government Documents

Abbott, Carl. *The New Urban America: Metropolitan Growth and Politics in the Sunbelt.* Chapel Hill: Univ. of North Carolina Press, 1981.

Adamson, Walter. *Hegemony and Revolution: A Study of Antonio Gramsci's Political and Cultural Theory.* Berkeley: Univ. of California Press, 1980.

Agnew, John A., John Mercer, and David E. Sopher, eds. *The City in Cultural Context.* Boston: Allen and Unwin, 1984.

Agronsky, Jonathan I.Z. *Marion Barry: The Politics of Race.* Latham, N.Y.: British American Publishers, 1991.

Almond, Gabriel A., and Sidney Verba. *The Civic Culture: Political Attitudes and Democracy in Five Nations.* Princeton, N.J.: Princeton Univ. Press, 1963.

Alterman, Rachelle, ed. *Private Supply of Public Services: Evaluation of Real Estate Exactions, Linkage, and Alternative Land Policies.* New York: New York Univ. Press, 1988.

Andrich, Mark C. "Planned Unit Development in the District of Columbia, 1958-1990: A Mechanism for Enlightened Flexibility or a Zoning Loophole for Overdevelopment?" Master's thesis, George Washington Univ., 1991.

Arblaster, Anthony. *Democracy.* Minneapolis: Univ. of Minnesota Press, 1987.

Barber, Benjamin. *Strong Democracy: Participatory Politics for a New Age.* Berkeley: Univ. of California Press, 1984.

Barker, Ernest, ed. and trans. *The Politics of Aristotle.* Oxford: Oxford Univ. Press, 1979.

Barnekov, Timothy, Robin Boyle, and Daniel Rich. *Privatism and Urban Policy in Britain and the United States.* New York: Oxford Univ. Press, 1989.

Barnes, Samuel, Max Kaase, et al. *Political Action: Mass Participation in Five Western Democracies.* Beverly Hills, Calif.: Sage Publications, 1979.

Barone, Michael, and Grant Ujifusa. *The Almanac of American Politics, 1992.* Washington, D.C.: National Journal, 1991.

Bartelt, David W. "Renewing Center City Philadelphia: Whose City? Which Public Interest?" In Squires, *Unequal Partnerships*, 80-102.

Beauregard, Robert A., ed. *Atop the Urban Hierarchy.* Totowa, N.J.: Rowman and Littlefield, 1989.

Binder, David. "Public Opinion Survey of City of San Francisco." August 21, 1990.

Bluestone, Barry, and Bennett Harrison. *The Deindustrialization of America: Plant Closings, Community Abandonment, and the Dismantling of Basic Industry.* New York: Basic Books, 1982.

Boggs, Carl. *Social Movements and Political Power.* Philadelphia: Temple Univ. Press, 1986.

———. *The Two Revolutions: Gramsci and the Dilemmas of Western Marxism.* Boston: South End Press, 1984.

Borchert, James. *Alley Life in Washington: Family, Community, Religion, and Folklife in the City, 1850-1970.* Urbana: Univ. of Illinois Press, 1980.

Brooks, Clem, and Jeff Manza. "Do Changing Values Explain the New Politics? A Critical Assessment of the Postmaterialist Thesis." *Sociological Quarterly* 35, no. 4 (1994): 541-70.

Broussard, Albert S. *Black San Francisco: The Struggle for Racial Equality in the West, 1900-1954.* Lawrence: Univ. Press of Kansas, 1993.

Brown, Archie. "Ideology and Political Culture." In *Politics, Society, and Nationality Inside Gorbachev's Russia,* ed. Seweryn Bialer, 1-40. Boulder, Colo.: Westview Press, 1989.

Brugmann, Bruce B., and Greggar Sletteland, eds. *The Ultimate Highrise: San Francisco's Mad Rush toward the Sky.* San Francisco: San Francisco Bay Guardian, 1971.

Buechler, Steven M. "New Social Movement Theories." *Sociological Quarterly* 36, no. 3 (1995): 441-64.

Caro, Robert A. *The Power Broker: Robert Moses and the Fall of New York.* New York: Random House, 1974.

Catlin, Robert A. *Racial Politics and Urban Planning: Gary, Indiana 1980-1989.* Lexington: Univ. Press of Kentucky, 1993.

Caves, Roger W. "Seattle, Washington: Capping Downtown Growth." In *Land Use Planning: The Ballot Box Revolution,* 166-94. Newbury Park, Calif.: Sage Publications, 1992.

Clavel, Pierre. *The Progressive City: Planning and Participation, 1969-1984.* New Brunswick, N.J.: Rutgers Univ. Press, 1986.

Cohen, Paul. "San Francisco Commercial Real Estate Industry." *San Francisco Business,* April 1985, 16-22.

Collin, Robert, and Michael Lytton. "Linkage: An Evaluation and an Exploration." *Urban Lawyer* 21 (1989): 413-46.

Costain, Anne N. *Inviting Women's Rebellion: A Political Process Interpretation of the Women's Movement.* Baltimore: Johns Hopkins Univ. Press, 1992.

Cronin, Thomas E. *Direct Democracy: The Politics of Initiatives, Referendum and Recall.* Cambridge, Mass.: Harvard Univ. Press, 1989.

Cummings, Scott, ed. *Business Elites and Urban Development: Case Studies and Critical Perspectives.* Albany: State Univ. of New York Press, 1988.

Cushman and Wakefield, Inc. "Downtown Plan Monitoring Report, 1985-89." San Francisco Department of City Planning, Jan. 1991.

Dalton, Russell, and Manfred Keuchler, eds. *Challenging the Political Order: New Social and Political Movements in Western Democracies.* New York: Oxford Univ. Press, 1990.

Deakin, Elizabeth A. "The Politics of Exactions." In Alterman, *Private Supply of Public Services,* 96-110.

DeLeon, Richard E. *Left Coast City: Progressive Politics in San Francisco, 1975-1991.* Lawrence: Univ. Press of Kansas, 1992.

DeLeon, Richard E., and Sandra Powell. "Growth Control and Electoral Politics in San Francisco: The Triumph of Urban Populism." *Western Political Quarterly* 42 (June 1989): 307-32.

Development Review and Outlook, 1984-1985. Washington, D.C.: Urban Land Institute, 1986.

Diner, Stephen J. "From Jim Crow to Home Rule." *Wilson Quarterly* 13, no. 1 (1989): 90-101.

Donahue, John D. *The Privatization Decision: Public Ends, Private Means.* New York: Basic Books, 1989.

Dreier, Peter, and Bruce Ehrlich. "Downtown Development and Urban Reform: The Politics of Boston's Linkage Policy." *Urban Affairs Quarterly* 26 (March 1991): 354-75.

Eisinger, Peter K. *The Rise of the Entrepreneurial State: State and Local Economic Development Policy in the United States.* Madison: Univ. of Wisconsin Press, 1988.

Elazar, Daniel J. *American Federalism: A View from the States.* 2d ed. New York: Crowell, 1972.

Elberling, John H. "Community Origins of the Downtown Plan." Photocopy in author's possession since July 1991.

Elkin, Stephen L. *City and Regime in the American Republic.* Chicago: Univ. of Chicago Press, 1987.

Ellis, Richard. *American Political Cultures.* New York: Oxford Univ. Press, 1993.

Fagen, Richard R. *The Transformation of Political Culture in Cuba.* Stanford, Calif.: Stanford Univ. Press, 1969.

Fainstein, Susan S., and Norman Fainstein. "Economic Restructuring and the Rise of Urban Social Movements." *Urban Affairs Quarterly* 21 (Dec. 1985): 187-206.

Feinstein, Dianne. "Commentary." *San Francisco Business,* Jan. 1982, 3.

Femia, Joseph V. *Gramsci's Political Thought: Hegemony, Consciousness, and Revolutionary Process.* Oxford: Clarendon Press, 1981.

Ferman, Barbara. *Challenging the Growth Machine.* Lawrence: Univ. Press of Kansas, 1996.

Fetterman, David M. *Ethnography: Step by Step.* Newbury Park, Calif.: Sage Publications, 1989.

Finegold, Kenneth. *Experts and Politicians: Reform Challenges to Machine Politics in New York, Cleveland, and Chicago.* Princeton, N.J.: Princeton Univ. Press, 1995.

Fisher, Robert, and Joseph Kling. "Community Mobilization: Prospects for the Future." *Urban Affairs Quarterly* 25 (Dec. 1989): 200-211.

Fitzpatrick, Michael Andrew. "'A Great Agitation for Business': Black Economic Development in Shaw." *Washington History* 2, no. 2 (fall-winter 1990-91): 49-73.

Fogelson, Robert M. *The Fragmented Metropolis: Los Angeles, 1850-1930.* Cambridge, Mass.: Harvard Univ. Press, 1967.

Frieden, Bernard J., and Lynne B. Sagalyn. *Downtown, Inc.: How America Rebuilds Cities.* Cambridge, Mass.: MIT Press, 1989.

Gale, Dennis E. "Neighborhood Resettlement: Washington, D.C." In *Back to the City:*

Issues in Neighborhood Renovation, ed. Shirley Bradway Laska and Daphne Spain, 95-115. New York: Pergamon Press, 1980.

———. *Washington, D.C.: Inner-City Revitalization and Minority Suburbanization.* Philadelphia: Temple Univ. Press, 1987.

Garreau, Joel. *Edge City: Life on the Frontier.* New York: Doubleday, 1991.

Gatewood, Willard B. *Aristocrats of Color: The Black Elite, 1880-1920.* Bloomington: Indiana Univ. Press, 1990.

Gaventa, John. *Power and Powerlessness: Quiescence and Rebellion in an Appalachian Valley.* Urbana: Univ. of Illinois Press, 1980.

Geertz, Clifford. *The Interpretation of Cultures.* New York: Basic Books, 1973.

Gillette, Howard. *Between Justice and Beauty: Race, Planning, and the Failure of Urban Policy in Washington, D.C.* Baltimore: Johns Hopkins Univ. Press, 1995.

Goetz, Edward G. *Shelter Burden: Local Politics and Progressive Housing Policy.* Philadelphia: Temple Univ. Press, 1993.

———. "'Type II Policy' and Mandated Benefits in Economic Development." *Urban Affairs Quarterly* 26, no. 2 (1990): 170-90.

Goldfield, David R. "Private Neighborhood Redevelopment and Displacement: The Case of Washington, D.C." *Urban Affairs Quarterly* 15, no. 4 (June 1980): 453-68.

Golding, Sue. *Gramsci's Democratic Theory: Contributions to a Post-Liberal Democracy.* Toronto: Univ. of Toronto Press, 1992.

Goodwyn, Lawrence. *The Populist Moment: A Short History of the Agrarian Revolt in America.* New York: Oxford Univ. Press, 1978.

Gramsci, Antonio. *Selections from the Prison Notebooks of Antonio Gramsci.* Ed. and trans. Quintin Hoare and Geoffrey Nowell Smith. New York: International Publishers, 1971.

Green, Constance McLaughlin. *Washington: Capital City, 1879-1950.* Princeton, N.J.: Princeton Univ. Press, 1963.

Gutheim, Frederick. *The Federal City: Plans and Realities.* Washington, D.C.: Smithsonian Institution Press, 1976.

Harris, Charles Wesley. *Congress and the Governance of the Nation's Capital: The Conflict of Federal and Local Interests.* Washington, D.C.: Georgetown Univ. Press, 1995.

Hartman, Chester. *The Transformation of San Francisco.* Totowa, N.J.: Rowman and Allanheld, 1984.

———. *Yerba Buena: Land Grab and Community Resistance in San Francisco.* San Francisco: Glide Publications, 1974.

Hartz, Louis. *The Liberal Tradition in America.* New York: Harcourt, 1955.

Henig, Jeffrey R. "Collective Responses to the Urban Crisis: Ideology and Mobilization." In *Cities in Stress*, ed. M. Gottdiener, 221-45. Beverly Hills, Calif.: Sage Publications, 1986.

——. "Race and Voting: Continuity and Change in the District of Columbia." *Urban Affairs Quarterly* 28, no. 4 (June 1993): 544-70.

Henrikson, Marcene. "No Place to Grow." *San Francisco Business*, May 1981, 6-10.

Henry, William A. *In Defense of Elitism.* New York: Doubleday, 1994.

Hippler, Arthur E. *Hunter's Point: A Black Ghetto.* New York: Basic Books, 1974.

Inglehart, Ronald. *Culture Shift in Advanced Industrial Society.* Princeton, N.J.: Princeton Univ. Press, 1990.

———. *The Silent Revolution: Changing Values and Political Styles among Western Publics.* Princeton, N.J.: Princeton Univ. Press, 1977.

———. "The Silent Revolution in Europe: Intergenerational Change in Postindustrial Societies." *American Political Science Review* 65, no. 4 (1971): 991-1017.

Jackson, Kenneth. *The Crabgrass Frontier: The Suburbanization of America.* New York: Oxford Univ. Press, 1985.

Jacobs, Allan B. *Making City Planning Work.* Chicago: American Society of Planning Officials, 1978.

Jacobs, John. "The Delicate Balance," *San Francisco Business,* Feb. 1982, 3.

———. "Power in America's Cities." *San Francisco Business,* Oct. 1983, 3.

Jaffe, Harry S., and Tom Sherwood. *Dream City: Race, Power and the Decline of Washington, D.C.* New York: Simon and Schuster, 1994.

Jenkins, J. Craig. "Resource Mobilization Theory and the Study of Social Movements." *Annual Review of Sociology* 9 (1983): 527-53.

Jennings, James, and Mel King, eds. *From Access to Power: Black Politics in Boston.* Cambridge, Mass.: Schenkman Books, 1986.

Johnson, Thomas Reed. "The City on the Hill: Race Relations in Washington, D.C., 1865-1885." Ph.D. diss., Univ. of Maryland, 1975.

Johnston, Allen. *Surviving Freedom: The Black Community of Washington, D.C., 1860-1880.* New York: Garland Publishing, 1993.

Kann, Mark E. *Middle Class Radicalism in Santa Monica.* Philadelphia: Temple Univ. Press, 1986.

Kantor, Paul. *The Dependent City: The Changing Political Economy of Urban America.* Glenview, Ill.: Scott, Foresman, 1988.

Kantor, Paul, and H.V. Savitch. "Can Politicians Bargain with Business? A Theoretical and Comparative Perspective on Urban Development." *Urban Affairs Quarterly* 29, no. 2 (Dec. 1993): 230-55.

Kavanagh, Dennis. *Political Culture.* London: MacMillan, 1972.

Keating, W. Dennis, and Norman Krumholz. "Downtown Plans of the 1980s: The Case for Equity in the 1990s." *Journal of the American Planning Association* 57 (spring 1991): 136-52.

Kincaid, John, ed. *Political Culture, Public Policy, and the American States.* Philadelphia: Institute for the Study of Human Relations, 1982.

Knox, Paul L. "The Restless Urban Landscape: Economic and Sociocultural Change and the Transformation of Metropolitan Washington, D.C." *Annals of the Association of American Geographers* 81, no. 2 (1991): 181-209.

Larana, Enrique, Hank Johnston, and Joseph R. Gusfield, eds. *New Social Movements: From Ideology to Identity.* Philadelphia: Temple Univ. Press, 1994.

Lassar, Terry Jill. *Carrots and Sticks: New Zoning Downtown.* Washington, D.C.: Urban Land Institute, 1989.

Lee, Barrett A., Daphne Spain, and Debra J. Umberson. "Neighborhood Revitalization and Racial Change: The Case of Washington, D.C." *Demography* 22, no. 4 (Nov. 1985): 581-602.

Lesko, Kathleen, Valerie Babb, and Carroll R. Gibbs. *Black Georgetown Remembered.* Washington, D.C.: Georgetown Univ. Press, 1991.

Lessof, Alan. *The Nation and Its City: Politics, "Corruption," and Progress in Washington, D.C., 1861-1902.* Baltimore: Johns Hopkins Univ. Press, 1994.

Levine, Mark V. "Downtown Redevelopment as an Urban Growth Strategy: A Critical Appraisal of the Baltimore Renaissance." *Journal of Urban Affairs* 9, no. 2 (1987): 103-23.

Lipset, Seymour Martin. *Political Man, The Social Bases of Politics.* Garden City, N.Y.: Doubleday, 1960.

Logan, John R., and Harvey Molotch. *Urban Fortunes: The Political Economy of Place.* Berkeley: Univ. of California Press, 1987.

Longoria, Thomas, Jr. "Empirical Analysis of the *City Limits* Typology." *Urban Affairs Quarterly* 30, no. 1 (1994): 102-13.

Lortie, Francis N., Jr. *San Francisco's Black Community, 1870-1890: Dilemmas in the Struggle for Equality.* San Francisco: R and E Research Associates, 1973.

Lowe, Jeanne R. *Cities in a Race with Time: Progress and Poverty in America's Renewing Cities.* New York: Random House, 1967.

Lowi, Theodore J. *The End of Liberalism: The Second Republic of the United States.* 2d ed. New York: Norton, 1979.

Massey, Douglas S., and Nancy A. Denton. *American Aparteid: Segregation and the Making of the Underclass.* Cambridge, Mass.: Harvard Univ. Press, 1993.

McAdam, Doug. *The Political Process and the Development of Black Insurgency.* Chicago: Univ. of Chicago Press, 1982.

McCarthy, John D., and Mayer N. Zald. "Resource Mobilization and Social Movements: A Partial Theory." *American Journal of Sociology* 82, no. 6 (1977): 1212-41.

McGovern, Stephen J. "Mayoral Leadership and Economic Development Policy: The Case of Ed Rendell's Philadelphia." *Policy and Politics* 25 (April 1997): 153-72.

Meyer, David. *A Winter's Discontent: The Nuclear Freeze and American Politics.* New York: Praeger, 1990.

Milbrath, Lester, and M.L. Goel. *Political Participation.* 2d ed. Chicago: Rand McNally, 1977.

Miller, John C. *Alexander Hamilton and the Growth of the Nation.* New York: Harper and Row, 1964.

Mollenkopf, John H. *The Contested City.* Princeton, N.J.: Princeton Univ. Press, 1983.

Molotch, Harvey. "The City as Growth Machine." *American Journal of Sociology* 82 (Sept. 1976): 309-32.

Morten, Richard. "Can San Francisco Afford the Anti-Highrise Initiative?" *San Francisco Business,* Oct. 1979, 20-24.

———. "Warning: The San Francisco Planning Initiative Endangers Our City's Health." *San Francisco Business,* Sept. 1983, 26-29.

Mouffe, Chantal, ed. *Gramsci and Marxist Theory.* London: Routledge and Kegan Paul, 1979.

National Capital Downtown Committee. *A Report and Sketch Plan for the Revitalization of Downtown Washington, D.C.* Washington, D.C., 1961.

National Capital Park and Planning Commission. *Washington Present and Future: A General Summary of the Comprehensive Plan for the National Capital and Its Environs.* Washington, D.C.: National Capital Park and Planning Commission, 1950.

National Capital Planning Commission. *The Nation's Capital: A Policies Plan for the Year 2000.* Washington, D.C., 1961.

———. *Worthy of the Nation: The History of Planning for the National Capital.* Washington, D.C.: Smithsonian Institution Press, 1977.

Nickel, Denise R. "The Progressive City? Urban Redevelopment in Minneapolis." *Urban Affairs Review* 30, no. 1 (1995): 355-77.

Olson, Mancur. *The Logic of Collective Action.* Cambridge, Mass.: Harvard Univ. Press, 1965.

Pacifico, Michelle F. "'Don't Buy Where You Can't Work': The New Negro Alliance of Washington," *Washington History* 6, no. 1 (spring-summer 1994): 66-88.

Paolantonio, S.A. *Frank Rizzo: The Last Big Man in Big City America.* Philadelphia: Camino Books, 1993.

Paul, Brad. "San Francisco's Growth Management." Graduate School of Design, Harvard Univ., 1988. Photocopy in author's possession.

Peterson, Paul. *City Limits.* Chicago: Univ. of Chicago Press, 1981.

———. *The New Federalism.* Washington, D.C.: Brookings Institution, 1995.

Polanyi, Karl. *The Great Transformation: The Political and Economic Origins of Our Time.* Boston: Beacon Press, 1957.

Porter, Douglas. "The Linkage Issue: Introduction and Summary of Discussion." In *Downtown Linkages,* ed. Douglas Porter, 2-22. Washington, D.C.: Urban Land Institute, 1985.

———. "Mission (Almost) Impossible: Winning Approval for Mission Bay." *Urban Land* 51 (Jan. 1992): 27-32.

Pye, Lucian W. "Political Culture and Political Development." In *Political Culture and Political Development,* ed. Lucian W. Pye and Sidney Verba, 3-26. Princeton, N.J.: Princeton Univ. Press, 1965.

Ramsay, Meredith. *Community, Culture, and Economic Development: The Social Roots of Local Action.* Albany: State Univ. of New York Press, 1995.

Reps, John W. *The Making of Urban America: A History of City Planning in the United States.* Princeton, N.J.: Princeton Univ. Press, 1965.

———. *Monumental Washington: The Planning and Development of the Capital Center.* Princeton, N.J.: Princeton Univ. Press, 1967.

Robinson, Tony. "Gentrification and Grassroots Resistance in San Francisco's Tenderloin." *Urban Affairs Quarterly* 30, no. 4 (1995): 483-513.

Rosdil, Donald L. "The Context of Radical Populism in U.S. Cities: A Comparative Analysis." *Journal of Urban Affairs* 13, no. 1 (1991): 77-96.

Sassoon, Anne Showstack. *Gramsci's Politics.* 2d ed. Minneapolis: Univ. of Minnesota Press.

Savage, James. "Postmaterialism of the Left and Right: Political Conflict in Postindustrial Society." *Comparative Political Studies* 17, no. 4 (1985): 431-51.

Savas, Emanuel S. *Privatization: The Key to Better Government.* Chatham, N.J.: Chatham House Publishers, 1987.

Sbragia, Alberta. "The Pittsburgh Model of Economic Development: Partnership, Responsiveness, and Indifference." In Squires, *Unequal Partnerships*, 103-20.

Schmeckebier, Laurence F. *The District of Columbia: Its Government and Administration.* Baltimore: Johns Hopkins Univ. Press, 1928.

Schumpeter, Joseph. *Capitalism, Socialism and Democracy.* New York: Harper, 1942.

Scott, Mel. *American City Planning since 1890.* Berkeley: Univ. of California Press, 1969.

Sedway/Cooke. "Downtown San Francisco Conservation and Development Planning Program, Phase 1: Reconnaissance and Programming." San Francisco, October 1979.

Shearer, Derek. "In Search of Equal Partnerships: Prospects for Progressive Urban Policy in the 1990s." In Squires, *Unequal Partnerships.*

Skocpol, Theda. *States and Social Revolutions: A Comparative Analysis of France, Russia and China.* Cambridge: Cambridge Univ. Press, 1979.

Smith, Michael P. *The City, State and Market.* New York: Basil Blackwell, 1988.

Sobolik, Michael C., and Jeanette I. Rice. "A Tale of Recovery." *Mortgage Banking* 55 (July 1995): 24-37.

Spitzer, Neil. "A Secret City." *Wilson Quarterly* 13, no. 1 (1989): 102-15.

Squires, Gregory D., ed. *Unequal Partnerships: The Political Economy of Urban Redevelopment in Postwar America.* New Brunswick, N.J.: Rutgers Univ. Press, 1989.

Steinberger, Peter J. *Ideology and the Urban Crisis.* Albany: State Univ. of New York Press, 1985.

Stoker, Robert. "Baltimore: The Self-Evaluating City?" In Stone and Sanders, *The Politics of Urban Development*: 244-66.

Stone, Clarence N. "The Politics of Urban Restructuring: A Review Essay." *Western Political Quarterly* 43 (March 1990): 219-31.

———. *Regime Politics: Governing Atlanta, 1946-1988.* Lawrence: Univ. Press of Kansas, 1989.

———. "Systemic Power in Community Decision Making." *American Political Science Review* 74 (Dec. 1980): 978-90.

Stone, Clarence N., and Heywood T. Sanders, eds. *The Politics of Urban Development.* Lawrence: Univ. Press of Kansas, 1987.

Swanstrom, Todd. *The Crisis of Growth Politics: Cleveland, Kucinich and the Challenge of Urban Populism.* Philadelphia: Temple Univ. Press, 1985.

Tarrow, Sidney. *Power in Movement: Social Movements, Collective Action and Politics.* Cambridge: Cambridge Univ. Press, 1994.

Taub, Theodore C. "Exactions, Linkages, and Regulatory Takings: The Developer's Perspective." *Urban Lawyer* 20 (1988): 515-96.

Teaford, Jon C. *The Rough Road to Renaissance: Urban Revitalization in America, 1940-1985.* Baltimore: Johns Hopkins Univ. Press, 1990.

———. *The Twentieth-Century American City.* 2d ed. Baltimore: Johns Hopkins Univ. Press, 1993.

Temko, Allan. "San Francisco Rebuilds Again." *Harper's*, April 1960, 51-59.

Thompson, Michael, Richard Ellis, and Aaron Wildavsky. *Cultural Theory.* Boulder, Colo.: Westview Press, 1990.

Tucker, Robert C. *Political Culture and Leadership in Soviet Russia: From Lenin to Gorbachev.* New York: Norton, 1987.

United States Bureau of the Census. *Census of Population and Housing: Characteristics for Governmental Units and Standard Metropolitan Statistical Areas.* Washington, D.C.: Government Printing Office, 1982, 1992.

Urban Land Institute Market Profiles. Washington, D.C.: Urban Land Institute.

Vogel, Ronald K., and Bert E. Swanson. "The Growth Machine versus the Antigrowth Coalition: The Battle for Our Communities." *Urban Affairs Quarterly* 25 (Sept. 1989): 63-85.

Walsh, Edward J. "Resource Mobilization and Citizen Protest in Communities around Three Mile Island." *Social Problems* 29, no. 1 (1981): 1-21.

Warner, Sam Bass. *The Private City: Philadelphia in Three Periods of Its Growth.* Philadelphia: Univ. of Pennsylvania Press, 1968.

White, Stephen. *Political Culture and Soviet Politics.* New York: St. Martin's Press, 1979.

Wildavsky, Aaron. "Choosing Preferences by Constructing Institutions: A Cultural Theory of Preference Formation." *American Political Science Review* 81, no. 1 (1987): 3-21.

Williams, Juan. "A Dream Deferred: A Black Mayor Betrays the Faith." *Washington Monthly,* July-Aug. 1986, 24-39.

Wirt, Frederick. *The Power in the City: Decision Making in San Francisco.* Berkeley: Univ. of California Press, 1974.

Wolin, Sheldon S. *Politics and Vision.* Boston: Little, Brown, 1960.

Personal Interviews

(all conducted by the author, in the interviewee's city, unless otherwise indicated)

Adams, Gerald, journalist, *San Francisco Examiner,* San Francisco. June 28, 1991.

Aebersold, Paul, activist, Logan Circle Citizens Association, Washington, D.C. Dec. 15, 1992.

Badiner, Larry, Department of City Planning, San Francisco. June 5, 1992.

Bash, Alec, Department of City Planning, San Francisco. June 13, 1991.

Bass, Dennis, activist and president, Dupont Circle Citizens Association, Washington, D.C. April 22, 1992.

Bell, James, attorney, National Youth Law Center, San Francisco. July 2, 1991.

Bierman, Sue, City Planning Commission, 1976-92, San Francisco. June 18, 1992.

Blakeslee, Elizabeth, activist, Logan Circle Citizens Association, Advisory Neighborhood Commission member, Washington, D.C. Dec. 16, 1992.

Blazej, Lu, Department of City Planning, San Francisco. July 1, 1991.

Brugmann, Bruce B., editor and publisher, *San Francisco Bay Guardian,* San Francisco. June 17, 1992.

Carlson, Dale, activist, vice president of Pacific Stock Exchange, San Francisco. June 13, 1991.

Cazenave, Rene, activist, Council of Community Housing Organizations, San Francisco. May 31, 1991, July 9, 1992.
Chin, Gordon, activist, Chinatown Resource Center, San Francisco. June 25, 1992.
Clarke, David, chair, District Council, Washington, D.C. May 18, 1992.
Coleman, Eugene, Department of City Planning, San Francisco. June 11, 1991.
Colyer, George, activist, Coalition for a Living Downtown, Washington, D.C. April 29, 1992.
Cox, Darryl, activist, San Francisco. June 26, 1991.
Coyle, Stephen, director, Boston Redevelopment Authority, 1984-91. Washington, D.C., May 11, 1992.
Davis, Martha, activist, Project WISH, Washington, D.C. April 23, 1992.
DeLuca, Joe, developer, Empire Group and Aculed Group, San Francisco. June 27, 1991.
Dickerson, Jim, housing advocate, executive director of MANNA, Washington, D.C. April 30, 1992.
Duffy, Pamela, attorney, Coblentz, Cahen, McCabe, and Breyer, San Francisco. June 18, 1991.
Duskin, Alvin, activist, San Francisco. June 22, 1992.
Eisen, Rick, attorney, counsel to Coalition for Nonprofit Housing, Washington, D.C. April 28, 1992.
Emerson, Ed, activist, San Francisco Tomorrow, San Francisco. June 7, 1991.
Engmann, Doug, City Planning Commission, 1988-92, San Francisco. June 9, 1992.
Fondersmith, John, Office of Planning, Washington, D.C. May 18, 1992.
Giloth, Robert, executive director, Southeast Community Organization/Southeast Development, Inc., Baltimore. Telephone interview, Sept. 5, 1990.
Glenn, Marcia, activist, Coalition for Nonprofit Housing, Washington, D.C. May 7, 1992.
Gonzales-Burns, Julie, public relations officer, Catellus Development Corporation, San Francisco. June 27, 1991.
Grandis, Ed, ANC commissioner, Dupont Circle, Washington, D.C. April 15, 1992.
Greene, Fred, director, Office of Planning, Washington, D.C., 1984-91. May 6, 1992.
Gresham, Zane, attorney, Morrison and Foerster, San Francisco. June 18, 1991.
Grosboll, Dick, activist, San Francisco Tomorrow, San Francisco. June 6, 1991.
Gross, Nate, chief of comprehensive planning implementation, Office of Planning, Washington, D.C. Dec. 15, 1992.
Harris, Michael, attorney, Lawyers Committee for Urban Affairs, San Francisco. June 3, 1992.
Hayes, Knox, chief of strategy and policy development, Department of Housing and Community Development, Washington, D.C. May 20, 1992.
Heller, Jeff, president, Heller and Leake Architects, San Francisco. June 25, 1991.
Hernandez, Ricardo, activist, Latino Democratic Club, San Francisco. June 17, 1991.
Hestor, Sue, activist, San Francisco. June 5, 1991.
Hitchcock, Con, activist, Dupont Circle Citizens Association, Washington, D.C. April 17, 1992.
Hubbard, Harriet, activist, Washington, D.C. April 18, 1992.
Jefferson, Jim, president, Jefferson Company, San Francisco. July 9, 1991.
Johnson, Geraldine, activist, San Francisco. July 9, 1991.
Jones, Tom, Mayor's Office of Housing, San Francisco. July 5, 1991.

Kilroy, Tony, activist, San Francisco Tomorrow, San Francisco. June 19, 1991.

Lazarus, Jim, vice president, Chamber of Commerce, San Francisco. July 3, 1991.

Looman, David, political consultant, San Francisco. June 14, 1991.

Lord, Paul, Department of City Planning, San Francisco. Telephone interview, June 24, 1992.

Lynch, Terry, activist, Downtown Cluster of Congregations, Washington, D.C. April 14, 1992.

Macris, Dean, director, Department of City Planning, San Francisco, 1980-92. June 15, 1992.

Martin, Clarene, ANC commissioner, Downtown, Washington, D.C. May 8, 1992.

McCarthy, Denise, activist, Telegraph Hill Dwellers, San Francisco. June 11, 1991.

McGrath, Dorn, activist, president of Committee of 100, Washington, D.C., professor of urban planning, George Washington University. Dec. 15, 1992.

Miller, Rob, legislative assistant, District Council, Washington, D.C. May 14, 1992.

Moore, Robert, director, Department of Housing and Community Development, 1978-83; executive director, Columbia Heights Community Development Corporation; Washington, D.C. April 20, 1992.

Moylan, Peter, activist, San Francisco Tomorrow, San Francisco. June 4, 1991.

Nash, Andy, activist and president, San Francisco Tomorrow, San Francisco. June 12, 1992.

Nettler, Richard, attorney, Melrod, Redmen, and Gartlan, Washington, D.C. April 20, 1992.

O'Donoghue, Joe, president, Residential Builders Association, San Francisco. June 17, 1991.

Okamoto, Rai, director, Department of City Planning, San Francisco, 1976-80. June 4, 1992.

Omerberg, Mitch, activist, Affordable Housing Alliance, San Francisco. July 2, 1991.

Pettit, Bruce, journalist and editor, *The Pettit Report,* San Francisco. June 15, 1992.

Prowler, David, City Administrative Office; activist, Chinatown Resource Center, 1984-88; San Francisco. June 15, 1992.

Richards, Laura, activist, Citizens Planning Coalition, Washington, D.C. April 21, 1992.

Rolfe, Norm, activist, San Francisco Tomorrow, San Francisco. May 28, 1991.

Rosen, Marcia, attorney, Lawyers Committee for Urban Affairs, San Francisco. June 4, 1991, June 3, 1992.

Sanger, John, Public Utilities Commission; attorney, Pettit and Martin; San Francisco. June 16, 1992.

Sher, Steven, land use consultant, Wilkes, Artis, Hedrick, and Lane, Washington, D.C. May 21, 1992.

Smith, Jim, activist, Logan Circle Citizens Association, Washington, D.C. Dec. 15, 1992.

Smith, Lloyd, Zoning Commission, Washington, D.C. April 22, 1992.

Starbuck, Charles, City Planning Commission, San Francisco, 1976-81. Telephone interview, June 21, 1992.

Steen, Leslie, activist, nonprofit housing developer, Washington, D.C. Dec. 14, 1992.

Stumberg, Robert, activist, professor of law, Georgetown Law School, Washington, D.C. April 28, 1992.

Thompson, Bob, attorney, Pettit and Martin, San Francisco. June 11, 1992.

Toney, Causton, D.C. Chamber of Commerce; attorney, Arnold and Porter; Washington, D.C. May 11, 1992.
Wachob, Jim, activist, District 8 Democratic Club, San Francisco. June 12, 1991.
Welch, Calvin, activist, San Francisco. May 29, 31, 1991; June 23, 1992.
Williams, Deirdre, activist, Coalition for Economic Development Organizations, Washington, D.C. May 13, 1992.

Index